CRICKET

CRICKET

W. G. GRACE

GYAN

Published by

GYAN

Gyan Publishing House
5, Ansari Road
Daryaganj, New Delhi-110002
Phone: 011-47034999, 9811692060
E-mail: books@gyanbooks.com

Distribution Network
gyanbooks.com
India, USA, Canada, UK, Australia, France

ISBN : 978-81-212-9566-6 (PB)
First Published, 1891

2nd Impression 2023

Printed at: Gyan Press, Delhi.

CRICKET
Author: W. G. GRACE

CRICKET

BY

W. G. GRACE

1891

The Author and Publisher beg most cordially to express their thanks and obligations to the following gentlemen who have so heartily co-operated with them, either by lending pictures or in other ways giving such assistance as will make "CRICKET" *a lasting and permanent record of the game:*

C. P. GREEN, Malvern.
Rev. ROBERT STRATTEN HOLMES, Wakefield.
THOMAS PADWICK, Redhill.
FREDERICK GALE, Mitcham.
Messrs. E. HAWKINS & Co., Brighton.
Mr. PROTHEROE, Bristol.
PROPRIETORS OF *The English Illustrated Magazine.*
Messrs. STEARN, Cambridge.

I think it right my readers should know

that I have been

much aided in the preparation of this book

by my friend,

W. Methven Brownlee,

who has worked with me over every page,

and thus helped me to place this History of Cricket

before lovers of

Our National Game.

W. G. Grace.

CONTENTS.

LIST OF ILLUSTRATIONS.

CRICKET.

CHAPTER I.

HISTORICAL.—1300 TO 1845.

I CANNOT remember when I began to play cricket. Respect for the truth prevents me from saying I played the first year of my existence, but I have little hesitation in declaring that I handled bat and ball before the end of my second. My family was known as a cricketing family a quarter of a century before I was born. My brothers Henry, Alfred and E. M. were respectively 15, 8 and 7 years of age when I appeared, and though my mother did not lay claim to being considered a player, I am inclined to believe, judging by the light of later years, she knew how to play as well as any of them; she was certainly most enthusiastic, and ever ready with sound counsel and cheering words. And I know in her heart she hoped that I should be a credit to the family.

I have been told that I was an easy subject to teach; always willing to listen to words of wisdom, but rather casual in carrying them out, and looking as if I had a theory of my own about playing the game. Perhaps even at that age I realised the duty resting on every cricketer who desires to add a page or two to cricket history.

This much, then, may be safely accepted, that not a year has passed since 1850 in which I have not, in some form or other, played the game. That must be my justification for giving my experiences to the cricket-reading public.

But I have been asked to say something about the history of cricket; to touch upon the remote past, about which every writer has an opinion of his own, and upon which very few agree. Where wiser and more learned heads have failed I cannot be expected to succeed. I am a player pure and simple, and have been all my life more interested in the doings of players than in reading this and the other account of how the game began and where it was first played. I would rather read a hundred pages of Frederick Lillywhite's Scores and Biographies any day than half a dozen pages which try to prove it is absolutely untrue that the game had its origin in Rome, or Greece, or indeed anywhere but in England.

CLUB-BALL was played in the thirteenth century, and the Rev. J. Pycroft, author of *The Cricket Field*, and a friend of my own family, has little doubt of it being single-wicket cricket in its earliest form. He also quotes from Strutt, who wrote to this effect, fifty years later:—"In the Bodleian Library at Oxford is a MS., No. 264, and dated 1344, in which a female figure is represented bowling a ball of the size of a cricket-ball to a man who is raising a bat to strike it; behind the bowler are figures, male and female, waiting to catch the ball. The game is called Club-ball, and the score is made by running and hitting as at Cricket." A modern writer, who examined the MS. also, takes exception to Strutt's assertion that some of the figures in the picture are females, and says: "All the figures are monks, with their cowls up and down alternately."

In 1477 HAND-IN-AND-HAND-OUT was mentioned as a kind of cricket, and identical with Club-ball.

The word CRICKET is said to have been first used in the year 1550. John Parish, an innkeeper in Guildford, enclosed a piece of waste land that year, but was ordered to give it up in 1593. John Derrick, one of Queen Elizabeth's coroners for Surrey, aged fifty-nine, said: "When he was a scholler in the free school of Guldeforde, he and severall of his fellowes did runne and play there at *crickett* and other plaies." That has been accepted by writers generally on the authority of Russell, a local historian, who transcribed it from the old records of the borough of Guildford; but another and more careful reading has shown that Russell must have, innocently or intentionally, substituted *crickett* for *quoits*.

The seventeenth century was half through before the word was again heard of. Bishop Ken, in his thirteenth year, entered Winchester College in 1650, and Lisle Bowles, writing of him, says: "On the fifth day our junior is found attempting to wield a *cricket bat*." Eight years later Edward Phillips, John Milton's nephew, in his poem entitled "Treatment of Ladies at Balls and Sports," says: "Would that my eyes had been beaten out of my head with a *cricket ball* the day before I saw thee." In 1670 the British sailor added his testimony. The chaplain on board H.M.S. *Assistance* wrote to the effect that while they were lying at Antioch, on May the 6th of that year, "Krickett" and other games were played. This is his letter: "This morning early at the least 40 of the English, with his worthy the Consull, rod out of the city about 4 miles to the Greene Platte, a fine valley by a river side, to recreate themselves with such pastimes and sports such as duck hunting, fishing, shooting, hand-ball and *Krickett*, and at 6 we returne all home in good order, but soundly tyred and werry."

What is considered as the beginning of the double-wicket game was played in Scotland in 1700 under the name of Cat and Dog. Dr. Jamieson, in his Dictionary, 1722, says:—

"This is a game for three players at least, who are furnished with clubs. They cut out two holes, each about a foot in diameter and seven inches in depth, and twenty-six feet apart; one man guards each hole with his club; these clubs are called Dogs. A piece of wood, about four inches long and one inch in diameter, called a Cat, is pitched by a third person from one hole towards the player at the other, who is to prevent the cat from getting into the hole. If it pitches in the hole the party who threw it takes his turn with the club. If the cat be struck, the club bearers change places, and each change of place counts one to the score, like *Club-ball*."

If we are to accept that as authentic, then small beginnings have had great developments, and something may be said in favour of English Tipcat as having made its mark on the game.

Strutt, in his *Sports and Pastimes*, quotes from Thomas D'Urfey's *Pills to Purge Melancholy* (1710):

> "Her was the prettiest fellow
> At football and at *Cricket*."

In 1736 all doubt of the game being firmly established is at an end, for Horace Walpole on the 6th of May of that year, two years after he had left Eton, wrote:

"An expedition against bargemen, or a match at *Cricket*, may be very pretty things to recollect; but, thank my stars, I can remember things that are very near as pretty." And again, in 1749, he says: "I could tell you of Lord Montford's making *cricket-matches*,

CRICKET.

(From a Picture by F. Hayman, R.A., belonging to the Marylebone Club.)

and fetching up parsons by express from different parts of England to play on Richmond Green."

Clubs were now springing up rapidly, the most important of them being in the counties of Kent, Hampshire, Surrey, Sussex and Middlesex. Matches were of frequent occurrence, and according to several accounts large sums of money were staked on the result, and not unfrequently lawsuits followed. It said well for the popularity of the game that it fought through that stage and reached its present pure and healthy position in the hearts of the English people.

The oldest recorded score is:—

KENT *v.* ALL ENGLAND.

Played in the Artillery Ground, London, 1746.

ALL ENGLAND.

1st Innings.		2nd Innings.	
Harris, b Hadswell	0	b Mills	4
Durgate, b Hadswell	3	b Hadswell	11
Newland, b Mills	0	b Hadswell	3
Cuddy, b Hadswell	0	c Danes	2
Green, b Mills	0	b Mills	5
Waymark, b Mills	7	b Hadswell	9
Bryan, st Kips	12	c Kips	7
Newland, not out	18	c Lord J. F. Sackville	15
Harris, b Hadswell	0	b Hadswell	1
Smith, c Bartrum	0	b Mills	8
Newland, b Mills	0	not out	5
Byes	0	byes	0
	40		70

KENT.

1st Innings.		2nd Innings.	
Lord J. F. Sackville, c Waymark	5	b Harris	3
Long Robin, b Newland	7	b Newland	9
Mills, b Harris	0	c Newland	6
Hadswell, b Harris	0	not out	5
Cutbush, c Green	3	not out	7
Bartrum, b Newland	2	b Newland	0
Danes, b Newland	6	c Smith	0
Sawyer, c Waymark	0	b Newland	5
Kips, b Harris	12	b Harris	10
Mills, not out	7	b Newland	2
Romney, b Harris	11	c Harris	8
Byes	0	byes	3
	53		58

Kent winning by one wicket.

It will be seen that the match was closely contested, and the long-stopping exceptionally good. Only 3 byes were scored in the whole match, and those were in the last innings of Kent.

Up to 1700, and for some years after, the stumps were two in number, one foot high and two feet wide, surmounted with a bail. Between the stumps a hole was cut in the ground, large enough to contain the ball and the butt-end of the bat. In running, the striker was required to put his bat into the hole to score a notch; and the wicket-keeper had to place the ball in the hole before he could run the striker out. Wicket-keeper and bowler had many severe knocks on the hand from the bat; and the present mode of placing the bat inside the crease was substituted, and in force in the match I have given.

The following have been the changes in the size of the wicket:

1700.—Two stumps, 1 foot high, 2 feet wide.
1775.—Three stumps, one bail, 22 inches by 6.
1798.—Three stumps, one bail, 24 inches by 7.
1816.—Three stumps, one bail, 26 inches by 7.
1817.—Three stumps, two bails, 27 inches by 8.

There has been no change in the laws respecting the size of the wicket since 1817; but in the Gentlemen *v.* Players' match in 1837 the Players by arrangement had to defend wickets 36 ins. by 12 ins.

The distance between the wickets has been always twenty-two yards.

All bowling was underhand, and of very indifferent quality; pace without length was the aim of everyone.

The strongest club at this stage of the game was undoubtedly the Hambledon Club, in Hampshire, holding a position somewhat similar to the M.C.C. to-day. It was formed in the year 1750, and held its

THE ROYAL ACADEMY CLUB IN MARYLEBONE FIELD.

(From a Picture by F. Hayman, R.A., belonging to the Marylebone Club.)

own against all comers until 1769. Meeting with many reverses that year, it was on the point of dissolution the year after: but in 1771 its supporters determined to make another effort; and against Surrey County, in September of that year, they were successful by the narrow majority of one run. The next ten years saw them add to their laurels. Out of fifty-one matches played against England during that time, they won twenty-nine. They have been immortalised in one of the earliest and most charming of all books published on the game—Nyren's *Cricketers' Tutor.* Nyren gives the names of the most eminent players when the club was at its best, and says of them: "No eleven in England had any chance with these men, and I think they might have beaten any two-and-twenty." The Eleven were:

David Harris,	Tom Walker,
John Wells,	— Robinson,
— Purchase,	Noah Mann,
William Beldham,	— Scott,
John Small, jun.,	— Taylor.
Harry Walker,	

Beldham and Harris were the great men of the team—Beldham as a batsman, Harris as a bowler. Of Beldham, Nyren says: "We used to call him 'Silver Billy.' He was a close-set, active man, standing about five feet eight inches and a half. No one within my recollection could stop a ball better, or make more brilliant hits all over the ground; besides this, he was so remarkably safe. I hardly ever saw a man with a finer command of the bat, and he rapidly attained to the extraordinary accomplishment of being the finest player that has appeared within the latitude of more than half a century. One of the most beautiful sights that can be imagined, and which would have delighted an artist, was to see him make himself up to hit a ball. It was the *beau ideal* of grace, animation, and concentrated energy."

Of Harris, he says: "He was a muscular, bony man, standing about five feet nine and a half inches. It would be difficult, perhaps impossible, to convey in writing an accurate idea of the grand effect of Harris's bowling; they only who have played against him can fully appreciate it. First of all, he stood erect, like a soldier at drill; then, with a graceful curve of the arm, he raised the ball to his forehead, and drawing back his right foot, started off with his left. His mode of delivering the ball was very singular. He would bring it from under the arm by a twist, and nearly as high as his armpit, and with his action *push* it, as it were, from him. He never stooped in the least in his delivery, but kept himself upright all the time. His balls were very little beholden to the ground when pitched: it was but a touch and up again; and woe be to the man who did not get in to block him, for they had such a peculiar curl that they would grind his fingers against the bat."

Harris may be considered the first bowler who knew the power of a good-length ball. Until he appeared, daisy-cutters were about the only balls bowled. Everyone knows the result of hitting at a ball on the rise—that is off the wicket; or how easy it is to get a batsman out who can only play back. The two best batsmen of that time, Beldham and Lord Frederick Beauclerk, could play both back and forward, and the display was considered of a very high order when Harris was bowling against them.

Tom Walker was another of the Hambledon worthies, the coolest fellow in existence. Patience and imperturbability were his chief virtues; and he had the reputation of keeping up his wicket from the beginning to the end of an innings, and playing his first ball as he would play the last. Tom's appearance on a cricket-field would startle the carefully-dressed player of to-day. "He was the driest and most rigid-limbed chap I ever knew," says Nyren. "His skin was like the rind of an old oak, and as sapless. I have seen his knuckles knocked handsomely about, from Harris's bowling, but never saw any blood upon his hands. You might just as well attempt to phlebotomise a mummy. He had a wilted, apple-john face; long, spider legs, as thick at the ancles as at the hips, and perfectly straight all the way down." Tom was not satisfied with underhand bowling, and was the first to raise the arm above the level of the elbow; but he got no encouragement from the Hambledon Club, who decided it was throwing, and he had to give it up.

Nyren, while strong in the opinion that the Hambledon Club was head and shoulders above every other, was not blind to the merits of his opponents. He is great in praise of Lumpy—Stevens was his real name—a Surrey man. Lumpy could bowl the greatest number of length-balls in succession of any bowler he knew. He had a great reputation as a single-wicket player; but was completely and unexpectedly sat upon on a certain occasion. The match in which he was playing having been concluded early in the day, "a long, raw-boned devil of a countryman came up, and offered to play any of the twenty-two at single-wicket for five pounds. Lumpy was persuaded to accept the challenge, but would not stake more than a pound; the rest was subscribed. The confident old bowler made the countryman go in first, for he thought to settle his business in a twink; but the fellow having an arm as long as a hop-pole, reached in at Lumpy's balls, bowl what length he might, slashed and thrashed away in the most ludicrous style, hitting his balls all over the field, and made an uncommon number of runs before he got rid of him. Lumpy was not much of a bat, and the countryman quickly upset his wicket with a fast daisy-cutter, and won very easily, amidst the uproarious laughter of those present. Lumpy swore he would never play another single-wicket match as long as he lived, and he did not."

Nyren's description of a match is as hearty and enthusiastic as his sketch of the players. "Little Hambledon pitted against All England was a proud thought for the Hampshire men. Defeat was glory in such a struggle; victory, indeed, made us only a little lower than the angels. Half the county would be present, and all their hearts were with us. And whenever a Hambledon man made a good hit, worth four or five runs, you would hear the deep mouths of the whole multitude baying away in pure Hampshire, 'Go hard! go hard! *Tich* and turn! *tich* and turn!'"

We can shout to-day when occasion requires, but the players of the past seem to have had rather the best of us there.

The Hambledon Club played first on Broad-halfpenny Down, afterwards on Windmill Down, both close to the village of Hambledon. An old painting gives the eleven in their club costume of knee-breeches, stockings, buckles, shoes, and velvet caps. Lord Winchelsea's team some years later played in silver-laced hats.

Harris's introduction of good-length bowling caused the bat to be altered from the hockey shape to a straight form, and playing with a straight bat was now cultivated. There was no law in existence as to its size, and a player named White, of Reigate, appeared at a match with a bat larger than the wicket; but a rule was immediately passed regulating the size, and the Hambledon Club had an iron frame made through which every bat was passed before it was allowed to be used. Leg-guards now came into use, but they were very simply and imperfectly made. They consisted of two pieces of wood placed anglewise to protect the shins, and were anything but comfortable.

There were laws of a kind governing the game about the year 1700; but umpires had not the powers they possess now, and few matches were played without bickerings and quarrellings. Those of us who have had any experience of country cricket know that the umpires' decisions do not always receive the respect due to them, and that many a match has terminated in a dispute. That was not an uncommon ending to many a close match from 1700 to 1708. No man was ever justly out; many claimed to go in twice; catches were often disputed. The side going from home had the right of pitching the wickets, and a good general took care they were pitched to suit his own bowlers. One maxim of Nyren's will show that each side was only too anxious to steal an advantage over the other in the preliminary arrangements. He says: "In making a match you should be careful to *stand on higher terms than you have an absolute occasion for*, that you may the more easily obtain such as are necessary; keeping in mind the old adage, 'A match well made is half won.'"

The following laws are the oldest published, and remained in force until the beginning of 1774:

"THE GAME OF CRICKET, AS SETTLED BY YE CRICKET CLUB AT YE STAR AND GARTER IN PALL MALL.

The pitching ye first wicket is to be determined by ye cast of a piece of money when ye first wicket is pitched and ye popping crease cut, which must be exactly 3 Foot 10 inches from ye Wicket. Ye Other Wicket is to be pitched directly opposite, at 22 yards distance, and ye other popping crease cut 3 Foot 10 inches before it. The Bowling Creases must be cut in a direct line from each Stump. The Stumps must be 22 inches long, and ye Bail 6 inches. The Ball must weigh between 5 and 6 ounces. When ye wickets are both pitched and all ye Creases Cut, the party that wins the toss-up may order which side shall go in first at his option.

LAWS FOR YE BOWLERS—4 BALLS AND OVER.

The Bowler must deliver ye Ball with one foot behind the Crease even with ye wicket, and when he has bowled one ball or more shall Bowl to ye number 4 before he changes wickets, and he Shall Change but once in ye same innings. He may order ye Player that is in at his wicket to Stand on which side of it he Pleases, at a reasonable distance. If he delivers ye Ball with his hinder foot over ye Bowling crease ye Umpire shall call no Ball, though she be struck or ye Player is Bowled out; which he shall do without being asked, and no Person shall have any right to ask him.

LAWS FOR YE STRIKERS, OR THOSE THAT ARE IN.

If ye wicket be bowled down its out. If he Strikes, or treads down, or falls upon ye wicket in striking (but not in over running) its out. A Stroke or Nip over or under his Batt or upon his hands (but not arms), if ye Ball be held before She touches ye Ground, though She be hugged to the Body, its out. If in Striking both his feet are over ye popping Crease and his Wicket put down, except his Batt is down within, its out. If he runs out of his Ground to hinder a Catch, its out. If a Ball is nipped up and he Strikes her again Wilfully before She comes to ye Wicket, its out. If ye Players have crossed each other, he that runs for ye Wicket that is put down is out. If they are not Crossed, he that returns is out. If in running a Notch ye Wicket is struck down by a Throw before his Foot, Hand, or Batt is over ye Popping Crease, or a Stump hit by ye Ball, though ye Bail was down, its out. But if ye Bail is down before, he that catches ye Ball must strike a Stump out of ye Ground, Ball in Hand, then its out. If ye Striker touches or takes up ye Ball before she is lain quite still, unless asked by ye Bowler or Wicket Keeper, its out.

BATT, FOOT, OR HAND OVER YE CREASE.

When ye Ball has been in Hand by one of ye Keeper or Stopers and ye Player has been at Home, He may go where he pleases till ye next Ball is bowled. If Either of ye Strikers is crossed in his running Ground designedly, which design must be determined by the Umpires. N.B.—The Umpires may order that notch to be scored. When ye Ball is hit up either of ye strikers may hinder ye catch in his running ground, or if She is hit directly across ye Wickets ye Other Player may place his Body any where within ye swing of his Batt so as to hinder ye Bowler from catching her, but he must neither Strike at her nor touch her with his hands. If a striker nips up a Ball just before him he may fall before his Wicket, or pop down his Batt before Shee comes to it, to save it. The Bail hanging on one stump, though ye Ball hit ye Wicket, its not out.

LAWS FOR WICKET KEEPERS.

The Wicket Keeper shall stand at a reasonable distance behind ye Wicket, and shall not move till ye Ball is out of ye Bowler's Hands, and shall not by any noise incommode ye Striker; and if his knees, foot, or head be over or before his wicket, though the Ball strike it, it shall not be out.

LAWS FOR YE UMPIRES.

To allow 2 minutes for each man to come in when one is out, and 10 minutes between Each Hand to mark ye Ball, that it may not be changed. They are sole judges of all outs and ins, of all fair and unfair Play, of frivolous delays, of all hurts, whether real or pretended, and are discretionally to allow whatever time they think Proper before ye Game goes on again. In case of a real hurt to a striker, they are to allow another to come in, and the Person hurt to come in again, but are not to allow a fresh Man to Play on either side on any Account. They are sole judges of all hindrances, crossing ye Players in running, and Standing unfair to Strike; and in case of hindrance may order a notch to be scored. They are not to order any man out unless appealed to by one of ye Players. These Laws are to ye Umpires Jointly. Each Umpire is ye Sole Judge of all Nips and Catches, Ins and outs, good or bad runs at his own Wicket, and his determination shall be absolute; and he shall not be changed for another Umpire without ye Consent of both Sides. When ye 4 Balls are bowled he is to call over. These Laws are separately. When both Umpires shall call Play 3 Times 'tis at ye Peril of giving ye Game from them that refuse Play."

"Notch" was the term used for a run in those days. Scorers generally were not sufficiently educated to enter in writing the runs as they were made, and the primitive form of cutting a notch in a piece of wood was resorted to. A deeper notch was made every tenth run. Rarely were individual innings recorded in other than first-class matches; and it is difficult to say when the important clubs began to keep complete and reliable results of their matches.

The year 1774 left its mark upon the game. A committee of noblemen and gentlemen, from the counties of Kent, Hampshire, Surrey, Sussex, and Middlesex, met at the Star and Garter, Pall Mall, on February the 25th, and revised the Laws. Compared with those already given, they showed distinct progress, though falling short of the completeness and comprehensiveness of those in existence to-day. The great point gained was, that an authoritative body of players, chosen from the chief clubs in the kingdom, had spoken out, and their decisions were sure to be respected. Very few of them have stood the criticism of the 117 years that have elapsed since they were drawn up; but they were the outcome of the united wisdom of the best players of that time, and met the demands of the game for a good many years afterwards. The foot-notes with regard to betting would not be tolerated to-day; but, if we are to accept the statements of different writers, that nearly every important match played then was for a sum of money varying from £50 to £1000, we can see the need for them and understand why they were added.

The year 1775 saw the abolishment of placing the ball in the hole between the wickets, and the increase in the number of the stumps from two to three. At an important match that year, Lumpy, one of the best bowlers of the day, two or three times bowled balls which passed between the stumps. This was naturally considered hard upon Lumpy, and the third stump was added, and placed so that the ball could not pass between them without knocking the bail off. Two years later, 1777, what was considered a phenomenal score was made by James Aylward, for the Hambledon Club, against England. He scored 167 runs out of a total of 403. Individual performance and aggregate score were reckoned among the sensational doings; and it was thought that the former would stand as record for a century at least; as for the same individual exceeding it, no one dreamt of it. The same year saw the last match played on the Artillery Ground, Finsbury Square, the scene of many great and exciting contests for a considerable number of years.

The first recorded match of the White Conduit Club was played in 1785; and two years later the Marylebone Club was started. Farther on I have written more fully upon the rise and progress of the club, which has been looked upon as the authority upon all points of the game for more than a century. This much will suffice here: In 1779 a number of gentlemen—among them Lord Winchelsea, Sir Horace Mann, Sir P. Burrell, Lord Strathaven, and others—were in the habit of playing matches in the White Conduit Fields, and in the Artillery Ground, Finsbury. They formed the White Conduit Club the year after, and continued playing until some misunderstanding arose amongst the members. Thomas Lord, an attendant and enthusiastic player, was one of their bowlers, and he was instructed to look out for a ground, and promised support if he succeeded. By some writers Lord is given as a Scottish Jacobite; by others as a native of Yorkshire. It matters little to which country he belonged: he possessed the enterprising qualities which both Yorkshiremen and Scotchmen have the credit of; and in 1789 Lord's Cricket Ground, and the foundation of the M.C.C. on the site of Dorset Square, were accomplished facts. Here he remained for some years, until driven out by encroaching builders, when he and the club moved, about the year 1811, to another ground, where South Bank, Regent's Park, now stands. The cutting of the Regent's Canal compelled him to move a second time; and 1814 saw him and the M.C.C. established for good in St. John's Wood Road. The M.C.C. played matches in 1789, but there is no published record of their doings

A YOUNG CRICKETER.

(From a Picture ascribed to GAINSBOROUGH, *belonging to the Marylebone Club.)*

until the year after; and until 1791 a club match-book was not kept.

The year 1791 saw the dissolution of the Hambledon Club and the dispersion of its members over the counties of Surrey, Hampshire, Kent, and Middlesex.

Lord FREDERICK BEAUCLERK (height, 5 ft. 9 ins.; weight, 11 st. 12 lbs.) played his first match at Lord's in the same year for the M.C.C. *v.* Kent. He was in his eighteenth year, but gave no promise in that match of the skill which attracted the cricketing public a few years later, and which stamped him as the best amateur batsman of his day. He was a fair bowler, and kept up his form for nearly a quarter of a century.

Surrey, Kent, and M.C.C. were now the crack clubs in England, and before the end of the eighteenth century they were in turn strong enough to play an eleven of All England. County matches were of frequent occurrence: Surrey played Kent, Hampshire, and Middlesex; Kent and Middlesex played Essex; and Nottingham played Leicester.

The first twenty years of the nineteenth century introduced seven names which will live in the memories of cricketers as long as the game is played. To belong to the M.C.C. even in those days was the aim of most players; to be considered good enough to play for or against it, was to stamp the player as belonging to the first flight. W. Lambert made his first appearance at Lord's in 1801, playing for Surrey *v.* England; E. H. Budd in 1802, playing for Middlesex *v.* Surrey; George Osbaldeston in 1808, playing for M.C.C. *v.* Middlesex; W. Ward in 1810, playing for England *v.* Surrey; Jas. Broadbridge in 1817, playing for Sussex *v.* Epsom; George Brown in 1818, playing in a single-wicket match; and Fuller Pilch in 1820, when only seventeen years of age, playing for Norfolk *v.* M.C.C.

W. Lambert (height, 5 ft. 10 ins.; weight, 15 st.) was a good all-round player: first-class as a batsman, possessing tremendous hitting powers, a good bowler and wicket-keeper, and one of the best single wicket players of his time.

Mr. Edward Hayward Budd (born at Great Missenden, Buckinghamshire; height, 5 ft. 9 ins.; weight, 12 st.) excelled as a batsman, but was good all round: he used a bat 3 lbs. in weight, hit terrifically, and played cricket from his seventeenth year until his seventieth.

Mr. George Osbaldeston (born 1786 or 1787; height, 5 ft. 6 ins.; weight, 10½ st.) was a splendid batsman; but made his mark more as a bowler, being considered the fastest who had yet appeared. His reputation as a single-wicket player was only second to Lambert's, and together they were equal to any pair in England. A good story is told of a single-wicket match made between Osbaldeston and Lambert on one side, and Lord Frederick Beauclerk and Howard on the other. It was a p. p. match for fifty guineas, and the result was thought to determine which was the strongest pair of that time. On the day of the match Osbaldeston was ill, and Lord Frederick was asked to postpone the match.

"No! Play or pay," said his lordship.

"I won't forfeit," said Osbaldeston. "Lambert may beat you both; and if he does, he shall have the money."

His lordship would not hear of it. "Nonsense," he said, "you don't mean it."

"Yes; play or pay, my lord. We are in earnest and shall claim the stakes."

Score: Lambert—First innings, 56; second innings, 24; total, 80. Lord Beauclerk and Howard—First innings, 24; second innings, 42; total, 66.

MR. GEORGE OSBALDESTON.

(From an old Print.)

It was a great victory for Lambert, and he displayed excellent judgment. Wides did not count in those days; so he bowled them to his lordship until he lost his temper, and then catching him napping, bowled him with a straight ball. But Lambert will be remembered as being the first to score the century twice in a first-class match—in the year 1817—which stood as a record for over fifty years.

Mr. William Ward (born at Islington, London, 24th July, 1787; height, 6 ft. 1½ in.; weight, 14 st.) was a better batsman than bowler, and will be remembered for his great score of 278, when playing for the M.C.C. against Norfolk, in 1820. He played with a bat 4 lbs. in weight, and was one of the few who accommodated himself quickly to the change from underhand to round-arm bowling. Indeed, the change made little difference to him; and after it was introduced, he continued to score as freely as ever.

Jas. Broadbridge (height, 5 ft. 10 ins.; weight, 12 st.) could bat, but his name stands out as one of the two great bowlers of his time. Lillywhite and he were the two great exponents of round-arm bowling, and by their exceptional skill raised Sussex to a very high position in the cricketing world.

George Brown (born at Stoughton, Surrey, 27th April, 1783) is supposed to have been the fastest underhand bowler that ever played. He was so very fast that two longstops were needed for him, and nearly all the fieldsmen were placed behind the wicket. At Lord's a man once tried to stop the ball with his coat, but Brown bowled through it and killed a dog on the other side! Jackson, Tarrant, and Freeman, of later years, we can most of us remember, but Brown's pace at his best is said to have been faster than theirs. His height was 6 ft. 3 ins.; weight, about 16 st.

Fuller Pilch, as a batsman, was head and shoulders above the others, and was undoudtedly the crack from 1820 to 1850. His height was 6 feet 0½ in.; and he possessed an exceptionally long reach, which he used to the fullest advantage. He played forward, and was thoroughly at home against all kinds of bowling. He was born at Horningtoft, Norfolk, 17th March, 1803, but migrated to Town Malling in 1835, and by his personal skill raised Kent to the position of being able to play an eleven of England. He scored the century at least ten times in his career, which was considered a remarkable and exceptional performance then. He was past playing when I saw him first; but I can remember the pleasure it gave me when I met him at Canterbury, and we talked about the past, present, and future of the game. His star had set: mine was in the ascendant; but the light of battle was still on his face, and I could see what manner of man he had been.

Those were the players who made cricket history from 1800 to 1825; and I can quite believe they would give an excellent account of themselves to-day on our improved wickets against our best bowling.

Eton and Harrow played against each other at the beginning of the present century; but the earliest published score in existence is of the year 1805, when Eton won by an innings.

The Gentlemen and Players commenced in 1806; but then and for some years afterwards it was a case of the Players giving one or two of their best men, or playing against odds. The first match of that year the Gentlemen had Lambert and Beldham given them, and won; the second match Lambert only, which they won also. For years the Gentlemen struggled to make a fight, but all in vain. Various suggestions were made to make the match interesting and give them a chance

FULLER PILCH.

of victory, but the results were still the same; and it became an accepted fact that if anyone desired to establish a reputation for prophecy, he could do it easily by naming the Players as certain winners in their match against the Gentlemen. Apathy began to pervade the ranks of the Gentlemen, and a collapse seemed inevitable. Here and there enthusiastic players kept advocating the claims of the match, Mr. Ward among them. The year 1837, at his suggestion, the Players defended wickets 36 inches by 12; the Gentlemen, 27 inches by 8. The result was still unsatisfactory, the Gentlemen scoring 54 and 35 to the Players' single innings of 99. Like all innovators, Mr. Ward got little thanks for his invention, and the match was dubbed the "Barn-door Match," or "Ward's Folly."

The year 1817 saw a great decline in the powers of Surrey. Considered good enough to play thirteen of England some twenty years before, it was not able now to play eleven, and did not attempt it again until 1852.

The year 1822 was an important one. It saw Mr. JOHN WILLES at Lord's on the 15th and 16th July, playing for Kent *v.* M.C.C., make a big bid for the introduction of round-arm bowling. He was only allowed to bowl a few balls before he was "no-balled," and he left the ground, declining to go on with the match. A substitute was found, and Kent won easily by an innings.

Mr. Willes has the credit of introducing round-arm bowling, and there can be little doubt his attempt in this match created the agitation which led to its adoption a short time afterwards. This is the story told of how he learned it. He had been very ill, and to recover strength fell back upon the game he loved so dearly. He was not quite strong enough to bowl, so he enlisted the aid of his sister to bowl to him. The straight ones troubled him more than the old style of bowling; rising more quickly off the pitch, and travelling differently. A little reflection revealed that his sister in delivering the ball turned her hand over it, hence the change. As soon as he got well he practised it, and found he could do more with the ball. Unfortunately his temper was stronger than his respect for the laws; for not only did he leave the match, but made up his mind to give up playing altogether—a decision which he adhered to. It will not do to condemn his action too severely. He is not the first who has had a pet theory pooh-poohed, and given it up in a moment of petulance. Five years later, if he had retained his proficiency, he would have been a perfect godsend to the Gentlemen, and have helped to speed the good cause with F. W. Lillywhite, J. Broadbridge, and Mr. G. T. Knight. It should be remembered that Tom Walker, of the Hambledon Club, practised it also.

The year 1827 saw the new bowling having a fair trial. Lillywhite and Broadbridge were the most proficient at it, and placed Sussex in the position of being able to play All England. The first match came off on the 4th June, at Darnall, Sheffield, and was looked upon as a comparative test of the two styles of bowling—England being represented by underhand bowlers. Alas! for the underhand representatives! they were out of it altogether, Sussex winning by seven wickets. Why the match was played in Yorkshire I do not know, unless it be that the cricketing authorities in the South were desirous, in the interests of the game, to give cricketers in the North an opportunity of witnessing first-class play. Cricket had made tremendous strides in Nottingham, Sheffield, Liverpool and Manchester in the last half-dozen years, and the policy of the M.C.C. in playing a representative match there was in keeping with the forward spirit it has ever shown since the welfare of the game was placed in its hands.

The second match was played at Lord's a fortnight

later, Sussex again winning, but only by two wickets. The defeat upset some of the players who represented England, and a number of them, with more temper than judgment, met and signed the following document: "We, the undersigned, do agree that we will not play the third match between All England and Sussex, unless the Sussex bowlers bowl fair—that is, abstain from throwing."

Fuller Pilch's name was amongst the signatories, but reflection brought wisdom, and the third match was played at Brighton, the 23rd, 24th, 25th July, England winning by 23 runs. Ten years later Pilch, playing for Town Malling *v.* Reigate, scored 160 against Lillywhite's bowling. Round-arm bowling had now taken a hold, and here will be the place to say a word on behalf of one of the earliest and finest exponents it has ever had.

FREDERICK WILLIAM LILLYWHITE was born at West Hampnett, near Goodwood, Sussex, June 13th, 1792. There is no record of his doings until he was thirty years of age, and his first appearance at Lord's was on June 18th, 1827, in his thirty-sixth year, playing for Sussex *v.* England. His height was only 5 ft. 4 ins.; but he was substantially made (weighing 11 st. 8 lbs.), and possessed exceptional stamina. He played right up to the day of his death, August 24th, 1854. The introduction of round-arm bowling was his opportunity, and no one then had a greater command over the ball. His pace would be considered slow to-day, but his accuracy of pitch was something marvellous, and a ball off the wicket was a rare thing. A wide ball from him was not expected and rarely given; he only bowled some half-a-dozen in his whole career. He was what is now called a "head bowler," always on the look-out for a weak spot in the defence of the batsman, and trusting more to catches than to wickets bowled down. He

W. LILLYWHITE.

MR. ALFRED MYNN.

(From an old Print.)

knew that the batsmen of that time had not been used to over after over of straight, good-length balls, and that sooner or later he would tempt them to hit. For years Broadbridge and he carried everything before them. Broadbridge was medium-pace also, and had been before the public as a good man some ten years before. The batting for some years had had the upper hand of the bowling; but Lillywhite and Broadbridge restored the balance, and showed the importance of being able to defend one's wicket as well as hit.

In 1832 Mr. ALFRED MYNN appeared at Lord's. In his way, he was quite as celebrated as Lillywhite, and was certainly a more striking figure. He was born January 19th, 1809; height, 6 ft. 1 in.; weight, 18 st. He was of the most lovable temper, and no player was cheered more heartily by the cricket-loving public; and he was a rare good batsman, hitting severely, and scoring faster than any player of his time. The hitting of his time compares unfavourably with the rapidity of the scoring to-day, thirty runs an hour being considered fast. His bowling was round-arm, very fast, but in the early part of his career very erratic—aiming at beating the batsman by sheer pace. His delivery was peculiar,—described by one writer as noble and majestic. He walked up to the crease, head erect like a soldier on parade, and the ball shot from his hand at a pace worthy of so strong a man.

Mynn and Lillywhite were the two bowlers who were now looked up to as possessing the styles to be copied—Mynn, very fast, relying on his pace; Lillywhite, a good length, relying on his accuracy. Mynn had the greater number of followers for a time—followers who bowled at a pace much beyond their strength and went quickly to pieces. Lillywhite's accurate length appealed to the thoughtful player, and raised both bowling and batting to a more scientific position.

Sir FREDERICK HUTCHISON HARVEY BATHURST was born June 30th, 1807. Height, 6 ft.; weight, 13 st. He was a first-rate round-armed bowler, and, like one or two fast bowlers I have mentioned, had rather a low delivery. Very few amateurs have continued playing at so advanced an age, and with such great success; for when he was 53 years old he represented the Gentlemen of Hampshire on several occasions, bowling in most of their matches, and rarely failing to come off: one match in particular, against the United England Eleven, he showed that he had lost little of his wonderful command of the ball.

He represented the Gentlemen *v.* Players in 1837, the "Barn Door" match, and continued to do so until 1854, when he was in his 48th year. Most years he bowled for them with more or less success; but in 1853, at Lord's, he carried everything before him, bowling unchanged in both innings—a feat which had never been performed before by either Gentleman or Player in those matches. In the first innings he bowled 132 balls, 24 maidens, 19 runs and captured 5 wickets; in the second, 140 balls, 20 maidens, 31 runs, 6 wickets; and there can be little doubt the Gentlemen were indebted to him and Mr. Kempson for winning the match on that occasion.

He was not a scientific bat, going in for hitting, and taking little trouble about defence, like many of the great bowlers of that time, and I do not remember any very large scores to his name. But he was a very fine fieldsman, and one of the greatest supporters of the game we have had. He was President of the M.C.C. in 1857, and a constant attendant for many years at the great matches played at Lord's.

Mr. C. G. TAYLOR (height, 5 ft. 9 ins.; weight, 10 st.), two years later, made his first appearance at Lord's, playing for Eton *v.* Harrow, and for the next twelve years shared the amateur batting honours with Mynn. He belonged to Middlesex, and was born 21st November, 1815.

July 11th, 1836, at Lord's, was the beginning of North *v.* South matches; the North winning by six wickets. Lillywhite was ill, and did not play, or the result might have been different. In the return at Leicester, six weeks later, the South won by 218 runs. Mynn was in his best batting form, scoring 21 not out, first innings; 125 not out, second. In his last four innings he had scored 283 runs, twice not out—a feat which was considered a record for four consecutive innings in great matches. Lillywhite was just as effective with the ball in this match, capturing five wickets first innings, six second. Fuller Pilch played on the side of the North; but 1837 saw him batting for the South, which he continued to do for the remainder of his career.

Messrs. W. MARCON and H. W. FELLOWS, as exceptionally fast bowlers, attracted attention in 1841. Both played for Eton *v.* Winchester at Lord's, 29th, 30th July of that year, and in the fulness of strength were contrasts physically. Mr. Marcon was 6 ft. in height; weight, 11 st. He was born at Swaffham, 28th March, 1824. Mr. Fellows was 5 ft. 9¾ ins. in height; weight, 15 st. He was born at Rickmansworth, Hertfordshire, 11th April, 1826. Mr. Marcon played a great deal, and, like George Brown of Stoughton, required two longstops, and tested the nerve of every wicket-keeper who tried to take his bowling. It is said of him that, with a very fast ball, he broke a batsman's leg at Oxford. As a player, I should like to have seen this particular fast ball and the unfortunate batsman who tried to play it. My medical experience has shown me that some legs are easily broken; but I have been always of the opinion that the legs, like the heads, of 'Varsity men have been exceptionally hard nuts to crack. I have had many an interesting chat with Mr. Fellows; but, as far as I know, he has no such extraordinary testimony to his powers, although his bowling was considered dangerous to bat against, and the ball as it travelled hummed like a top. On one occasion he hit a stump so terrifically hard that it fell into the longstop's hands eleven yards distant! Both gentlemen had rather a low delivery, something between under-hand and round-arm.

The year 1845 was another of the eventful years. GEORGE PARR played for the North *v.* M.C.C. at Lord's. He was then in his twentieth year, and, though he did not score largely, eventually became the best batsman in England—a position which he held for many years. He had splendid defence, and hit particularly well all round, but excelled in hitting to leg. He had also a good knowledge of the game, and made an excellent captain; and his name was on the lips of every player for twenty years. He was born 22nd May, 1826, at Radcliffe-on-Trent: height, 5 ft. 9 ins.; weight, 12 st. 12 lbs.

The 17th July of that year is the date of the first match played at Kennington Oval. Originally a market garden, the Montpelier Club secured the ground in 1844, and formed themselves into the Surrey Club the year after. After a number of ups and downs in the next ten years, Surrey suddenly blossomed into a most powerful club, and became second only to its next-door neighbour, the M.C.C., in power and influence. The members in 1855 numbered 230, income £500; in 1861 they had increased to 1,000, income £2,000; and every year since they may be said to have increased.

The 25th August, 1845, is another landmark. On that date the now famous club, the I Zingari, began its wanderings over the face of the earth, seeking for rising

4

clubs; but more particularly for *gentlemen* bowlers who should wrest the supremacy from the professionals, and make the Gentlemen *v.* Players match a closer contest.

The club became a most popular one, and did good work for the game whenever it played. Crowds naturally flocked to see an eleven which comprised most of the best amateur bats of the day. Originally small in number, its strength to-day is something to be proud of, and to be enrolled amongst its members is considered a very high honour. I have in my possession a copy of its first Rules and Regulations, and give a selection:

RULE III.

A candidate for election shall be placed at a wicket, with or without a bat as the club may decide, and be bowled at. One straight ball to exclude. The number of balls given not to exceed the number of members of the I *Z.*

RULE V.

That the entrance be nothing, and the annual subscription do not exceed the entrance; but that the expenses of a match (*i.e.* of the I *Z.* umpire, &c.) be defrayed by the members engaged therein.

RULE VII.

That all directions connected with the game *may* be conveyed in the French or Italian languages.

SUPPLICATION.

Members playing in I *Z.* matches are more than most earnestly requested to abstain from wearing *any* coloured shirt, jacket or trousers. A Zingari belt or cap or ribbon should be the only distinguishing badge.

IRRITATION.

I *Z.* batsmen and fieldsmen being hit are not entitled to scratch or rub.

PROHIBITION.

Health drinking and dry toasts.

REITERATION.

Keep your promise, keep your temper, keep your wicket up.

The club flourished at a great rate, and in 1862 was made up of Active Members, Agents, Half-play Members liable to be called out, Members unattached to Cricket but attached to the I *Z.*, and Candidates for the Asylum for Aged and Decayed Zingari.

CHAPTER II.

THE ALL-ENGLAND AND OTHER ELEVENS.

THE All-England Eleven was formed in **1846**. Before that time cricket in England was confined to certain districts. It had always flourished in such counties as Kent, Hants, Surrey, Notts, and Sussex; but outside of them it had been limited to a few country clubs, which were more or less attached to some nobleman or gentleman's residence, and were in fact supported by them. Such for instance was the Kingscote club, in Gloucestershire, under the auspices of the good old cricketing family of that name. Lord Ducie had a club at Tortworth, and the Marquis of Lansdown at Bowood. True, there were important clubs in such large towns as Liverpool, Manchester, and one or two others; but the members were mostly in good positions, and were usually elected by ballot. At the weekly meetings of those clubs, the younger members came to play, the older ones to criticise, and sides were picked. A few matches were played during the season with clubs of the same strength who were within driving distance.

The dinners played no insignificant part at those gatherings, and many a good bottle of port was cracked before the evening was over. It is related that the Kingscote club nearly ruined itself by its hospitality to the Epsom club after a friendly match. Three haunches of venison were consumed, besides other delicacies, and the cellar ran dry. The chairman is said to have closed the innings of the claret with the remark: "Gentlemen, I am sorry to say there is only one bottle left, and as it would be ridiculous to divide that among so many, with your permission I'll drink it myself." That sort of social cricket existed, and very enjoyable cricket it was; but cricket amongst the people was scarcely known until the All-England Eleven appeared.

Amateur efforts do not, as a rule, meet with success, for the reason that too often no one is responsible and the element of self-interest wanting. The I Zingari club has been a brilliant exception; but since it was formed a hundred clubs could be named which, conducted on somewhat similar lines, have died after a few years of struggling existence. The All-England Eleven was started by one man, and conducted on business principles; and while it lived it was exceedingly active, and helped to spread a knowledge of the game. William Clarke was the founder; the majority of the players who composed it were the best professionals in England in every branch of the game, and under his leadership were open for engagements anywhere, as long as they obtained their price. As the Eleven grew in strength and popularity, the desire to be considered worthy of a place in it became the aim of every young and rising cricketer, and on more than one occasion some of the most celebrated amateurs were to be found playing in its ranks for the honour alone. Of course the difficulty was to find clubs of any strength to compete against. Usually the number of their opponents was twenty-two; but very often that was found inadequate to make a fight against so strong a combination of talent, and recourse was had to players outside of the club. In many cases two or more professional bowlers were allowed, and by that means interesting contests were played, and the Eleven compelled to put its best foot forward.

Every player of the twenty-two was naturally anxious to do his best against such celebrated players, for well he knew that his success would be talked about over the length and breadth of the land. To keep up one's wicket for half-an-hour, even without scoring, against the best bowling in England, was to create a reputation locally; to score a double figure and be praised by one of those great men, was something to boast of for a lifetime. A good many of us can date our first experience of first-class play from witnessing the famous All-England Eleven, and hundreds will tell with glistening eyes of the good old times when they were considered worthy of a place against it.

The first match played was against twenty of Sheffield, on August 31st, September 1st and 2nd, 1846, Sheffield winning by five wickets. The All-England Eleven players were:

Mr. A. Mynn,
W. Clarke,
J. Dean,
W. Dorrinton,
F. Pilch,
J. Guy,
W. Martingell,
T. Sewell,
G. Butler,
V. C. Smith,
W. Hillyer.

That was a team that could hold its own against any eleven in England; but not to be compared with the team of 1847, or a year or two later, which had such good men in it as G. Parr, F. W. Lillywhite, and J. Wisden.

Clarke was the central figure, and for years met with phenomenal success as a slow underhand bowler. As a leader he knew the value of a change of bowling, believing the greater the difference of style

DEAN
CLARKE
HILLYER
DORRINGTON
PILCH
SEWELL

the greater the chance of success. Mynn, Lillywhite, Hillyer, Wisden and he, ranging from fast round to slow underhand, were variety enough for all purposes, and there can be little doubt that their opponents were in many cases paralysed by it. It was an amusing sight in those days to watch the procession of local players to and from the wicket, dismissed by fast round-hand at one end and insinuating slow underhand at the other. I cannot think of a time when the All-England Eleven, during the first twenty years of its existence, did not possess slow and fast bowling, and in that lay half its strength against weak twenty-two's who had only been accustomed to one extreme or the other. Clarke's personal success was the astonishing part to his opponents. They could understand being bowled by a fast ball of indifferent length, which they but dimly saw after it pitched; but to be clean-bowled by slow underhand was a mystery to them. They forgot the head that was behind Clarke's bowling. Just as F. W. Lillywhite was the first to prove the power of a good-length medium pace, round-arm ball, so was Clarke the pioneer of good-length slow underhand. Both had thoughtful heads on their shoulders, could tell very quickly what a batsman could play and what he could not, and when they found a weak point bowled at it until they got their man out. I question very much if we have had a slow underhand bowler of the quality of Clarke since. His pitch was so accurate that when he made up his mind to bowl at a particular spot, he could bowl within two inches of it as long as he desired.

Clarke's Eleven visited something like forty different districts the first three years of its existence, and many other fresh places were visited in later years. It is difficult to get at a trustworthy statement of the bowling averages, but in 1850 Clarke bowled in thirty matches and captured 303 wickets.

William Clarke was born at Nottingham, 24th December, 1798, so that he was in his 48th year when he started the All-England Eleven. His height was 5 ft. 9 in.; weight, about 14 stone. He appeared, for North *v.* South, at Lord's in 1836, when he was 37 years old; but he made little impression then. Twenty years previously his name appears in the Nottingham Eleven, showing that he must have played at a very early age; but the advent of the All-England Eleven was his opportunity, and he bowled with great success until the year of his death in 1856. Like Lillywhite, he was well advanced in years before he made his mark, and it was the occasion that created the man. The success which had attended such fast bowlers as Sir F. Bathurst and A. Mynn, fast roundarm, and Messrs. Fellows and Marcon, fast underhand, had created a rage for fast roundarm bowling, and slow underhand had been completely neglected. Clarke saw that, and his accurate length, precision of pitch, and curl from the leg to the off, completely baffled the batsmen. Most of them were in two minds about playing back or running out, and he generally managed to bowl them before they got out of their indecision. But like most bowlers who are also captains, he had the weakness of keeping himself on too long. Against Pilch, and one or two others who collared him at times, he would try just another over, which invariably did more harm than good. Success brought him the usual number of followers, who jumped to the conclusion that the secret of his bowling success lay in his pace, not in his length. Slow underhand bowling became the rage for a year or two, and clubs were just as diligent in practising slows without length, as they had been in cultivating pace without length.

The appearance of the All-England Eleven at Bristol against twenty-two of West Gloucestershire, in June,

WILLIAM CLARKE.

1854, was my first experience of first-class play. I was nearly six years old, and had paid more than one visit in the spring of that year to the field at the back of the "Full Moon" Hotel, Bristol, while it was being relaid for this special match, and the names of Clarke, Parr, Caffyn, Julius Cæsar, Anderson, and Willsher, were discussed constantly at home. My father, uncle Pocock, and brother Henry, were playing, and with boyish eagerness and delight I sat in the pony-carriage by the side of my mother and watched the play. Bickley and Clarke were in great bowling form, particularly the former. He bowled:

1st Innings	...	38 overs,	30 maidens,	10 runs,	8 wickets.
2nd ,,	...	13 ,,	12 ,,	2 ,,	5 ,,

Clarke captured eleven wickets first innings, seven second. And how Parr and Caffyn hit our bowling all over the field! Clarke's figure stands out in my memory yet.

The year after they came again to the same field, and met the same club, but Clarke was not in the Eleven. He wrote to my father some time before the match, saying that, owing to ill-health and failing sight, he would be unable to play. He was present as an onlooker during the three days, and was so delighted with E. M.'s performance as longstop that he presented him with a bat. E. M. had owned many a bat before; but this one had a spliced handle with a strip of whalebone down the centre of it, and was very much prized. My father, uncle, brothers Henry, Alfred, and E. M., all played in this match, and the twenty-two got dreadfully beaten. Bickley was again the most successful bowler, and at one part of the match was unplayable. His analysis was:

1st Innings	...	38 overs,	24 maidens,	24 runs,	16 wickets.
2nd ,,	...	41 ,,	23 ,,	30 ,,	10 ,,

His first 14 overs in the first innings made almost a record:

14 overs, 0 runs, 4 wickets;

and the next five showed:

19 overs, 17 maidens, 2 runs, 6 wickets.

Three of the All-England Eleven played in top-hats.

At the conclusion of the match Clarke presented my mother with a copy of "Cricket Notes by W. Bolland, with a letter containing Practical Hints by William Clarke." He had remembered my mother's enthusiasm the year before, and the group of boys who gathered round when he talked to her, and he knew the book would give her and them pleasure. I have the book in my possession now; it is before me as I write, and his handwriting stands out distinctly—

PRESENTED TO MRS. GRACE

BY WILLIAM CLARKE,

SECRETARY, ALL-ENGLAND ELEVEN.

You can imagine how that book was treasured and read by the younger members of the family.

Between the years 1850 and 1860 a large number ot first-class players appeared. The All-England Eleven created great interest everywhere, and it brought to light names which otherwise might never have been heard of. I have only to mention Lockyer, Julius Cæsar, Caffyn, John Lillywhite, Wisden, Anderson, Willsher, Tinley, H. H. Stephenson, Jackson, Carpenter, Daft, T. Hayward, and Tarrant. All of them I have met at some time ot my career, and I can say without hesitation they could have held their own against any combination of the present time.

Four other players might be mentioned who appeared in the decade I have been referring to—James

Grundy, James Lillywhite, W. Slinn, and Isaac Hodgson. Grundy was much the best of the four, and a good all-round man. The other three did not play so prominent a part as those I have already named. They were frequently engaged by twenty-twos in their contests against the All-England Eleven, and did some good performances in bowling.

With such an array of talent as I have enumerated, and a large number of young promising players, it will be readily conceived that there was little difficulty in finding players enough to fill up the All-England Eleven. Indeed there were more than enough to fill up two elevens; and very soon a second was formed, under the title of the United England Eleven. There had been a good deal of grumbling in the early part of 1852 about Clarke's management of the All-England Eleven. One or two of the players were dissatisfied with his treatment of them, and did not hesitate to say so. Clarke had formed the Eleven, conducted it in his own way, and successfully; and, like most successful men, he was a little bit arbitrary, and disinclined to changes which did not agree with his mode of thinking, and which would affect his future management. A little consideration to the opinions of the grumblers might have kept the original team longer together, although the increasing number of good players every year would very likely have led to the same result in a year or two. Clarke did not see his way to making the changes desired, and so the United England Eleven was formed that year.

The United England Eleven played its first match against Twenty Gentlemen of Hampshire at Portsmouth, August 26th, 27th, 28th, 1852. The eleven representing it on that occasion was certainly not of the strength of the All-England Eleven; but there were three players in it who had done good work for Clarke's team, and whose places it would be difficult to fill. Wisden, Grundy, and John Lillywhite were the three, and Wisden and Dean were appointed joint secretaries of the new eleven. Quite evidently the two teams were not on the best of terms, or rather I should say the members of the United were on terms of proclaimed hostility to Clarke; for at a meeting of the members of the United Eleven at Sheffield, 7th September, the following agreement was drawn up and signed:

"That neither of the members of the United Eleven shall at any time play in any match of cricket, for or against, wherein William Clarke may have the management or control (county matches excepted), in consequence of the treatment they have received from him at Newmarket and elsewhere."

The manifesto did not have any effect upon Clarke, or weaken the interest attached to the All-England Eleven matches, for both he and the club continued their successful career. Of course the two elevens were eager to stand well with the public, and the managers of both tried to enrol in their list of members the best players of the day. The All-England Eleven seems to have been the more attractive; for Willsher, after playing for the United in 1853, went over to the All-England in 1854. There was plenty of room for both, and the cricketing public had now greater opportunities of witnessing first-class play. Caffyn left the All-England for the United in 1854; but it was not until 1858, when Carpenter appeared, that the United was seen at its best.

After Clarke's death, Parr became manager of the All-England Eleven, and a better feeling prevailing, a match was arranged between the two elevens, at Lord's, on the 1st, 2nd, 3rd June, 1857, for the benefit of the Cricketers' Fund, which the All-England Eleven won by five wickets. The teams were made up entirely of professionals on that occasion. Messrs. F. P. Miller and F. Burbidge were down on the list of the United; but the All-England objected on the ground of their being amateurs.

The Cricketers' Fund was originated in 1857, and matches on its behalf were played annually at Lord's, between the All-England and United Elevens, down to 1867. In 1864 it was re-established on a sounder basis, and it has made satisfactory progress since; especially after 1884, when Lord Harris became president. I have taken the following from a print in my possession:—

THE CRICKETERS' FUND FRIENDLY SOCIETY.

President: LORD HARRIS.

PROVIDES FOR

THE RELIEF OF CRICKETERS,

being Members of the Society, who, from

OLD AGE, ILLNESS, ACCIDENT, OR OTHER INFIRMITY,

are incapable of following their profession; and the temporary assistance of

WIDOWS AND CHILDREN

Of such Members, who have been left destitute.

Qualification for Membership:

Any person earning a livelihood from the game of Cricket can be admitted on filling up the necessary forms.

The Society numbered nearly 120 Members on January 1st, 1891.

CLAIMS PAID TO THE SAME DATE: £3,000.

Donations will be thankfully received by the President and the undermentioned, who are Trustees of the Society:

V. E. WALKER, Esq., Arnos Grove, Southgate.
C. E. GREEN, Esq., 13 Fenchurch Avenue, E.C.
A. J. W. BIDDULPH, Esq., The Chalet, Burton Park, Petworth, Sussex.
J. MCLAREN, Esq., Old Trafford Cricket Ground, Manchester.
THOS. HEARNE, Sec., M.C.C. House, Ealing Dean, W.

I cannot find words strong enough to express my appreciation of the good work the Society is doing, or the interest that is taken in it by all classes of cricketers; but it is to be hoped that still more professional cricketers than is now the case will become members. A deservedly high compliment was paid to it by the M.C.C. and Australian Elevens in 1890, when they played a match for its benefit at Lord's, from which the Society received close on £600.

The United Eleven had to go through a similar experience to the All-England before it disbanded in 1869, seventeen years after it was formed. Some of its prominent members seceded, and formed themselves into the United South of England Eleven.

The United South of England Eleven played its first match on the 11th, 12th, and 13th May, 1865, against Twenty-two of Ireland, and gave evidence that it was likely to prove a formidable rival to the other two elevens. I give the original team, from which it will be seen that it was made up entirely of Southern Players and comprised some of the best bowling and batting talent of the time:

T. Humphrey,	T. Lockyer,
H. Jupp,	T. Hearne,
G. Griffith,	T. Sewell, jun.,
W. Mortlock,	John Lillywhite,
Julius Cæsar,	E. Willsher.
James Lillywhite,	

Willsher was made secretary; John Lillywhite, treasurer.

The split affected the All-England as well; in fact, it might almost be considered a split between the Players of the North and the Players of the South. In the year 1862, Northern and Southern Players were continually bickering, and county matches suffered

POOLEY. JOHN LILLYWHITE. GRIFFITH T. HUMPHREY. SILCOCK. JAS. LILLYWHITE.
CHARLWOOD. G. F. GRACE, ESQ. W. G. GRACE, ESQ. SOUTHERTON.
JUPP. R. HUMPHREY.

accordingly. The formation of the United South of England Eleven was the final wrench, and the All-England Eleven was composed entirely of Northern players afterwards.

The All-England, the United, and the United South were the three principal elevens which travelled over the United Kingdom between 1846 and 1876. They had many imitators, the most important being:

The "United All-Ireland Eleven," which started in 1856, and broke up in a few years.

The "New All-England Eleven" in 1858, which lived two or three years only.

Another "New All-England Eleven" in 1862, which died the same year.

A "North of England Eleven" in 1863, which played one match only.

The "United North and South of England Eleven" in 1867, which played two matches.

The "New United South of England Eleven" in 1875.

Others sprang up from time to time; but they were of mushroom growth and existence, and need not be given.

It is impossible to state the number of wandering amateur elevens which existed at that period. They were nearly all conducted on similar principles to those of the I Zingari, without grounds of their own, and playing anywhere. Of course they were not of the strength of that famous club. As there is always a rage for extraordinary titles amongst young clubs, I have no doubt the few I give will be of interest. I would just remind hon. secs. that some of them are still in existence, and that the names may have been registered. I should be sorry if any rising and enterprising club were to be accused of appropriating the property of older and established ones:

The Knickerbockers, Accidentals, Inexpressibles, Dingle Wanderers, Anomalies, Gnats, Perfect Cures, Active Fleas, Perambulators, Et Ceteras, Limits, X.Y.Z., Owls, Rouge et Noir, Jolly Dogs, Odds and Ends, Caterpillars, I. O. U., Waifs and Strays, Butterflies, Desperadoes, Eccentrics, Hic et Ubique, Gryphons, Nonentities, Grasshoppers, Casuals, Harum Scarum, I Vagabondi, Idle Boys, Variegated Annuals, Rose of Denmark, Unmitigated Duffers, Fossils, Cock-a-doodle-doo, Pelicans, Don Quixotes, Cochin Chinas, Bohemians, The Fly by Nights, The Calves, Will-o'-the-Wisps, Lavender Kids, Spiders, Anythingarians, The Witches, The Wretches, Omnium Gatherums, Incapables, Rovers, and The Other Johnnies.

There can be very little doubt that for some years the All-England and United Elevens spread a knowledge of cricket, and in that way did good to the game; but by-and-by, when county and other important matches began to suffer, opinions rapidly changed, and travelling professional elevens, in the minds of the cricketing authorities, came in for a certain amount of condemnation. The jealousies of the two elevens had little sympathy at head-quarters or anywhere else when important matches were spoiled by them. Occasionally when a player was asked to play for his county he demurred, on the ground that he would be playing for one or other of the elevens on that day. It was not a very pleasant state of affairs, and rather a difficult one to solve. County cricket between 1846 and 1860 was not of sufficient interest to draw large crowds. A professional had to consider the gate: it was his means of living; and when that is remembered, it can be easily understood he would go where the greatest remuneration was to be had. It certainly was to be had in connection with the All-England Eleven, for its engagements lasted from May to September. Nor was the remuneration a question of weather, or in any way affected by the result of the match. A sum was guaranteed by the club played, and each player had his share, and could rely on a steady engagement as long as he kept up his form. It was not likely a player would throw up an engagement of that kind to play a county match, even though he were offered the same remuneration, unless he obtained permission from the manager of his eleven. Unfortunately, as I have already said, the managers of the two elevens were not too complaisant, and so county cricket suffered.

The cricketing authorities were alive to the difficulty; but could not see their way out of it, as there were not sufficient counties at that period for committees to work together and promise players even half the number of engagements a travelling eleven fulfilled.

The counties which played between the years I have mentioned were few in number. The Gentlemen *v.* Players was an annual match, and the M.C.C. was doing excellent work all over the country. Then, as now, the premier club sent its eleven all over England, and even across the Channel, keeping in view the sacred trust of fostering the game which had been placed in its hands. Oxford *v.* Cambridge had their yearly contests, and were now considered the most likely nurseries for recruits to strengthen the amateurs.

But, undoubtedly, the contests of the year were the All-England Eleven *v.* The United Eleven, and the North *v.* South, at Lord's, especially the former. When the two famous elevens met reputation was at stake, and both strove to put their best teams in the field. There was no half-hearted play then. Thought was put into every ball bowled, and neither batsman nor fieldsman spared himself. It was the match of the year from a player's point of view, and crowds testified to it by turning out in thousands. It was not always so in the North *v.* South matches. More than once an eminent player cried off at the last moment, and occasionally the sides were poorly represented.

And now it began to be realised that the game had taken a hold outside of England. September, 1859, saw Parr's team batting against Twenty-two of Lower Canada: and two years afterwards, on the 20th October, 1861, the first English team, under the captaincy of H. H. Stephenson, sailed for Australia. Little thought we then that 17 years later Australia should have progressed sufficiently to be able to send a team to us which should hold its own against the strongest of our clubs!

On the 18th and 19th July, 1861, my brothers, Henry and E. M., made their first appearance at Lord's, playing for the South Wales Club *v.* M.C.C. Both gave a fine display of cricket, Henry scoring 63 not out, first innings; E. M., run out 14 first, and 41 not out, second. E. M. was still more successful with the ball, capturing eight wickets first innings (six of them clean bowled), and seven second. He was in his twentieth year, and bowled both roundarm and underhand. South Wales won by seven wickets.

Between 1846 and 1862 few changes were made in the laws. The M.C.C., while it has always been watchful in the interests of the game, has never been hasty in altering or amending laws which had worked smoothly, wisely preserving a position of neutrality to outside appeals, and only acting when it became absolutely necessary. There were grumblings about this or the other bowler infringing the law in raising his hand above the shoulder in delivering the ball; and some of the umpires were accused of favouritism, or want of firmness, in not speaking out. It was well enough known that most of the bowlers offended occasionally; but as long as they did not make a practice of it, the umpire was silent. Possibly he had been a bowler himself, and knew how difficult it was for a roundarm bowler to bowl over after over with a horizontal arm and keep a good length; and what a relief it was to raise the arm now and then a little bit above the prescribed position, and how much quicker it made the ball come off the pitch.

Grumbling was pretty general in the beginning of 1862, and no one was surprised that an explosion occurred before the end of it. England was playing Surrey at the Oval on the 25th, 26th, 27th August of that year; and a memorable match it turned out to be in more ways than one. England commenced batting on the Monday, and kept possession of the wicket until 5.30 the next day, compiling the exceptionally large total of 503. Hayward headed the list with 117; Grundy came next, with 95; Carpenter third, with 94; and Willsher fourth, with 54. There was only one "duck" in the score; and that, strangely, was to Daft's name, caught at the wicket. Right glad were Surrey when that innings was over. With them it was not now a question of winning the match, but a question of saving it. It was one of those charming evenings we are occasionally favoured with in the month of August—not a breath of wind, the sun fast setting, and the shadows stealing over the ground; and one of the largest crowds ever present at the Oval. Mortlock and T. Humphrey appeared at the wickets about six o'clock. Mr. V. E. Walker and Willsher were the bowlers; and John Lillywhite and T. Sewell, the umpires. Only a few balls were bowled when Humphrey hit out at a curly one of Walker's, and the ball travelled at a great rate to

Grundy, who was standing at deep short-leg. Grundy sprang into the air, and with his right arm fully extended brought off a magnificent catch. The cheering was immense. Willsher was bowling steadily, as usual, at the other end; and Mr. F. Burbidge, who had taken Humphrey's place at the wicket, and Mortlock had to play carefully. Willsher commenced his third over, and immediately the ball left his hand Lillywhite cried "No ball!" Willsher continued to bowl; but after being "no-balled" six times in succession, he threw down the ball, and walked away. With the exception of Messrs. V. E. Walker and C. G. Lyttelton, the remainder of the eleven representing England followed suit.

To say that the excitement was intense is to convey but a faint idea of the sensation amongst players and spectators. Nobody knew why Willsher had been "no-balled;" his delivery looked as fair the third over as it did the first, or at any time in his bowling career. Lillywhite thought otherwise: in his opinion his hand was above the shoulder when the ball left it, and it was his duty to call "No ball." Play was stopped for the day. There was no demonstration, but it was generally believed that a very big nail had been knocked in the coffin of the law bearing on the point, and that the law would have to be either stretched or altered. A night's reflection found Lillywhite in the same belief; and to enable the match to proceed, Street was put in his place. There is no need to say if the action was a wise one. Lillywhite was made the scapegoat; but he could console himself with the thought, a year or two afterwards, that by his firmness on that occasion he had caused the law-makers to act.

A fortnight before that match my brother E. M. had caused a sensation of another kind at Canterbury. His score of 118 against Wootton and Grundy at Lord's,

EDGAR WILLSHER.

for the South Wales Club, had set the critics talking, and his doings the previous two years were recalled.

In 1860 he played 44 innings, average 41; his principal scores being:

150 for West Gloucestershire *v.* Clifton.
114* „ Lansdown *v.* Trowbridge.
183* „ Lansdown *v.* Plummer's XI.
118* „ Ashton School *v.* Ashton.

In 1861 he played 60 innings, average 34; his principal scores being:

102* for Lansdown *v.* Batheaston.
112 „ Lansdown *v.* Frenchay.
100* „ Berkeley *v.* Knole Park.
119* „ Lansdown *v.* Clifton.

They were not first-class matches, but good enough to show that he possessed batting powers of a very high quality.

For years, during the cricket week, my father and mother had visited Canterbury, where they had many friends, and were cordially welcomed in cricket circles. The match, the first part of the week in 1862, was England *v.* Fourteen of Kent; the second part, M.C.C. *v.* Gentlemen of Kent. The Hon. Spencer Ponsonby Fane, who was managing the matches for the M.C.C., had experienced great difficulty in getting together a good team for England; and at the last moment Hayward was taken ill and could not come.

In the evening my father suggested E. M. to the Hon. Spencer Ponsonby, who promptly said: "Communicate with him at once, please; and I shall try to arrange with Mr. Baker, the Secretary of the Kent County Club, that he shall be allowed to play as an emergency for the M.C.C. in the second match." Mr. Baker acceded to the request very heartily, and E. M.

turned up at Canterbury on Tuesday, and for England scored a "duck" first innings, 56 second. Willsher, Sewell, and Mr. Lipscomb were the bowlers, and his 56 included 9 fours and 6 twos.

There was a little friction over the second match. The Captain of the Gentlemen of Kent objected to E. M. playing for M.C.C., not being a member; but Mr. Baker very firmly said: "I have given my promise to the Hon. Spencer Ponsonby that Mr. Grace shall be allowed to play; and if you insist upon your objection being enforced, then I have no alternative but to resign the Secretaryship of the County Club." That put an end to the discussion, and E. M. carried everything before him.

Kent scored 141 first innings. E. M. went in first for the M.C.C. at one o'clock on Friday, and after seeing four wickets go down for 65 runs, he began to hit. He hit all that day, and was 105 not out at the end of it. A good deal of rain fell during the afternoon, and the wicket became heavy, but he made the ball travel at a great rate. Next morning he was in the same vein, and finished up with 192 not out; total, 344. His score was made up of 26 fours, 7 threes, 9 twos, and singles. He broke one bat in compiling it; but Lord Sefton, on behalf of the M.C.C., presented him with another.

The story of his being out first ball, and Fuller Pilch giving him "not out" on the ground that he "wanted to see the young gentleman bat," is a myth. In the early part of the innings the bowler appealed for a catch at the wicket, but Pilch unhesitatingly said "Not out." He was chaffed for his decision afterwards, but said he had no doubt about it. Then laughingly added, "Perhaps I should not have given him out if I had. I wanted to see Mr. Grace do a bit of hitting."

The second innings of the Kent Gentlemen lasted a little over three hours, E. M. capturing all ten wickets.

He bowled both roundarm and lobs, but was most successful with the latter.

The Hon. Spencer Ponsonby had the ball mounted with silver, and presented it to E. M. on behalf of the M.C.C.

I can remember E. M. in his twenty-first year. He is now in his fiftieth, with more than the average share of energy and activity left; at twenty-one he was as agile as a cat, and could field at point better than any player I have met. A very good judge said of him once:

"The only thing that man cannot do in the cricket field is keep wicket to his own bowling!"

The fame of E. M.'s doings spread everywhere, and his style of batting was freely criticised. The critics found fault with his cross hitting, and said he was not above hitting a straight, good-length ball; but all agreed that his hitting was something wonderful. It has always been a mystery to me how he timed the ball so accurately. Good-lengths, half-volleys, and long-hops were all the same to him. He got them on the right part of the bat, and neither bowler nor fieldsman could tell to which part of the field the ball was going. One hit they might expect. Give him a ball a little bit up, about a foot to the off, and they could depend upon it travelling to long-on. Many a fieldsman was placed there for a catch, but very rarely was the ground large enough for that particular hit, and a rough wicket made little difference to him. Do not imagine he could not play with a straight bat, or a defensive innings if he wanted. I have seen him defend his wicket as correctly and patiently as any one. From his twentieth to his thirtieth year his eyesight and quickness were exceptional, partly owing to his temperate and active habits.

In 1862, and for a good many years afterwards, his scores and averages were certainly remarkable; and when we compare them with the doings of the great players of the past and of his own time, we can understand the sensation he created between 1862 and 1865.

Mynn and Pilch were two of the best batsmen between 1830 and 1850. I give their doings in 1843 and 1844:—

Mynn in 1843 played 28 innings, scored 471 runs, average 16.23; most in an innings, 73.

In 1844 he played 36 innings, scored 439 runs, average 12.7; most in an innings, 48.

Pilch in 1843 played 22 innings, scored 525 runs, average 23.19; most in an innings, 89.

In 1844, 41 innings, 592 runs, average 14.18; most in an innings, 50.

In 1862 and 1863, Anderson, Hayward, Daft, Parr, and Carpenter were the crack batsmen:—

R. Carpenter	in 1862	averaged	31.20	for 38	innings.
R. Daft	"	"	22.6	" 22	"
T. Hayward	"	"	21.12	" 62	"
G. Anderson	"	"	19.5	" 53	"
G. Parr	"	"	13.39	" 43	"

E. M. GRACE.

1862 .. 40 innings, 2190 runs; average, 40.30.

The year 1862 is hardly a fair comparison, for the majority of the matches in which E. M. played were not first-class. The year after, when he played for the All-England Eleven, South *v.* North, and Gentlemen *v.* Players, is a fairer test:—

1863.—*First-class Matches only.*

R. Daft	... 9	innings, 313	runs,	average 34.7
G. Anderson	... 10	" 287	"	" 28.7
T. Hayward	... 16	" 392	"	" 24.8
R. Carpenter	... 22	" 447	"	" 20.7
G. Parr	... 16	" 204	"	" 12.12

E. M. GRACE.

27 innings ... 964 runs ... average 35.19

The result was sufficient to stamp E. M. as the most successful batsman of that year. An average of 20 was considered remarkable in 1850. In 1860 it did not create so much astonishment; in 1863 E. M. raised it to 35. In the matches in which he took part that year, he played 78 innings, scored 3074 runs, and averaged 39.32.

CHAPTER III.

MY FAMILY, HOME, AND EARLY CRICKET DAYS.

MY father, Henry Mills Grace, was born at Long Ashton, in Somersetshire. He was a fair cricketer, though not possessing the skill of either of my brothers. When a boy he played a great deal, and if he had had the opportunities afforded to his children, he would have attained a good position as an all-round player. Clubs were few in number in his boyhood, and grounds were fewer still. For one that possessed a ground of its own, a dozen had to be content with the open common. Nor were schools so considerate about playing cricket in his time, and players had many difficulties in the way of practising and learning. The greatest difficulty he had to contend against was the distance to the ground. Clubs in the neighbourhood of Bristol were singularly fortunate in one respect: they had plenty of open ground then, as they have now. Durdham Downs were available, and, though not looked after as they should have been, a very fair pitch could be obtained.

When my father became a medical student, it was impossible for him to get away during the afternoon or evening, as most students do in the present day, and if he had not resorted to extraordinary hours he would have been compelled to give up playing. Two to three days a week throughout the cricketing season, he and a number of companions were in the habit of going to the Downs and practising between the hours of five and eight in the morning. In that way only could he continue the game he loved so well; and I remember we tried to follow in his footsteps in after years, at not quite so early an hour. He had the great qualities of perseverance and concentration, and he diligently impressed upon us the need for cultivating them.

I can remember his words now:

"Have patience, my boy; where there's a will there's a way; and there is nothing you cannot attain, if you only try hard enough."

My father and mother were married in the year 1831, and settled down in Downend, Gloucestershire, where they lived the rest of their lives. Downend is about four miles from Bristol, and was not a more important village sixty years ago than it is now. At the time my father made it the place of his labours, it was a small scattered village, and tourists when they travelled that way rarely paid it the compliment of staying long in it.

My father had to make his way in life, and was at the beck and call of every sick person within a radius of twelve miles. He had not an hour he could call his own. The early morning saw him riding six miles eastward; at midnight he was often six miles to the west.

There was not much time for cricket. The village had not a club of its own; so my father had to be satisfied with running into Bristol now and again, to look at the matches of the Clifton and Bristol clubs—about the only two at that time within available reach.

My brother Henry, the eldest of the family, was born on the 31st January, 1833. At eight years of age he was sent to school, and every time he came home would talk of nothing but cricket. My father realised that he would be compelled sooner or later to create time to help him, if he desired to keep in touch with him physically as well as mentally. He was strong in the belief that if you want to educate and influence a boy thoroughly it is as important to play with him as to work with him; so he took time by the forelock, and had a cricket-pitch laid in front of the house. It was not much of a pitch, nor was it full size; but it was sufficient to teach the rudiments of the game.

The villagers and surrounding neighbours began to take an interest in cricket, and nothing would satisfy them but that my father must take the initiative in forming a club. Why should not Downend have a club of its own? It was not strong enough to form one; so the neighbouring villages were invited to help, and a club was established, and named "The Mangotsfield." Rodway Hill was the most convenient spot for the majority of the players, and, indeed, about the only place where ground could be had. It was common ground; but the members set to work with a will, and levelled and railed in about forty yards square at considerable expense. The West Gloucestershire club was formed about a year later by Mr. Henry Hewitt and the students living with the Rev. Mr. Woodford, the clergyman at Coalpit Heath.

And now my father became more enthusiastic than ever, and prevailed upon some of his old Bristol friends to come over and help the good cause. My uncle Alfred Pocock responded heartily, and walked twice a week between the two places, a distance of twelve miles. He was a first-class racquet player; and, though he had not played cricket until he was twenty-three years of age, was not without hope that he might become a first-class cricketer also. He, too, possessed my father's enthusiasm and perseverance; so it can be readily understood the Mangotsfield Club began to improve rapidly.

My father was 5 ft. 10 ins. in height; weight, about

13 st. He batted right-handed; but bowled and threw in with his left. No man was more alive to the importance of choosing an eleven carefully for match play. A week or two before a match, he would take out his note-book and write down his team:

"First," said he, "I must have two good bowlers.

"Also two good change-bowlers.

"A wicket-keeper and long-stop.

"The rest, as long as they can bat and field, will make up a fair team."

Good fielding was his strong point, and he used to insist upon his team practising throwing and catching all round the field. Another important order was that, one night a week at least, sides should be chosen, and every one play as if it were a match.

My uncle Alfred Pocock was 5 ft. 9 ins. in height; weight, 12 st. 7 lb. When he first played for the Mangotsfield Club, he did not possess the skill which made him so valuable to E. M., Fred, and myself; but, infected by my father's earnestness, he practised diligently and acquired great power with both bat and ball. He made many good scores for the club, and his bowling won many a match. Nothing pleased him so much as watching a correct style of play; and he would bowl willingly for hours to a promising youngster, and was delighted to see him punish an indifferent ball. He bowled roundarm, medium pace, could break both ways, and was very straight. I have known him hit a single stump six times in twenty balls, and he was not satisfied unless he did it.

There is no need to say that, with two such enthusiasts as my father and uncle, the Mangotsfield Club increased in numbers and began to hold its own in contests. The West Gloucestershire Club held a distinct lead for a year or so, pretty much owing to the skill and influence of Mr. Hewitt, who was ably supported by the pupils of the Rev. Mr. Woodford, at Coalpit Heath. Mr. Woodford about this time had half-a-dozen college boys reading with him, who had learned their cricket under able teachers, and who were much more proficient with bat and ball than the majority of local talent. About the year 1845 the Mangotsfield was much strengthened by the appearance of two nephews of my mother, Mr. William Rees and Mr. George Gilbert, who came to stay with us during the holidays. The holidays lasted nearly two months, and my cousins showed both clubs that they had a great deal to learn in every branch of the game. Both were almost in the first class as batsmen, much above the average as bowlers, and fielded with dash and certainty.

The "Mangotsfield" became too much for its sister club and the majority of the clubs which played against it. The year 1846 saw it still improving, and the West Gloucestershire had to admit its superiority. Amalgamation was agreed upon the year after, and the West Gloucestershire Club chosen as the more dignified and most suitable name. Rodway Hill was the more convenient ground, and there they played for the next twenty years.

The principal clubs in the neighbourhood of Bristol about that period were Clifton, Kingscote, Lansdown, Westbury-on-Trym, and Bedminster. Lansdown had been in existence since 1825, and was the strongest opponent of the West Gloucestershire; the others had very little chance against it. In later years Cheltenham College was included in the list, and became the most exciting match of all. Forty years ago there was not the same limit as to age at Cheltenham, and the XI. were often nearer twenty years than sixteen. The College XI. became a thorn in the side of the West Gloucestershire, in proving that it was not omnipotent. Mr. M. Kempson was in residence at that time, and by his fine all-round play gave the West Gloucestershire many a hard day's work. He gave them a taste of the bowling skill which was to be of so much service to his side in the Gentlemen *v.* Players match in 1853. Mr., now Sir Henry, James was there also, and helped with both bat and ball, and altogether the match was the most exciting and enjoyable of the year. I ought to say matches; for most years two were played. The annual fixture was in the month of June; but hardly a year passed in which a second was not played in September or October when the boys returned from the holidays.

The year 1846 was the club's first experience of very fast bowling. Mr. Marcon was in the neighbourhood that year, and played against them. Their wickets went down like ninepins, and half of the batsmen never saw the ball when he bowled. Every fieldsman was behind the wicket, and there were two longstops: the first stood fifteen yards behind, and was supposed to be the wicket-keeper; and the second about thirty yards farther away. Mr. Marcon did not trouble about the length of the ball. He aimed at the wicket, and the ball flew straight from his hand to it without touching the ground; and nearly every time it hit the bottom of the stump, the stump was smashed. Runs were scored now and then from a snick to leg or slip, but not one of them could hit him in front of the wicket. A member of the team said it could be done—ought to be done, and *he* would do it!

"It is no use grounding your bat and waiting until he bowls," said he. "No! have your bat in the air in hitting position, and let fly at him." He was certainly big enough and strong enough to do as he said; so in he went, and stood waiting with the bat in the air, ready to hit.

Mr. Marcon came with a rush, and our enterprising member hit. The ball hit the bat high up about the shoulder, and bat and ball went right through the wicket.

My brother Henry was fifteen years of age when he played his first match for the club in 1848. He did not make much of a show that year; but two or three years later he could show an average of 17 for seven innings, and was very successful with the ball also. My cousins were at their best then, and the West Gloucestershire had now become a very strong club.

The year 1852 saw the departure of my cousins. They had begun the work of life, and holidays of two months' duration had become a thing of the past. The brunt of the fight had again to be undertaken by my father and uncle; but they faced it pluckily, for the sake of the boys who were springing up. Henry was still improving in his play, and my uncle and he were considered the two best all-round players in the district. They could both bowl very straight: my uncle was the steadier, with plenty of patience, but my brother was the faster, and on a rough kicking wicket met with great success. They would go any distance to play, whether the match were good, bad, or indifferent, and some of their experiences of country cricket were rather amusing.

Mr. Williams, a player of University reputation, who was living at Thornbury, got together an eleven; but he could not lick them into match form, and almost gave up in despair. He did not like to cry "Beaten," and thought he might as well have a try against some of the clubs, about the end of the season, when one or two of their best men were away holiday-keeping. Bristol was the club chosen; but, unfortunately for Mr. Williams, Henry and my uncle had been asked to play, and they were on the ground waiting when the Thornbury team appeared. The chances were about 100 to 1 against Thornbury, and the certainty came off on that occasion; for Mr. Williams and his hopeful lot were ignominiously defeated. With more pluck than judgment, and doubtless to encourage his disheartened eleven, Mr. Williams said at the conclusion of the match:

"The result was a piece of luck. My lot could play the same team any day, and I should not mind putting twenty-five pounds on the result."

"Do you mean it?" said the captain of the Bristol.

"I do!" said Mr. Williams; and the match was fixed for a fortnight later, the first week in October.

My father was told of the match, and blamed both Henry and uncle for allowing it to be made, and considered it was nothing short of robbery. They said they had nothing to do with the making of it, and had not a sixpence on the result. My father, however, did not like the look of matters, and said he would play for Thornbury and pay part of the money.

"Understand now and for good, you boys," said he, "I shall not allow you in future to take part in any match which is played for money, as it is introducing a form of gambling into the game, which is wrong and must do harm to it."

Mr. Williams turned up on the appointed date. The Bristol team was even stronger than on the first occasion, and could not keep from laughing at the team opposed to them. Mr. Williams and my father chatted together, without the slightest sign of dismay on their faces. The remainder of the Thornbury eleven were nearly all strangers, and hardly one of them had been seen in a good match before.

Some of the Bristol eleven suggested to their captain that the money should be posted before the match commenced. He had no intention of proceeding to that extremity; but the spirit of mischief prevailing was too much for him, and he was compelled to approach Mr. Williams and make the request. Mr. Williams put his hand in his pocket and produced notes to the amount, much to the surprise of the Bristol captain, who had to make the humiliating confession that he had omitted to bring his part.

Such a scene as followed has not often been witnessed at the beginning of a match. Mr. Williams and my father waxed indignant; and did not hesitate to tell the Bristol captain that his conduct was far from gentlemanly, and unworthy of so manly a game; and they declined to go on with the match until the amount was produced. The whole team could not raise the sum among them; but a few watches and what money they had in their pockets were accepted as an equivalent, and deposited in safe hands.

Thornbury won the toss.

"What shall we do, doctor?" asked Mr. Williams.

"We may as well bat," said my father: "it is a one-innings match, and we shall have the best of the wicket."

Mr. Williams and my father went in first, and my uncle and Henry bowled. There was no tempting my father to hit; for he had made up his mind to keep up his wicket. At the end of an hour and a half, when Mr. Williams was bowled, the score was 60, of which he had made 45 in brilliant fashion. My father was not out 12, and they had run three byes. Half an hour later the innings was at an end: the total 75, my father not out 17.

The match began rather late in the day, and it was 3.30 when Bristol began to bat. With the exception of my father, there was not one of the Thornbury lot who had ever been known to bowl, and it was thought the match would be over by 5 o'clock. It was over earlier than that.

My father bowled the first over, and a good one it was; not a run scored off it. Laughing was general when Mr. Williams commenced at the other end. He fell back on the old, old resource when everything else has failed—underhand grubs! There was not quite so much laughing at the end of the over, when he had clean-bowled one man, and the scoring-sheet was still blank.

Snow had fallen during the day, and the wicket cut up badly. My father bowled as steadily and patiently as he had batted; and Mr. Williams slung in his grubs, and got a wicket nearly every other over. The match was all over by 4.45, and Bristol had scored something less than 50 runs. To say that the Bristol XI. were laughed at, is to express very faintly what took place.

My uncle and Henry, when they got back to Downend, were chaffed unmercifully; and it was many a long day before they heard the last of that match.

During the rise and progress of the Mangotsfield and West Gloucestershire Clubs, great changes had been taking place in our home.

There was, as I have already mentioned, Henry, born 31st January, 1833. Then followed Alfred, born 17th May, 1840; Edward Mills, born 28th November, 1841; myself, born 18th July, 1848; George Frederick, born 13th December, 1850; and four girls between Henry and myself.

Downend House, where my father and mother had been living since Henry's birth, had now become rather straitened in accommodation, and a move was made to "The Chesnuts" across the road sometime in 1850, where my father and mother lived for the rest of their lives.

The change was an improvement in many ways. For one thing there was an orchard attached to it, which meant for my brothers and myself a more convenient pitch on which to practise. My father, Henry, and uncle set to work early in 1851, and had a good wicket ready by the beginning of the cricket season. The orchard was about eighty yards in length, and thickly studded with apple trees, a few of which had to be sacrificed. On the left of it was a high wall; on the right, Mr. Cave's wood and a deep quarry full of water.

The first year or two the pitch was small; but E. M. enlarged and improved it as he grew up, and I cannot remember when it was not in a condition worthy of a first-rate club. There was no restriction in our hitting, but undoubtedly the situation was its greatest attraction: we had only to step out of the house and begin play, and that to a medical family whose duties took them so far from home was a priceless boon. Many a time my father and brother Henry returned from their work too pressed for time to be able to go to Rodway Hill, and so had to give up the desire of half-an-hour's practice. That was obviated now. They could partake of a hasty lunch, and join in the practice that was carried on most days during the season. I should say during most months in the year, for we commenced as early as March and did not leave off until October. To my father and mother there was a great charm in the new arrangement, for it kept the entire family together. Rarely did we practise without my mother being present as an onlooker. My sisters did not play the game, as has been so often stated; but my mother and they fielded the ball if it travelled their way, and bowled a ball or two occasionally to Fred and myself when we were boys. That was the extent of their efforts.

My memory carries me back to my sixth year. Most boys at that age have more to do with the nursery than a cricket ground; but it must be remembered that my family was a cricketing one in every sense of the word, and a cricket ground in front of one's home at that time rare and exceptional. It was as natural for me and every one at home to walk out to the ground, as it is for every boy in England to go into his nursery; and what boy with a choice at his command would prefer the latter? Alfred and E. M. were showing great promise, though not quite good enough to play for the club, and spent every moment of their spare time practising.

My uncle made a point of coming to Downend frequently to coach us, and an excellent coach he made. His bowling was not fast enough to frighten us, but straight and accurate enough to enable us to learn the first principles of batting; viz., good defence. Very fortunately, at that period of my life I was given a bat to suit my strength. I say fortunately, for my uncle and Henry tell me a mistake had been made with regard to E. M. in that respect. Who was to blame, I know not; but E. M., long before he reached manhood's years, was in the habit of using a full-sized bat, and to that they attribute in some measure his cross-hitting. A little thought will show that there is a deal of reason in their argument. It is possible for a boy to handle a bat a little bit over his weight, and even play straight with it; but it is impossible for him to do so when it is inches too long. That is a point that cannot be considered too carefully in coaching a boy, if a correct style and freedom be aimed at. Good players can be reckoned by the score, who will tell you that a mistake of that kind was made with them in their early days, and that they never got thoroughly over it.

To my uncle great credit is due for teaching me, and I sincerely wish that every boy who reads this may possess a teacher as patient and as capable. His first piece of advice was:

"Use a bat suited to your height and strength, and

if you stand properly and play straight, you ought to be able to keep the ball from hitting your wicket."

Then he would show me how to hold the bat so as to use it freely; give me guard according to the side of the wicket he bowled; place my feet in the proper position, and impress on me the need to stand upright. For months, for years I might say, I had to be content with simply stopping the ball, happy if I could keep it away from the wicket.

"Keep your left shoulder well forward, and get over the ball," he kept drumming into our heads; "until you do that, you will never do any good. And keep your eye fixed on the bowler, and never lose sight of the ball from the time it leaves his hands. There must be no playing or hitting wildly."

I did all that—in my own mind—as conscientiously and persistently as any boy works at anything he loves; but somehow I could not make the progress I longed for. Too soon would come a ball on the blind spot, and I was beaten. I should like to be able to say that I had no difficulty in learning, and that proficiency came to me much easier than it comes to other boys. The reverse is the truth. I had to work as hard at learning cricket as I ever worked at my profession, or anything else. Very quickly I learned that there was no royal road there, and that if I wanted to be a good cricketer I must persevere. I was fortunate in having a good tutor, and a strong gift of perseverance; that is as much as I can say to students of the game.

For the next two or three years I had to be satisfied with short innings in family practice games. The rule was, fifteen minutes each to the senior members, five minutes to the juniors or more if time allowed; however, I had plenty of fielding, and worked hard at it. E. M. kept us busy in that way; and as Mr. Cave's wood and the quarry were in the direction of long-on, it suited his pull from the off beautifully, and he took a special delight in hitting the ball there.

From first to last we had three dogs, whose services were invaluable: Don, Ponto, and Noble. Noble was a most intelligent retriever, and would go into the water for the ball without hesitation. Ponto took his position at the side of the bowler, and watched the flight of the ball with as much care as the batsman; and when it was hit over the trees, would listen carefully until he heard it crash among the branches and then make straight to the spot where it fell. His instinct was remarkable, and with a little training we got him to do wonders. A ball bowled to the off he expected to be hit on that side, and he did not take kindly to E. M.'s pulling. They had plenty of pluck, too; for they would present their chest to the ball, no matter how hard it was hit, and time after time I have seen them catch it on the bound with their mouth.

By the time I was nine years old I had got over the elementary stage of stopping the ball, and was slowly acquiring power in meeting it firmly and playing it away. Playing with a straight bat had become easy to me; and my uncle told me I was on the right track, and patiently I continued in it. In my tenth year I could play a ball from my wicket with a fair amount of confidence. "Do not allow the bowler to stick you up, or it is all over with you," he said. I could now play forward as well as back; but, of course, had to be content with less firmness in that stroke, quite satisfied if I could meet the ball with a straight bat.

The next year saw me still improving, and I was considered good enough to play for the club. My cousin, W. Rees, was staying with us for a week or two. His appearance was of great interest to me, and I watched his play most carefully. It was six years since he played last for the West Gloucestershire, and his old skill had not deserted him; for he played three innings, and scored 102 runs. He was one of my godfathers; and, after seeing my defence, thought me such a promising young player that he presented me with a bat before he left. My godfather was of the same opinion as my father and uncle about the bat being suited to the height and strength of the player, for the one he gave me was not full size. But it had what I had long wished for, a cane handle.

What was I doing in the way of bowling? will be asked. A great deal; though perhaps not giving it the thoughtful attention I bestowed on batting. I was not blind to the fact that, if I wished to become a good cricketer, I must cultivate every branch of the game. A year or two ago there was some talk of training boys to begin bowling at a shorter distance than twenty-two yards. With that suggestion I heartily agree; for I am perfectly certain that very few boys between the years of ten and fifteen have strength enough to bowl the regulation distance any length of time without becoming tired and bowling short. Eighteen yards was the distance we were taught to begin at, and a good length was the principal point drilled into our heads. I pegged away very perseveringly, and I believe in my twelfth year was paid the compliment of being considered the forlorn hope when the regular bowlers of the club had failed. A very dubious compliment, I admit, but I considered it a very high one. It was very encouraging to me, and I did my little best to justify it.

The year 1860 saw E. M. in great batting form for the West Gloucestershire Club, and I too helped to swell the total of the scoring-sheet. Against Clifton the Club did a good performance, scoring an aggregate of 381, and winning easily. E. M. and my uncle went in first, and made 126 before they were parted.

Altogether E. M. scored 150, without the semblance of a chance, and his hitting was clean and hard. I was down on the sheet as eighth man, and at the end of the first day scored 35 not out—very patiently and correctly, they say; and next day added 15 more. I was not quite twelve years of age, and played with the bat my godfather gave me. A little later the same year we played Gloucester and Cheltenham combined, and won by an innings and 27 runs.

The year 1861 was not an encouraging one to me or my teachers; for in ten innings played I only scored 46 runs. The matches were principally for West Gloucestershire, against Clifton, Lansdown, Knole Park, and Bedminster—then, as now, the best clubs in the neighbourhood of Bristol. I was now very tall for my age, and could get well over the ball. The club had one or two peculiar experiences that year, which were strongly illustrative of country cricket.

In the Lansdown match scoring was very one-sided. Partly owing to the weather, only seven men put in an appearance for Lansdown when the match began, and my uncle and E. M. disposed of them for 33 runs. There was little in that to discourage them; but at the end of the day, when the same pair had scored 147 without being parted—E. M. 75, uncle 69,—one or two of the Lansdown players did not hesitate to say that there was neither reason nor fun in the match, and hoped that the West Gloucestershire eleven would not mind if they abandoned it. The West Gloucestershire only laughed; for they could remember a similar experience against the same club in 1847, when Lansdown had the laugh on their side. Then Lansdown scored 74 first innings; West Gloucestershire, 6 only. Only nine overs were bowled, and it was a most inglorious procession. At the end of the day Lansdown had scored 128 for five wickets in their second innings; and West

Gloucestershire, considering the task too much for them, said they would give them the match. At that time, when a match got very one-sided, giving it up was a common occurrence, and neither side thought it unsportsmanlike.

But the match of matches for a startling and unexpected finish was West Gloucestershire *v.* Redland, at Rodway Hill, on 28th July, 1858. With the exception of Fred, all the members of the family, uncle included, were playing, and a good match was expected. We were on the ground practising before the Redland turned up, and had a fair number of spectators even at that early hour. One onlooker, who had been drinking rather freely, lay full-length unpleasantly close to where we were playing, and all our persuasions to get him to move further away were unavailing. When the Redland eleven arrived, an attempt was made to clear the ground, but our noisy critic resented, and my father, much against his will, had to resort to force of arms. Calling up my brother Alfred, who had a fair reputation as a boxer, he ordered him to remove the obstinate individual; he did not seem to object, and the unusual sight of a fight *before* a cricket-match was witnessed. Two minutes proved that Alfred had a very easy undertaking, and he dealt very lightly with his opponent who had the sense, or feeling, to cry "Enough," and left the field altogether. The little preliminary excitement added to the interest of the match, and a keen and enjoyable one it became.

Redland scored 51 first innings, 116 second. West Gloucestershire scored 67 first, and were 84 in the second for five wickets, with about an hour remaining to play, when our friend of the morning turned up again. This time he brought his friends with him, who asserted that he had been unfairly treated. It seemed absurd that a cricket-match should be delayed a second time for so small a matter; but there was no alternative. Alfred had a tougher task this time; but, rising to the occasion, he polished off his opponent in an artistic and satisfactory manner.

That did not satisfy him or his friends; for they betook themselves to a convenient heap of stones, and a free-fight ensued. For a little while the West Gloucestershire and Redland, fighting side by side, had rather the worst of the contest; but, charging shoulder to shoulder with stumps and bats, they drove the crowd from the heap of stones, and assumed the offensive. A lively state of affairs prevailed the next half-hour. In the meantime my father had ridden off hurriedly to the nearest magistrate, who returned with him, and threatened to read the Riot Act if they did not disperse. Fortunately for the reputation of the two clubs and the villagers, so extreme a measure was unnecessary, and the opposition collapsed; but the match had to be abandoned.

The year 1862 found my father aiming at the formation of a County Club; and his suggestion being well received, what was undoubtedly the first match of Gloucestershire County was played at Clifton that year, under the title of The Gentlemen of Gloucestershire *v.* Devonshire. That was a step in the right direction, and on the high-road to first-class play.

The West Gloucestershire Club, while it owed much of its early success to my cousins, W. Rees and George Gilbert, was at its best between 1860 and 1867. In those years E. M. was a host in himself; Henry, Alfred, and my uncle as good as they had ever been; and Fred and I improving every year. We all played in the eleven in 1863, and I could show at the end of that season an average of 26.12 for nineteen innings.

That year the club was strong enough to play Twenty-two of Corsham, and win; and in 1866, Ross, Hereford, and Monmouth were also included. The last three were played in succession, commencing at Ross on the 10th and 11th September, and finishing at Hereford on the 14th and 15th. It was a most enjoyable week. The Twenty-two of Ross and District scored 35 and 40 to West Gloucestershire's single innings of 129. E. M. and myself bowled right through: E. M. had ten wickets for 14 runs first innings, and twelve for 21 runs second; I had ten for 18 first, and eight for 14 second.

The Twenty-two of Monmouth did rather better, scoring 47 and 57 to our 85 and 84. E. M. and I again bowled unchanged throughout. E. M. had thirteen wickets for 24 runs first, and twelve for 29 second; I had seven for 23 first, and eight for 25 second. Rather an amusing incident occurred in that match: E. M. and myself had taken our positions at the wicket to commence batting, when the captain of the Monmouth Twenty-two asked if we had any objection to playing with a ball which was slightly soiled and had been in use for a few overs. I did not see any particular objection to it, and was willing to go on; but E. M. insisted upon the rules of the game being observed, and would have none of it. There was no alternative but to send down to the town for another, and we had to wait patiently for over a quarter of an hour until the messenger returned. I was bowled first ball, much to the delight of my opponents.

The Twenty-two of Hereford was much the strongest combination, and defeated us by 43 runs.

The year 1867 was the last of the West Gloucestershire club. It had lived for more than twenty years, and held its own against all the clubs in the neighbourhood. Its last match was against Twenty-two of

Holt, and proved a very one-sided affair. The Twenty-two scored 56 and 109; West Gloucestershire scored 413 in a single innings, of which E. M. scored 200, Henry 17, and my share was 93.

	Overs.	M.	R.	Wkts.
The first innings E. M. bowled	—25	7	28	12
,, ,, W. G. ,,	—25	13	26	7

The second innings we stepped aside, and allowed Fred to bowl—

Overs.	M.	R.	Wkts.
40	18	44	15

At that period Henry was in his 35th year, E. M. in his 27th, Fred in his 17th, and I in my 20th.

I have dwelt at some length on the doings of the West Gloucestershire Club, as it had almost become a family club for some years before it stopped playing; and it was in connection with it that E. M., Fred, and I gained much of our skill. It ceased to exist owing to the many first-class engagements which we had offered to us, and which my father and mother thought we ought to accept in the interests of the game. It had fulfilled what my father had in view when he formed the Mangotsfield Club—to spread a knowledge of the game in the district, and teach his boys to play. That its success as a club gave him pleasure I do not require to say. My uncle and he little thought their efforts would bear such fruit, or that the orchard at Downend would be cherished so dearly. They had watched their boys grow into men, able to hold their own in the cricket-field, and accepting defeat and victory in the right spirit. It was a stern school to learn in, but it was thorough. We pursued it earnestly, never grumbling at the work to be undertaken.

The matches played by the West Gloucestershire

Club against the following clubs, from 1846 to 1867 resulted as follow:

	Total Matches.	Won.	Lost.	Drawn.
Lansdown	14	8	4	2
Knole Park	12	9	2	1
Clifton	15	10	4	1
*Cheltenham College	12	3	3	6
Bedminster	13	12	1	0
Westbury	11	10	0	1
Kingscote...	3	2	0	1

The Gentlemen of Gloucestershire *v.* Gentlemen of Devonshire, at Clifton on the 8th and 9th July, 1862, was our first county match, and the result was very gratifying, and encouraged us to proceed. We did not lay claim to first-class form; but after defeating Devonshire by an innings and 77 runs, we naturally considered that we were not far from it. E. M. was undoubtedly the hero of that match; for he scored 57 out of a total of 219 runs, and captured 6 wickets for 47 runs first innings, and 7 for 21 second. Mr. J. J. Sewell, of Marlborough College fame, played a splendid innings of 65 runs, and with E. M. put on 115 runs for the first wicket. Rarely had any county club made so favourable a start, and my father was delighted with the result. My uncle, Henry and Alfred played; but I was not considered good enough, although I watched every ball bowled.

The return, at Teignbridge on the 25th and 26th August, was rather disappointing to us, for we lost it by 33 runs. It was the first important match I played in, and I scored 18 runs, but did not bowl. Henry made 19, and our total first innings was 92. In the second, with the exception of E. M., 21, and my

* Cheltenham College matches were always one day matches which explains the large number drawn.

brother-in-law, Dr. Bernard, 21, everyone came to grief, and our total was 68.

In the year 1863 I made great progress in batting, scoring freely against our crack local clubs—Clifton, Lansdown, and Knole Park,—and was looked upon as one of the principal bowlers of the West Gloucestershire Club. Our first match against the Gentlemen of Devonshire illustrated the changing fortune characteristic of cricket. It was played at Tiverton on the 24th and 25th July. Devonshire winning the toss, batted first, and scored 227; two players, Messrs. J. H. Coplestone and A. D. Gill, scoring 141 runs between them. We scored 135—of which I made 15, not out,—and had, of course, to follow our innings. E. M., Henry, Alfred, and my uncle grumbled terribly at the condition of the wicket, and spying a big roller at the extreme corner of the field, all hands were enlisted to bring it up, and we spent the time allowed between the innings in rolling. A change came over the look of affairs; for E. M. was in one of his uphill fighting moods, and played magnificently. He hit very hard, and scored 132 out of a total of 294. Mr. J. J. Sewell scored 42, my brother Alfred 32, and Henry and uncle 23 each. Devonshire was left with 203 to win, certainly not an impossible undertaking; but they were not equal to it. My uncle did one of his finest bowling performances, capturing 7 wickets for 36 runs, and getting rid of our opponents for the small total of 78.

The return match, played at Clifton 20th and 21st August, proved even more disastrous to us than the return match the previous year; for we were defeated by an innings and 61 runs.

Three days later we played Somersetshire at the Sydenham Fields, Bath, and won by 87 runs. I was top scorer with 52 not out, and obtained 4 wickets for 17 runs first innings; 2 for 26, second.

MR. E. M. GRACE.

On the 31st August, 1st and 2nd September, of the same year, I played my first match against first-class professional bowling. The All-England Eleven played Twenty-two of Bristol, at Durdham Down, on those days, and I was eager to measure my strength against players who ranked so high. Nine years had elapsed since the All-England Eleven played its second match at the back of the Full Moon Hotel, and great changes had taken place in the team. Clarke, the founder, was dead, and Bickley, owing to ill-health, was unable to play. Willsher, H. H. Stephenson, Anderson, Julius Cæsar, and A. Clarke had played in 1855; but Tarrant, Hayward, Jackson, Tinley, and the others we had not seen. It was well known that cricket in Bristol had made great strides in the last half-dozen years; how much, we could not say. The team representing the All-England Eleven was considered as strong as the two previous ones, and the result would indicate the extent of our improvement.

E. M. was our captain, and had now played for and against the All-England Eleven; Messrs. Sewell, Daubeny, and Bramhall had good local reputations, and altogether the Twenty-two was representative of cricket in the neighbourhood. Personally, I was anxious to do well, and practised diligently with bat and ball for weeks before. I knew right well that the contests in which I had played the last year or two were not to be compared with the contest on this occasion.

E. M. showed that the All-England bowling had no terrors for him; for he began hitting the first over, and made 37 altogether. One hit rather amused us. It went almost straight up and mountains high to Jackson, the bowler. "I have got it!" said Jackson, running up the pitch; but thinking he had misjudged it, he ran a yard or two back again, then ran forward again, and allowed the ball to fall a yard or two behind him. Messrs. Sewell and Daubeny played splendidly for 38 and 44. I batted tenth man.

"Have you ever felt nervous at the beginning of an innings?" has been repeatedly asked of me; but I believe I have always parried the question. Well, I did feel very nervous, or anxious—call it which you like; and if it is any encouragement to young players, I may say that I experienced the same feeling for many years afterwards. When any player of note tells you that he plays the first over or two without a slight feeling of that kind, and that he is as cool and confident then as he is the last over, do not be discouraged if it be different with you, or say, "That accounts for his scoring more freely than I do." Perfect command of nerve at the beginning of an innings is much to be desired, if it do not lead to over-confidence; but the very few I have met who *said* they possessed it have always given me the impression of being too eager to score the first over or two, and hit rather wildly to accomplish their end. That, in my opinion, is not so likely to lead to long scores as a slightly nervous feeling, as long as it does not have the mastery of you.

Before I began batting in this match I practised for a little during the luncheon hour, and Tarrant was kind enough to bowl to me for five or ten minutes, a kindness which turned out very useful. When I began my innings Jackson and he were the bowlers; and being nearly of the same pace, in an over or two I felt quite at home, played confidently, and hit out. Tarrant was shunted, and Tinley took his place and bowled lobs. A change from fast round-arm to lob-bowling has never affected the rate of my scoring. E. M. bowled lobs at home as long as I can remember, and I used to hail the change with delight.

Tinley's first over I played carefully; in the second I decided to hit, and hit him into the scoring-tent. The hit was loudly cheered; I was pleased, felt elated, got over-confident, and paid the penalty. In my haste to repeat the stroke, I ran out too far in the third over, missed the ball altogether, and was clean bowled. I had scored 32, at 15 years of age, against the All-England Eleven, the heroes of the cricket world, and there is no need to say that I was delighted.

But my delight did not cause me to slacken my desire to progress. On the contrary, I realised that I had given promise of excellence, and must strive harder—not only to justify it, but to improve on it.

The All-England Eleven made a poor show in its first innings, Jackson and H. H. Stephenson scoring 33 between them, the others 53; total, 86. A small total we thought, and due to the effective bowling of E. M. and E. T. Daubeny, who divided the wickets.

E. M. justified his selection as captain. When E. Stephenson and Willsher got set in the second innings, I was put on to bowl, and E. M. went out to the long-field. "Throw up one or two for Stephenson to hit," said he, which I promptly did, and E. M. brought off a magnificent catch the first over.

The All-England Eleven was defeated by an innings and 20 runs.

To be asked to play for the All-England Eleven may be considered a distinct step forward. That was my position in the early part of 1864, when I was in my sixteenth year. E. M. had not returned from Australia with the other members of Parr's team, and I received an invitation to play against Eighteen of Lansdown on the 30th of June. For some reason or other, Lansdown had not then asked me to play, and I accepted the All-England Eleven invitation with much pleasure. Henry was equally pleased, though playing for the Eighteen, and was anxious that I should acquit myself creditably. Lansdown batted first, but did not do well against Tarrant and Hayward, only scoring 75. Mr. J. W. Haygarth scored 27, and Henry was nct out 11. In the second innings they did better, making 162—E. T. Daubeny, 78. John Lillywhite, for the Eleven, did what he liked with the Lansdown bowling, scoring 105 out of a total of 260. I batted sixth man, which I considered rather a high compliment in so strong a team, and was in for over half an hour while I made 15. Just when I got set an unfortunate mistake of Lillywhite's caused me to be run out. But I did not mind that: I had played for the All-England Eleven, and had helped to defeat a strong local Eighteen by an innings and 22 runs.

Ten days later I made my first appearance in London, playing at the Oval for the South Wales Club. Henry and E. M. had played repeatedly for the same club; but E. M. was still on his homeward journey from Australia, and they had to do without him this match. My uncle and brothers were well known in Wales, having played at Newport, Cardiff, and elsewhere against the All-England Eleven, and that led to their connection with the South Wales team, with whom they made an annual trip to town for years. Henry suggested that I should take E. M.'s place; and I was booked to play against Surrey Club and the Gentlemen of Sussex. My engagement nearly fell through. I was on the ground, with Henry, ready to play in the Surrey match on the 11th July. The captain of the South Wales team approached Henry, and asked him if he objected to my standing out against the Gentlemen of Sussex at Brighton, as he had the offer of a very good player, and he believed their opponents were exceptionally strong. Henry objected very much. "To begin with," he said, "the boy was asked to play in both matches, and he shall play in both matches or none;

and I only hope every member of the team will do as well as I expect him to do." Henry scored 11 and 49 against the Surrey Club: I scored 5 and 38, and nothing further was said about my standing out.

The Brighton match was played on the old Hove Ground, on the 14th, 15th, and 16th of July, and it was my first appearance at that famous watering-place. The wicket was in excellent condition, as it was always there; and after the discussion between Henry and the South Wales captain, I was eager to do well. Henry was not playing, and I felt that the entire responsibility of the family credit was resting on my shoulders. Up to the last moment we hoped E. M. would turn up; and I desired it eagerly, if only to give me heart. His ringing voice and cheery tones would have been invaluable to me; but I had to be content with a paragraph in the newspapers to the effect that the *Rev.* Mr. Grace, who had done such wonders in Australia, was expected to play. We have had E. M. described times and forms innumerable; but that was the only occasion we ever had him given as the "Rev.," and we never could make out whether he considered it in the light of a compliment or as a bit of sarcasm. The match has been reported and criticised more than once, so I need not enter into minute details. South Wales won the toss, and I batted first wicket down. Before the second wicket fell, Mr. Lloyd, the South Wales captain, and myself raised the score to close upon 200 runs; and at the end of the first day the total was 356 for nine wickets, of which I had scored 170—made up of 19 fours, 9 threes, 17 twos, and singles—without giving a chance. I was out in attempting to cut a wide ball—getting over it too much, and cutting it into my wicket. We had news the same afternoon that E. M. had stepped on English soil, and he was wired to turn up next morning. He did not; possibly satisfied that there was no need for him after our long score.

The Gentlemen of Sussex scored 148 first innings, and had to follow on. They gave us a fine bit of leather-hunting in their second innings, scoring 341, and leaving us 134 to win. Time did not permit us to finish; but at the end of the third day we had scored 118 for five wickets, of which I had made 56 not out.

They gave me a bat, which I have to-day and am very proud of. The handle and the blade are of one piece of wood: it was the only one to be had on the ground at the end of the innings; however, I value it for the reason that it marks the date of the beginning of my long scores. I was not quite sixteen years of age, and had gained my first experience in playing steadily and consistently through a long innings.

A week later I played for the same club at Lord's against the M.C.C.; and before the end of the month against the I Zingari. In the first match I scored 50; in the second, 34 and 47; and for South Wales Club that year I had an average of 48 for nine innings. In first-class matches I scored 402 runs for seven innings, average 57; and at the end of the season I had an aggregate of 1079. I had played well enough to merit an opinion from John Lillywhite's *Companion*, in its summary for the season:

> "Mr. W. G. Grace promises to be a good bat: bowls very fairly."

That was my progress and position at the end of 1864, when I had completed my sixteenth year. The lesson I have desired to convey to young players is, that my doings in the cricket world at that period of my life, if they are of any value, were owing to my father and uncle's stimulating examples, and perseverance on my own part. When the associations and surroundings are favourable, there can be little doubt that perseverance will work wonders, if love and enthusiasm go with it. Love and enthusiasm we all possessed from the oldest to the youngest, and we possess it to-day.

And we have always been a temperate family. Intemperate smoking, in my opinion, has more to do with nervousness and small scores than moderate drinking. E. M. and I have never smoked. Another point to be considered is constant exercise of some kind throughout the year. We were known to be fond of hunting, shooting, and fishing, as well as cricketing. Immediately we laid down the bat, we took up the gun or rod; and my father, brother Alfred, and E. M. hunted as long as professional duties permitted. I find a day's shooting or fishing, or a run with the harriers or beagles, of great use during the winter months, and I take care to have plenty of walking. In the months of February and March I begin to prepare for the season, increasing the amount of exercise, and by the beginning of May I feel fit enough to face the cricketing season.

The spring and dash of life have somewhat abated in me, and perhaps I am less careful to-day in the matter of sleep than I was ten or fifteen years ago; but I cannot remember when I did not at the beginning or middle of the season take care to have a fair amount of rest. Every player must judge for himself whether he require six, eight, or ten hours. It has happened on many occasions that I have been up half the night, and scored heavily next day; but that proves nothing, unless, perhaps, that I possess exceptional physical powers.

A good story comes to my mind, which, while it goes against my theory, is too good to be lost. It occurred during the Scarborough week, where good cricket and good cheer go hand-in-hand. Three or four of us were on the way to our rooms in the early morning, after an enjoyable dance; and being more in the mood for chatting than sleep, we, with one exception, decided to spend an hour or two longer comparing reminiscences. The "exception" had commenced his innings that day, and was not out when play stopped.

"You can do what you like," said he; "but I'm off to bed, as I mean to make a hundred to-morrow."

I forget how long we sat up—certainly later than we should have done in the beginning of the season,—but next day every one of us scored largely; while our friend was out first over, without adding to his overnight's score! I sincerely hope young players will not follow our example, though it was not attended with disastrous results.

I have assumed that what I have been saying about my family and home, and early training, my readers would equally apply to the training of my youngest brother, Fred. He was just as enthusiastic as any of us, and practised as diligently at home as E. M. or I did, though he lacked some of our opportunities. My brothers Henry and Alfred had married, and were living some miles away from Downend, when he was old enough to begin; and E. M. was very much away. Fred had to fall back upon the services of the boot-boy and nursemaid, and he kept them busy bowling to him all day long. My mother looked after his progress, and saw that he had every encouragement to improve, and he showed promise of excellence at quite as early an age as I did. I remember we had some difficulty in getting him out of the habit of practising left-handed. He was strong for his age, and played with a determination worthy of a much older boy. School training brought him forward rapidly, and before he had completed his tenth year he had played his first match and distinguished himself as a bowler locally, clean bowling ten of his opponents' wickets, and having two caught off him. Steadily he grew in skill and strength, and at the end of 1864, when E. M. and I had done sufficient to attract attention outside of Gloucestershire, he, in his fourteenth year, was a well-known figure to every cricket club in the district. He did not play with so straight a bat as I did, but, for his age, he was much more resolute in his hitting, and in the field showed something of the dash and certainty which characterised him in that branch of the game in after years.

There was a marked difference in the batting styles of E. M., Fred, and myself. I do not require to particularise E. M.'s again. He went in for hitting in his peculiar way as long as I can remember him, and he invariably brought it off. There was one special feature in it which helped him in his long scores; the flight of the ball after he hit it. When he got the ball clean on the bat it travelled low and fast, and the fieldsman had to be on the spot to have any chance of catching it. His strong nerve was invaluable to him and the side he played on, and the quality of the bowling made little difference to him. I have seen more than one bowler, who had been performing splendidly, go all to pieces as soon as E. M. had hit him once or twice; and one match I shall not readily forget. Gloucestershire was playing Notts, in 1877, when Morley and Barnes were at their best. The first dozen overs or so Morley was simply unplayable, and four of the Gloucestershire wickets were down for less than thirty runs—Fred's, Townsend's, and my own among them—when E. M. went in to bat. "Keep your eye on Morley, and play carefully, Ted," I said. "All very well to talk," said he. "I should like to know what good the steadiness of you fellows has done for the innings? It looks to me like a clear case of funk, and I am going to stop it!" And stop it he did. In his very first over, Morley gave him one slightly to the off, which he promptly cracked to the boundary at long-on. In the next he pulled a good-length straight one to the same spot; and Morley lost his head and did not know where to bowl to him. Afterwards, Moberly and E. M. put on runs at a great pace, and eventually we beat them by an innings.

Gloucestershire *v.* Lancashire, in 1889, at Liverpool, was another illustration of it. Lancashire scored 73 and 102; Gloucestershire 80 first, and had lost five wickets for 42 second, the wicket unplayable. E. M. was our last resource, and he justified it. Very early in his innings Briggs favoured him with a ball about a foot to the off, which was sent to leg. Two or three extra fieldsmen were placed on that side for him, and Briggs tried him again. He gave him a good-length ball, a little outside the off stump, which E. M. hit between cover-point and mid-off and scored four by it; and then, to show it was no fluke, repeated it an over or two later. Briggs was all at sea, and E. M. had the measure of him afterwards, and, with the help of A. C. M. Croome, won for us a splendid and unexpected victory by three wickets.

It was hitting and nerve of that kind which made E. M. the terror of local clubs when he played for West Gloucestershire, between 1860 and 1867; and it was more than once seriously proposed that he should not be allowed to play. And he was just as successful with the ball. I give some of his exceptional performances, to show the quality of his play at that time:

Aug., 1861.—For Berkeley *v.* Knole Park, he scored 100 not out in a total of 119, and took every wicket 2nd innings.

Aug., 1861.—For Lansdown *v.* Clifton, 119 not out, and took every wicket 2nd innings.

Aug., 1862.—For M.C.C. *v.* Gentlemen of Kent, 192 not out, and took every wicket 2nd innings.

Aug., 1863.—For Lansdown *v.* Clifton, 61 not out, and took every wicket 2nd innings.

May, 1865.—For an Eleven *v.* an Eleven, at Clifton, 69 not out, and took every wicket 2nd innings.

Aug., 1867.—For Marshfield *v.* Corsham School Club, 98 not out, and took every wicket 2nd innings.

April, 1864.—Single-wicket Match, E. M. Grace *v.* Six of Maryborough, Australia. E. M., 106 not out; the Six not being able to get him out.

Fred's hitting was quite as clean, but more orthodox, and he had better defence. He stood very upright, but had the habit of placing part of his left foot in front of the wicket. He, too, scored heavily against local clubs, and met with great success as a bowler; but somehow he did not frighten his opponents so much as E. M. I do not think I frightened them so much either; for local clubs have always welcomed me, when I could find time to play with them. If I might be allowed to compare my own style with E. M.'s and Fred's, I should say I had the advantage in height, and played straighter; and I think I have always had greater patience.

A word or two more, and I have done with the Family Sketch and our early training. When we took to first-class cricket, play and practice suffered to some extent in the orchard at Downend; but we kept the wicket in good condition until the home was broken up, and always used it a month or two before the season began. We kept in constant touch with the home-circle right through the season; either wiring the result of every first-class match, or posting the scoring-card at the end of every day's play. That much they expected, and I think we rarely disappointed them.

My father died in the year 1871. He had lived to

MR. G. F. GRACE

see his sons grown to manhood's years, taking part in the duties of life, and occupying a high position in the game he loved so dearly. His last effort was to establish the Gloucestershire County Club on a sound basis, which he was successful in doing in the year 1870. My mother remained among us thirteen years longer, and was present at every county match at Clifton College. She took great interest in cricket all round the neighbourhood, and treasured every telegram and report of our doings. Local papers did not give much space to cricket twenty years ago, and rarely reported matches played outside of the county; and as London papers did not reach Downend till late in the day, we made a point of telegraphing or writing to her the result of every match played from home. E. M. and I were playing for Gloucestershire *v.* Lancashire, at Manchester, on 25th July, 1884, when we received the telegram announcing her death. It came with painful surprise to us, and for the moment we knew not what to do; but my friend and comrade of many years, A. N. Hornby, the captain of the Lancashire Eleven, grasped the situation, and, with a promptness and consideration which E. M. and I can never forget, immediately stopped the match, and we hurried home to have the last look at her who had loved us so wisely and well.

CHAPTER IV.

CRICKET SCHISMS AND THE PROGRESS OF COUNTY CRICKET—1863 TO 1869.

COUNTY Cricket made satisfactory progress in the year **1863**. A number of county clubs were then formed, which took root, and have flourished with more or less success since. They had to contend against the popularity of the All-England and United Elevens, who still received liberal encouragement wherever they appeared; but lovers of the game could see, even at that date, that a county club was more likely to establish the game on a firm footing than a travelling eleven which owed its existence entirely to gate-money. The success of the two Elevens was no doubt owing to the quality of the players representing them; but their jealousies and constant bickerings began to tire their supporters, and when the North and South took sides, matters for the moment looked serious. I suppose we shall never get to the bottom of the various schisms which created so much ill-feeling about that time, and which spoiled so many important matches; and I question if it be worth the trouble to try. A short recapitulation of them will be sufficient.

First, we had Clarke's management of the All-England Eleven called into question, which led to the formation of the United Eleven; second, there was jealousy on the part of the northern men about the selection of H. H. Stephenson for the captaincy of the first English Eleven which went to Australia; then we had the Nottinghamshire dispute with Surrey for first place in county honours, which caused them to steer clear of meeting each other for years; and, finally, we had the divisions of the different elevens into North and South.

It was not an uncommon thing for two or three members of an eleven to combine and object to another member playing. For some reason or other, G. Atkinson absented himself from the Yorkshire team against Nottinghamshire on the 9th, 10th, and 11th July, 1863. Seven days afterwards, eight of the most prominent Yorkshire players wrote to the Honorary Secretary:

"We, the undersigned, have made up our minds that we will not play in the forthcoming Yorkshire *v.* Surrey match if George Atkinson plays."

It was a most unhappy position for a Secretary to be placed in; but the eight gained their point, for Atkinson did not play in the Surrey match.

The North *v.* Surrey match at the Oval, 3rd, 4th, and 5th August the same year, was also spoiled, owing to Parr's "combination" objecting to play. Parr, Anderson, Daft, Hayward, Carpenter, Tarrant, and Jackson were all absent, and it was not a case of their being unable to play, but that they would not play against Surrey. When England played Surrey a fortnight later, they were in the same mood, and remained in it in the North *v.* Surrey match, at Manchester on 20th, 21st, and 22nd August. In the latter match the North, though playing a weak team, was strong enough to win, and a certain amount of satisfaction was felt that the team should have been able to do it without the dissentient players. A lively newspaper correspondence ensued, and it must have been unpleasant to the players who stood out to read:

"The Northern Managers have experienced great difficulty in getting together their strength, and whilst endeavouring to smooth down the feeling which exists between certain players and the Surrey authorities, they have shown that they are not wholly reliant upon a particular division to supply an eleven to represent the North."

In the early part of **1864** an agitation was set going in one of the leading sporting papers which had for its aim the formation of a "cricket parliament" to depose the Marylebone Club from its position as the authority on the game; but it met with little countenance, and the old club, which had now played on its present ground for fifty years, was allowed to carry on the work which it, and it alone, seemed to be able to do with firmness and impartiality. If evidence were wanting of the M.C.C.'s interest and consideration for the game at that period, we have only to look at the number and quality of matches played by it. During the year 1864 it played as many as 34 matches, including such clubs as Cambridge and Oxford Universities; Eton, Harrow and Rugby Schools; the Army Club, Royal Artillery, and some of the minor counties. Show us how we can do good to the game and we shall endeavour to do it, has always been the aim of the Committee of the M.C.C., and it would have been a thousand pities if the Club had been deprived of its powers at that critical period of cricket history.

June the 10th of the same year saw an important alteration in the laws. The Willsher episode of 1862 was still fresh in the memories of players, and after vainly trying to get umpires to "no-ball" a bowler when he raised his arm above the shoulder, it was finally decided that Law X. should read thus:

"The ball must be bowled; if thrown or jerked, the umpire shall call 'no-ball.'"

That settled for good the vexed question of the height of arm in delivering the ball, and bowlers and umpires breathed more freely afterwards.

Surrey and Nottinghamshire met in July, and it was thought their differences were at an end; but when England met Surrey a month later, the crack Northern players would not come; and they also absented themselves from the North *v.* South match, in September. In the last match the North was poorly represented, and the South won very easily. So indignant were the Southern players that at the end of the first day's play they met and drew up the following protest:

"We, the South of England, decline playing at Newmarket on the 6th, 7th, and 8th October, as they, the North of England, refused to play in London. *(Signed)* T. Lockyer, W. Mortlock, E. Pooley, James Lillywhite, jun., G. Bennett, T. Humphrey, H. Jupp, C. H. Ellis, T. Hearne, T. Sewell, jun., G. Griffith, John Lillywhite, and Julius Cæsar."

That did not improve matters; in reality it widened the breach, and created a schism between North and South, which led to the formation of the United South Eleven, and the North of Thames *v.* South of Thames matches; and in after years the All-England and United Elevens were seen very little in the south.

It was a most unhappy state of affairs and, but for the firmness of the M.C.C. and the leading amateurs of the various counties and clubs, might have had serious consequences. Fortunately, a love for the game was springing up all over the United Kingdom, and good players were increasing in number rapidly. Very soon equally good players could be seen outside of the famous elevens, and the demands of the different players—in some cases reasonable, in others unreasonable—could either be granted or firmly refused. The M.C.C. was now playing the Colts of England, for the purpose of discovering rising talent; and county clubs were doing the same thing. Public schools, colleges, and other clubs were also adding to the number. The Na Shuler Club, holding pretty much the same position in Ireland as the I Zingari in England, was formed in 1863; and there was another and more powerful combination, named the Free Foresters, which had been in existence since 1856, and which for seven years could show a record of 102 matches played, 62 of them won. Then there was the Southgate Club, which, owing to the famous Walker family, had a great reputation in the neighbourhood of London and out of it. It was very busy about that time, playing almost a first-class eleven, and sixteen of it were strong enough to defeat the United England Eleven by an innings and 65 runs.

A very pleasing and encouraging feature at that time was the growth and interest taken in the game outside of England. Scotland and Ireland were developing rapidly, and began international matches with each other; and an English eleven, under the leadership of Parr, was causing great interest in Australia. England *v.* Twenty-two of Victoria, on the 1st, 2nd, 4th and 5th January, 1864, at Melbourne, brought out a great crowd, as many as 40,000 attending during the four days. For a parallel to it in England we have to go to the Eton and Harrow match at Lord's, in the height of the London season, when something approaching 20,000 were present in two days.

The All-England *v.* United England, and Gentlemen *v.* Players matches, though far ahead of the Eton and Harrow match in a cricketing sense, were not to be compared with it in attendance. The Players were still far ahead of the Gentlemen, and that year's defeat made the eighteenth in succession.

But, undoubtedly, the most encouraging feature of that season was the progress made by the counties. Surrey county had a very fine record: 14 matches played—8 won, 1 lost, 5 drawn.

Middlesex ...	8 played	: 5 won, 2 lost, 1 drawn.
Sussex	8 ,,	: 5 won, 2 lost, 1 drawn.
Cambridgeshire	3 ,,	: 3 won (2 against Yorkshire, 1 against Notts).
Notts	7 ,,	: 3 won, 4 lost.
Yorkshire ...	7 ,,	: 2 won, 4 lost, 1 drawn.
Kent...	9 ,,	: 9 lost.

A very sad show for Kent, considering that 13 of that club played an Eleven of England twice that year.

Lancashire played 9: 3 won, 3 lost, 3 drawn; most of them against minor counties and local clubs. Hampshire played 11 matches of one kind and another, and Buckinghamshire played two against Middlesex. Amateur Elevens were quite as busy; the I Zingari playing 23 matches, the Incogniti 23, and the Free Foresters 14.

I began to take an active part in first-class cricket in **1865.** I was only sixteen years of age, but I was over 6 feet in height and 11 stone in weight. Before the end of the season I had played for the Gentlemen of the South, the Gentlemen of England, England *v.* Surrey, and for the Gentlemen *v.* Players twice, with what success will be seen later on. Before touching upon the doings in 1865, it will be useful to revert for a little to the past.

The All-England and United All-England Elevens were still in full swing, playing as many as thirty matches during the season. Scotland and Ireland were now included in the list of their engagements; but rarely was either eleven seen in the South. They still possessed the cream of the professional talent; and when they played against each other, the display was still the finest of the season. Down to the year 1864 the two elevens had met fourteen times, and results showed six wins each, two drawn. And, so far, not a single member of either eleven had scored a hundred runs in an innings. Carpenter scored 97 in the 1859 match; but that was the nearest approach to it. The reason, no doubt, was owing principally to the quality of their bowling and the rough wickets which were played on then. It is told of Clarke's Eleven that on one occasion when it visited Cornwall a man fielding at long-on flushed a covey of partridges, and that a patch 40 yards by 10 was the only part of the ground that was ever cut or rolled. But it might, in a degree, be attributed to the fact that professional players did not cultivate batting as much as bowling, knowing that, however good they might be at the former, they must excel in the latter to secure an engagement with a club of any importance. The aim of every club was to engage a good bowler as soon as its finances permitted. The player who averaged a double figure at the end of the season was considered to have batted exceptionally well; and when a good bowler did it he was looked upon as an all-round first-class cricketer indeed, and could command a very high price for his services.

The averages of a number of the prominent batsmen of both elevens in the annual matches played against each other from their inauguration in 1857 will show the quality of the batting at that period. At the end of 1864:

R. Carpenter	had played	19	innings,	average 25.6
G. Parr	,,	21	,,	,, 24.18
T. Hayward	,,	18	,,	,, 16.13
R. Daft	,,	18	,,	,, 16.11
T. Hearne	,,	17	,,	,, 16.13
H. H. Stephenson	,,	24	,,	,, 16.2
G. Anderson	,,	14	,,	,, 13.9
J. Jackson	,,	18	,,	,, 13.11
W. Caffyn	,,	24	,,	,, 12.5
J. Grundy	,,	24	,,	,, 11.11
R. C. Tinley	,,	21	,,	,, 10.5
E. Willsher	,,	24	,,	,, 10.3
J. Wisden	,,	17	,,	,, 8.6
G. Tarrant	,,	9	,,	,, 7.6

Those were the most celebrated players of both elevens.

When we turn to the doings of the Gentlemen and Players there is a different story to tell. These matches were commenced in 1806. At the end of 1864 results showed that the Players had won 39, the Gentlemen 14, and 3 were drawn; and that the century had been exceeded 8 times; seven of them to the credit of the Players, one to the credit of the Gentlemen.

If we remember that in the majority of the matches won by the Gentlemen, they were either playing extra men, or had one or two players given them, it will be easily seen that the best of our amateur talent was very far behind the best of our professional. From 1854 to 1864 the Gentlemen were completely out of the running. Out of the 19 matches played between those years, the Players won 18, and 1 was drawn.

That was the state of affairs at the end of 1864; and when it was announced that 60 young players had applied and been recommended to play in the Nottinghamshire Colts' Match on Easter Monday, 1865, and that other counties were full of promising talent also, the prospects of professional players looked very rosy. University and public school cricket were in full swing also, and the number of first-class amateur batsmen was rapidly increasing.

At the end of 1865 County Cricket showed that Nottinghamshire and Surrey were at the head of the poll.

In purely county matches Surrey won 7, lost 3, and 2 were drawn; Nottinghamshire won 6, lost 1; Middlesex won 3, lost 1, and 1 was drawn; Kent won 2, lost 3, and 2 were drawn; Sussex won 1, lost 4, and 2 were drawn; Cambridgeshire won 1, lost 1, and 1 was drawn; Yorkshire won 0, lost 6, and 2 were drawn. Buckinghamshire, Hampshire, and Warwickshire played against each other with varying results.

Nottinghamshire's performance was a very fine one; four wins being ridiculously easy, especially that against Sussex at Trent Bridge, 1st, 2nd, and 3rd June, which was won by an innings and 86 runs. Parr and Daft batted consistently for their county all that season; the former doing specially good work with the bat, considering that he was now in his fortieth year, and had represented Nottinghamshire for 21 years. Then they had such good bowlers as Grundy, Wootton, Jackson, Alfred Shaw, and Tinley. Grundy was very successful on that occasion, the Sussex batsmen being perfectly helpless against him. In the second innings he bowled 100 balls, took 5 wickets, and only 6 runs were scored off him. The one match lost was the return against Surrey at the Oval on the 13th, 14th, and 15th July, and there was a tremendous amount of excitement and feeling over it. Parr declined to play, which did not make matters pleasant to begin with; and rarely have two counties fought so keenly as those two did on that occasion. Surrey in the second innings had 14 runs to make to win when the ninth wicket went down. They obtained them; but the Nottinghamshire players and some spectators alleged that Sewell, the last batsman, had been run out, and spoke bitterly of the umpire's decision. Quite a crowd gathered in front of the pavilion at the finish, and neither of the elevens measured their language, nor forgot to rake up old sores. The relationship between the two counties had become so strained, that the committees of both clubs decided to abandon the match in 1866, and contests between them were not resumed for three years.

Yorkshire's performances were sadly disappointing to its supporters; but the committee had to contend against internal dissensions, and on more than one occasion were without their full strength. Five of the regular eleven refused to play against Surrey at Sheffield on the 19th, 20th, and 21st June; and afterwards the committee tried all in their power to do without them, with the result that every match was lost. The county had commenced the season with satisfactory hopes, too; and amongst their fixtures was a match against the All-England Eleven, which turned out to be the most humiliating defeat a good eleven had experienced for years, the county losing by an innings and 255 runs. Carpenter and Hayward scored over a hundred runs each for the All-England Eleven, and every member of the team made a double figure; and in the second innings Wootton took all ten wickets.

On the 22nd June I played my first representative match. The Gentlemen of the South met the Players of the South at the Oval on that day, and it was my good fortune to be on the winning side, the Players being defeated by an innings and 58 runs. Mr. I. D. Walker was the successful batsman, scoring 91 out of a total of 233. I need not say I was anxious to do well, and was chagrined at being stumped without scoring.

THOMAS HAYWARD. ROBERT CARPENTER.

The captain of the team sent me in first wicket down, a compliment which I keenly felt I had not justified; but I was on better terms with myself at the end of the match, after having bowled with success unchanged through both innings. In the first innings I took five wickets for 44 runs, in the second eight wickets for 40.

Ten days later I made my first appearance for the Gentlemen *v.* Players at the Oval, in response to the invitation of the committee of the Surrey Club. On that occasion I was placed eighth on the batting list, and scored 23 first innings, 12 not out second. Mr. R. D. Walker scored 92 the second innings; Mr. R. A. H. Mitchell, 53 first and 33 second: but we lost the match by 118 runs; and I realised that whilst there were as good batsmen in the Gentlemen's eleven as in the Players', the former were still much behind in bowling. It was the ninth time that this match had been played at the Oval, and on each occasion the Players had won rather easily. It was easy to understand that against such an array of talent as the Players then possessed, the Gentlemen had a formidable task before them to win one of the two matches that were now played annually between them. Our defeat was all the more annoying that the Players' eleven was not at all representative on that occasion; for the northern cracks—Daft, Parr, Jackson, Hayward, Carpenter, Tarrant, and Anderson—had all declined to come.

The return match, at Lord's, on the 10th and 11th July, was more encouraging to us; the Gentlemen winning it by eight wickets. It was their first win since the year 1854. Hayward, Carpenter, and Parr were amongst the Players, and this added considerably to our satisfaction in defeating so strong an eleven. I batted first, with my brother E. M., in both innings. Mr. B. B. Cooper made 70 for the Gentlemen, and Mr. R. A. H.

Mitchell 44 not out; and G. Parr was highest for the Players, making 60 in their second innings.

I had another, and what I considered a very high, compliment paid to me on the 17th, 18th, and 19th July. The second of those dates was my eighteenth birthday, and I spent it playing for The Gentlemen of England *v.* The Gentlemen of Middlesex, on the Middlesex County Ground, at Islington. The result showed that both teams had plenty of batting strength, for 822 runs were scored for 36 wickets. My brother E. M. was most successful for England, scoring 12 and 111; and my share was 48 and 34. Mr. A. J. Wilkinson scored 28 and not out 84 for Middlesex; and Mr. C. F. Buller made 71 for the same side.

At the Oval, on the 21st and 22nd August, I played for England *v.* Surrey, and going in first with E. M., raised the score to 80 before we were parted.

I have dealt more fully with my own doings in those matches than I had intended; but, as it was the first year in which I contended against the best of the amateur and professional talent, I believed it might be of interest and encouraging to beginners to have the results. It will be seen that, at times, I was fairly successful with both bat and ball; but that now and then I shared the common experience of doing very little with either. First-class professional bowling I found to be a widely different thing from the amateur bowling which I had played chiefly against in the last year or two against local clubs. My slight experience against the All-England Eleven had in a measure prepared me for it, and I took no liberties: but most of the bowlers were new to me, and their styles varied; and I learned that before I could do much against a man, I must know something about his bowling. It was trial enough to be compelled to play over after over of straight, good-length balls; but I had to watch tricky ones as well. Patience I found to be my greatest friend, and before the season was over I had gained something in confidence. But, of course, I was disappointed at not scoring a hundred runs at least once during the year, although I knew that was a feat rarely accomplished at that time against first-class bowling. My highest score was 85, for the South Wales Club *v.* I Zingari; but my most encouraging performance was in bowling for the Gentlemen of the South *v.* Players of the South, in the match I have already mentioned, and for which the Surrey Club presented me with a ball, with the following inscription on it:

> "Presented to W. G. Grace, Esq., by the Surrey County Cricket Club, for his great performance in the match of Gentlemen of the South *v.* Players of the South at the Oval, June 22nd and 23rd, where he bowled 5 wickets first innings for 44 runs, and 8 second for 40."

I had plenty of cricket of one kind and another that year, playing in all 54 innings, and scoring 2169 runs; and one of the innings was for Suffolk County Club. It came about in this way. The M.C.C. was playing that county at Lord's, and I was in London at the time. I strolled on to the ground the second day; and Suffolk being two men short, very kindly asked me to play. I did not wait to be asked twice, and could have wished to have done better for them. We were sadly defeated, only scoring 58 and 62; while the M.C.C. scored 269 in a single innings. E. M. scored 82 for them, and knocked the Suffolk bowling all over the ground.

There were two or three good individual performances during the year; one of them being Jupp's 216 for the Players of the South *v.* Fourteen Gentlemen of the South, at Southampton in September. The Gentlemen were a very weak lot; but Jupp's score was made without a chance. Pooley scored 111 by hard hitting in the same match. Another fine effort was my brother E.M.'s against the United England Eleven, for Eighteen of the Lansdown Club, at Bath in the month of June. Out of a total of 299 he made 121; and he, my eldest brother Henry, and myself took all the wickets in both innings.

Over a hundred runs in an innings, in good matches, was scored by Messrs. C. G. Lyttelton, R. D. Walker, A. Lubbock, Spencer Leigh, S. A. Leigh; and among the Players, by W. Oscroft (twice), H. H. Stephenson, Bennett, T. Humphrey, Hayward, and Carpenter.

My brother E. M. came in for a hot reception at a match played at the Oval on the 28th, 29th, 30th September. Playing for Eighteen Gentlemen of the Surrey Club against the United South of England, he scored 64 and 56, and received his 75th presentation bat; it being the custom of the committee of the Surrey Club at that time to give a bat for every score of 50 runs. Mr. I. D. Walker and he bowled unchanged in both innings; Mr. Walker's underhand lobs and E. M.'s fast round completely beating the United South batsmen. Jupp was most at home with them, and got set in the second innings. "The problem is to get Jupp out," said I. D. to E. M. "All right!" said E. M.; "I can do it with a lob." Very shortly after he gave him a lofty one, which fell right on to the top of the wickets, and a scene followed. Cries of "Shame!" and "Unfair bowling!" were shouted all over the ground; and a large number of the spectators advised Jupp not to go out. The match was stopped for the greater part of an hour, finally resuling in a win for the Eighteen by 155 runs.

THE ALL-ENGLAND ELEVEN played 30 matches that year: won 19, lost 5, drawn 6.

Carpenter was at the head of the averages with 31 innings, average 24.23; G. Parr, 28 innings, average 17.16. In bowling: J. Jackson captured 206 wickets, average 5.21 per innings; G. Tarrant, 250 wickets, average 5.40 per innings; and Tinley, 301 wickets, average 7.28 per innings.

THE UNITED ALL-ENGLAND ELEVEN played 9 matches: won 3, lost 3, drawn 3.

Carpenter played 14 innings, and averaged 17.2; J. Thewlis played 14 innings, and averaged 16.5.

In bowling: G. Atkinson captured 61 wickets, average 5.1 per innings; J. Grundy, 48 wickets, average 5.3 per innings; G. Wootton, 35 wickets, average 4.3 per innings; Tarrant, 33 wickets, average 8.1 per innings.

THE UNITED SOUTH ELEVEN played 14 matches: won 4, lost 4, drawn 6.

Jupp and Humphrey were the most successful batsmen; Willsher and Jas. Lillywhite the most successful bowlers.

A marked improvement was witnessed in batting in the year **1866.** Hardly a week passed without an individual innings of a hundred runs in an innings being recorded in some match or another; and before the season was at an end, 200 runs was exceeded four times. The averages reached a figure undreamt of a few years before, and the once-coveted double figure had become quite common. An aggregate of 1000 runs, which was at one time considered a very exceptional feat, was accomplished by eighteen batsmen, ten of them amateurs; many of the batsmen, however, played few or no first-class matches.

The All-England Eleven again showed excellent results: 30 matches played—won, 15; lost, 6; tie, 1; drawn, 8. The United All-England played 22—won, 14; lost, 2; drawn, 6. The United South played 17—won, 4; lost, 7; drawn, 6.

In County Cricket, Surrey, Middlesex, Kent, Sussex, Cambridgeshire, and Lancashire were well represented: but Yorkshire was again a failure, only playing three matches, and losing two of them; the other was unfinished. Nottinghamshire only played six matches—home and home with Cambridgeshire, Yorkshire, and Middlesex; winning 2, losing 1, whilst 3 were drawn.

The All-England Eleven *v.* United All-England Eleven match was played, as usual, at Lord's, for the benefit of the Cricketers' Fund, on 21st, 22nd, and 23rd May, and a large crowd witnessed the contest. The teams were composed entirely of northern players: both elevens were well represented, and a very good match took place, the United winning, and making the record of matches played between them 7 wins each, 2 drawn. But after that, representative matches—North *v.* South, and Gentlemen *v.* Players—were completely spoiled, owing to the northern players declining to play. No less than thirteen players in the North refused, and at last the committee of the Marylebone Club spoke out clearly and firmly. At a committee-meeting of that club, held on May 21st, the following resolutions were passed:

> "1. That as the committee must decline to enter into the disputes among the professionals, or take the part either of northern and southern players, another eleven be selected to play in the North *v.* South match.
>
> "2. That the selection of players for the match Gentlemen *v.* Players having been considered in reference to the refusal of the northern players to meet the southern men, the players in all matches at Lord's be selected from those who are willing to play together in a friendly manner in the matches on that ground."

Of course, the resolutions were passed too late to have any effect that season; but they bore fruit two or three years later.

The match between the Gentlemen and Players at Lord's, on the 25th June, was not representative of the players; although it was strong enough to beat the

Gentlemen by 38 runs, chiefly owing to the magnificent batting of Tom Hearne, who scored 122 not out in the second innings.

The return match at the Oval was no better, but the Gentlemen turned the tables, and won by 98 runs.

The South *v.* North, at Lord's, on the 2nd July, was a miserable failure. There were only a few players in the North team that could be called first-class, and the match was robbed of all interest. The North scored 95 and 65, to the South's single innings of 203, and the spectators who witnessed it did not hesitate to speak out about the conduct of the absent northern players.

I cannot say that I played a very important part with the bat in any of these three matches. In the first and second I scored 77 runs for four innings; in the third I made 19 in my single innings. But I met with fair success with the ball in both matches against the Players, obtaining six wickets in the first and nine in the second.

I have often been asked if I had much faith in myself before I commenced my big innings of 224 not out for England *v.* Surrey, at the Oval, on the 30th July of that year. My memory is a blank in that respect. I was a little over eighteen years of age at the time, and the years that followed were busy ones; and that particular match, and one or two others, have become dim memories. I know I travelled up to town the same morning, and felt slightly nervous the first over or two; everything afterwards I have forgotten, except the shouting which followed at the end of the innings, late in the afternoon of the second day. And I remember Mr. V. E. Walker, the captain of the England team, was kind enough to let me off the last day to compete in the 440 yards' hurdle-race of the National Olympian Association Meeting at the Crystal Palace, which I won in 1 minute 10 seconds over 20 hurdles.

GEORGE PARR.

(From an old Print.)

My score of 173 not out, for the Gentlemen of the South *v.* Players of the South, at the Oval, 27th and 28th August, is also a hazy remembrance. I have a faint idea that there was more hitting in it than in the previous match, and that I played more confidently. I had been thinking hard, during the season, that the arrangement of the field in first-class matches was not quite what it ought to be. There was a prevailing opinion at the time that as long as a bowler was straight, a batsman could not score off him, and that no men in the long field were necessary. The opinion had, I believe, been handed down from old W. Lillywhite's time, who, when a straight ball was driven over his head, used to take off his hat, rub his pate, and say: "That's a very pretty game, but it aint cricket." My brother E. M. was the first to upset that theory, and I determined to copy him, and so every time I had a ball the least bit over-pitched, I hit it hard over the bowler's head, and did not trouble about where it was going. My height enabled me to get over those that were slightly short, and I played them hard: long-hops off the wicket I pulled to square-leg or long-on, without the slightest hesitation.

The year altogether was a busy one, and the game had now taken a greater hold than ever.

I have been repeatedly asked when I played first in the Midland and Northern counties, but was at a loss to answer. I stumbled across an old score the other day, which recalls the date and circumstances. It was on the 4th and 5th of June, 1866, at the old Hyde Park Ground, Sheffield, when I captained Eighteen Colts of Nottingham and Sheffield against the All-England Eleven. I have represented many a team in my life, but this seems to my mind the most curious, and I shall not readily forget the impression the match made on me. The ground was on the top of a hill which took some climbing to reach, and everything in connection with it was of the most primitive description. I am more used to Yorkshire ways and arrangements now; but at the time I felt as if I had got to the world's end, and a very black and sooty end it seemed! I was only a boy of 17, and had never before had the honour of leadership on my shoulders against an eleven of world-wide fame. My brother E. M. had been asked to undertake the responsibility, but could not go, and recommended me to take his place. The All-England Eleven beat us by an innings and 8 runs, and I was very much impressed with Parr's leg-hitting. The ground was not much to look at, but the wicket was a good one; and after scoring 9 and 36, I was complimented on having captained the team and with playing creditably.

Scorers of 1000 *Runs in all Matches in* 1866.

	Runs.	No. of Innings.	Not out.	Highest in Innings
Mr. W. G. Grace	2168	40	7	224*
Mr. C. F. Buller	1647	54	6	196
Mr. M. A. Troughton ...	1526	46	14	91
Mr. J. J. Sewell	1466	44	7	166
Mr. R. A. Fitzgerald... ...	1420	60	6	147
Mr. A. Lubbock...	1383	34	9	220
Mr. E. B. Fane	1265	37	3	151*
Captain Taylor	1237	56	7	99
Mr. Ashley Walker	1213	47	1	126
Mr. C. F. Lucas...	1081	36	3	135
H. Jupp	1605	68	8	165
Sergt. W. McCanlis	1580	45	8	172*
T. Hearne	1335	52	2	146
J. Smith	1163	62	2	80
H. Holmes	1118	42	10	105
R. Carpenter	1102	37	11	97*
J. W. Burnham	1060	42	7	115
T. A. Mantle	1010	44	9	93

* Not out.

The Marylebone Club opened the season of 1867 with a match on the continent. It sent twelve of its members across the Channel to play a friendly game against twelve of the Paris Club, on the new ground in the Bois de Boulogne, in the hope, no doubt, of spreading a knowledge of the game. It was the first time the M.C.C. had played out of the United Kingdom, and judging by the names of the players who represented Paris, it might have been a contest between two English elevens. The M.C.C. won very easily, defeating their opponents by an innings and 135 runs; Mr. A. Lubbock scoring 102 in brilliant form. The match took place on the 22nd and 23rd April, and on the two succeeding days the I Zingari played on the same ground, against the same club, and won just as easily; Mr. A. Lubbock again being the top scorer with 72 not out. History does not report that the French nation was stirred or excited over the visit of two such important clubs, nor does it say that cricket clubs were formed and flourished on account of it.

A month later, on the 23rd, 24th, and 25th May, the All-England and United All-England Elevens met at Manchester for the benefit of the Cricketers' Fund. The match had been played on Whit-Monday at Lord's since 1857; but as both elevens were now composed entirely of Northern men, and the schism which had raged for years between North and South was still active, very little surprise was felt when the fixture was announced to take place on the old Trafford Ground. The M.C.C. realising that the two elevens meant to travel their own way respecting that match, as they had done in the North *v.* South matches, met in the early part of the season and passed the following resolution:

"Taking into consideration the conduct of certain of the professionals of England during the season of 1866, it is no longer desirable to extend the patronage of the Marylebone

Club to the Cricketers' Fund exclusively; but a fund has now been formed which shall be called 'The Marylebone Professional Fund,' which shall have for its object the support of the professional players who, during their career, shall have conducted themselves to the entire satisfaction of the Committee of the M.C.C."

The first match on its behalf was played at Lord's on the 10th and 11th of June, between an Eleven of England and Middlesex County, and was largely attended. I had the pleasure of playing for England, and helping to speed the good cause. It was the first time Middlesex had played against England, and the result was far from encouraging to the county; for it lost by an innings and 25 runs. Mr. A. Lubbock was top scorer with 129, and I supported him with 75; and while we were together runs came at a great pace. So far Mr. Lubbock had shown that he was likely to take a high place in batting honours at the end of the season, his hitting and defence in the matches he had already played being consistently good.

At Lord's on 17th and 18th of June, North of the Thames *v.* South of the Thames was substituted for the old North *v.* South Match, and the wrench between Northern and Southern players was, for a time, complete. The match was one of the curiosities of a remarkable scoring season. Batting generally had so much improved that a total score of 400 runs created as little surprise as a total of 200 had done a year or two previously. The season, so far, had been dry, and favourable for tall scoring, and before the match commenced the opinion prevailed that this match would prove no exception. But the weather has spoiled many a match, and it spoiled that one—for three innings were completed on the first day for a total of 195 runs. The South batted first, and were all out in an hour and seventeen minutes for a paltry 32. Wootton and Grundy were the bowlers, the former capturing 7 wickets for 18 runs. The North did very little better; the first 4 wickets fell for 7 runs, and six of them were down for 16 in thirty-six minutes. They were all out in an hour and a-half; total 61: for this I was mainly responsible — obtaining 6 wickets for 23 runs.

The second innings of the South realised 102 runs; Mortlock being the highest score with 22 not out. Alfred Shaw did the mischief this time—bringing off three remarkably good catches, and capturing 3 wickets in 39 balls for 2 runs. The North began their second innings next morning with a balance of 73 against them, and were all out in an hour and three-quarters for 46. The highest score was 8, and there was not a "duck" in the innings. Not a single extra was scored; and the fielding was magnificent. My brother E.M. brought off four very fine catches at point, Pooley was brilliant behind the wickets, and James Lillywhite took 4 wickets for 18 runs, and myself 6 for 28. It was a most exciting and sensational match from start to finish, and the keenness and closeness of it will be remembered for many a long day.

The match between the Gentlemen and Players, played at Lord's on the 8th and 9th of July, was almost a repetition of the one I have just described. The Players batted first, and were all out in an hour and fifty minutes for 79; Mr. Appleby taking 6 wickets for 33 runs. The Gentlemen scored 87 in the first innings. Wootton was the most successful bowler —capturing 6 wickets for 41 runs.

The second innings of the Players was more disastrous than the first, for they only scored 61; and three innings had been completed a little before seven o'clock on the first day. I was the successful bowler this time—capturing 8 wickets for 25 runs. The

Gentlemen were left with 54 to win. A little over an hour sufficed to finish the match next day, on a difficult wicket; the Gentlemen winning by 8 wickets.

There was no need to complain of the weather on that occasion. From beginning to end it was perfect; but, as Lillywhite said in his summary of the year, "the wickets were decidedly bad even for Lord's ground."

The return match between the Gentlemen and Players was spoiled by the weather, and could not be completed; but it will be memorable for the finely-played innings of 107 not out—in the second innings—by Mr. A. Lubbock, the hard-hit 71 of my brother E. M., and the wicket-keeping of Mr. J. Round. But I took no part in it, or in any match for over six weeks.

On the 14th of July I was laid up with scarlet fever, and was unable to play until the end of August, and I did not feel very fit then. It was a bitter disappointment to me; for while my bowling efforts had been quite up to my expectations, I had not scored so heavily as I had desired, and I was hoping for better things before the season ended. That was my most successful bowling year. I bowled faster than I do at present—now and then putting in a slower one, which often deceived the batsman.

The year was a great one of individual performances with both bat and ball; 200 runs in an innings was scored by Messrs. E. B. Rowley, E. M. Grace, and H. Clement, though not in first-class matches; and 100 runs was scored 171 times, but only eleven of them against first-class professional bowling. Mr. W. Townshend scored 100 runs twice in a match for Rossall School. But, undoubtedly, the great batting performance of the year was Mr. Lubbock's, who scored over a hundred runs three times—two of them in first-class matches—and who had the very fine average at the end of the season of 72.4 for 5 innings.

Wootton and Southerton both captured over 100 wickets in first-class matches; but Grundy, Emmett, Freeman, and one or two others bowled with finer results. Emmett and Freeman proved invaluable to their county, and it was owing entirely to their all-round efforts that Yorkshire, after being at the bottom of the poll in 1866, was raised to the top in 1867—not losing a single match in the six played.

Neither Surrey, Kent, Cambridgeshire, nor Middlesex kept up its 1866 form; but Sussex and Lancashire showed improvement, and Nottinghamshire was still well to the front. Nottinghamshire played one match against the North of England, which practically meant the combined strength of Lancashire, Yorkshire, and Cambridgeshire, but was beaten by 112 runs. Freeman and Tarrant bowled unchanged in both innings against them, dividing the wickets and clean-bowling nine of their opponents.

Batting generally advanced with rapid strides in the year **1868**. Total scores and individual performances exceeded everything in the past, and the cry was that the batting had now become too strong for the bowling. Two innings of 689 and 630 runs were scored; Mr. Tylecote scored his memorable 404 not out at Clifton, and Mr. W. J. Batchelor scored 289 for the Long Vacation Club at Cambridge. Totals and individual scores were the highest yet recorded in the history of the game. Altogether over 200 runs in an innings were scored by six players, and the century was exceeded at least 200 times. It was very much owing to the lovely weather which prevailed the greater part of the season, making the wickets dry and fast.

An eleven of Aboriginal Players of Australia visited

England, and played their first match at the Oval on 25th and 26th May. They played 47 matches during the season; winning 14, losing 14, and 19 were drawn. In strength they were about equal to third-class English teams; and the result of their visit was satisfactory and encouraging to them in every respect. I had not the pleasure of playing against them; but I believe it was generally admitted that two players, Mullagh and Cuzens, showed very good all-round form.

County Cricket still progressed; Yorkshire holding its own, but not shining so conspicuously over the others as it did the previous year. Nottinghamshire played Lancashire for the first time, and home-and-home matches were resumed with Surrey.

Gloucestershire made a start, playing the M.C.C. at Lord's on the 25th and 26th June, and winning by 134 runs; but it was two years later before the club was formed on a sound basis, and engaged in contests with other counties.

My brother Fred played on this occasion; but he had made his first appearance at Lord's on the 1st and 2nd of the same month, playing for England *v.* M.C.C. He was only 17 years of age at the time; but he had already earned a great reputation in local cricket, and had represented the South of the Thames *v.* North of the Thames in 1866. I was of the same age when I first played for England, and I believe we are the only two players who have represented England so young. Fred had played for the United South also, and was thought good enough to go in first with me; and we now continued to represent that Eleven most years.

Before the season was over I accomplished two or three good batting performances. On June the 1st and 2nd, for England *v.* M.C.C., at Lord's, played for the benefit of the Marylebone Cricketers' Fund, I scored

29 out of 96 first innings, and 66 out of 179 second; and we defeated the old club by 92 runs. The M.C.C. had not played England since 1856, and did not again until 1877.

The North of the Thames *v.* South of the Thames was played, in place of the North *v.* South match, at Lord's, on the 8th of June, and was one of the curiosities of those contests. The North Eleven was not a particularly strong one, and the match was finished in one day, the South winning by nine wickets. A shower of rain in the early part of the day caused the ground to kick, and in five hours thirty-one wickets were disposed of for 260 runs. Mr. A. N. Hornby appeared in the North team on that occasion.

At Lord's on the 29th and 30th June the Gentlemen defeated the Players by eight wickets, and I scored 134 not out in a total of 201. It was my first hundred in those matches; and the wicket was very hard and fast, which suited me splendidly. I hit very hard, and rarely made a mistake; and I believe even to-day that it was one of the finest innings I have ever played. The wicket played queerly, and everything was run out at Lord's in those days, and not once in the innings did Willsher, Grundy, Lillywhite or Wootton cause me any trouble; and I very seldom allowed the ball to pass the bat. I captured six wickets for 50 runs first innings; four for 31 second.

The return match at the Oval on the 2nd and 3rd July saw Mr. I. D. Walker in magnificent batting form. He scored 165 out of a total of 379, and never played a better innings in his life. Every bowler was hit all over the ground by him, and Lillywhite and Willsher were on four times. In his score there were two 6's, three 5's, and seventeen 4's. The bowling of Mr. David Buchanan in the second innings was another feature of the match. He captured nine wickets for 82 runs—

a very fine performance, considering that he was now 38 years of age, and that it was his first appearance in those contests. The Gentlemen won by one innings and 87 runs, this being their second win at the Oval. Their first win on that ground was in 1866, and Mr. Burrup, the Secretary, was so elated over it, that he presented every member of the eleven with a bat. There was less excitement on this occasion, and at last the happy time had come when the Gentlemen could hold their own in these contests.

The return match between the North of the Thames and the South of the Thames, on the St. Lawrence Ground at Canterbury, August 3rd, 4th, and 5th, was a remarkable, and in one respect historical, match. For the North the Rev. J. McCormick scored 137 in the first innings in two and a half hours, and hit our bowling all over the field; in the second innings, Mr. R. A. H. Mitchell scored 90, and Mr. H. N. Tennant 45 not out. For the South, I scored 130 first innings; 102 not out second. Altogether, 1,018 runs were scored in the three days; and it was the first time I scored two centuries in a match. It should be remembered that the St. Lawrence Ground was always an easy scoring one; and on that occasion, being hard and dry, it was particularly so, and suited me exactly. Besides, there were boundary hits at that date there, and I did not have anything like the running I had for my 134 at Lord's.

The year **1869** showed no decline in high scoring; in reality it showed an increase in three-figure innings and averages. The century was made close upon 250 times: nine times by myself; five times each by my brother Fred and Jupp; four times by Mr. I. D. Walker; and three times each by Messrs. B. B. Cooper, E. L. Fellowes, A. N. Hornby, C. I. Thornton, F. W. Wright, B. Pauncefote,

C. J. Ottaway, T. Wise, Lieut. Scott, Daft and Rowbotham. My brother Fred also scored 206, and Mr. L. C. Howell 201.

I had the honour of being elected a member of the M.C.C., and played my first match on the 13th of May, against Oxford University, at Cowley Marsh, and scored 117 out of a total of 229; and by the end of the season my results for that club were:

In batting—12 innings, 724 runs; average, 60.4.
In bowling—426 overs: 209 maidens; 570 runs; 44 wickets; average, 12.42.

And I scored over a hundred runs in an innings four times for it.

County Cricket was in favour of Nottinghamshire and Yorkshire that year, they running a dead heat for first honours. Surrey played as many as twelve county matches; but was defeated by both Nottinghamshire and Yorkshire. Cambridgeshire had ceased to exist as a county; although a match under that title was played against Yorkshire at Leeds, on the 10th and 11th July, which resulted in a great defeat for Cambridgeshire. Tarrant was seized with illness in the early part of the season, and did not play again, and Cambridgeshire without him was far below the best county form. Lancashire, Sussex, and Kent did not improve on their 1868 form; and Middlesex having lost their ground at Islington, only played two matches against Surrey—one at Lord's, the other at the Oval.

The North *v.* South matches were resumed; but again Parr, Carpenter, and Hayward declined to play. With Freeman and Emmett at their best, however, the North could hold its own without them, and the contests ranked next in importance to those between the Gentlemen and Players. They met three times during the season, and the South won two out of the three. I batted six times, and scored altogether 258 runs. My best innings was in the second match played at Sheffield, when I scored 122 out of a total of 173, against Freeman, Emmett and Wootton. And I was fairly successful with the ball in the same match, capturing six wickets for 57 runs first innings. But Southerton's seven for 34 runs in the second innings put all other bowling performances in the shade; although in the whole match Freeman took 13 wickets for 86 runs.

The most remarkable match of that year was The Gentlemen of the South *v*. Players of the South, at the Oval on the 15th, 16th, and 17th July. It had been a scoring match most years; but 1869 outshone its predecessors, and at the end of the three days only 21 wickets had fallen for a total of 1,136 runs. The Players won the toss, and on a perfect wicket, and in favourable weather, batted all the first day and until 1.50 the next, for the large total of 475. Pooley and Jupp commenced the innings, and scored 142 before they were parted. Charlwood batted seventh man, and hit our bowling everywhere in his score of 155. Eight of us had a try at him; but it fell to the lot of my brother Fred to clean bowl him. My bowling average did not come out particularly well in that match. "At last," said the Players, "we have got the best of them!"

Mr. B. B. Cooper and I batted first for the Gentlemen, and the Players had close upon four hours of it before they parted us for a total of 283. Six of their regular bowlers nearly broke their hearts in trying to part us; but Mantle, the unexpected and about the last resource, caught and bowled both of us in six balls, Mr. Cooper having scored 101, while my share was 180. But that was not the end of it. Mr. I. D. Walker came afterwards, and smote them to the tune of 90; and it was five o'clock on the Saturday before the innings was at an end, for a total of 553. The 283 was a record for first wicket in a first-class match, and it is so to-day. The Players had an hour and forty minutes left to play, and in that time scored 108: Pooley, 50; Jupp, not out 43.

The All-England Eleven played 23 matches; 8 won, 6 lost, 9 drawn.

The United All-England Eleven played its last match that year. It was founded in 1852, and held its own against the All-England Eleven and odds; but somehow or other it had never been so popular as its formidable rival and predecessor.

The Gentlemen won both matches against the Players: the first at the Oval by 17 runs, the second at Lord's by three wickets. The brunt of the batting was borne by Messrs. I. D. Walker, A. Lubbock, and myself; the bowling by Messrs. Absolom, Buchanan, and Appleby.

CHAPTER V.

CRICKET IN MY MANHOOD—1870 TO 1877.

MOST men who have lived active mental or physical lives have had their memories taxed to remember the various incidents in them. It has been so in my case, for the doings of some years stand out more clearly than others.

The year **1870** I can remember as being one of my best; indeed, I may say it saw me almost in my best batting and bowling form. Nine times I scored over a hundred runs in an innings, the majority of them in first-class matches.

For the M.C.C. I played 12 innings, and averaged 55.6; for Gloucestershire County, who played first-class county matches for the first time that year, I played 4 innings, and averaged 91.2; for the Gentlemen *v.* Players I played 4 innings, and averaged 85.1; and altogether during the season I batted in 33 innings in first-class matches, scored an aggregate of 1,808, and averaged 54.26.

It will be inferred from those scores that the season was everything that could be desired in the matter of weather. And so it was. Wickets were dry and fast the greater part of it, and I scored at a great pace. My defence had grown stronger, and my hitting powers had improved also.

On the 9th and 10th of May a match, Left-handed *v.* Right was played at Lord's; but the Left-handed were not in it. The match was noteworthy from the fact that Carpenter, Hayward, and J. Smith again appeared on that ground, and it looked for the moment as if the North and South had once more clasped hands and blotted out the past. The South *v.* North, at the same ground on the 6th and 7th June, confirmed the good feeling; for all the Northern cracks, with the exception of Freeman, were present, and he was only absent on account of the first match played by the North of England eleven, at Dewsbury, of which Iddison he and were joint secretaries. That was G. Parr's last appearance at Lord's; he was 44 years of age, and scored 41 in fine form.

An important change in the laws affecting bowlers was passed at a special meeting of the M.C.C. on the 4th of May. Before that date a bowler could change ends once only in an innings. The alteration now enabled him to change twice; but he was not allowed to bowl more than two overs in succession. The new rule was first carried into effect in the M.C.C. and Ground *v.* Yorkshire match at Lord's on the 30th and 31st May.

M.C.C. and Ground *v.* Nottinghamshire, at Lord's on the 13th, 14th, and 15th June, will be memorable for the unfortunate injury to Summers, one of the most promising players that Nottinghamshire had produced for years. They batted first, and scored 267, of which Daft made 117. The M.C.C. scored 183 first innings, of which I made 117 not out. We had to follow our innings, and I resumed after ten minutes' interval, and was bowled first over for a duck by J. C. Shaw. Messrs. I. D. Walker, J. W. Dale, and C. E. Green came to the rescue, however, and we totalled 240. Nottinghamshire won a close match by two wickets. The injury to Summers occurred early in the second innings. The first ball bowled to him by Platts was a little bit short, and it bumped and hit him on the head, and concussion of the brain followed. Platts was in no way to blame, for the ball did not bump higher than many I had to play in the same match; but unfortunately Summers treated the blow too lightly, appearing on the ground next day in a hot sun, and afterwards travelling by rail to Nottingham, which shook him terribly, and developed symptoms which subsequently proved fatal.

It used to be said that the Gentlemen were seldom fully represented in the Gentlemen *v.* Players' matches: but it was the opposite that year, for the Players' eleven was far from being representative; and the consequence was, that the first was drawn very much in the Gentlemen's favour, while the second was won. In the match at the Oval, I scored 215 out of a total of 513 in the second innings—so far, the highest individual performance yet recorded in those matches—and Mr. W. B. Money played two brilliant innings of 70 and 109 not out. In the return match at Lord's, I scored 109 in the first innings. It was my brother Fred's first appearance for the Gentlemen, and he was fairly successful with the ball; but he failed with the bat, having two ducks to his name in the first match, and only scoring 8 and 3 runs in the second.

A very good match was played at Beeston, Nottingham, on the 18th, 19th, and 20th August, between the Gentlemen of the North and the Gentlemen of the South, which showed Messrs. A. N. Hornby, I. D. Walker, and my brother Fred at their best. The North batted first, and scored 287; Mr. Hornby's contribution being 103, in which there were one 8 and seventeen 4's. As usual, I commenced the batting for the South. I played what I thought a brilliant 77, and nearly every one of the eleven said so too; but I. D. Walker afterwards scored 179, and Fred carried out his bat for 189, very little was, therefore, thought about my performance. My lot, however, was not quite so unhappy an one as Mr.

G. Strachan's. For six hours he sat patiently with the pads on, waiting for I. D. or Fred to come out, and when his turn came he had to be content with two balls: the first he hit for 2; the second he was c and b Hornby. I ought to have said that Fred hit thirty-four 4's in his score; I. D. Walker, one 5 and twenty-five 4's; and that the other eight batsmen scored 19 runs amongst them.

Another good bit of scoring was 166 for first wicket by Fred and myself, for the United South *v.* Twenty-two of Sleaford with R. Iddison, at Sleaford, 9th, 10th, and 11th June. It is curious how some innings leave a greater impression than others. That one is vivid to me on account of an accident which happened to one of the Twenty-two. He was fielding at short-leg to Iddison's lob-bowling, and was standing a little in front, about twelve yards from the wicket. Iddison would have him closer in, and eventually he was placed four yards nearer. I did not say anything at the time, but could not help thinking the position would have to be abandoned before Fred and I had finished batting.

Iddison pitched the first or second ball of the over a little too far up, and I stepped out and hit it on the full pitch. It went straight to the unfortunate fieldsman, hit him on the ankle, and then travelled far enough to enable us to run four. "He must be hurt," I thought; but he did not show it. He was a rare plucked one, and never winced; but, as Jas. Lillywhite said, "It is not in cricket human nature to hide that stroke, and I'll keep my eye on him;" and, sure enough, when the fieldsman moved to the long-field at the end of the over, and thought no one was looking, he began to rub vigorously. We saw little of him next day, and I believe he was laid up for some time afterwards. I think it cured Iddison of placing a man so near when bowling lobs.

Yorkshire was the most successful county that year, entirely owing to the very fine bowling of Freeman and Emmett. Lancashire showed a slight improvement; but Nottinghamshire, Kent, and Sussex did not come out favourably; while Surrey had an unprecedented run of ill-luck. I threw all my energies into Gloucestershire matches, and felt specially gratified at the results of our first year's play. We played Glamorganshire once, Surrey twice, M.C.C. and Ground once, winning them very easily. The first match we played was against Surrey, 2nd, 3rd, and 4th June, on Durdham Downs. Our eleven was made up entirely of amateurs, while Surrey played ten professionals and one amateur. It was the closest match we played, and created considerable interest in Gloucestershire. Quite a large crowd turned out, and we had some difficulty in getting them to stand far enough back. I remember that in the first innings Pooley, who was batting very well, would not go on until they were moved. Eventually they did go, and he said he could now hit out to leg to his heart's content; but the change worked in another way—it enabled long-leg to go farther out, and the first or second ball bowled Pooley hit into his hands, to the delight of the spectators.

Reference to the batting averages will show that Messrs. W. B. Money, A. N. Hornby, I. D. Walker, and W. Yardley were in great form. Nearly every innings played by them was full of dash, and they scored at a great pace against all kinds of bowling. Mr. Hornby, in particular, hit very hard, and exceeded the hundred eight times during the season, two of them in first-class matches. That feat I performed, as I have said, nine times, five of them in first-class matches; the highest and best being 215 for the Gentlemen *v.* Players, at the Oval.

The year **1871** was my most successful year with the bat. I was twenty-two years of age, and had played against every first-class bowler in England. Nearly all nervous feeling at the commencement of an innings had left me; but I guarded against over-confidence, and invariably played the first over or two carefully until I got my eye in. Grounds had improved wonderfully everywhere, and I aimed at placing every ball, however straight and good the length of it; for that was about the only way to score at all rapidly against the crack bowlers of the day, who could bowl over after over every ball on the wicket.

In the middle of May, I scored 181 for M.C.C. *v.* Surrey; and I kept up my form right to the end of the season, exceeding the century ten times, all of them in first-class matches. The weather was rather unfavourable, and occasionally the ground caused the ball to kick badly; but I never lost patience, and in one or two matches in particular I very much desired to score largely. Willsher, H. H. Stephenson and John Lillywhite had benefit matches that year, and I was anxious to do well for them; for they had done excellent work for the game for many years, and were highly respected by all classes of cricketers. Willsher was unfortunate in the matter of weather in the match Single *v.* Married, played at Lord's on the 10th, 11th and 12th July, on his behalf; but I scored 189 not out for him, and got up another match in September, which helped considerably to increase the fund. In the second match, W. G. Grace's XI. *v.* Kent, I scored 81 not out first, and 42 not out second; and W. Yardley played a magnificent innings of 126 not out in the second innings of Kent.

North *v.* South, at the Oval on 31st July, 1st and 2nd August, was the match played on behalf of Stephenson; and I shall not readily forget his disappointment when I was given out l.b.w. to J. C. Shaw the first ball bowled in the match. I was rather disappointed by it also; for there was a tremendous crowd present, and the wicket and the weather were perfect. "Keep up your heart, H. H.," I said; "I shall take care that it does not occur in the second innings." Fortunately the weather kept favourable all through, and I started my second innings about 4.30 the second day. After the first over or two I began to hit at a rare pace, and I paid particular attention to J. C. Shaw. At the close of the day's play my score was 142 not out, and only two wickets had fallen for 195. Stephenson was happy that night; and he was happier next morning, when the sun shone brilliantly and another large crowd came to witness the finish. I was out for 268, in a total of 436, at 4 o'clock on the third day, and had hit three 5's and twenty-eight 4's. Stephenson was immensely pleased, and presented me with a gold ring.

The Gentlemen *v.* Players was the match on behalf of John Lillywhite. It was played on the old Hove Ground at Brighton, 14th, 15th and 16th August, in splendid weather; and with the third ball of the match J. C. Shaw clean-bowled me. Lillywhite's heart was sad indeed, particularly as he it was who gave me out l.b.w. to Shaw in the first innings of Stephenson's match.

"I am terribly sorry, Lillywhite," I said; "I did want to do well for you."

"Better luck next time!" he replied.

I cannot explain it; but, personally, I was not hopeful, and said so. Lillywhite did not share my misgivings; for he took two sovereigns out of his pocket, put them into my hand, and said:

"You take these, and pay me a sixpence back for every run you make in the second innings. I call it a fair bet."

It was the greatest compliment I have ever had paid

to my batting skill; and my fears vanished as I realised the fulness of it. You may guess how I laid on after the first over or two to wipe out the eighty runs which were required to pay off the two pounds. I commenced my second innings at three o'clock on the second day. The first wicket fell for 35, then my brother Fred joined me, and we raised the total to 275 before we were parted; and scored 240 in two hours and a half. After the first hundred runs, I forgot all about the bet. At the end of the day's play, the total was 353 for three wickets; my score being 200 not out. I had a great reception when I reached the pavilion, Lillywhite being particularly warm.

"I'll trouble you for five pounds on account," he said.

"All right, Lillywhite, here it is," I replied; "but if you do not let me off for the rest of the bet, I shall knock down my wicket first over to-morrow!"

He made a virtue of necessity and cried "Quits!" I added 17 runs to my score next day.

No part of my cricket experience has given me more pleasure than my batting success in benefit matches. I always hoped to do something extraordinary on those occasions; and it is particularly gratifying to me to-day to remember that I nearly always accomplished it.

George Parr played his last match that year. He had been before the cricketing public for 27 years; and he finished his brilliant career at Trent Bridge on the 29th, 30th, and 31st May, in a manner worthy of his best days, scoring 32 not out, and 53 for Nottinghamshire *v.* Fourteen Gentlemen of Nottinghamshire.

In the Gentlemen *v.* Players' matches, the former had the best of it, winning one, while the other two were drawn slightly in their favour.

Amongst the counties, Gloucestershire held its own.

Sussex did exceptionally well, but Surrey was again at the bottom.

I made a first appearance on four grounds that year, and scored well on all of them. At West Brompton I scored 118 in my only innings, and I do not remember having played there since. At Fenner's Ground I played for Gentlemen of England *v.* Cambridge University, and scored 162 in my only innings. Mr. W. N. Powys had a great reputation as a fast bowler then, and he was expected to slaughter us. He did not. Mr. C. I. Thornton, for the University, hit 20 off one over of Mr. D. Buchanan's. At Trent Bridge I scored 79 first innings and 116 second against Nottinghamshire: the latter score was the first century scored on that ground. At Maidstone I scored 81 not out first, and 42 not out second, and did not play on it again until 1890, when I scored 109 not out, and 37.

And I played my last match on the old Hove Ground, Brighton, and scored 0 first, 217 second. It was on the same ground that I scored 170 and 56 not out for the South Wales Club in 1864, and I said good-bye to it rather regretfully.

The early part of the season of **1872** was unsuitable for heavy scoring, and the bowlers had the best of it until the end of June. Snow, sleet, and frost in May did not help the grounds, and scores up to the middle of the season were smaller than they had been for years. Like other batsmen, I suffered by it, and did not do so well as the previous year. I scored the century twice in May—once for the M.C.C., the other for the United South; but my best displays began on the 1st of July, for the Gentlemen *v.* Players, at Lord's, and during the succeeding eight days I scored at a rate that I have rarely equalled and but once exceeded in my career. In two matches for the Gentlemen *v.* Players.

in one week, I scored in three innings 77, 112, and 117; and two days later I made 170 not out for England *v.* Nottinghamshire and Yorkshire.

I was again fortunate in benefit matches. For Gloucestershire *v.* Yorkshire, at Sheffield, 29th, 30th, and 31st July, for the benefit of Roger Iddison, I made 150, and with Mr. T. G. Matthews put on 208 runs the first day, our wickets still standing at the end of it. For the South *v.* North, at the Oval the end of July, I played for Griffith's benefit, and scored 114.

Eight times I scored over a hundred runs in an innings, and at the end of the season my batting results were:

For M.C.C.—13 innings, 528 runs, average 40.8.

For Gloucestershire County—6 innings, 284 runs, average 47.2.

For Gentlemen *v.* Players—3 innings, 306 runs, average 102.

For South *v.* North—6 innings, 285 runs, average 47.3.

For Gentlemen of England (Canadian Tour)—11 innings, 540 runs, average 49.1

In First-class Matches—26 innings, 1,485 runs, average 57.

In all matches—63 innings, 3,030 runs, average 48.

For the United South Eleven, principally against Twenty-two's, I scored 316 runs for 8 innings: average, 39.4. I also played for Twenty-two of Melton Mowbray against the All-England Eleven, and for Sixteen of Grantham *v.* The United North Eleven. My brother Fred and Jas. Lillywhite played for Melton Mowbray in the same match, and we caught Carpenter napping when he was batting for the Eleven. Lillywhite was bowling and I was wicket-keeping, and Fred, I believe, was fielding at long-leg; anyhow, Carpenter hit one to leg, for which he ran two. Immediately he turned for the third run I ran out about ten yards to meet the ball, and caught it first bound; and while he was trotting quietly up the pitch in fancied security, with his back to me, I let fly at his wicket. I could throw in those days, and was not surprised when the middle stump went flying out of the ground. The surprise was on Carpenter's side, the laugh on ours.

"Well, well! there's no fool like an old fool," said he. "To think I should have played cricket all these years, and get out in that way!"

Surrey came out excellently in county contests that year, and headed the list: Kent dropped to the bottom.

Lancashire made good progress also, and was much indebted for its success to two bowlers—W. McIntyre and Watson. So well did those two perform, that Mr. A. Appleby, almost at his best, played a comparatively small part in bowling for his county. Mr. Hornby, too, was a host in himself, batting with great dash and invariably scoring. Daft and Selby did great things in batting for Nottinghamshire; and Mr. W. Yardley was very successful also. He had one exceptional experience at Lord's on the 20th and 21st May, playing for the South *v.* North: he was out first ball in both innings, earning his spectacles in a way that he will not readily forget!

An experiment was made at Lord's on the 9th May, in the match M.C.C. *v.* Next Twenty. The wickets were fixed an inch higher and slightly broader than the law prescribed. The experiment was not a success.

The year **1873** was my tenth of first-class cricket, and my best display of all-round form. I could show a higher batting average in 1871; but my bowling average was not so good, although I captured exactly the same number of wickets. The early part of the season was very wet, and batting generally was not up to the standard of previous years. Two amateurs--Messrs. Frank Townsend and J. M. Cotterill—took a high position, and Messrs. C. J. Ottaway, I. D. Walker, A. N. Hornby and C. I. Thornton were consistently good; but the number of batsmen who averaged 25 runs per innings was below that of 1871. The proportion of amateurs in the list was greater than ever. Daft and Jupp were now the only two professionals who could be classed with the best of the amateurs; for at last the years began to tell upon Carpenter, and his wonderful skill was beginning to desert him. Emmett proved that he could handle the bat as well as the ball, and Charlwood and Lockwood were doing excellent work also.

But a colt appeared that year who was to raise the standard of professional batting far above everything yet reached. Arthur Shrewsbury made his first appearance at Trent Bridge Ground on the 14th and 15th of April, playing for Twenty-two Colts against Notts County. He was 17 years of age, and scored 35 by scientific cricket, against A. Shaw, J. C. Shaw, M. McIntyre and F. Morley, four of the very best bowlers of that or any time. His defence was perfect, and his patience, for so young a player, exceptionally good. A month later at Lord's he confirmed the good opinions formed of him, scoring 4, and not out 16 for Fifteen Colts of England *v.* M.C.C.

The amateurs were to receive quite as valuable a recruit in their ranks before the season was over. Mr. W. W. Read was but 17 years of age when he was considered good enough to represent his county. Before the season was over, he played for Surrey *v.* Yorkshire at the Oval on the 11th and 12th of August. Few cricketers have delighted the cricketing public more than Mr. W. W. Read and Shrewsbury during the last ten years. For their counties and in representative matches they have won many a great victory, and

ARTHUR SHREWSBURY.

averted many a defeat. By-and-by I shall have occasion to describe their styles, and touch upon their brilliant performances.

The Gentlemen *v.* Players' matches were great victories for the former that year. The first was played at Lord's, and was won by the Gentlemen by an innings and 55 runs; the second at the Oval, which was won by an innings and 19 runs; and the third at Prince's, which was won by an innings and 54 runs. The results were entirely owing to the superiority of the Gentlemen in batting. Mr. Hornby played a grand innings of 104 in the match at Prince's, and in my three innings I scored 158, 163, and 70.

Four matches were played between the North and South; the South winning 2, losing 1, and 1 was drawn.

Gloucestershire and Nottinghamshire divided honours in county cricket. The Gloucestershire eleven was composed entirely of amateurs; Nottinghamshire, of professionals only.

Individual scores of a hundred runs and over in an innings were made about 230 times; and the number to my credit was seven, all of them in first-class matches. At the end of the season I took a team out to Australia. It was the third which had gone there, and, while we found cricket generally much improved, there was little doubt that England was still considerably ahead of Australia in playing the game, though very little in enthusiasm over it. I had the pleasure of meeting three players then who afterwards created great reputations—Messrs. H. F. Boyle, F. R. Spofforth and C. Bannerman. Of course, neither showed the form then which he displayed in later years.

The season of **1874** opened favourably: the weather was delightful, and continued so the greater part of it; and the consequence was, that the bat had again the best of

MR. W. W. READ.

the ball, and that century-scoring exceeded everything yet recorded. In matches of all kinds, individual innings of a hundred runs was scored close upon three hundred times; and over two hundred was scored twelve times. Very little was thought of the first figure now, unless in first-class cricket; and the increase in the number was owing more to the improvement in the grounds than to any decadence of bowling. By the end of the season I had scored over 200 runs once, and over a hundred twelve times: the greatest number of centuries I have ever scored in one year. Nine of them were in first-class matches. Jupp exceeded the hundred three times in first-class matches; and, in my estimation, played finer cricket that year than he ever played before or afterwards. Thirty-seven completed innings for an average of 36.15 was a wonderful improvement on the professional batting form of 1862, and showed how the game had advanced.

Shrewsbury was considered good enough to represent his county; but no one was surprised that he failed to do much the first year. It takes more than one year's experience to master, or even fight successfully against, first-class bowling, as I found to my cost when I began to play in the great matches; and a very successful colt may be a very indifferent county representative for some time. The same may be said with regard to Mr. W. W. Read.

Another and fine all-round cricketer commenced his brilliant career that year, and made his mark very quickly in first-class matches. I refer to Mr. A. G. Steel, whose performances with both bat and ball have been the admiration of the thousands who have had the pleasure of witnessing them. I shall have occasion to speak at some length about him farther on; but I cannot help saying here, that I never envied a county the possession of any cricketer so much as I envied Lancashire the possession of Mr. A. G. Steel. He was 15 years of age when he played his first match at Lord's on the 29th and 30th July for Marlborough College *v.* Rugby School, and scored 41 not out first innings.

The Players made rather a better fight against the Gentlemen that year, winning one match out of the three played, and losing the other two by 48 and 61 runs. Only one individual innings of a hundred runs was scored in the six innings played by both sides, and that fell to my credit.

One of the closest and most exciting matches of that year was the North *v.* South, played at Prince's on the 4th and 5th June for the benefit of the Cricketers' Fund. The South in its second innings had 27 runs to make to win, with five wickets standing, and yet lost by 3 runs.

I was again successful in a benefit match, scoring 167 for Gloucestershire *v.* Yorkshire at Sheffield on behalf of Luke Greenwood.

University cricket was now a different thing from what it had been ten or twenty years before; and very rarely were the Gentlemen without one or two University players in their eleven when they met the Players. A match entitled "Gentlemen of England who had not been educated at the Universities *v.* Gentlemen of the Universities, Past and Present" was played at the Oval on the 15th and 16th June. A University education has always been considered a distinct aid to success, mentally and physically; but this match did not show that University men were better cricketers than non-University men, for their representative eleven got severely beaten by an innings and 76 runs. But then their opponents had among them such players as A. N. Hornby, I. D. Walker, V. E. Walker, A. Appleby, G. F. Grace, and myself.

What was described as an "American Invasion" took place early in the month of August. Eighteen

American Baseball Players (who visited us with the idea of introducing the game of baseball) played seven cricket matches, and showed that they knew something of that game as well as baseball. Unfortunately they had been much underrated, and the engagements made on their behalf were against very third-class teams. They won four out of the seven played, and the other three were drawn. There was one individual score of 50, but 25 was nearer the form of the best of them; and only once did the total of their innings reach as high as 130. Their fielding was exceptionally smart; and though their efforts to create a love for baseball were not rewarded, their skill was undoubtedly appreciated.

The All-England, United South, and United North Elevens were still travelling all over the country; but county cricket was taking a greater hold, and they did not excite so much interest as they used to. With the United South, I visited Ireland for the first time, and against Twenty-two of Leinster my brother Fred and I did a good performance, scoring 272 runs. My 153 was, so far, the highest innings made against a twenty-two; and I had now scored the century in England, Scotland, Ireland, Canada, and Australia.

Cricketers all over the country had occasion to grumble at the weather in **1875**. It was both wet and miserably cold the greater part of the year, and wickets everywhere were sticky and very often unplayable. Batting averages went down considerably, and bowlers got great break on the ball. Slow and medium round-arm bowlers had their opportunity, and improved to some extent, and batsmen who had only been used to straight fast were a little bit abroad in playing them. Alfred Shaw at times did what he liked with the ball; and I shall never forget his wonderful performance for Nottinghamshire *v.* M.C.C., at Lord's, on the 14th and

15th June—166 balls for seven runs and seven wickets, six of them clean bowled, my own among them. It took me an hour to make 10 runs, and I thought—and still think—as much of that hour's play as I do of many an hour in which I scored close upon a hundred. Mr. G. Strachan did a very fine performance with the ball also. For the Gentlemen *v.* Players, at the Oval, he with 21 balls got 5 wickets, and no runs were scored off him.

That year was my greatest success with the ball; the sticky wickets suiting my bowling as nicely as the fast suited my batting, and I captured 192 wickets during the season, for an average of 12.166 runs. I had never done so well before, nor have I since.

Batting, as I have said, suffered in consequence. One young player, Mr. A. J. Webbe, however, came to the front with a rush, and played two or three very fine innings during the season. For the Gentlemen *v.* Players, at Lord's, in the second innings, he and I put on 203 runs for the first wicket, and his defence and patience were perfect. He was 20 years of age at the time.

Two great bowlers dropped out of first-class cricket that year—J. C. Shaw and E. Willsher. Freeman had dropped out a year or two before; so that three of the very best bowlers we have ever had had now left the ranks. I question if we have had three such really good fast bowlers since. Just about that time medium-pace bowling began to be cultivated, and very fast was neglected by both amateur and professional.

The Players won one out of the three matches played against the Gentlemen and one was drawn. The North *v.* South matches were not quite so interesting as in former years. When only two matches were played, the interest and excitement were great; but this year as many as seven were played in different parts of the country, and the public and the players themselves got tired of them.

County cricket flourished, and Nottinghamshire came to the front again.

My batting average dropped down to 32 that year, the reason being the weather. Quite naturally, critics thought "I had gone off;" but in my heart I did not think so, for I felt as fit as I ever felt in my life. Two or three times that remark has been made about Messrs. A. N. Hornby, W. W. Read, Shrewsbury, and myself; and I have been rather amused when one or the other scored a hundred runs the next match.

Charming weather prevailed during the greater part of the season of **1876**, and at the end of it batting averages were very much higher than they had been for years. The bowlers had a very trying time, and were unfeignedly glad when the last ball was bowled. It was a year of exceptional batting performances for me, though my average was not quite so high as in two or three years I have already given. About this time I began to find that, in batting in particular, it took me longer to get into form and condition than in previous years. Increase of years and increase of weight may possibly account for it. I was close upon 28 years of age, and in weight about 15 st.

During the month of May I played 8 completed innings, scored 163 runs; average, 20.3. In June I played 12 completed innings, scored 464 runs; average, 39.5. In July I played 11 completed innings, scored 637 runs; average, 57.10. In August I played 10 completed innings, scored 1278 runs; average, 127.8. The month of August of that year was, I believe, the highest run-getting month in my whole cricket career; and I sincerely hope I shall not be considered egotistical in touching at some length upon one or two of the matches played.

It is now well known how Kent County scored 473

runs in its first innings against the Gentlemen of the M.C.C. at Canterbury on the 10th August—Lord Harris being the top scorer with a grandly-played 154 —and then got the M.C.C. out the day after for 144. The M.C.C. had to follow its innings a few minutes before five the same evening, and Mr. A. P. Lucas and myself started the batting. Every one believed that the match was now a hopeless thing for the old club; and I was exceedingly anxious to get off that night, so that I might reach Clifton next day, and have a quiet Sunday's rest before meeting Nottinghamshire on the Monday. It was no use trying to play carefully; so I made up my mind to hit. I risked a little more than usual, helped myself more freely than I would have done under different circumstances, and everything came off. The 100 was scored in forty-five minutes, and when stumps were drawn at 6.45 the total was 217 for four wickets, made in an hour and fifty minutes. My share was 133 not out; extras, 17.

Saturday was one of the hottest days of a very hot month; and I thought I might as well put my best foot forward in the early morning. My partner was Mr. P. C. Crutchley, and he being in the scoring mood also, we kept the ball travelling at a great pace. The ground was in rare order, and from noon to luncheon-time we put all we knew into our hitting, only stopping for a few minutes while I borrowed a bat, having broken the one which had served me so well. The new bat was a good one, but much too small in the handle for me, and the pace slackened slightly; however, during the luncheon-hour the Hon. Spencer Ponsonby Fane very kindly got hold of some thick twine, which he wrapped round it and brought it up to the right size. Tired nature began to tell its tale during the afternoon: but relief came from the officers' tent in the form of champagne and seltzer; and at it we went again, and were not parted until we had put on 227 runs, and raised the total to 430 for five wickets. The opinion of the Kent Twelve, Mr. Absolom's in particular, was, "that it had been a very hot day!" The total was 546 before I was out, my score being 344, made in 6 hours and 20 minutes, without a chance.

I had to travel by train to Bristol on Sunday; but by Monday morning the effects of it had worn off, and when I started the Gloucestershire innings against Nottinghamshire I felt very fit. I scored 177 in 3 hours and 10 minutes; and in it there were one 7, two 6's, one 5, and twenty-three 4's. My wicket went to the credit of Selby, and showed the value of a change, however indifferent the bowler. Alfred Shaw and Morley had been trying all they knew, and failed; so Selby was called upon. He said he did not want any long-leg to *his* bowling; so my brother Fred promptly hit his first ball in that direction, and we ran 7 for it. The same over I hit him in the same place for 6; but in attempting it a second time, I got under the ball and was caught at long-on rather square. I believe the fieldsman was Barnes. He was in his right position at long-on when Fred and myself hit the 7 and 6 to long-leg, and had to go after the ball; for there was no boundary on the sloping side of the College Ground in those days. He quietly took his position almost square with the wicket and brought off the catch, and remarked afterwards that "he knew something about placing the field to a third-rate bowler, if Selby did not." Our total score was 400. Daft and Oscroft batted in magnificent form the first innings, but could not save the follow on; and on the evening of the third day Gloucestershire were left with 31 to win, which E. M. and Fred hit off in 25 minutes.

The Nottinghamshire men on the home journey met the Yorkshire Eleven travelling down, and told them to look out for squalls at Cheltenham. Tom Emmett laughed, and said the "big 'un has exhausted himself, and cannot do the century trick thrice in succession. If he does, I mean to shoot him, in the interests of the game; and I know there will be general rejoicing, amongst the professionals at least!"

I do not think I ever played on a better wicket than the one which had been prepared at Cheltenham, and I was not surprised that runs came at a great pace. At the end of the first day the score was 353 for four wickets: Mr. Moberly, 73 not out; myself, 216 not out; and when we were parted about two o'clock next day, the total was 429; Mr. Moberly having batted in his very best form for 103. It was rather a curious coincidence that the long stand should have been made by the 6th man and myself both in this and the Canterbury match. Our total was 528, and my score 318 not out. Yorkshire made 127 for seven wickets.

I can say little about my 400 not out, for United South *v.* Twenty-two of Grimsby, that has not already been said. I can just remember that the Twenty-two thought our team rather a weak one; that the wicket was perfect; and that the grass was closely cut for about forty yards square, but the rest of it a little bit long. Holmes, one of the eleven, had occasion to grumble when he was given out l.b.w. to a ball that was far from being straight; but consoled himself the third day when the same umpire served one of the Twenty-two just as badly. "A perfectly fair umpire," he said, "but decidedly incompetent." I did not feel half so tired at the end of my Grimsby score as I did after the Canterbury or Cheltenham scores.

There is another match I must say a word about —the North *v.* South, played at Nottingham for Daft's benefit. The South had a very good team, and so had the North, and every one was anxious that the match should turn out a real success. The weather was on its best behaviour; and I was upset at only scoring 16 first innings; in fact, neither side did much the first day: the first innings closing thus—North, 102; South, 155. The third day was the exciting one. Splendid batting on the part of Messrs. A. N. Hornby, R. P. Smith, Lockwood, and Daft himself, made the North score 242 in the second innings, and left the South 190 to win, and 3½ hours to do it. "Rather a heavy task," was the general opinion. Mr. A. J. Webbe and myself hit 100 runs in 66 minutes; then he left at 101, for 41—a real good bit of batting. Mr. I. D. Walker 20, and my brother Fred 10 not out, enabled us to score the necessary runs. They were made in 2 hours and 25 minutes; and I had the satisfaction of scoring 114 not out for one of the most popular and scientific cricketers of his or any age.

The Gentlemen *v.* Players' matches were decidedly in favour of the Gentlemen that year. Two were won by them, the other drawn. The North *v.* South matches were played as usual; the South winning 1, and 2 were drawn; and the All-England, United South of England, and United North were busy all the season.

Individual innings of 300 runs and over in an innings were scored 3 times; of 200, 14 times; of 100 runs, more than 400 times.

I had the pleasure of seeing Gloucestershire at the head of the counties again. My batting and bowling performances during the season showed that I had played:

	Completed innings.	Runs.	Average.
For M.C.C.	7	494	70.4
For Gentlemen *v.* Players	5	309	61.4
For South *v.* North	7	474	67.5
For Gloucestershire County	11	890	80.10
In first-class matches... ...	42	2622	62.18

Bowling in first-class matches:

Overs.		Maidens.		Runs.		Wides.		Wickets.		Average.
1550.1	...	638	...	2388	...	0	...	124	...	19.32

MR. A. J. WEBBE.

In 1877 County cricket had taken a firm hold, and created greater interest than the All-England and United South Elevens ever did. There were as many as nine first-class counties playing: their contests were very exciting, and their doings were followed carefully from the beginning to the end of the season. "Who is going to take first place in county honours this year?" was a question that was repeatedly asked. But it was one that required special knowledge to answer. Gloucestershire did great things in 1876, and was conceded pride of place; and when it was announced that Midwinter, an Australian of high reputation in both bowling and batting, had returned to England, and would now play for that county, every one concluded that it would again be well to the front. Midwinter was the first professional who played for Gloucestershire, and his bowling considerably strengthened it.

For some years Gloucestershire and Middlesex had been called the counties of amateurs, and it was entirely owing to their great batting skill that they had held their own against what may be called the professional counties. We have only to refer to the batting averages to find that the professionals were still very far behind the amateurs in that branch of the game. The fact seems to have impressed itself rather strongly upon the Lancashire and Surrey Committees about this time; for we find their elevens with a good sprinkling of amateur talent in them, by which they were much benefited. Mr. A. N. Hornby, at the head of the Lancashire eleven; Mr. G. Strachan, at the head of Surrey; and Lord Harris, at the head of Kent, were infusing vigour into their teams, and producing good results. Nottinghamshire and Yorkshire, while possessing the very best professional bowling talent of the day, were lacking in amateur batting, and did not do so well as they would have done if they had possessed both.

The Gentlemen *v.* Players, North *v.* South, and University contests were quite as interesting and exciting as county contests; but at last the All-England Eleven, United South, and United North began to lose their attractions; for no one thought of going out of his way to watch the skill of a first-class professional bowler pitted against indifferent country batsmen, when he could witness county matches fought out from start to finish by the very best professional and amateur talent. The All-England Eleven played two or three matches in 1876, but very little afterwards, and died out for lack of gate support. The United South lived two or three years longer; but after 1877 my medical studies demanded more of my time, and I could only play for Gloucestershire, M.C.C., and in the great matches. I believe the United South played its last match at Stroud in 1880.

Messrs. W. W. Read, A. P. Lucas, A. J. Webbe and F. Penn had now taken a very high position amongst the amateurs, and batted in very fine style. Mr. W. W. Read and Jupp, for Surrey *v.* Yorkshire at the Oval, scored 206 for first wicket, the second highest yet recorded in a county match; and Mr. J. M. Cotterill and myself put on 281 runs between the fall of the first and second wickets for the South *v.* North at Prince's. Individual performances of 200 runs in an innings were scored 10 times, and the century was scored more than 500 times. G. Hearne, Mycroft, Morley and myself were very successful with the ball. For M.C.C. and Ground *v.* Oxford University, Morley bowled 33.1 overs for 14 runs and 13 wickets—a feat that has not often been surpassed.

For Gloucestershire *v.* Nottinghamshire at Cheltenham, at the end of the match, I bowled 25 balls for no runs and 7 wickets.

CHAPTER VI.

AUSTRALIAN ELEVENS AND FIRST-CLASS COUNTY CRICKET.

IT seems a good many years ago since, in 1878, the first Australian eleven visited England, and it is rather difficult to remember the exact feeling which prevailed about it at the time. I can just recollect we were very glad to see them, but not very much alarmed about being defeated by them. We had their victory against Lillywhite's team the previous year in Australia fresh in our memories, and inferred from it that the game had advanced rapidly in that country; but we never for a moment thought of classing them with an English representative team; although we thought that they might do fairly well against the best of our counties. Their first match was against Nottinghamshire; and A. Shaw and Morley being in their best form, they were defeated by an innings and fourteen runs. Their bowling, batting, and fielding did not impress us very favourably in that match; and good judges of the game very naturally shook their heads, and predicted a weary and trying time for them before the season was over.

Their match *v.* M.C.C. and Ground, on the 27th May, was a great surprise. It was all over in one day; the Australians winning by nine wickets, against one of the strongest batting and bowling teams in England, or anywhere else. M.C.C.—first innings, 33; second, 19. Australians—41 first innings; 12 for one wicket, second.

The wicket was as bad as it could be, and small

scoring was expected; but no one dreamt for a moment that in the Australian eleven there were two bowlers possessing the powers which Messrs. Spofforth and Boyle displayed. For the rest of the season the Australian matches rivalled county matches in interest; and though the wickets were more or less moist all the year, exceptionally good cricket was shown. Results at the end of the trip showed that they were a match for the best of our counties, but not yet up to the form of a representative English team: that in bowling and fielding they could hold their own with us; but in batting were a good distance behind. Their proficiency in bowling was, undoubtedly, the strength of their play, and impressed us greatly. An amateur capable of holding his own against the best of our professional bowling had been a rare thing among us for many years, and the proportion had been about four professionals to one amateur. The Australian bowling was entirely in the hands of amateurs, and it did not suffer by comparison with English professional bowling.

Their batting was their weak point. C. Bannerman averaged, in eleven-a-side matches, 24.1 for 30 completed innings; the rest were under 20.

County cricket in England did not suffer much by the Australian invasion, and some very interesting and exciting matches were played. Middlesex, with a very strong batting team, took first place, and Gloucestershire and Nottinghamshire were close up.

Mr. A. G. Steel's performance with the ball was equal, if not superior, to anything ever shown either by professional or amateur; and two professionals, Selby and Ulyett, handled the bat in a way worthy of Daft in his best days.

The Gentlemen won both matches against the Players; and, altogether, the year was one of great interest.

Over 200 runs in an innings was scored by ten amateurs, and the century was scored about 350 times.

Before the first Australian eleven had completed its tour in England it was decided that a fifth eleven of English players should go out to Australia. On this occasion it was an invitation from the Melbourne Cricket Club to the amateurs of England; but a team made up of amateurs entirely was found impracticable, and two most popular professionals, Emmett and Ulyett—both belonging to Yorkshire,—had to be included. Ulyett was a good all-round player, but not a very successful bowler on good wickets; and it was not expected that the eleven would show such favourable results as those which had preceded it. And so it turned out; for, while the batting generally was quite up to the quality of anything the Colonials had yet seen, the weakness of the bowling caused the tour to turn out rather an uneventful one.

An English eleven, made up of professionals from Nottinghamshire and Yorkshire, which visited Canada and America at the end of the season, had a different tale to tell when it returned. Of twelve matches played, nine were won and three were drawn; and it was the bowling that did it!

The season of **1879** in England was a very wet one from beginning to end, and the bowling beat the batting; Alfred Shaw, Morley, and Peate, in particular, showing grand results.

County contests were more exciting than ever, and the struggle for supremacy was a close and keen one.

Amongst the amateur batsmen, Messrs. A. N. Hornby, Hon. A. Lyttelton, A. G. Steel, and A. P. Lucas did particularly well; and amongst the professionals, Flowers, Bates, Barnes, and Scotton showed excellent promise of things to come. I was still busy with my medical studies, and could not play so much as formerly, but in batting and bowling I did better than in the previous year.

A very gratifying feature of the year to me was the presentation of a national testimonial at Lord's, on the 22nd of July, by Lord Fitzhardinge, who had been one of the chief movers in getting it up. Two years previously the Duke of Beaufort, then President of the M.C.C., suggested the presentation, and the Committee of the old club taking it up heartily, a very liberal response came from every part of the kingdom. I need not say I was pleased. I had played the game from the time I could handle bat and ball, because I liked it; but I did not know until this year that in doing so I had given pleasure to so many and made so many friends. Lord Chas. J. F. Russell uttered words at the presentation which I shall never forget. Comrades and players, both amateurs and professionals, showered their heartiest wishes upon me; and I felt, more than I could express—and feel it still,—that everyone had been very kind to me, and that helping to speed the interests of the game so dear to us all was something to be proud of.

Very little surprise was expressed when another Australian XI. appeared on English grounds in **1880.** Their first tour had been very successful, and it was only natural they should seek to strengthen the favourable impression they had made. We had been told to expect a great improvement in their batting, and wonderful performances with the ball by a bowler new to English players. Expectations were realised: for at least two of them, W. L. Murdoch and P. S. McDonnell, showed a conspicuous inprovement in their batting skill; and the new bowler, Palmer, was a great acquisition, and at times bowled with great success.

MR. WM. LLOYD MURDOCH.

Results showed that they were quite up to our best county form, but still unable to cope with a picked eleven. The memorable match against an Eleven of England, at the Oval on the 6th, 7th, and 8th September, in which Murdoch batted so grandly for 153 not out in the second innings and Spofforth was unable to play, may be advanced as an argument to the contrary; but I thought then, and I think still, that if three matches had been played between the same elevens, England would have won all three. The composition of the English team will be most interesting to students of the game, and will show how broadly county cricket was represented. There were three players selected from Nottinghamshire; three from Gloucestershire; two from Kent; one from Lancashire; one from Middlesex; and one from Yorkshire.

Two things were clearly revealed: that the Australians had in Spofforth and Murdoch a bowler and batsman of the very first class. Spofforth could show in eleven-a-side matches a bowling average equal to Alfred Shaw, who was undoubtedly the most successful English bowler that year; and in all matches, his 391 wickets for an average of 5.63 per wicket will bear comparison with anything recorded in the history of the game. Murdoch's average of 25.8 for 19 completed innings, while not quite up to the standard of our first-class batsmen, was a great advance on his 1878 performances.

County cricket was in no way affected by the Australian visit; for, if anything, the interest displayed during the season was greater than in any previous year. Nottinghamshire deservedly came out first, for it was the only county that lowered the colours of the the Australian eleven.

Gloucestershire had now played for eleven years, and had held its own against all comers. I had taken a particular pride in its success, as every lover of the game does in the county he represents, and was pleased to know that my individual efforts with bat and ball had helped to give it a high position. But then I had been supported by a team of amateurs that many a captain might envy. To name them, and give their doings, would take more space than can be well afforded: but I cannot allow this year to pass without saying something about my brother Fred's share in the good work, for it was his last amongst us. He died before the season was over, and before he had completed his 30th year. The blow to my family and Gloucestershire county was more than I can find words to express; indeed, no words can express it. But I know that not only Gloucestershire, but the cricketing world, sustained a heavy loss by his death. I think I may be allowed to say of him, with pardonable pride, that he was a brilliant field, a splendid batsman, and a fairly successful bowler in first-class company; and that his memory is cherished by every player who knew him. I give his batting performances for his county, and will let them speak for themselves.

He played—

	Completed Innings.	Runs.	Most in an Innings.	Average.
1870 to 1874	34	1199	165*	35.26
1875	12	430	180*	35.83
1876	12	297	78	24.75
1877	15	441	98	29.40
1878	14	418	73*	29.85
1879	15	211	57	14.06
1880	13	320	83	24.61

The Gentlemen *v.* Players' matches resulted in a win to each. The first, at the Oval, the Players won by 37 runs, in a great degree owing to the fine bowling of Alfred Shaw and Morley, who bowled in great form, as they did the greater part of that year. The return, at Lord's, the Gentlemen won by five wickets, owing to consistently good batting of the eleven and the successful bowling of Mr. H. Rotherham.

Very few of the old names now remained in the batting averages, and another generation of bowlers was springing up. A reference to the bowling and batting averages at the end will show a remarkable improvement on previous years. The doings, in particular, of Alfred Shaw, Morley, and Peate will bear more than one perusal. For years the first two had stood head and shoulders above every other bowler in the quantity and quality of the work done; and Shaw, in particular, might be called the bowler of the century. Other bowlers have been as successful in one or two seasons; but for consistent brilliancy, for ten years at least, he has had no equal in England, or out of it.

Lord Harris, the Hon. Alfred Lyttelton, the Hon. Ivo Bligh, and Mr. A. J. Webbe were now batting in grand form; and the amateur batting of that year was of a very high quality. Professional batting came out favourably also; Barnes, Charlwood, and Ulyett showing excellent results.

Mr. Renny-Tailyour scored 331 in a single innings for the Royal Engineers. Over 200 was scored 18 times by other players, and a 100 close upon 500 times.

The year **1881** saw Lancashire at the top of the tree. That County played brilliantly in all its matches, and came out very far ahead of the others. To begin with, it possessed in its captain, Mr. A. N. Hornby, one of the ablest and most popular cricketers in England, who never spared himself, whether he were playing a winning or a losing game, and whose enthusiasm infected every member of the team. As a batsman, he had no superior that year; for not only did he perform grandly for his county, but he came out first in the averages in first-class cricket.

It was difficult to find a weak spot in the eleven. In batting and bowling they could compare favourably with any county; but it was very much owing to their brilliant fielding that such good results rewarded their efforts. It may be advanced against their success that five of the professionials were playing under residential qualifications; but it must not be forgotten that other counties would have been only too glad to have had them on similar conditions, and that it was owing to the Committee of the County Club and the excellent judgment of Mr. Hornby that they had been originally selected and their powers developed.

Surrey was trying hard to recover its old position, and the Committee invited colts from all parts of the county to practise at the Oval under the eyes of good and competent judges. The old arrangement of having a colts' match once or twice a year had not produced favourable results, many a promising colt failing to do himself justice through nervousness or some other cause. Constant practice for a week or two was a better test, and showed whether they had the making of county players in them.

Nottinghamshire was in the unfortunate position of having good players and not being able to use them. Seven of the eleven after playing one match refused to play again unless they were all engaged for the rest of the season. It was a blow to the Committee, but one that had to be faced; for, if the malcontents had succeeded in their demand, county cricket would have suffered in Nottinghamshire and elsewhere. It said a great deal for the rising talent of the county that they could make a fair show against the other counties without the aid of the seven. Before the season was over, however, five of them admitted they had made a mistake, and were reinstated in the eleven, and afterwards the county showed something of its true form.

Yorkshire had a very good season, although during a part of it they were without the services of Hill and Ulyett; but they possessed a very successful and good bowler in Peate, whilst Bates and the evergreen Emmett did their share of the work.

Gloucestershire had a promising bowler in Woof that year. Middlesex was considerably strengthened by the bowling of Burton; and Mr. C. T. Studd's all-round form, the brilliant wicket-keeping of the Hon. A. Lyttelton and Mr. Vernon's dashing batting all helped to give it a good place. Kent suffered by the absence of Lord Harris a part of the season; and Sussex showed little sign of improvement.

The Gentlemen won their matches against the Players at the Oval and Lord's; but the latter were without their best eleven, owing to the Nottinghamshire rupture. They were both won by small majorities, however, and few better contests were played during the year. A third match, played at Brighton for the benefit of James Lillywhite, who had represented Sussex in every contest for twenty years, had a very exciting finish. The Gentlemen were left with 113 runs to make in the second innings, and after making 50 without the loss of a wicket every one naturally thought the match was a gift to them; but, on Alfred Shaw going on to bowl, a complete change occurred, and, amidst the greatest excitement, the Players pulled off an unexpected victory by one run. I was unable to play in this match, and was rather sorry for it; for I knew how serviceable Lillywhite had been to his county.

Jupp also had a benefit this year—South *v.* North, at the Oval,—but a county engagement kept me away, and I had to be content with sending all manner of good wishes for the success of one of the finest cricketers Surrey ever produced.

Individual scoring was good during the months of May, June, and July while the weather was dry and the wickets hard; but heavy rains set in early in August, and continued for the remainder of the season, which caused the pace to slacken considerably. A record was established by Mr. W. N. Roe, on the 12th July, playing for Emmanuel L. V. C. against Caius L. V. C. at Cambridge, when he scored 415 not out, exceeding Mr. Tylecote's score at Clifton in 1868 by 11 runs. Medical work took up much of my time that year, and I played less than formerly.

In **1882** the visit of the third Australian team was of great interest. Only eleven-a-side matches were arranged, an indication that the visitors meant to test the full strength of English cricketers. Murdoch was again at the head of the eleven and said to be batting better than ever. His huge score of 321 for New South Wales *v.* Victoria, in the early part of the year, proved that, and led us to expect greater things of him than he had done in 1880. He brought with him the best of the first team, and the weak members had been replaced by such good names as G. Giffen, T. W. Garrett, H. H. Massie, and S. P. Jones.

Their first match against Oxford University was a revelation of their powers, and established the reputations of three of the new members—Massie, Giffen, and Garrett. Their second match, played against Sussex, just as clearly showed that the old members, Murdoch, Palmer, Spofforth, and Bannerman, had gone forward and not backward. How well they fought against the best of our county elevens is a matter of history; not meeting with a single defeat, and conclusively proving that they were worthy of being classed not far behind the best of our representative teams. The Gentlemen of England succumbed to them; but they were defeated by the Players, North of England and Cambridge University. Their great match against the combined strength of England at the Oval, on the 28th and 29th of August, will always be a pleasant memory to them.

Australia	—first innings,	63;	second innings,	122.
England	„	101;	„	77.

England only wanted 85 to win in its second innings, and actually scored 51 for one wicket, and yet lost by 7 runs. Spofforth has done many great performances with the ball; but the finish of that innings will always be a good one to recollect, for the wicket was in fair condition, and he was fighting an uphill game against half-a-dozen of the best batsmen in England. Never bowler fought more successfully or pluckily than he did that day; and, supported by Boyle, he landed a victory for his side that stirred the hearts of his opponents and every one present. The shouting and cheering that followed I shall remember to my dying day, as I shall remember the quick hearty recognition of English cricketers over the length and breadth of the land that the best of Australian cricket was worthy of the highest position in the game.

In all, 38 matches were played during the tour, of which the Australian team won 23, lost 4, and 11 were drawn.

That, to my mind, was the best eleven of the seven which have now visited us, having no equal for all-round form. Their fielding and bowling were quite up to the English standard; their batting, slightly under it; and Blackham's wicket-keeping perfection.

It will not do to say that county cricket was not affected by the excitement which prevailed over the engagements of the Australian eleven that year. Undoubtedly it was. Lancashire and Nottinghamshire were equal for first place, the latter playing in its old form, owing to the perfect harmony which now prevailed between the committee and all the members of the eleven. Alfred Shaw and Morley were as effectual as ever with the ball; but Shrewsbury was not in the best of health, and did not play up to the form expected of him. Peate, of Yorkshire, had now become the acknowledged best slow bowler of England, and Emmett was as good as ever. Crossland, for Lancashire, strongly illustrated the usefulness of a fast bowler on a side. So good had become the wickets everywhere, that slow bowling was losing its sting, and good judges were of the opinion that it was the pace of the Australians' bowling which produced such excellent results.

Gloucestershire, Middlesex, Surrey and Kent were much in want of bowling of all kinds, and Sussex and Derbyshire were still far behind the others.

The Players won the first match against the Gentlemen at the Oval by 87 runs; but magnificent batting on the part of Messrs. A. P. Lucas and C. T. Studd turned the tables on them in the return match at Lords, the Gentlemen winning by 8 wickets.

A record score was made by the Orleans Club *v.* Rickling Green Club, at Rickling Green on the 4th and 5th August, the total amounting to 920. The first wicket fell for 20 runs; then Mr. A. H. Trevor joined Mr. G. F. Vernon, and they raised the score before they were parted to 623.

Individual innings of over 300 were scored 4 times; of 200, 19 times; and of 100 close upon 700 times.

For some years previous to **1883** grumbling had been general against the Law which admitted of the wicket being rolled only between the innings. Very often winning the toss meant that one side had a good wicket to play on the greater part of the first day; while the other had, perhaps, but an hour left before the stumps were drawn. If rain fell during the night, the wicket became unplayable next morning, owing to the in-side not being allowed to roll the pitch before resuming its innings. That grievance was now redressed; for early in this year the M.C.C. passed an addition to the Law, which allowed the wicket to be rolled on the second and third mornings of a match, and a valuable addition it turned out to be.

A change was also made in the appointment of umpires. No one was now selected to umpire in a match in which his own county was engaged.

County cricket had a better chance in the absence of the Australian eleven, and it was very encouraging to notice the increase of spectators. Travelling elevens were rarely heard of now, and county matches were fulfilling the aim of their promoters. Yorkshire and Nottinghamshire were well ahead of the others, both being strongly represented in batting and bowling. Middlesex came next; and at last Surrey began to creep up again, owing to the magnificent batting of Mr. W. W. Read and the bowling of Jones. It was noticed that those counties which were lacking in good professional bowling were invariably low down on the list; Sussex, Kent, and Gloucestershire being in that unfortunate position. Midwinter's return to Australia weakened the Gloucestershire eleven, and there was no one springing up to take his place.

Professional batting was improving rapidly, and Shrewsbury and two or three others were in excellent form. If anything, they were playing over-carefully. The desire to show well in the averages was creating a school of slow scorers whose aim was to keep up their wicket and let the runs come. Twenty to thirty runs an hour was a good pace of scoring with them. It was sound enough cricket, but rather tedious to look at.

The power of fast bowling had another exponent in Harrison, of Yorkshire, who met with great success; and Crossland was quite as successful as in the previous year: but those were about the only two fast bowlers who had a first-class reputation, and curiously they both had doubtful actions.

The first match between the Gentlemen and Players, at the Oval, 28th, 29th, and 30th June, resulted in a tie —the only tie ever recorded in those matches. Owing to a professional engagement I was absent from the ranks of the former, for the first time since 1867. The return, at Lord's, was productive of heavy scoring, and the Gentlemen won it by seven wickets.

The fourth Australian team, which visited England in **1884**, was considered the equal of its predecessors by many judges; but, weighing everything carefully, I still hold to the opinion that the third was the best we have yet had. The new men—Alexander, Cooper, and Scott—were not up to the form of those left behind—Garrett, Jones, Horan, and Massie; and results will bear me out. In all, 32 matches were played: 18 won, 7 lost, 7 drawn, which was not quite so good a show as the 1882 team made. Three matches were played against the full strength of England, two of which were drawn, and England won the third. It was an unsatisfactory ending; for everyone desired to have three matches fought out to the end.

Spofforth was as effective as ever with the ball; Murdoch, McDonnell, Giffen, and A. Bannerman had lost nothing of their skill with the bat; and Blackham gave the finest display of wicket-keeping the cricketing world had yet seen.

MR. P. S. McDONNELL. MR. G. ALEXANDER. MR. G. GIFFEN. MR. G. E. PALMER.
MR. F. R. SPOFFORTH. MR. W. L. MURDOCH. MR. W. MIDWINTER. MR. H. F. BOYLE.
MR. J. McC. BLACKHAM. MR. G. J. BONNOR. MR. A. C. BANNERMAN.
MR. W. H. COOPER. MR. H. J. H. SCOTT.

THE AUSTRALIANS, 1884.

I must speak favourably of the Philadelphians, who visited England that year for the first time, considering that they defeated the Gentlemen of Gloucestershire under my leadership, and enabled Lord Harris to have the laugh at me. It was a little bit unfortunate that they came the same year as the Australians; for while they played quite up to the expectations formed of them, their doings were discounted by the brilliant performances of Murdoch's Eleven. They were certainly a good lot, and gave an excellent account of themselves against the amateur teams played; but they were not up to English county form. The most successful batsmen were, Messrs. Scott, R. S. Newhall, Thayer, and Stoever; the bowlers, Messrs. Lowry, MacNutt, and C. A. Newhall.

Nottinghamshire had a great year among the counties, not losing a single match; but then it had in its team Shrewsbury, Barnes, Gunn, Flowers, Selby, Scotton, A. Shaw, Attewell, Wright, and Sherwin, players who have made great reputations in all departments of the game. Middlesex and Yorkshire were in good form also; and Surrey took a step upward. G. Lohmann played for the last named county, and gave evidence of good all-round form; his bowling impressing the critics very favourably. Sussex was not quite so low as formerly, due in some degree to the fine batting of Mr. W. Newham; and Lord Harris was the mainstay of Kent. Gloucestershire had to take a very humble position for want of bowlers; but could still hold its own in batting, being strengthened in that department by Messrs. Brain and Pullen, two promising young players.

The Gentlemen *v.* Players' matches resulted in a win to each. Ulyett batted brilliantly in both, scoring 292 runs for three completed innings.

Mr. A. G. Steel was in great form with the bat

PULLIN (UMPIRE). PEATE. MR. A. P. LUCAS. HON. A. LYTTELTON. SHREWSBURY. FARRANDS (UMPIRE).
MR. A. G. STEEL. LORD HARRIS. MR. W. G. GRACE. MR. W. W. READ. ULYETT.
MR. S CHRISTOPHERSON. BARLOW.

ENGLAND (v. AUSTRALIANS) 1884.

and took first place in the averages. His best displays were against the Australians. He twice exceeded the century against them.

The wickets were hard the greater part of the season, and century-scoring was far in advance of anything yet recorded. Spofforth's bowling performances was the best of the year, and Emmett's results were very good, considering the number of years he had played.

The year **1885** was one of Mr. W. W. Read's best; his batting being consistently good throughout the season. His hitting was brilliant against all kinds of bowling when he got his eye in and was well set. Shrewsbury and Gunn showed great improvement also, and were at the head of professional batting that year, as indeed they are at the present time.

A glance at the averages will show the marked change that was creeping over professional batting. For the first time since Carpenter, Hayward, Daft, and one or two others were the most prominent batsmen, the professionals could show a larger number than the gentlemen in the list of the averages. For more than ten years the gentlemen could show a proportion of two to one; in 1885 it was the other way. Shrewsbury had much the best average of the year, though it will be seen that he did not play half the number of innings which Mr. W. W. Read played. His defence had become stronger than ever, and his wicket was about the most difficult one in England to capture. He did not go in for rapid scoring, but his hitting all round was clean and safe. Gunn's style was also admirable, but rather freer than Shrewsbury's.

Another professional who did great things that year was Briggs, of Lancashire. For years he had batted with success, and his fielding at cover-point had been most brilliant; but now he came out as a bowler, and by the end of the season proved that he had no superior as an all-round player. Lohmann, of Surrey, confirmed the good opinion formed of his bowling the previous year: and though his name did not appear high up in the batting list, he performed well enough to stamp him as a player of all round excellence. There were half-a-dozen other professional players, belonging chiefly to Surrey, Lancashire, Nottinghamshire, and Yorkshire, who all displayed good form; so it will be gathered that the Gentlemen had now a hard nut to crack when they met the Players.

Three matches were played between them that year. The first, at the Oval, was drawn in favour of the Players: Gunn, Briggs, and Shrewsbury being very successful with the bat; while Mr. W. W. Read played a brilliant 159 for the Gentlemen. The second, at Lord's, was won by the Players by four wickets: Gunn, Shrewsbury, and Briggs being again the highest scorers; whilst Messrs. F. M. Lucas and A. G. Steel did well for the Gentlemen. The Players had not won a match at Lord's since 1874. The third was played at Scarborough late in the season, and resulted in a crushing defeat of the Players by an innings and 25 runs. Neither side was fully represented; but I happened to be in my best batting form, and scored 174 out of a total of 273, while Messrs. Christopherson and Evans were very successful with the ball. The Players scored 59 and 179—Gunn, 88 in the second innings.

Three matches were played between North and South, and all were benefit matches. The first was played at Lord's, on the 25th and 26th May, for the benefit of the widow and children of F. Morley, and was won by the South by nine wickets; the second was played at the Oval on the 25th, 26th, and 27th June, for the benefit of R. Humphrey, and was won by the North by eight wickets; the third was played at Manchester for the benefit of Watson, and was drawn very much in favour of the North, Shrewsbury scoring largely in both innings.

There was no abatement in the interest taken in county cricket. Nottinghamshire did not show up so well as in the previous year, but was again at the head of the poll.

Mr. J. S. Carrick created a new record by scoring 419 not out for the West of Scotland Club, at Priory Park, Chichester, on the 13th and 14th July, the total being 745 for four wickets; and Messrs. L. Wilson and G. Wyld, for Beckenham *v.* Bexley Park, at Beckenham on the 1st August, scored 470 runs for no wicket. Barnes and Gunn distinguished themselves also, scoring 330 runs between the fall of the third and fourth wicket, for the M.C.C. and Ground *v.* Yorkshire, which was record in a first-class match. It was a great year of individual performances, 200 and over being scored 33 times, and the century about 800 times.

Very little need be said about the fifth Australian Eleven which came to us in **1886**. A great deal was expected; but very little of importance was accomplished. The summary of the tour showed that 38 matches had been played: 9 won, 7 lost, 22 drawn. That was far below the standard of the previous teams, and the Australians were all more or less disappointed. Spofforth was not up to his old form, owing to an accident which caused him to play the part of a spectator for one month of the trip.

Giffen was the mainstay of the eleven, and without him the team would have fared very badly. Three representative matches were played, with the result that England asserted its undoubted superiority. Two of them were won by an innings, the other by four wickets. The opinion at the end of the tour was that they were up to County form, certainly not beyond it. The number of drawn matches was neither encouraging nor interesting. Giffen, Jones, and Scott had an average of 26, 24, and 21 respectively for the whole of the tour; but eight English players had an average of from 30 to 40 against them. Four of their team exceeded the century, while that figure was scored against them eight times by English players. I did it thrice, Maurice Read twice, and six other players did it once.

Giffen was also very successful with the ball, considering the amount of work he did; but his average was below both Emmett's and Lohmann's. Spofforth, Garrett, and Boyle did not show up so favourably as in former years, but Blackham at the wicket was finer than ever, and was, without doubt, far ahead of English wicket-keepers. The work he did was astonishing; and how his hands stood it was a mystery to everyone. He was as brilliant and safe in the last match as he was in the first.

An Eleven of Parsees also visited England that year; and though they only won one match, yet they gave evidence of becoming good players, and they were as heartily received as either of the Australian or Philadelphian teams. There was no desire to be critical, for every Englishman took it as a compliment that the noble game should have taken root in India. I played once against them at Lord's, and shall never forget their unbounded demonstrations of joy when they got me out. Any criticism of their play at that time would be out of place; they have made considerable progress since, and I may have occasion to speak more freely about them later on.

The season was a favourable one for scoring; but it could not be said that the batting was too good for the bowling. The professionals still held their own with the gentlemen in batting, and had almost a monopoly of the bowling in first-class matches. Brilliant things were done with the bat by nearly all the old players; and Mr. A. E. Stoddart caused more than common interest. His 485 for Hampstead *v.* Stoics, at Hampstead, on the 4th of August, exceeded every individual performance yet recorded; and though it was made against very second-rate bowling, it will stand out in the history of the game as a remarkable display of well-timed vigorous hitting. He hit sixty-three 4's; and when he left the total was 813 for 7 wickets, made in the very quick time of six hours and a quarter.

Individual scoring was higher that year than any year since the game began: over 200 being exceeded no less than thirty-six times, and 100 more than a thousand times.

Nottinghamshire and Surrey had a very close race for first place in county honours, and finished about equal. Both now possessed very strong teams, the Surrey committee in particular straining every nerve to obtain promising recruits.

The Players won their match against the Gentlemen at Lord's by five wickets; whilst that at the Oval was drawn, very much in their favour. The opinion was gaining ground about this time that unless the Gentlemen cultivated bowling more, the Players would shortly have much the best of the contests.

In **1887** the old saying that "It is a long lane that has no turning" was strikingly verified by Surrey. After a period of twenty-three years, the Committee of that County Club could breathe more freely, and realise that their efforts had been attended with success, for Surrey was again at the head of the Counties, and very fine results it showed. The eleven was a strong one, including such players as Messrs. J. Shuter,

W. W. Read, Roller and Key, with Lohmann, M. Read, Abel, Beaumont, Bowley, Jones and Wood. The batting and bowling could compare favourably with that of any other county. Lohmann was worth playing for his batting and fielding alone; but his bowling undoubtedly was then, as it is now, the backbone of the team. I cannot remember any county which has been so fortunate with its wicket-keepers during the last twenty-five years as Surrey. Lockyer created a great reputation; Pooley was a worthy successor, and Wood has proved that he might be classed in the same company.

Lancashire was second on the list, and owed its position to its bowling. Watson, Briggs and Barlow had few equals as all-round players; and Mr. A. N. Hornby had lost none of his skill as a batsman, or enthusiasm and judgment as a leader.

Nottinghamshire was compelled to take third place—a position lower than it had occupied for many years. Shrewsbury in batting had a fine average for it, having played 18 completed innings for 1,388 runs; average, 77.2: and he was well supported by Gunn and Barnes. His average, with the exception of my own in 1874 and 1876, when I played 7 and 11 completed innings for averages of 84 and 80, is, I believe, far in advance of any other player's average for his county since county cricket was played. Against Middlesex at Nottingham on the 15th and 16th August, he scored 267 in an innings, made without a chance, which occupied him ten hours and a quarter. Before the season was over, he scored over the century on six other occasions for his county; and that year, although he did not play in so many matches as he did in some years, was the most successful in which he had yet played. His display in first-class matches was a fine one indeed, and put in the shade all professional performances:

21 completed innings, 1,653 runs; average, 78.15.

Individual batting performances were as brilliant as in any previous year, and we have to go far to find as good results as the following:

Over 200 in an innings, in *first-class matches*, was exceeded 6 times: twice by Mr. W. W. Read, and once each by Messrs. K. J. Key, A. J. Webbe, Shrewsbury, and Gunn. Over 100 in an innings, in *first-class matches*, was scored 123 times: six times by Shrewsbury, six times by myself (twice in one match), and more than once by two or three others. My two centuries in one match were made against Kent, at Clifton, on the 25th, 26th, 27th August, and it was the second time I had done it in first-class cricket.

The Players won both matches very easily against the Gentlemen: the first, at Lord's, by an innings and 123 runs; the return, at the Oval, by an innings and 16 runs. Shrewsbury, in the first match, batted excellently for 111; but it was owing to the fine all-round play of the team that they did so well, and asserted their undoubted superiority. The successful bowlers were also successful with the bat, and their fielding was quite as brilliant as that of the Gentlemen. It was the strongest all-round team that had ever represented them. The bowling of the Gentlemen was their weak spot, and their eleven was over-matched in both contests.

Perhaps this would be the proper place in which to trace the steps which led to the formation of the County Cricket Council.

As long ago as 1868, when it was no unusual thing for a player to represent two or even three counties in the same season, Nottinghamshire, at a General Meeting, passed a resolution as an instruction to its Committee to this effect:

"Under the impression that County Cricket, to be thoroughly appreciated by the public, a return ought to be made as near as may be to the manner in which those contests were formerly conducted, when no title but birth enabled any player, whether gentleman or professional, to take part therein; and that, consequently, it be an instruction to the Committee, in the selection of our future matches, to give preference to those counties who adopt that rule.

"Secondly, that so long as the title to play in county matches is by residence as well as birth, the same may be acquiesced in by the Committee, on the understanding that no such player shall play in any respect of each such qualification during the season.

"Lastly, that it be a further instruction to the Committee that they endeavour to prevail upon all the counties who do not at present do so, to adopt the principle of the last resolution. It is believed that Kent, Sussex, Yorkshire, Cambridgeshire and Nottinghamshire, at the present time, play only those who are county-born; and it is thought other counties would follow in their wake if the subject were properly introduced to their notice, as tending to promote a real and appreciable contest between county and county."

Four years later the Surrey Committee raised the question also; and at a meeting of the representatives of the leading counties in December, 1872, a resolution was passed:

"That no player, either amateur or professional, play for more than one county during the season; but that he shall be free to choose at the beginning of the season whether he shall play under the birth or residential qualification."

A copy of the resolution was sent to the M.C.C., who weighed it carefully, and eventually the following rules were passed at a meeting of County representatives held in the Surrey County Pavilion at the Oval, on the 9th June, 1873, and confirmed at a meeting of the M.C.C. held in the Pavilion at Lord's on the 1st of July.

RULE 1.—"That no cricketer, whether amateur or professional shall play for more than one county during the same season.

2.—"Every cricketer born in one county and residing in

another shall be free to choose at the beginning of each season for which of those counties he will play, and shall, during that season, play for that county only.

3.—"A cricketer shall be qualified to play for any county in which he is residing and has resided for the previous two years, or a cricketer may elect to play for the county in which his family home is, so long as it remains open to him as an occasional residence.

4.—"That should any question arise as to the residential qualification, the same shall be left to the decision of the Marylebone Club."

A further discussion of those rules arose at a meeting of County Secretaries held at Lord's in December, 1881, when Lord Harris moved, "That the Committee of the M.C.C. be requested to consider whether the two years' residential qualification might not be safely reduced to one year;" but the motion was rejected by 14 votes to 3.

At a largely-attended meeting of County Delegates, held at Lord's on the 12th July, 1887, Lord Harris in the Chair, it was moved and carried:

1.—"That a County Cricket Council be formed.

2.—"That the Council consist of one representative each from the counties of Nottinghamshire, Yorkshire, Surrey, Kent, Lancashire, Sussex, Gloucestershire, Middlesex, Derbyshire, Essex, Warwickshire, Norfolk, Leicestershire, Staffordshire, Somersetshire, Northamptonshire, Hampshire, Durham, Hertfordshire, and Cheshire.

3.—"That it shall be competent for the Council to alter or amend the rules of County Cricket Qualification.

4.—"That upon all questions raised under the rules of County Cricket Qualification the Committee of the M.C.C. shall adjudicate."

That was undoubtedly a step in the right direction; for the birth and residential qualifications had agitated the minds of County Club Committees for many years.

The air was full of rumours about the sixth Australian team which landed in England in **1888**.

I have noticed that a really good bowler appears in the ranks of the professionals about once in half-a-dozen years, and amongst the amateurs about once in twelve. Australian cricketers have shown that the remark does not apply to them; for in the six teams which have visited us from 1878 down to 1888, at least half-a-dozen amateurs may be classed as great bowlers. There may be some difference of opinion respecting the positions which Allan, Palmer, Garrett, Giffen, Boyle, and Evans will occupy in cricket history; but there can be none about Spofforth, Turner, and Ferris. They will be emphatically classed amongst the great bowlers of the century.

Giffen, acknowledged to be the best all-round player who had yet represented Australia, was not with them on this occasion, and the number of players new to English soil was unusually large. By some the team was considered up to the standard of its predecessors, by others much below it; but nearly all were agreed that Turner and Ferris would uphold the reputation of Australian bowling. I question if any team started so favourably as that one did. Mr. Thornton's Eleven, Warwickshire, Surrey, Oxford University and Yorkshire went down before it in startling succession, the last four being defeated in a single innings, and quite a panic set in amongst certain cricketers. Turner and Ferris came off in bowling, and showed that they could bat also; and nearly all the other members of the team played up to their best form. Lancashire stayed the rot; then the Gentlemen of England scored heavily against them, and the Players defeated them by ten wickets, and the believers in English supremacy began to breathe more freely.

The play of the team was very much in-and-out afterwards, and before the season was over their form could be safely classed. Forty matches were played—of which they won 19, lost 14 and 7 were drawn. There is little need to analyse the matches; and the team may be put down, with one or two others, as being up to county form, but below English representative form. It is true that they met with a very sad stroke of bad-luck when Jones, their best bat, was stricken with illness; but they were, undoubtedly, taken as a whole, below the quality of either of Murdoch's teams, and by a good many thought weaker than Scott's.

The bowling of Turner and Ferris will be remembered, but everything else will be forgotten. How those two slaved and toiled from the beginning to the end of the tour, and with what remarkable effect, is still fresh in the memories of most of us. Rarely have two bowlers been called upon to do so much work in one season, or acquitted themselves so admirably; Turner bowled over 10,000 balls; Ferris close upon 9,000; and Turner's average will compare favourably with Spofforth's, or any bowler that ever lived. Without them the team would have been a failure. McDonnell, the captain, was blamed for working them too much; but he had a very difficult problem before him, and it is easy to be wise after the event. If we are to judge by the results of the others when they were called upon to bowl, we cannot blame him; for not one of them could be compared with the famous pair. Blackham was as good at the wicket as ever; McDonnell hit brilliantly now and then; and Bonnor, when he made up his mind to hit, was still very effective.

There was quite as much interest displayed over county cricket as over the Australian contests; and Surrey came out far ahead of the others. Lohmann was in great form with the ball; and the batting of Messrs. W. W. Read, J. Shuter, M. P. Bowden, and Abel and M. Read, who averaged over 30 runs each against the first-class counties, was also a great source of strength. Mr. W. W. Read outshone himself in individual performances, scoring 338 in a single innings against Oxford University, which was the second highest ever obtained in a first-class match.

Kent and Yorkshire were next on the list, and Gloucestershire made a distinct step forward. For Gloucestershire against Yorkshire, in the return match at Clifton, I made 148 and 153, and it was the third time I scored the century twice in the same match. Nottinghamshire was lower down than it had been for years, and missed greatly the services of Shrewsbury, who was in Australia looking after the business arrangements of an English football team.

The two matches played by the Gentlemen and Players resulted in a win to each. The first, at Lord's, on the 9th and 10th of July, was finished in two days, the Gentlemen winning it in a most sensational way by 5 runs. The wicket was in favour of the bowlers, and low scoring was the rule on both sides. The Players were left with 78 to make to win. They scored 71 for six wickets, and then collapsed; Mr. S. M. J. Woods, who played for the first time, doing most execution with the ball. His ten wickets for 76 runs in the whole match was a fine performance, and clearly showed how well the Gentlemen could hold their own in these or any contests when their fine batting was backed up by good bowling. The return match, at the Oval, was won by the Players by an innings and 39 runs, and their luck in winning the toss had much to do with it. Heavy rains prevented a start until the second day; and after the Players batted the wicket played badly.

A second team of Parsees visited England that year, and displayed much better form than the first did in 1886. They played 31 matches; winning 8, losing 11, and 12

MR. J. A. DIXON. MR. M. P. BOWDEN. MR. W. NEWHAM. LORD GEORGE SCOTT.
MR. J. ECCLES. MR. J. SHUTER. MR. W. G. GRACE. MR. A. G. STEEL. MR. W. W. READ.

were drawn. That was a great improvement on their first visit when everything went against them. In one thing they showed excellent promise—their consistent efforts in playing an uphill match. More than once, when disaster stared them in the face, and everything seemed to be going against them, they played most pluckily, and made a close match of it.

Second-class county cricket showed considerable development. In all ten counties were represented, and Leicestershire, Somersetshire, and Warwickshire were the most successful.

Two English teams visited Australia in 1887-8: one was under the leadership of Mr. G. F. Vernon, who went out at the invitation of the Melbourne C.C.; the other was under Shrewsbury. Both teams were very successful in their contests, but came to grief financially —at which no one was surprised. On one occasion the best of the two teams played against a combined Eleven of Australia, and upheld the credit of the old country with marked success.

At the annual meeting of the County Cricket Council on December 10th, 1888, the following resolution was passed and added to the rules of County Cricket:

> "That a man can play for his old county during the two years that he is qualifying for another."

In 1889 Shrewsbury's presence in the Nottinghamshire eleven made a great difference to that County. Gunn and Barnes were also in excellent form; and up to the end of July results pointed to their taking a very high position. But the wet wickets which prevailed the greater part of August upset more than one member of the team who had been doing exceptionally well, and their brilliant performances in the early part of the season were greatly discounted.

Surrey did not play up to its 1888 form, its batting

being the weak point. Neither Mr. W. W. Read, Mr. J. Shuter, nor Abel did so well as he had done in the past; but, fortunately Lohmann was very effective with the ball, and he was well supported by Beaumont, Bowley, and a promising colt—Sharpe.

Lancashire came out better than it had done for a year or two. Two importations, Mold and A. Ward, had qualified by residence, and valuable additions to the eleven they proved to be; Mold as a fast bowler, and A. Ward as a batsman. Briggs was as successful as ever with both ball and bat; and Watson showed that, though he had played for nearly twenty years, his bowling had lost none of its sting.

Gloucestershire was not so successful as in the previous year; but at last it possessed a ground of its own, which was admitted to be one of the best in the world, and the Committee became hopeful of improvement at no distant date. It was still lacking in first-class bowling.

Yorkshire met with disaster after disaster, and the season was the worst the county had experienced since it was formed.

Sussex had a most disappointing year also.

An English eleven sailed from England to South Africa at the end of 1888, and played till the end of March, 1889. Australia and Canada had been visited repeatedly; but this was a new departure, and indicative of how the game spreads wherever Englishmen congregate. The arrangements were conducted by Major Warton; and the team was captained by Mr. C. A. Smith, of Sussex. The team was not a representative one, but it had in it such well-known players as Abel, Ulyett, Maurice Read, and Briggs, who gave the colonists a fine illustration of all-round cricket. Abel's doings with the bat were noteworthy—22 completed innings, 1,075 runs, average 48.19; while Briggs astonished everyone out there by his fine performance with the ball—1,220.3 overs, 628 maidens, 1,512 runs, 290 wickets, average 5.62. Two matches were played against a combined eleven of South Africa, which the English team won very easily.

The Gentlemen of Philadelphia visited us again in 1889, and gave a very fine batting display against second-class teams. Three of them had an average of over thirty runs per innings, and six more of over twenty. Like the majority of amateur elevens, their weak spot was bowling, and some very heavy scores were made against them. Mr. W. W. Read, in particular, did very well against them for the Gentlemen of Surrey, scoring 105 and 130, and so added the feat of two centuries in a match to his great performances. Twelve matches was the total number played; of which the Philadelphians won 4, lost 3, and 5 were drawn.

Three matches were played by the Gentlemen and Players in 1889: the first, at the Oval, on the 4th, 5th, and 6th of July; the second, at Lord's, on the 8th and 9th of July; the third, at Hastings, on the 16th, 17th, and 18th of September. The Oval match was productive of heavy scoring—the Gentlemen making 347 and 225, to the Players' 396 and 177 second for one wicket. Gunn, Barnes, and Quaife did great things in batting for the Players; and Messrs. O'Brien, Stoddart, Cranston, W. W. Read, Nepean and myself did best for the Gentlemen. The match at Lord's was another decisive victory for the Players, who won by ten wickets; Barnes batting in great form for 130 not out. At Hastings, the Gentlemen won by one wicket after a very sensational finish. It was too late in the season to expect heavy scoring throughout the match; and although the Gentlemen were only left with seventy-three runs to get to win, the state of the wicket rendered it rather difficult. Five wickets fell for twenty-five runs, Lohmann and Attewell doing what they liked with the ball; when the ninth man was out eight runs were still wanted, and the excitement all over the ground was intense. Mr. McCormick, of Sussex fame, was equal to the task, however; for, after playing carefully some time for seventeen runs, he finished up the match with two hits to the boundary.

The North *v.* South matches were again overdone, as many as five being played, the North having the best of it. The most interesting of all, though it was not finished, was that played at Scarborough on the 5th, 6th, and 7th of September. The North scored 360 in its first innings, the South 197. On the last day the South had to follow on against a majority of 163. The wicket was far from perfect, and the ball had to be watched carefully; but Abel and myself put on 226 for the first wicket, after three hours and three-quarters' play; and when the stumps were drawn the total was 278 for three wickets—of which Abel had scored 105 by careful and scientific cricket, while my share was 154.

Gunn and Barnes came out at the top of the batting averages, and Maurice Read was a good third. The Gentlemen were again well to the front, Mr. T. C. O'Brien showing up splendidly. It will be a very long time before his magnificent display for Middlesex against Yorkshire in the second innings, at Lord's on the 22nd of June, will be forgotten. Middlesex was left to get 280 runs to win and 3 hours and 35 minutes in which to do it. At half-past 5 four wickets were down for 129. When Mr. O'Brien went in 151 runs were wanted to win, and no one dreamt for a moment that it could be done in the time. He hit as no man had hit for many a long day; but at 6.15, 83 runs were still wanted. With the help of Mr. Vernon, he kept up the pace, and accomplished one of the greatest feats of batting ever performed since the game began, winning the match for his side with ten minutes to spare. The brilliancy of his hitting from first to last, the excitement over it, and the burst of enthusiasm which it produced, were worth a day's travel to witness. It was truly a great performance, and stamped him as one of the most dashing batsmen of his or any time.

Mr. J. Cranston was another amateur who did exceptionally well. He had been well known for years as one of the most reliable bats in the Gloucestershire Eleven, but that year saw him classed as the best left-handed batsman in England.

Two hundred runs and over in an innings was scored by 27 players, and over one hundred about a thousand times. The months of May and August were wet, but June and July enabled the batsmen to score rapidly. One very remarkable match was played at Lord's on the 9th and 10th August, for M.C.C. and Ground *v.* Northumberland. Gunn and Mr. Brodrick-Cloete began the batting for M.C.C. Mr. Brodrick-Cloete's wicket fell with the score at 9, and then Attewell took his place. The score was 325 at the end of the first day, Gunn and Attewell still in. Next day the score was increased to 428, when Attewell was caught, having made exactly 200. The innings was declared at an end, Gunn's score being 219 not out. Northumberland made 141 first innings, and 117 second.

At the third annual meeting of the County Cricket Council, on Dec. 6th, resolutions to the following effect were passed:

"1. In the interests of County Cricket it is desirable that an official classification of counties should be made annually by this Council, and that a committee of the County Council, consisting of the President, with three representatives from first-class and three from second-class counties, be appointed to recommend a scheme for this purpose; such scheme to include a scheme of promotion by merit, under which a county may rise from one class to another.

"2. That all three-day matches shall begin at twelve o'clock the first day, and not later than 11.30 following days."

Two or three important changes had been made in the laws at a meeting of the M.C.C., held in the month of May. They were as follow:

"1. That the over in future shall consist of five balls instead of four.

"2. That the bowler may change ends as often as he pleases, but may not bowl two overs in succession.

"3. That the Captain of the batting side may declare the innings at an end in a one-day match whenever he chooses to do so; but only on the last day of a match arranged for more than one day."

The alterations elicited a great number of opinions for and against; but by the end of the year it was generally admitted that they had worked satisfactorily. Declaring the innings at an end in one-day matches caused the greatest stir; and when one comes to think of it, it cannot be a very pleasing thing for the tail of an eleven to be told that there is no need for them to bat, and that they must be content with fielding for once in a way.

The seventh Australian team, which visited England in **1890**, under the leadership of Murdoch, might be classed in strength with McDonnell's, although it did not show such good results. For the first time since these teams came to us in 1878, they lost more matches than they won; and I need not say the result was alike disappointing to Australian and English cricketers. We had been led to expect one of the strongest elevens that had ever left Australia; and for a match or two, in the early part of the tour, it looked as if the prediction would be verified: but afterwards they met with defeat after defeat, and finished up the tour with 38 matches played: 13 won, 16 lost, 9 drawn. Their best wins were against Lord Sheffield's Eleven, Lord Londesborough's Eleven and Surrey; but they were defeated twice by England, twice by the Players of England, twice by the South of England, twice by the M.C.C., twice by Nottinghamshire and twice by Yorkshire: so that their claim to be classed with a representative English Eleven was completely disposed of. A third match against England, at Manchester, had to be abandoned owing to heavy rains, not a ball being bowled in the three days.

Murdoch showed that he had lost little of his skill with the bat, and he was ably supported by a new player, Dr. J. E. Barrett; but with these exceptions, the batting was weak, which indeed was the case with all the previous teams. Murdoch has always been considered a hard-wicket bat, and it was rather unfortunate for him that the season should have turned out a wet one; but considering he had given up the game for years, his display was very good, and it caused general satisfaction when he came out at the head of the averages.

Barrett, who ran him a close race for first place, confirmed the great reputation which he had made in Australia, and did much better than was expected. Very rarely, if ever, has any young player done so well on a first appearance; indeed, it is held very generally by the Australians themselves that young players never play up to their form the first tour, and we have only to look at the performances of Charlton, Walters, and others to see the truth of it.

His style was not very taking, but he watched the ball very carefully, and was something more than a stone wall type of batsman. His patience was un-tiring, and when the bowling was good there was no tempting him to hit; but immediately the bowler began to tire and sent up a loose ball, Barrett cracked it to the boundary as well as most batsmen. His fine score of 170 for once out, in the concluding match at Manchester, will be remembered for many a long day. He was a fair bowler also, and with practice will be yet heard of in that department.

Of the others, in batting, very little need be said. Lyons gave us occasional displays of lofty hitting, but he was not the equal of Bonnor in that respect; and for brilliancy, dash, cleanness and placing, was far behind McDonnell in his best days. Trott maintained his 1888 reputation, and at times did exceptionally well, but he lacked in consistency. Turner, Ferris, and Blackham, batted as well as they ever did; but the others met with only moderate success.

It is almost impossible to praise Turner and Ferris too highly for their great bowling performances. Murdoch, like McDonnell, found that they were head and shoulders above everybody else, and he must have had many an anxious quarter of an hour speculating what the team would do in the case of either breaking down. Turner, now and then, was irresistible, and carried everything before him on sticky wickets; but Ferris did better on the hard, good wickets, pegging away in his persistent, plucky way, never minding being hit, and determined at all costs to get the batsmen out. Rumours had reached us before the team appeared that Ferris had gone off, but he bowled better than ever; and it was a fitting finish to their grand displays that Turner and he should have ended the season with the same number of wickets, 215, to their credit.

Equally high praise may be bestowed on Blackham's wicket-keeping. It was finer than ever, and he did more work than ever; and he is still to-day, as he has been any time in the last twelve years, the finest wicket-keeper who ever donned gloves. Gregory, in the field, was conspicuous for quickness, certainty, and a wonderful return, and is worthy of a very high place amongst brilliant cover-points. Two or three batsmen who were ignorant of his powers had to pay the penalty of a run-out in attempting a short run.

First-class county cricket and representative matches suffered very little by the Australian visit. In the former, Surrey, as was expected, took a very decided lead in the early part of the season, and came out well ahead of the others. Ably led by Mr. J. Shuter, it scored victory after victory, and it was only at the end of the year that it suffered defeat. It had a very strong batting team, nearly every member of the eleven being good for runs; while in bowling, Lohmann and Sharpe were up to the form of any bowler in England. Lohmann's performance of taking over 200 wickets in first-class cricket for the third year in succession had never before been accomplished. Turner and Ferris reached that figure in 1888 and 1890, Southerton in 1870, Peate in 1882, and Spofforth in 1884; but these are the only names I can recall.

Lancashire did very well, and took second place; and both Kent and Yorkshire came out better than in the previous year. Greater things were expected of Nottinghamshire; but, with the exception of Shrewsbury and Gunn with the bat, and Attewell with the ball, hardly a member of the team played up to his 1889 form. Gloucestershire went through rather a peculiar experience: until the latter part of July it never won a match, but after it began its Northern tour it never suffered defeat. In batting, J. Cranston, my brother E.M., Painter, and myself were most successful; and Woof bowled very well on the slow wickets. Sussex had a very disastrous season, losing 11 of the 12 matches played.

Great improvement was displayed by one or two of the second-class counties: Somersetshire in particular played grandly, and went through the season without knowing defeat.

The Gentlemen were beaten by the Players at the Oval, but had the best of a drawn match at Lord's.

In the beginning of the season Shrewsbury and Gunn attracted great attention by their wonderful batting displays; but after the wet set in, the former fell off. Their grand stand for Nottinghamshire *v.* Sussex, in which they made 398 before being parted, was a new record for longest partnership in first-class cricket; and Gunn's 228 for the Players was the highest ever made against an Australian eleven in England. Messrs. A. N. Hornby, A. J. Webbe, and Hall and Ulyett, batted consistently the greater part of the season, and Abel finished up in fine form.

Mr. A. E. Stoddart played two very fine innings in the earlier part of the season: one for the South *v.* North, at Lord's, when he scored 115 out of 169 without a mistake on a difficult wicket; the other for the Gentlemen *v.* Players, at the Oval, when he hit a brilliant 85 on another difficult wicket; but later on he fell woefully off, and could hardly get a run.

Three young Cambridge University players came to the front, Messrs. G. McGregor, E. C. Streatfeild, and R. N. Douglas. McGregor's reputation as a wicket-keeper was made the year before, but 1890 saw him in improved form, and he was paid the very high compliment of being chosen to play for England *v.* Australia. All three played for the Gentlemen. Under the leadership of Mr. S. M. J. Woods, they helped very materially by their good form to give their University a high position. The four professionals,

MR. G McGREGOR.

Briggs, Lohmann, Peel, and Attewell, by their fine all-round play, maintained their great reputations.

On the evening of the 11th of August, a special meeting of the County Cricket Council was held in the pavilion of the Surrey County Club. There were present delegates from Surrey, Kent, Gloucestershire, Yorkshire, Sussex, Warwickshire, Derbyshire, Leicestershire, Hampshire, Northamptonshire, Norfolk and Essex. Mr. J. Shuter presided, and it was decided:

I. That for the season 1891 the counties be divided into three classes, namely:

FIRST CLASS.

Notts	Kent	Yorkshire
Lancashire	Middlesex	Sussex
Surrey	Gloucestershire	

SECOND CLASS.

Warwickshire	Somersetshire	Staffordshire
Derbyshire	Hampshire	Cheshire
Leicestershire	Essex	

THIRD CLASS.

Hertfordshire	Lincolnshire	Glamorganshire
Northamptonshire	Northumberland	Devonshire
Norfolk	Durham	

II. (*a*) That every first-class county be required to play matches with at least six other first-class counties. These to include matches with the Champion county of the previous year.

(*b*) That every second-class county play two matches with at least three other second-class counties, these three to include the Champion county in the second-class for the previous year.

(*c*) That every third-class county play two matches with at least three other third-class counties.

III. That in each of the three classes an order of merit be drawn up from the results of the season's play in 1891 and future years, and that this order be determined by the same method as that by which the Championship for the first-class counties is at present decided; viz., by subtracting wins from losses, and not counting drawn games.

IV. That in 1892 the lowest county in the first-class and the highest county in the second-class play each other home-and-home matches, these constituting a series which shall be termed the qualifying series. The same arrangement to apply to the lowest of the second-class and the highest of the third-class counties.

V. That if a county be, by these means, reduced in class, it shall, for the following season, be considered the highest in the class to which it has descended, and shall follow the course of procedure set forth in No. 4.

That, on the other hand, if a county, after playing in a qualifying series as the highest best of an inferior class, shall have to remain in the same class, it shall not be considered the highest for the next season unless it shall obtain such a position by virtue of its performances in that season.

The scheme of classification did not give general satisfaction, and a newspaper warfare was kept up for sometime afterwards. Later in the year delegates from the second-class counties—Hampshire, Warwickshire, Staffordshire, Essex, Cheshire and Derbyshire—met in the pavilion at Lord's, and passed a resolution to be submitted as an amendment by Warwickshire at the annual meeting of the County Cricket Council to be held in December.

The annual meeting was held in the pavilion at Lord's, on the 8th December, Mr. M. J. Ellison presiding. It was evident that special interest was taken in the points to be considered, for there was a large attendance of delegates from the first, second, and third-class counties. After the minutes of the previous general meeting and the special meeting in August were read, and a statement of accounts and balance-sheet were passed, Mr. Ansell, of Warwickshire, moved, on behalf of the second-class counties, the following amendments to the classification scheme:

In Rule II. (*b*) to omit the clause:—"These three to include the Champion County in the second-class for the previous year."

To strike out IV. and V., and substitute the following:

IV. That at the end of each season, in the month of August or September, the lowest county in the first-class shall play the highest of the second-class for right of place. One game only shall be played, and upon neutral ground, to a finish, the winner being placed in the superior class and the loser in the class below for the following year.

> NOTE (*a*).—In the event of two counties being equal at the top or bottom of either class, the question of their superiority shall first be decided on neutral ground, played to a finish, and followed immediately by the match for right of place in the superior class for the next year.
>
> NOTE (*b*).—In the event of three counties being equal, either at the bottom of the first or top of the second class, the matter shall remain in abeyance for that year.

V. Should the trial matches fail to define the positions of competing counties, the Cricket Council itself shall undertake the classification for the following year.

> NOTE (*c*).—This scheme shall apply also to the lowest of the second and the highest of the third-class counties.

The first motion, to omit II. (*b*), was carried with one dissentient, Gloucestershire; but when Mr. Ansell brought forward his second motion, to strike out Rules IV. and V., and substitute fresh matter, it became perfectly evident that a great diversity of opinion existed. A very animated discussion arose, and, in unmistakable tones, the majority of the delegates declined to pledge themselves to any classification scheme that would compel them to play more matches than they wished to. Mr. Ansell's motion that Rules IV. and V. should be struck out, was agreed to; but the meeting rejected the proposals of Warwickshire by 11 votes to 4. Mr. J. B. Wostinholm then moved that the rules of the Council be suspended for further discussion of the subject; but Mr. A. J. Webbe jumped up and moved as an amendment that the Council be suspended *sine die*. The voting for the amendment was 7 for and 7 against; and the Chairman giving his casting vote in favour of it, the meeting came to an abrupt ending.

* * * * * * *

To get at a clear idea of the progress which the game has made during the last forty years, I would refer my readers to the batting and bowling averages in the last chapter of this book. At the end of 1864 a batting average of twenty-five runs per innings was very exceptional, and rarely accomplished by other than a professional player. It may be explained in this way—that amateur bowling was lamentably weak, whilst professional bowling was very strong, and a carefully prepared ground the exception.

The year 1865 saw a slight change. Two or three of the amateurs gave evidence of marked improvement with both bat and ball; and, for the first time since 1854, the Gentlemen beat the Players. The batting averages leaped up considerably in 1866; seven amateurs had an average of thirty runs and over per innings, while only one professional reached that figure; and there were fifteen amateurs with an average of over twenty, to four professionals. But the professionals had quite as great a monopoly of the bowling; thirteen to four was their proportion in that department. And so it went on for twenty years; the amateurs keeping a strong lead with the bat, the professionals with the ball.

The year 1885 brought further change. The professionals not only maintained their superiority with the ball, but challenged the supremacy of the amateurs with the bat. For twenty completed innings in first-class matches, thirteen professionals had an average of over twenty-three runs per innings; while the number of amateurs who had it was only six. Nor was it a mere flash in the pan; for the years 1886 and 1887 saw the professionals still challenging the amateurs for first place in batting honours, while still retaining their high position with the ball. The year 1888 brought the amateurs to the front with the bat again; but 1889 and 1890 show it was again a close race between them.

Never, in any year, have the amateurs had a look-in with the professionals in bowling, so far as numbers are concerned, and only once or twice have they headed the list. Mr. A. G. Steel did very well for them in 1878; while my performances in the years 1867, 1874, 1875, and 1877 might be classed with first-class professional bowling.

And so we may face the fact that the professional standard of all-round play is higher to-day than at any time since the game began. The professionals are now the equals of the amateurs in batting and fielding, and their superiors in bowling. And I am very much afraid it is likely to continue so for a considerable time. Amateur bowling is weaker to-day than it has been for many years, while the outlook for the future is not particularly bright. It used to be said, some twenty years ago, that it was always safe to back the Players against the Gentlemen. After 1864 prophets were more modest in their utterances. The last two years have shown that the Players are taking their old position.

A careful reader will have noticed how, bit by bit, travelling elevens lost their attraction, and were slowly, but surely, effaced by the growing and absorbing interest taken in county matches.

The history of county cricket is worthy of a book to itself, and cannot have justice done to it here. Surrey,

Sussex, Kent, Middlesex, Hampshire and Nottinghamshire have been in existence for more than one hundred years; and all of them, at one time or another, were strong enough to play an Eleven of England. But county cricket pure and simple may be said to have reached its highest development in the last twenty years. Yorkshire was established in the early part of the present century, Lancashire in 1864, and Gloucestershire and Derbyshire in 1870. How those counties have fought against each other with varying success can be seen from the yearly results I have given. From 1870 to 1890 Nottinghamshire stands out pre-eminently amongst the first-class counties, having been at the head of the list seven times, while it will be seen Sussex has been at the bottom eight times.

I shall not trouble my readers by saying much about the future of the counties. Surrey and Nottinghamshire's prospects are as bright to-day as at any time in their history; but, then, the brightest prospects have often been shattered in cricket, and many a county that was expected to do well has done ill. It is never safe to prophesy when the unexpected happens so often. Counties in the South have greater difficulties to contend against in obtaining first-class bowlers than the counties in the North, but all of them are striving their utmost to meet the difficulty and keep their position in contests which are now looked upon as the most exciting of all: contests which have become the backbone of the game.

CHAPTER VII.

THE MARYLEBONE CLUB AND UNIVERSITY CRICKET.

MY connection with the Marylebone Club dates from the 13th of May, 1869, when I was not quite twenty-one years of age. I have said elsewhere that I considered it a very high compliment to be thought worthy of a place in the club which has done more than any other to develop the game, and I have nothing but the very pleasantest recollections of the twenty-two years I have played for it. The M.C.C. had been in existence 82 years when I joined it; there were 1,200 members, and the number of matches played during the season was something under 40. To-day it is 104 years old; the list of members has swelled to 3,500, and as many as 160 matches were played last year, of which 84 were won, 40 lost, and 36 drawn. It will be of interest to touch briefly upon the growth of the old club, which is now acknowledged to be the authority on cricket, not only in England, but wherever the game is played.

About the year 1780 the White Conduit Club was the most important in London, and Thomas Lord, a kind of half-attendant, half-ground bowler, was in the habit of bowling to the members. The White Conduit Club, like most cricket clubs, had to contend against internal dissensions, and some of the members decided to go elsewhere. But the difficulty in the way was a suitable spot for a ground, for there were at most only two of any importance in London at the time. Lord was asked to look about in the neighbourhood of Marylebone, and was promised influential support if he succeeded. The Earl of Winchelsea and Col. the Hon. — Lennox were the principal movers in the matter; and Lord, being a bit of an enthusiast, and realising that the speculation was likely to turn out well, at once proceeded to carry out the suggestion. By 1787 a suitable spot, now known as Dorset Square, was acquired, and Lord's Ground and the Marylebone Club became accomplished facts.

The Club must have had an influential membership even at that date, for the following year we find it revising the laws of the game. At once it began to play matches with the White Conduit and other clubs; but the first recorded is M.C.C. *v.* White Conduit Club, on the 27th June, 1788, which the M.C.C. won by 83 runs. Everything went smoothly for a period of twenty-two years; then Lord, owing to a dispute with his landlord about an increase of rent, had to leave Dorset Square. North Bank, Regent's Park, was next chosen, in 1810: but that was to be a very short abiding place; for in 1812 the making of Regent's Canal caused the ground to be cut up.

Neither the Club nor Lord was disheartened; for in 1814 the present site in John's Wood was secured, and there the club has played ever since. A year or two previously the Homerton Club, the next in importance, amalgamated with the M.C.C., and the playing eleven became a very strong one. But it should be remembered that before this some of the members of the old Hambledon Club, which broke up in 1791, had played for the M.C.C., and consequently strengthened it. Matches against England, London, Kent, Middlesex, Hampshire, and other clubs, had been of frequent occurrence before the end of the eighteenth century, and the fame of the M.C.C. had gone over the land.

Lord and the club committee must have thought highly of the turf on which they played at Dorset Square; for it was taken up and relaid on the North Bank Ground, and afterwards transferred to St. John's Wood Road. The earliest recorded match of the M.C.C. on its present ground was played against Hertfordshire on the 22nd June, 1814, the M.C.C. winning by an innings and 27 runs. In the eleven representing the winning side were four players who were well known all over the cricket world, and who maintained their reputation for many years afterwards—Lord Frederick .Beauclerk, Messrs. E. H. Budd, G. Osbaldeston, and W. Ward.

Harrow and Winchester played against each other for the first time at Lord's on the 27th and 28th July, 1825, and the match will be remembered for the disastrous fire which took place in the pavilion during the night of the last day. Valuable records of the game which could not be replaced were destroyed, and Lord suffered rather heavily. Something like £2,600 was due to him for subscriptions; but as the books had been burnt, it was difficult for him to remember who had paid and who had not.

It is just possible that Lord was discouraged by it: anyhow, we find he desired to retire, and for the moment it looked as if the ground would fall into the hands of the builders, who had coveted it for many years. Mr. Ward very generously stepped in and purchased the remainder of the lease at a very high price, and the club continued its prosperous career. The pavilion was quickly rebuilt, and two years later Oxford and Cambridge began their annual contests.

Mr. Ward unfortunately could not see his way to hold the lease after 1835, and Mr. J. H. Dark took it off his hands and became the proprietor in 1836. The club seems to have got on pretty smoothly under the proprietorship of Mr. Dark until 1863, when he proposed to part with the remainder of his lease of 29½ years for the sum of £15,000. The year after he accepted £11,000;

and Mr. Moses, the ground landlord, offered a renewal of the ground-rent for 99 years at the rate of £550 per annum. Considering that the old rent had only been £150, the club had now to face a considerable increase in its yearly expenses. Nothing daunted, the Committee accepted: but Mr. Moses came forward in 1865 with a new offer; viz., to sell the fee outright for a sum of £21,000. Eventually he accepted £18,150; and Mr. W. Nicholson, a member of the committee, in a very laudable spirit advanced the money on a mortgage of the premises at the rate of £5 per cent., which he afterwards reduced to £4 per cent., and conceded to the club the right to pay him off by annual instalments.

At last the club could call the ground its own, and the strides it made in the next twenty years were really remarkable. By 1878 the whole amount had been paid off, and the finances of the club established on a firm footing, which it has since maintained. In 1866, when Mr. Nicholson bought up the freehold, the club numbered 980 members, and had an income slightly over £6,000; to-day, as I have already said, it has 3,500 members, with a total income of £30,000. It is no secret that the committee, if they desired, could double the membership in a month's time; for applications for election come from all parts of the globe. However, they have no desire to do so, for it is their aim that the club shall not exceed the limit which would affect the comfort and enjoyment of the present members; and a rule has been passed which admits only of 156 members being elected yearly, active cricketers preferred, and half of them being specially selected.

There is no need to say that the club is in a prosperous condition. If proof were wanted of it, I have only to refer to the handsome pavilion which was recently built at a cost of £20,000. The Hon. Sir

Spencer Ponsonby Fane laid the first stone on the 17th September, 1889, and everything was completed by the beginning of 1890. It is capable of accommodating 3,000 people, and is a vast improvement on the old structure, which had weathered the storms of 65 years. The entire size of the ground is 12 acres; the enclosed part for playing matches, 6 acres. All round it improvements have been made and are being made yearly. Ten men are employed throughout the year to look after it, and everything in connection with it is in apple-pie order.

The Marylebone Cricket Club is the first in the world, and is held in deserved respect by everyone who plays the game. At home and abroad, every Englishman refers to it with pardonable pride, and upholds it as the chief bulwark of our national game.

The M.C.C. is everywhere acknowledged to be the maker and preserver of the laws. It has been accused of being too conservative in some respects, and of not marching quickly enough in the interests of the game; but my experience of the club has shown me that it has been quick to act immediately a grievance has been made clear. Rarely a year has passed in which some point of law has not cropped up, and received calm and careful consideration. Unfair bowling, the selection of umpires, county qualifications, disputes between players of the North and South—in fact, everything bearing on the welfare of the game—have in turn been discussed and decided; and the opinion is general to-day that the old club has been faithful to the trust which has been placed in its hands for upwards of a hundred years.

The centenary celebration, which was held on the 13th, 14th, 15th, 16th, 17th and 18th June, 1887, was an important landmark in the history of the club. The first three days were devoted to first-class cricket, M.C.C. and Ground *v.* England, when A. E. Stoddart and Shrewsbury batted in fine form for the latter. The last three days, the Gentlemen of the M.C.C. played Eighteen Veterans of Over Forty, and the giants of the past could be seen batting with some of the giants of the present. The dinner which was held in the tennis court in the evening of the 15th brought together a most distinguished company of players and lovers of the game, numbering about two hundred. Success to the Great Army of Cricketers, the Church, the Army, the Navy, the Bench and the Bar, Medicine and the Cricket Counties was proposed in turn, and no such memorable meeting has been held since cricket was first played.

The Committee of the M.C.C. have never lost sight of the interests of professional players. Young and promising players have always been encouraged, and the most successful have rarely failed to secure an engagement on the staff of ground bowlers. There are over 40 professional cricketers engaged at Lord's, many of them earning as much as £10 per week. The season lasts about 16 weeks. For country matches they are paid at the rate of £6 per match; for matches played at Lord's, £3 10s. if they win and £3 if they lose. The ground bowlers are paid from 30 shillings to 50 shillings per week, and they can always depend on handsome gratuities from the members. Every player selected by the Committee to play against the Gentlemen is paid at the rate of £10 per match; and after years of faithful service, nearly every first-class player can rely upon a benefit match, which may be expected to realise a goodly sum.

It will readily be understood that every player covets the position of ground bowler at Lord's, and avails himself of the first offer to play there, in the hope of creating a favourable impression. The M.C.C. is generous in another way: the expenses of county teams playing against it at Lord's being defrayed by the club, while the expenses of M.C.C. Elevens which visit the provinces come out of the club funds only.

The club can also show a most distinguished roll of office bearers, but no trustworthy record can be given before 1826.

Presidents:

1826 Charles Barnett, Esq.
1827 Henry Kingscote, Esq.
1828 A. F. Greville, Esq.
1829 John Barnard, Esq.
1830 Hon. G. Ponsonby
1831 Wm. Deedes, Esq.
1832 Henry Howard, Esq.
1833 Herbert Jenner, Esq.
1834 Hon. H. Ashley
1835 Lord Charles Russell
1836 Lord Suffield
1837 Viscount Grimston
1838 Marquis of Exeter
1839 Earl of Chesterfield
1840 Earl of Verulam
1841 Earl Craven
1842 Earl of March
1843 Earl of Ducie
1844 Sir John Bayley, Bart.
1845 Thos. Chamberlayne, Esq.
1846 Earl of Winterton
1847 Earl of Strathmore
1848 Earl of Leicester
1849 Earl of Darnley
1850 Earl Guernsey
1851 Earl Stamford and Warrington
1852 Viscount Dupplin
1853 Marquis of Worcester
1854 Earl Vane
1855 Earl of Uxbridge
1856 Viscount Milton
1857 Sir Frederick Bathurst, Bart.
1858 Lord Garlies
1859 Earl of Coventry
1860 Lord Skelmersdale
1861 Earl Spencer
1862 Earl of Sefton
1863 Lord Suffield
1864 Earl of Dudley
1865 Lord Ebury
1866 Earl of Sandwich
1867 Earl of Verulam
1868 Lord Methuen
1869 Marquis of Lansdowne
1870 J. H. Scourfield, Esq., M.P.
1871 Earl of Clarendon
1872 Viscount Down
1873 Earl of Cadogan
1874 Marquis of Hamilton
1875 Sir Charles Legard Bart., M.P.
1876 Lord Londesborough
1877 Duke of Beaufort
1878 Lord Fitzhardinge
1879 W. Nicholson, Esq.
1880 Sir Wm. Hart-Dyke, Bart., M.P.
1881 Lord George Hamilton
1882 Lord Belper
1883 Hon. Robert Grimston
1884 Earl of Winterton
1885 Lord Wenloch
1886 Lord Lyttelton
1887 The Hon. E. Chandos Leigh, Q.C.
1888 The Duke of Buccleuch
1889 Sir Henry James, Q.C.
1890 Lord W. de Eresby

Only one of them died in office, and that was the Hon. Robert Grimston in 1883, than whom no warmer supporter of the game ever lived. He closely identified himself in his later years with the I Zingari and Essex clubs; but he will be best remembered for his enthusiasm over the Eton and Harrow matches at Lord's. If you had wished to know what enthusiasm meant, you had only to keep your eye on him on these occasions. For the time being there was only one thing to him worth thinking about, and it was that particular match. He was oblivious to everything outside of it, and would listen to nothing that did not bear upon the past matches of the two schools, or the one going on. And as for cheering, coaching, and encouraging his own school, the majority of us were not to be compared with him. He desired a close, exciting match; but Harrow he would have win, and when it did, there was no happier man on earth.

The M.C.C. has always been fortunate in the gentlemen who have filled the offices of Treasurer and Secretary.

Past Treasurers:

F. Ladbrooke, Esq.	R. Kynaston, Esq.
H. Kingscote, Esq.	T. Burgoyne, Esq.

Present Treasurer:

The Hon. Sir Spencer Ponsonby Fane, K.C.B.

Past Hon. Secretaries:

1822 to 1841—Mr. B. Aislabie.
1842 to 1857—Mr. Roger Kynaston.
1858 to 1862—Mr. Alfred Baillie.
1863 to 1867—Mr. R. A. Fitzgerald.

On the 1st January, 1868, Mr. Fitzgerald became paid Secretary of the club at a salary of £400 per annum, which office he held until 1876. Mr. H. Perkins was elected in 1877 at the same salary, and is still in office.

ANNUAL LIST OF MATCHES PLAYED BY THE M.C.C. DURING THE LAST TWENTY YEARS.

Date.	*Matches.*	*Won.*	*Lost.*	*Drawn.*
1871	37	17	8	12
1872	44	21	10	13
1873	46	17	13	16
1874	50	19	18	13
1875	48	21	7	20
1876	60	23	16	21
1877	65	27	11	27
1878	77	33	18	26
1879	84	43	7	34
1880	95	42	17	36
1881	117	55	11	51
1882	123	47	24	52
1883	130	49	17	64
1884	121	59	34	28
1885	136	72	30	34
1886	128	76	26	26
1887	141	85	29	27
1888	147	75	23	49
1889	152	99	29	24
1890	160	84	40	36
	1961	964	388	609

UNIVERSITY CRICKET.

It will be very naturally asked, what do I know about University Cricket? Not very much, I admit; for I never was in residence at either Cambridge or Oxford. But I know something about University players, and I have made a point of watching the doings of both elevens with more than common interest; for well I know it is from them the Gentlemen must expect to improve in bowling strength to enable them to contend at all successfully against the Players. It may safely be said that, with two or three exceptions, the great amateur bowlers of the last 50 years have belonged to either Cambridge or Oxford, and, quoting from memory, I cannot remember a year in which the Gentlemen had not two or more players in their eleven from one or the other. And, speaking from my twenty-five years' experience of first-class cricket, I fail to see that it is likely to be otherwise in the future.

I know that good bowlers and batsmen are made long before the age at which public school boys usually go to Oxford or Cambridge, and that Eton, Harrow, Rugby, and one or two others ought to have the credit of having trained the eminent University players who have stirred the cricket world. Still there can be very little doubt that it is the hard discipline which comes after 17 or 18 years of age that develops the promising boy into a first-class player.

Cambridge has the credit of having produced more first-class bowlers than Oxford, and the names of the most prominent will come readily to the mind of every cricketer—Messrs. A. G. Steel and C. T. Studd in the past, and S. M. J. Woods and E. C. Streatfeild of to-day. Of course, if we go back farther, such great names as M. Kempson, C. D. Marsham, E. L. Fellowes, W. F. Maitland, R. Lang, H. M. Plowden, Hon. F. G. Pelham, W. N. Powys, D. Buchanan, S. E. Butler (who took all 10 wickets of Cambridge for 38 runs, in 1871), and others will be remembered. A still larger number might be mentioned; but those I have given are sufficient to prove what I have said—that the great amateur bowlers have mostly come from Oxford or Cambridge.

And the same may be said of our crack batsmen, though in a lesser degree. Such great names as J. Makinson, C. G. Lane, Hon. C. G. Lyttelton, R. A. H.

Mitchell, C. E. Green, W. Yardley, C. I. Thornton, W. H. Hadow, C. J. Ottaway, E. F. S. Tylecote, Lord Harris, A. J. Webbe, A. P. Lucas, Hon. A. Lyttelton, W. S. Patterson, Hon. E. Lyttelton, F. H. Buckland, A. G. Steel, C. T. Studd, Hon. Ivo Bligh, W. H. Patterson, Lord Hawke, J. H. Brain, T. C. O'Brien, K. J. Key, W. Rashleigh, Lord George Scott, H. J. Mordaunt, and others will be easily remembered: but they are by no means the only eminent batsmen who have helped materially to make cricket history during the last 25 years; for opposite them can be placed the names of a great many players of equal reputation who never belonged to either University. Nor is the reason for this far to seek; batting has always been the most popular branch of the game to the amateur, and it must be borne in mind that County Clubs, with their ground bowlers, have enabled him to keep up his form without drawing too much upon his time. Half-an-hour's practice twice a week is sufficient to keep most batsmen in form, and there are very few so placed who cannot obtain it.

Keeping up one's bowling form requires rather more attention. I know it is generally accepted that a really good bowler is born, not made; but that does not mean that he can trust to his natural talents alone to perform great feats. Nothing short of hard work, and plenty of it, will make a good bowler, however natural or exceptional his style; and, unfortunately, very few except University players seem to be able to give the necessary time.

About the best illustration I can remember at the moment is Mr. M. Kempson, with whom I have had many an interesting chat. His great desire was to play for the Gentlemen against the Players some day; and at Cambridge he used to bowl to the professionals, as well as have them bowl to him. In

1853, he bowled two hours a day for six weeks in preparation for the match; and it is now a matter of history how well he bowled, and, with Sir F. Bathurst, won the match for the Gentlemen. His careful preparation enabled him to do more with the ball than he ever did before or afterwards; and in that particular match he could almost do what he liked with it. And I remember he told me how smartly he got rid of Box, one of the most dangerous batsmen in the Players' eleven. Box's favourite hit was a smart cut between the slips, when he got the right ball. Mr. Kempson arranged with Mr. Nicholson, who was keeping wicket, to motion short-leg to third man as soon as he gave the signal. He did so before he delivered the last ball of the first over: bowled exactly the right ball, and Box cut it straight into Sir F. Bathurst's hands. Box's astonishment was something to be seen, not described.

The Universities have also given us some of the most brilliant of our amateur fieldsmen. Their name is legion; and I need not specify them, unless in the case of great wicket-keepers. The Hon. Alfred Lyttelton I have already referred to; but two others have since appeared who may claim the same excellence, Messrs. Philipson and McGregor. McGregor, in my estimation, is above the form of any amateur wicket-keeper who has yet represented his University, or played in any of the great contests.

The Oxford and Cambridge contests were begun in 1827, and except five have all been played at Lord's. The closest fights were in 1841, 1870, and 1875, when the victories were gained by the narrow majorities of eight, two, and six runs. On five occasions Oxford has won by an innings, whilst Cambridge has done the same thing thrice.

Not until 1870 did any player score 100 runs in an

innings; but it has been done thirteen times since. They are as follow:

Mr. K. J. Key (Oxford)	143 in 1886
Mr. W. Yardley (Cambridge)	130 in 1872
Mr. H. J. Mordaunt (Cambridge)	127 in 1889
Mr. G. B. Studd (Cambridge)	120 in 1882
Mr. F. H. Buckland (Oxford)	*117 in 1877
Mr. W. H. Game (Oxford)	109 in 1876
Mr. W. H. Patterson (Oxford)	*107 in 1881
Mr. W. Rashleigh (Oxford)	107 in 1886
Mr. W. S. Patterson (Cambridge)	*105 in 1876
Mr. E. Crawley (Cambridge)	*103 in 1887
Mr. C. W. Wright (Cambridge)	102 in 1883
Mr. H. W. Bainbridge (Cambridge) ...	101 in 1885
Mr. W. Yardley (Cambridge)	100 in 1870
Lord George Scott (Oxford)	100 in 1887

Eight of them go to the credit of Cambridge, six to Oxford.

The highest innings yet made in these matches have been—

Cambridge, 388 in 1872; 302 in 1876; and 300 in 1889
Oxford, 313 in 1887; 306 in 1881; and 304 in 1886

The Cambridge Eleven of 1878, under the captaincy of the Hon. E. Lyttelton, is considered to have been the strongest that ever played, and almost up to the form of an English representative eleven. Their defeat of the first Australian Eleven by an innings and 72 runs was the heaviest inflicted upon that team during the whole tour.

OXFORD v. CAMBRIDGE CONTESTS.

1827.	Played at Lord's, 4th June ...	Drawn.
1829.	Played at Oxford, 8th June...	Oxford won by 115 runs.
1836.	Played at Lord's, 23rd June...	Oxford won by 121 runs.
1838.	Played at Lord's, 6th July ...	Oxford won by 98 runs.
1839.	Played at Lord's, 17th June...	Cambridge won by an innings and 125 runs.

1840. Played at Lord's, 8th July ... Cambridge won by 63 runs.
1841. Played at Lord's, 14th July... Cambridge won by 8 runs.
1842. Played at Lord's, 9th June ... Cambridge won by 162 runs.
1843. Played at Oxford, 8th June... Cambridge won 54 runs.
1844. Played at Lord's, 4th July ... Drawn.
1845. Played at Lord's, 12th June... Cambridge won by 6 wickets.
1846. Played at Oxford, 11th June... Oxford won by 3 wickets.
1847. Played at Lord's, 17th June... Cambridge won by 138 runs.
1848. Played at Oxford, 15th June... Oxford won by 23 runs.
1849. Played at Lord's, 21st June... Cambridge won by 3 wickets.
1850. Played at Oxford, 6th June... Oxford won by 127 runs.
1851. Played at Lord's, 3rd July ... Cambridge won by an innings and 4 runs.
1852. Played at Lord's, 8th July ... Oxford won by an innings and 77 runs.
1853. Played at Lord's, 14th June... Oxford won by an innings and 19 runs.
1854. Played at Lord's, 3rd July ... Oxford won by an innings and 8 runs.
1855. Played at Lord's, 21st June... Oxford won 3 wickets.
1856. Played at Lord's, 16th June... Cambridge won by 3 wickets.
1857. Played at Lord's, 25th June... Oxford won by 81 runs.
1858. Played at Lord's, 21st June... Oxford won by an innings and 38 runs.
1859. Played at Lord's, 23rd June... Cambridge won by 28 runs.
1860. Played at Lord's, 25th June... Cambridge won by 3 wickets.
1861. Played at Lord's, 17th June... Cambridge won by 133 runs.
1862. Played at Lord's, 23rd June... Cambridge won by 8 wickets.
1863. Played at Lord's, 22nd June... Oxford won by 8 wickets.
1864. Played at Lord's, 13th June... Oxford won by 4 wickets.
1865. Played at Lord's, 26th June... Oxford won by 114 runs.
1866. Played at Lord's, 18th June... Oxford won by 12 runs.
1867. Played at Lord's, 1st July ... Cambridge won by 5 wickets.
1868. Played at Lord's, 22nd June... Cambridge won by 168 runs.
1869. Played at Lord's, 21st June... Cambridge won by 58 runs.
1870. Played at Lord's, 27th June... Cambridge won by 2 runs.
1871. Played at Lord's, 26th June... Oxford won by 8 wickets.
1872. Played at Lord's, 24th June... Cambridge won by an innings and 166 runs.
1873. Played at Lord's, 23rd June... Oxford won by 3 wickets.
1874. Played at Lord's, 29th June... Oxford won by an innings and 92 runs.
1875. Played at Lord's, 28th June... Oxford won by 6 runs.

1876.	Played at Lord's, 26th June...	Cambridge won by 9 wickets.
1877.	Played at Lord's, 25th June...	Oxford won by 10 wickets.
1878.	Played at Lord's, 1st July ...	Cambridge won by 238 runs.
1879.	Played at Lord's, 1st July ...	Cambridge won by 9 wickets.
1880.	Played at Lord's, 28th June...	Cambridge won by 115 runs.
1881.	Played at Lord's, 27th June...	Oxford won by 135 runs.
1882.	Played at Lord's, 26th June...	Cambridge won by 7 wickets.
1883.	Played at Lord's, 25th June...	Cambridge won by 7 wickets.
1884.	Played at Lord's, 30th June...	Oxford won by 7 wickets.
1885.	Played at Lord's, 29th June...	Cambridge won by 7 wickets.
1886.	Played at Lord's, 5th July ...	Oxford won by 133 runs.
1887.	Played at Lord's, 4th July ...	Oxford won by 7 wickets.
1888.	Played at Lord's, 28th June...	Drawn.
1889.	Played at Lord's, 1st July ...	Cambridge won by an innings and 105 runs.
1890.	Played at Lord's, 30th June...	Cambridge won by 7 wickets.

Matches played 56: Cambridge won 28, Oxford won 25, drawn 3.

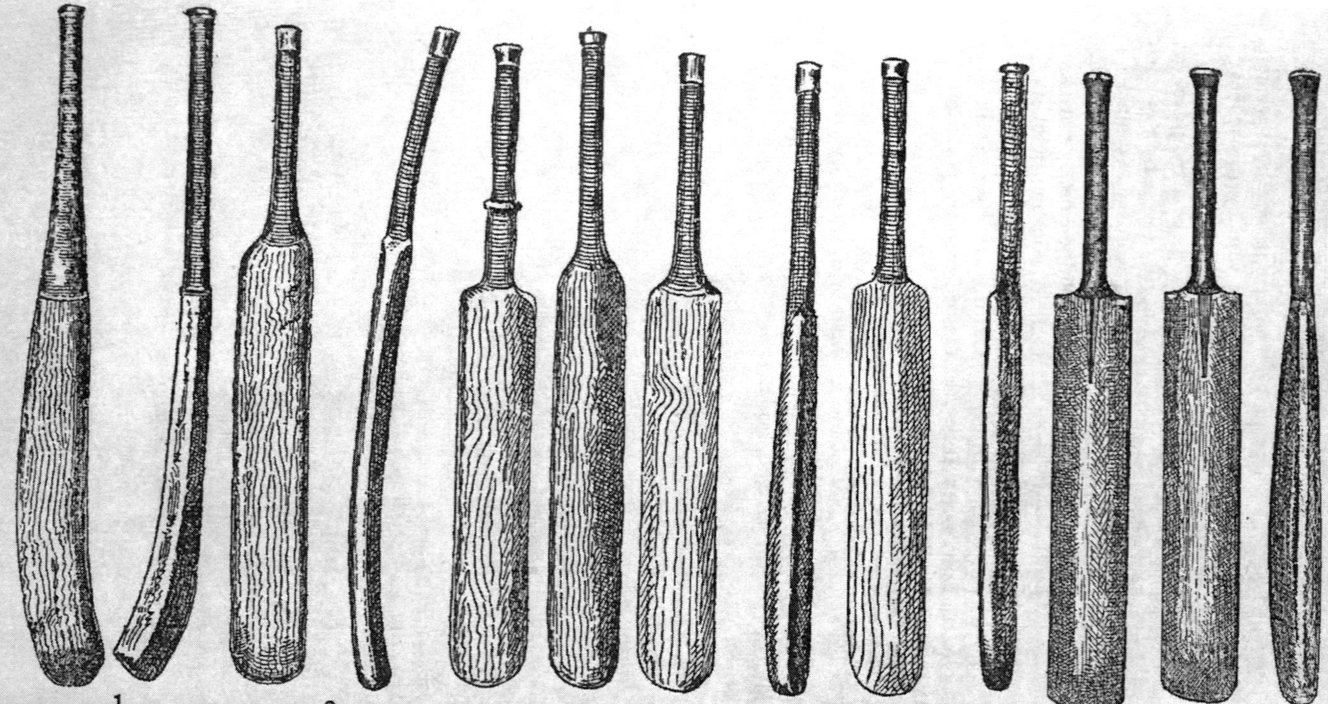

1 2 3 4 5 6 7 8

The drawings of Bats 1 to 6 are taken, by permission, from *Echoes from Old Cricket Fields*, by Mr. F. Gale. The approximate dates are as follow:—No. 1, *1743*; No. 2, weighing 5 lbs., *1771*; No. 3, *1790*—this is a double-handed bat, and belonged to Robinson, a man with a crippled hand, who wore an

CHAPTER VIII.

BATTING.

I SHOULD like to say that good batsmen are born, not made; but my long experience comes up before me, and tells me that it is not so. There are gifts of eye and wrist which nearly all good batsmen possess in a greater or lesser degree that enable them to play certain strokes with great effect; but, to acquire all-round proficiency, I am strongly convinced that constant practice and sound coaching have all to do with it. I try to remember the time when I first handled a bat, and I can recall nothing but the advice that was drilled into me — Stand well up to the wicket; keep your left shoulder well forward; practise constantly and put your whole heart into it.

Opinions vary as to the qualifications a player must possess to be classed as a first-class batsman, and I fear always will vary. Some of the players I have met possessed a beautifully free style, and gave the impression of being able to score largely; but somehow the runs never came. Some had a cramped and ungainly style, which provoked severe comments; but nevertheless the runs did come. Then there were others who kept up their wickets for hours for very small scores; while opposite them were free-hitters who made more runs in a tenth part of the time.

Now it will not do to say that all of them may not be described as first-class batsmen. To score 50 runs off one's own bat in an hour is a very fast rate of scoring, and if it be done in a free, hard-hitting style always commands our admiration. To score the same number in two or three hours by patient defence and quiet placing may not receive the same amount of praise, but under certain conditions it may be a more valuable innings to one's side. I do not sympathise with the batsman who plays only to keep up his wicket, and does not try to hit; but I do sympathise with those who, not possessing great hitting powers, keep adding quietly, though slowly, to the score as best they can.

I am now speaking to the young player, and will touch upon details that are too often neglected when he begins to play.

It may be safely laid down that the duty of a batsman is to make runs, and that he who can make them quickly or slowly as occasion requires belongs to the very highest class.

First let me urge upon him to practise in earnest from the outset, and if possible to get his first lesson from an experienced player. He need not have it from one who in his time made his hundreds against the finest bowling in England, and who talks about the glories of the past; a humbler individual, who has a real love for the game, will often be of more use, and will not be averse to showing how it is done. He has, in all likelihood, been through the mill himself, and knows that nothing short of patient practice will lead to success. That is the teacher worth listening to; but the pupil should not be content with his help alone. He should seek for every opportunity to witness the great players of the day, and watch their styles attentively, so that he may have both example and precept

One of the first essentials to the making of a good batsman is a good wicket. There are very few schools of any importance now without a cricket-ground, and the pitch is generally well looked after; but there are hundreds of beginners living in the country who are not so favoured, and who have to look after the pitch themselves. Let me impress on them the great need of doing so. I have said elsewhere that I cannot remember when we had not a good pitch at home; but let me say also that its condition was entirely owing to our own efforts. Many an hour we spent rolling it; and we had our reward. Once you have played on a good wicket, you will never be satisfied with an indifferent one.

You will be singularly fortunate if you have a piece of ground of any size at your home; but it is not absolutely necessary that it should be very large. Thirty to forty yards long, by fifteen to twenty broad, with stop-nets, will serve your purpose; and it will not be a disadvantage at that stage of your progress to be told that, for other than cricket reasons, you must keep the ball down when you hit. And you need not worry if the whole of the ground is not turfed over. As long as you have ten yards in good condition, carefully rolled in front of the wicket you are batting at, you have all that is needed for satisfactory practice.

Always play with a bat suited to your strength and height. Every boy longs for a full-sized bat, and thinks it a reproach to practise with anything else. I can assure you that you are going the wrong way to acquire a correct style if your wish be gratified, and may get into faulty habits that will stick to you all your life. Youth is the impressionable time for both mental and physical training, and in the majority of cases it is more difficult to unlearn than learn.

You may not always be able to get a bat the weight you desire, and very little mischief may result from playing with one two or three ounces too heavy, for weight does not affect your playing straight or driving properly; but it is better to err on the side of having one too light, for with a heavy one you cannot cut or time the ball correctly. A full-sized bat in the hands of a boy who is not very tall is an unwieldy weapon, and destructive of a free, sound style; and it is impossible to play straight with it. Is there any need for me to say that playing with a straight bat is more likely to protect your wicket than playing with a cross bat? If you have any doubt about it, get some one to hold a bat both ways in front of a wicket, and see for yourself which style covers it most.

As a rule, you will find that a bat is about the proper length for your height when you can ground it properly, and play perfectly straight while holding it about the middle of the handle, which is considered the best place to grip both for defensive and offensive purposes. A few stone wall players and some others play with the right hand close to the shoulder; but this, while admittedly good for defence, will undoubtedly cramp your hitting. E. F. S. Tylecote was the best first-class player I ever met who held the bat in that way. Going to the other extreme of holding it at the top of the handle will admit of loftier and more vigorous hitting, but it will weaken your defence. I believe in holding it with the right hand about half-way up, and the left just above it. With the hands in that position you are able to defend your wicket against all kinds of bowling and still hit freely.

While you are waiting for the ball, make sure that the hands are in the right position; grip the handle firmly, and keep the left shoulder well forward, or you will never play with a straight bat. But try to get some one to show you how to hold the bat and place the hands, and you will in five minutes get a better idea of the right and wrong ways of doing it than you would get in an hour from the most elaborate treatise ever written on batting. Indeed, this advice might be applied to many other details, as it is difficult to give a clear idea without drawings.

The next point is a very important one—where and how to stand at the wicket. It makes very little difference whether you take guard to cover middle stump or middle and leg; but the position of the feet cannot be too carefully studied and practised. Place the right foot just inside the crease, and make sure that the toes are clear of the wicket. The left foot should be outside the crease, clear of the wicket, at a distance to enable you to stand easily and move it backward or forward comfortably. Some players, and good players too, place the foot in front of the wicket; but that I am certain is a mistake, and with a bad umpire at the bowler's end may cause you to lose your wicket. The players themselves will be the first to tell you it is a bad habit; but it was one they acquired in their boyhood, and it has stuck to them since.

You must not go to the other extreme of standing too wide of the wicket, or you will give the bowler an opening to bowl you off your pads. I have always tried to keep my feet clear of the wicket, but so close that it was impossible for a ball to get past between the pads and the wicket. Sometimes I have drawn a line from the leg stump to the crease, so that I might see at a glance if my feet were clear, and it is not a bad habit for a young player to cultivate. Once he has got into the habit of standing correctly, he may drop doing it in a match, although I believe in taking every precaution whether practising or playing in a match.

Take your block a little more than a length of the bat from the wicket, and be sure to make a good mark so that you will not lose sight of it. If after playing for a little while it gets worn and dim, do not hesitate to ask the umpire to give it to you again.

You are now ready to play the ball, and will ground your bat in the block hole when the bowler begins his

MR. W. G. GRACE.

(Batting position as the bowler starts to bowl.)

run. One or two writers say: "Stand with your weight equally balanced on both legs." That I believe to be a grave mistake. The weight should be chiefly on the right leg, and kept there when you raise your bat to play the ball. For want of that being constantly drilled into the learner's head, he too often moves the right foot, which is opposed to all good play. Anything that will cause you to move the right foot when defending your wicket should be avoided, and I am inclined to think that standing with your weight equally balanced on both legs has a tendency that way. In fact, I believe it to be good advice that the beginner's right foot should be pegged down for some time, until he acquire ease and confidence in playing back and forward.

Another mistake committed is twirling or flourishing the bat after you have raised it from the block hole, preparatory to hitting or playing the ball. It serves no practical purpose, unless it be to cover your nervousness, and it is decidedly bad form. You have all your work cut out to keep your eye on the bowler's arm, and flourishing the bat does not help you; besides, I very much question if you can come down so quickly on a shooter with the bat constantly on the move, as you can holding it quietly a few inches from the ground.

And now we come to the first and important stage in the art of batting—how to keep up your wicket. That must be the aim of the beginner; for no one will ever score largely and consistently who cannot do it. It is better a thousand times to be able to keep your wicket up for an hour, even if you only score ten runs, than to make the same number of runs in the first over and be bowled the next. I admit that the addition to the total score is the same; but ten runs in an hour, if made by the first or fifth man of your side, are worth double that number made in a couple of overs; for in all probability you will have taken the sting out of the bowling, and paved the way for the batsmen who follow.

The art of defence may be summed up thus: the power to play both forward and back. It was not an uncommon thing years ago to hear it said of this and that player, "Oh, he plays everything back, and is wonderfully strong and patient in his defence." If you had asked, "Cannot he play forward also?" you would very likely have been told that he did not trouble about it, and that the wicket was too rough and bumpy to attempt it; besides, he had such a long reach that the balls he could not play back to he could invariably hit. Now if anyone were to make that statement to-day, he might escape ridicule, but believe me he would be very quickly classed as a second-rate batsman. The wickets are now too good to be used as an excuse, while so accurate has become the bowling, that a batsman who could only play back would very quickly get stuck up, and be caught at point or short-slip.

Both styles of play must be cultivated, and until the beginner has acquired proficiency in them his defence will be very imperfect. The grand essential is to keep the right foot firm and play with a straight bat. If you are compelled to play back, you will have to draw back the left foot; but on no account must you move the right. That you must keep as firm as if it were riveted to the ground, or you will very likely be driven on to your wicket. And do not forget to keep your left shoulder well forward and come down on the ball with firmness.

The great secret of good back play is a quick eye and watching the ball. Perhaps the bowler is bowling round the wicket, and you have taken guard for middle-stump. He may bowl on the off stump a ball not far enough up to play forward to, but with sufficient break to hit the leg stump; you will then have to change quickly to protect it. Or the ball may have break enough to hit the pads and cannon on to the wicket, if you are not quick enough with eye and wrist to meet it. Be sure to grip the bat firmly, and have the handle sloping slightly forward, and be on the look-out for an occasional shooter. They do not come so often as they used to, but that makes them all the more dangerous when they do come.

Whatever you do, do not get in front of the wicket when you play the ball. There is no need to give that bit of advice as long as you keep the right foot firm and in the position I have already advised you to place it when standing at the wicket; but unfortunately there are a few of our very finest batsmen to-day who step right in front to most balls, whose example you may be tempted to follow. You cannot be too much on your guard against it; for, sooner or later, a bowler with a good head on his shoulders will get a ball past your bat, and you will have to pay the penalty of l.b.w. There are others who get in front when the ball is pitched just outside the leg stump in trying to play it hard to square-leg. My experience has shown me that it is unnecessary even then, and that by keeping your right foot firmly in its place and drawing back the left until the heels are almost touching, you can resort to what is called the glide stroke and place the ball to leg.

To play forward, you must advance the left leg; but must take care not to over-reach yourself, or you will move the right foot. Keeping the right foot on the ground is even more important in playing forward than playing back; for you have to remember that it is just on the edge of the crease, and the slightest movement may cause you to lift it, and if you miss the ball a smart wicket-keeper will stump you before you can recover yourself. You can find out for yourself, by practising at a wicket without a bowler, how far you can reach with safety without dragging the right foot.

Another very important thing to remember in playing forward is, never to place the bat further forward than the level of the left foot, and to be sure to have the handle of it slanting, so that the top of it is nearer than the blade to the bowler. Upon that will depend whether you meet the ball firmly and correctly. Try to have the bat as close to the left leg as you can with safety, so that if the ball should break slightly back, it will not pass between the bat and the pads.

Forward and back play are the two strokes you must rely on to protect your wicket, and you must practise them diligently. Occasionally you will get a ball which puts you in two minds, and, for want of decision to play one way or the other, it may either beat you altogether, or cause you to play it in a half-hearted way and be caught. I have invariably found that when that occurred with me I had either been careless in watching the bowler's arm, or that he had deceived me by altering his pace without a change of action. Spofforth and Lohmann are good at that, and have taken in many batsmen the first time they bowled against them.

When that experience comes, you will have to be quick to get out of the difficulty; there is only one way that I know of, and that is, to meet it with the half-cock stroke. You have made up your mind to play forward, and taken the initial step; but at the last moment you find that the ball is going to pitch shorter than you at first thought. You must rely on your arms to extricate you from the difficulty by drawing back the bat until it is just over the popping-crease, a few inches from the ground. Drawing back the left foot alone will not help you; therefore concentrate upon a rapid use of the arms.

I shall now enumerate the wickets upon which I have found forward play and back play most effective.

A fast, dry and true wicket.
A fast, good wet wicket.
A slow, good wicket after rain.
A drying sticky wicket.

On a fast, dry and true wicket I never hesitate to play forward; for the bowler can get little or no work on the ball, and, what is more, the further it is pitched up and the faster it comes along the easier it is to play forward to it. My scores of 344 for M.C.C. *v.* Kent, and 318 not out for Gloucestershire *v.* Yorkshire, in 1876, were made on wickets of that kind, and I played forward to nearly every good-length ball.

I carry out the same principle on a fast, good wet wicket; for the bowler has much difficulty in getting work on the ball, owing to its wet, slippery state: but I watch the ball more carefully, for I know it will occasionally keep low and travel faster after it pitches, while shooters occur more frequently than on a dry wicket.

On a slow, good wicket after rain the bowler can get more work on the ball than on a good, fast wicket; but the ball does not come so quickly off the pitch, and it rarely rises higher than the bails. You can play either back or forward on a wicket of that kind, according to the pitch of the ball; but in playing forward you must not play too quickly, as the ball sometimes hangs a bit, and you may play it back to the bowler. Turner beat me with his second ball in that way in the first innings of the England *v.* Australia match at Lord's on the 21st July, 1890; and I candidly confess I felt, and I daresay looked, particularly foolish over it. Playing a little too soon at the ball, which got up and hung, I met it on the shoulder of the bat, and an easy catch to

Turner followed. In the second innings the wicket was much faster, and I felt quite at home and played forward with perfect confidence.

Back play is most effective on a drying sticky wicket. That is about the worst you can play on; for the ball not only gets up high, but the bowler can get a great amount of work on it, and you have no course but to watch it until the last moment and play back to it. Keep your eye on the bowler; watch how he holds the ball and runs up to the wicket before delivering it, and you may be able to detect any alteration in length and pace. And never get flurried whatever his action may be; for if you take your eyes off his arm or lose your head for a second, he has you at a disadvantage.

And now I come to a point which is fast becoming a characteristic of all good batsmen; and that is, playing the ball with the bat, and not allowing the ball to hit the bat. Your forward play and back play may be perfect; but if you can only stop the ball, you will never belong to the ranks of first-class batsmen. Make an effort to play the ball away from you with some force, and with practice you will do it as readily as merely stopping it and allowing it to roll a yard or two away. In Chapter III. I pointed out that it was years before I gained sufficient command of the bat to enable me to place the ball where I wished. At first I was content to be able to play it away anywhere; but with constant practice I gained the power of placing it between the fieldsmen.

I firmly believe most players can do the same if they only try hard enough. Eye and wrist will respond when the brain commands; but here and there you may find a batsman who seems to be able to do better than another. Timing the ball is the secret of all good play; and timing, as far as I can make out, means the harmonious working of eye, wrist, arms, legs, and shoulders, which can only be acquired by constant practice.

It may be said that keeping up one's wicket is all very well, but what about hitting and the making of runs? Well, let me tell you that if you can keep up your wicket and play the ball hard away from you, runs will come. There is a variety of hits that ought to be touched upon, such as the cut, the leg-hit, the drive, &c.; but they almost demand a treatise to themselves.

Of the cut, the most charming of all strokes, because it seems to be made with very little effort, I may say that it depends entirely on the perfect timing of the ball. The right foot should be moved to the front of the off stump, and the stroke should be made with the wrist when the ball is about a foot in front of the wicket. Half the secret of good cutting consists in hitting slightly over the ball, which will cause it to touch the ground at a short distance from the wicket without affecting its speed. The batsman should not be satisfied that it is a genuine cut unless the ball travels more in the direction of long-slip than point; of course, I am speaking of a fast good-length ball, a little outside the off stump. A long-hop should be hit hard between point and mid-off with a horizontal bat, and the batsman should advance the left leg in front of the wicket in doing it; or if the ball is not very wide, he should draw back the right foot: that is one of Mr. W. W. Read's best strokes.

There is very little leg-hitting now-a-days, owing to the wonderful accuracy of the bowling. The bowler, as a rule, has eight men on the off side of the wicket, and very seldom bowls to leg. Occasionally you may get a half-volley on the pads, or slightly inside of them; but that should be driven between short-leg and mid-on, instead of pulled to leg. When you get a good-length ball, or one a little over-pitched, just outside of the pads, the proper way to treat it is to throw out the left leg and hit as near to the pitch as possible with a horizontal bat, but be careful not to get under the ball; if it is a long-hop, then you should draw back the left leg and hit or play it to leg.

In driving, you should aim at getting well over the ball and playing with a straight bat, and not be satisfied unless you keep the ball well down. Of course you will notice if the fieldsmen are too close in, or if the boundaries are short, and may risk something in lofty hitting instead of driving. It used to be considered by some very good players bad cricket to hit a straight ball, whatever the length of it. On the faith of it, Wootton and Grundy, two of the very best bowlers of their time, placed all their fieldsmen, with the exception of long-leg, close in, and treated the batsmen to an occasional long-hop or half-volley with perfect complacence. I believe my brother E.M. was the first to upset that theory by hitting the ball as hard as he could over the bowler's head, or to long-on, and not troubling about the flight of it. I considered the example a good one and followed in his footsteps, and I do the same thing to-day under similar circumstances; but you very seldom have the chance now, as all bowlers have one or two men in the long field.

The great thing in hitting is, not to be half-hearted about it; but when you make up your mind to hit, to do it as if the whole match depended upon that particular stroke. That applies especially to slow round-arm or lob bowling. The fear of being stumped has deterred many a man from running out far enough, and a weak hit, followed by a catch, is the result. You may as well be hanged for a sheep as a lamb; so go out with a will, hit hard, and forget there is a wicket-keeper or fieldsman within a mile of you.

It is a mistake to hit at the pitch of slow round

or underhand bowling. There is generally sufficient twist on the ball to beat you, and if you do not miss it altogether, you will most likely get caught at cover-point. And the same may be said of a medium-pace good-length ball on the off stump, breaking slightly away from you. In my younger days, when I was quicker of foot than now, I often ran out to slow round and underhand bowling, and hit the ball full pitch, or waited and got it long-hop. I still consider it good play, and there is no doubt it has a demoralising effect on some bowlers.

There are two or three other hits that I might allude to; but those I have touched on are the principal ones, and the beginner should practise them as often as he can. He should also make a point of watching every first-class batsman, and make a note of his characteristic strokes. Very rarely will he find two batsmen hit in the same way, and it is always of interest to note where they differ. I also think it useful in practice to indulge in an occasional burst of hard hitting, but always try to keep the ball well down.

Judgment as to how and when to run is one of the characteristics of a good batsman. You should always back up two or three yards, but not before the ball is delivered, or the bowler may put down the wicket and run you out. Remember that it is the striker's duty to call if the ball is hit in front of the wicket, and the non-striker's, as a rule, if hit behind the wicket. When you call for a run, shout in a decided manner. Run hard directly your partner calls you, if you intend to go; if not, stop him at once. The great thing is to make up your mind instantly, and you will then be seldom run out. Do not run up the centre of the pitch, as you will cut it up; and to avoid collisions you and your partner should each, if possible, run on his own side, and certainly not cross more than once.

"Always run for a catch" is an old adage, and very good advice if the run is an easy one; but if there is any chance of a run-out, you should never do so. Never fail to run your bat along the ground for a yard or two before you reach the popping-crease. Many a batsman would have saved his wicket had he taken this precaution; for want of it, many have been run out. The first run should always be at your top speed: but do not rush past the wicket as some do; turn quickly, and be ready for another. When a ball is hit to the long field, and both batsmen are on the "look-out," a second run can often be obtained if the fieldsman fumbles the ball or throws it in slowly. It is astonishing what a sharp run can be made with safety by two good men who understand each other; when it is repeated two or three times, the field often becomes demoralised, and by mistakes and reckless throwing-in adds many runs to the score. A good example of this was shown last year by S. M. J. Woods and G. McGregor, who, for Lord Londesborough's XI. *v.* Australians, almost played tip-and-run for a few overs, and put on 24 runs for the last wicket.

There are many other points to be considered, such as knowing when to play a slow, patient game, or a forcing game; but these are the growth of time, and an experienced captain considers it a part of his duties to point them out to you. Just let me say that the prominent characteristic of all first-class batsmen is consistency in scoring. They display the same carefulness after having made a hundred runs as they do after scoring ten. Try to follow in their footsteps; for that is the only way to score largely. And never grumble if you have a run of ill-luck and fail to score heavily for weeks in succession. It is an experience which comes to us all at some time or other, and he is made of sterling stuff, and a real lover of our grand old game, who accepts it cheerfully. And—always be modest in the hour of success.

* * * * * *

I ought to have said something about the young batsman's outfit. Too little attention is paid to that by fairly good coaches; but, believe me, bad-fitting boots, or boots without proper spikes, may make all the difference in your play. No good cricketer is careless on that point; for he knows well that he must feel at ease, if he hopes to be at all successful. Pads that do not fit comfortably will tire you as much as hard hitting, and you should make sure before you begin your innings that they are carefully strapped, and not likely to get loose.

Gloves are even more important, and if they do not fit nicely, will affect your hitting. No player of any eminence now bats without a right-hand glove at least; but I strongly advocate both right and left being used. And you cannot be too careful about the quality of the rubber; for a blow on the back of the hand or fingers when imperfectly covered, will play sad havoc with your scoring, and may stop your cricket for some time. You should also make sure that the fastenings are all right, as carelessness there will make the hands uncomfortable; and a loose, flapping glove may be the cause of your losing your wicket, as the ball is more likely to hit a glove of that description than one firmly fastened.

And a belt instead of a scarf is sometimes an element of danger. The handle of the bat may come in contact with the buckle, and the noise be mistaken by the umpire for a snick off the bat. In fact, I once saw a man given out in that way. The ball passed so close to the bat, that the umpire, hearing a snick, thought it must have touched it; and, on being appealed to, unhesitatingly gave him out.

CHAPTER IX.

BOWLING.

THE majority of cricket writers whose opinions are worth reading are agreed that a first-class bowler is born, not made, and my experience of cricket has confirmed the truth of it. I have met but few bowlers in the first flight who did not possess the natural gift of making the ball come more quickly off the pitch than one would expect; but not one can tell how he does this. Mr. M. Kempson, whose bowling helped the Gentlemen to beat the Players in 1853, is of opinion that the secret of bowling is incommunicable, but a gift improvable by practice to any degree of perfection. I am not going to cry down perseverance and energy, for I owe too much to them; but I repeat, a first-class bowler must have the inestimable something which enables him to begin bowling as naturally as a duck takes to water. Afterwards it depends entirely on himself whether he is to make a great name or not. There is only one way of doing that, and it is by sheer hard work with muscle and brain.

Physical strength alone will not do on the perfect wickets we have nowadays: it must be accompanied with a good head. How often have we heard it said of this and the other bowler that he has not come up to the promise of his youth, although he has been a most diligent and exemplary worker! We have no need to go far for an explanation: it all lies in the not uncommon experience that he has the misfortune to be lacking in brain power, and will never be other than a member of the ding-dong "stuff-em-in" type if he were to practise for a hundred years. He can do what he is told, bowl straight and keep a good length; but he has not the power to read the batsman's thoughts, or the ingenuity to find out his weakness. He will always be a good change bowler, but will never reach the first class.

Several things should be impressed on the young bowler when he begins, but the following in particular:

> Bowl straight.
> Bowl a good length.
> Vary your pace and pitch.
> Try to get some break on the ball.
> Learn something about the nature and condition of the wicket on which you are bowling.
> Seek for the weak spots in the batsman's defence.

Anybody can bowl fairly straight is a truism; but how many can do it without tiring quickly? The young bowler should be taught to begin at eighteen or twenty yards, a distance at which he can bowl without over-extending himself, and not be satisfied unless he can hit the stumps pretty often. The length of run he must find out for himself; but one great point he must observe—not to stop for a second when he reaches the crease before he delivers the ball. I have seen a good many bowlers do that, who could only account for it by the fact that they had been taught badly and could not help doing it. Well, it is a very bad habit, for half the benefit of the run is lost. The young bowler should be corrected every time he does it. Years ago I rather fancied a short run, believing it tired the bowler less; but I have changed my opinion, and would advise something between six and ten yards or more. Nearly all the good bowlers we have to-day, no matter their pace, take a longish run, and the giants of the past did the same thing. Mr. S. M. J. Woods, Lohmann, Briggs, Peel and Attewell are the most prominent of our English bowlers at present, and all take a good run; and the Australians, Messrs. Spofforth, Boyle, Turner and Ferris, do the same.

The young player cannot do better than watch first-class bowlers carefully, make a note of their styles, and mark their points of difference.

Another point that used to be urged strongly was to present a full front to the batsman at the moment the ball left the hand. That has been considerably modified of late years, and there are now more advocates for a side position. Presenting a full front means that the bowler's arm can be seen plainly before the ball leaves the hand—a point in favour of the batsman; a side position means that arm and hand are hidden until the last moment—a point in favour of the bowler. I could mention the names of half-a-dozen bowlers, of whom it has been said that their delivery was a most puzzling one, and that it was pretty much owing to their being able to keep their arm out of sight. Of others, again, it has been said: "We have no difficulty with them—we can see them all the way."

I am not advocating the cultivation of a style merely for the purpose of distracting the attention of the batsman; but I would point out the great success that has attended such bowlers as Messrs. C. A. Smith, Spofforth, Giffen and Ferris, who have peculiar deliveries. When Smith begins his run he is behind the umpire and out of sight of the batsman; and I can assure you it is rather startling when he suddenly appears at the bowling crease. Spofforth goes to the other extreme, starting some yards on the off-side of the batsman, and giving the impression that he is aiming at a point nearer

MR. S. M. J. WOODS

short-leg than the wicket. G. Giffen is even more tantalising; for, just before the ball leaves his hand, his arm is completely hidden, and there is more of his back than his face to be seen. Ferris, the left-hander, starts his long run with his bowling-hand close to his leg; when he has got over three or four yards he brings both hands together almost on a level with his chin, and looks as if he were kissing the tips of his fingers to the crowd. Down goes the hand again, another trot of four yards and he brings his hands together above his head; and just as you get a little bit excited and wonder when he is really going to bowl, his arm disappears behind, to re-appear with startling rapidity to deliver the ball. J. C. Shaw, the famous left-hander, also puzzled most batsmen the first over or two. He brought his arm from behind his back, and caused me a lot of trouble in the early part of most innings I played against him. I could name many others who want careful watching; but those I have given are sufficient to prove what I say—that the bowler who delivers the ball sideways is more difficult to watch than the bowler who delivers it with a full front.

The next point to be considered is the height of the arm in delivering the ball. It may now be safely accepted that above the shoulder is more effective than under it; in fact, the higher the better. If the wicket be at all fast, the ball invariably comes quicker off the pitch, rises higher, and is more likely to lead to a catch. However, care must be taken to bowl with a free arm, or there will be very little sting—or "devil" as it is called—in the ball. Most of the great fast bowlers of the past had a beautiful arm action, and have not been surpassed in that respect by Lohmann, Turner, or Sharpe—three of the most prominent bowlers we have at the present time.

George Freeman, the best fast bowler I ever played

against, had a lovely free action, though he did not raise his arm much above the shoulder. He did not appear so fast as he really was; but he made the ball come quickly off the pitch, and he took many wickets with balls that kept low. John Jackson was slightly before my time, but his arm action delighted me the little I saw of it. Tarrant, with his long run all over the place, was another: then there was Allen Hill, whose beautiful delivery was a model for all time. Martin McIntyre, with his head-over-heels action, though not in the same bowling class as Freeman and Jackson, got up his pace entirely owing to his freedom of arm; and Mold and Sharpe, of the present time, are worthy of being watched. And amongst the amateurs may be mentioned, Messrs. C. D. Marsham, Foord-Kelcey, Christopherson, A. H. Evans, R. Lipscomb, and S. M. J. Woods.

The young bowler must not think because he can bowl straight that he is worthy of taking his place amongst good bowlers. He is still in the very elementary stage and not out of the alphabet of the game. A good length is the next thing to be studied, and though I have put it second on the list, it is really the key-note to all good bowling. Delivery, break, and pace are much to be desired, but without length they are utterly useless. There are some bowlers who, by their wonderful accuracy of length, stick up the batsmen and get wickets on the most perfect grounds, and I need only mention Attewell, who is without a superior to-day, as a fine example of what I refer to. Good wickets reduce most bowlers to a level, and it is only the good-length and head bowlers who can do anything on them. Willsher was past his best when I met him; but though he had lost much of his break and pace, he still kept a grand length, and was successful up to the last day he played. Break and pace may go, and very often do go earlier than one could wish, but as long as a bowler preserves his length he can do good work in most elevens.

A good-length ball may be described as one which very often finds the batsmen in two minds. He is in doubt whether to play forward or back to it, and while he is deciding, either the ball beats him altogether, or he spoons it to a fieldsman close in. It is difficult to say exactly the distance it should pitch from the batsman's wicket, but the opinion of very good and experienced players is, that for slow bowling it should pitch about four yards from the wicket ; for medium pace, four and a-half yards to five; for fast, from five to seven. Of course the quality of the batsman will always have to be considered; for what may be a good-length ball to a batsman with a short reach, will be almost a half-volley to a tall player possessing an exceptionally long reach. The beginner cannot do better, however, than to put a mark, say a feather or a piece of paper, at either of the distances I have mentioned, according to his pace, and practise diligently. Anything pitched within a foot of it will be a good-length ball, and will test the defence of any batsman.

I said that the young bowler should begin at a distance suited to his strength. Let me now press upon him the greater need not to exceed his strength when he is able to bowl the full length. Promising bowlers have been ruined for want of that caution, especially amongst the amateurs. The temptation to bowl just a little faster ought to be repressed rather than encouraged, for it is fatal to success and not unlikely to lead to a breakdown. Find out exactly what you can do in practice without tiring, and stick to it. It is a rule that cannot be too strongly taken to heart in learning; for on our vastly improved wickets to-day the innings are of longer duration, and the physical strain demanded of a first-class bowler is greater than at any time since the game began. I need only allude to the exceptionally hard work which Turner and Ferris went through for the Australian Elevens which came to us in 1888 and 1890. It would not have surprised anyone if either had broken down. Every player aiming at becoming a really good bowler for his county must face the fact that he may have to bowl for hours and days at a time, and that bowling above his strength will wear him out and lead to short-length balls which the most indifferent batsman can play with ease.

Vary your pace is my next bit of advice. That does not mean you are to bowl a lot of balls faster than you are in the habit of doing, but rather that you are to resort to slower ones. Of course you will indulge in a fast one occasionally; but remember that you will find it easier to keep your good length in attempting a slower one. You must try to hide a change of action in your delivery, or an acute batsman will at once perceive it, and be on his guard. The great Australian bowlers are very good at bowling a slower or faster ball without a perceptible change of action.

Spofforth, in particular, was a master of the art, and I question if anyone has surpassed him since. He was most successful with his medium-pace balls, which were rather slower than his usual deliveries. There was the same run, the same action, the same elevation; and so completely was the batsman deceived that he played seconds too soon and was completely beaten. Palmer was another who was very successful in the same way; and Alfred Shaw was for years the chief amongst English bowlers in that respect. Shaw was a model of beautiful style and accurate length, and, at his best, could stick up the best batsmen in England. His change of pace was generally to a slower ball; and now and then he changed his elevation, a device which put the batsman in two minds.

Lohmann to-day is equally effective; and it is simply ludicrous to watch batsman after batsman walk into the trap. After the trick was done one could not help saying, "What an absurdly simple ball to have been bowled by!"—but, all the same, it was a triumph of the bowler's art.

Try to get some break on the ball. That is the next stage for the young bowler, and must be acquired if he desires to reach the first class. There are times when the wicket is perfection, and straight good-length balls have little effect against a first-rate batsman. He keeps playing them with a straight bat, hoping to tire the bowler out, when loose ones will come and the runs with them. Professional batting is improved all round; but its strongest point is the unwearied patience and strong defence of its finest representatives. If the young bowler thinks he will tire out a Shrewsbury, a Gunn—I shall not say a Scotton—he is hugely mistaken; and if he has nothing but straight good-length balls in his attack, he may make up his mind for a long day's work.

As soon as he has mastered length, he must try to add to his skill the power of breaking the ball, and then he may safely believe that he is within measurable distance of becoming first class. The amount of break he can get on the ball will depend very much on his pace. Should he be fast he must not hope for too much, for the two rarely go together. Slow and medium-pace bowlers do most at that, and get from one inch to two feet on a favourable wicket. A very important point is, whatever amount one does put on, to try to have sufficient command of the ball so that if it beat the batsman it will hit the wicket. It is a confession of weakness trying to put on six inches and find it breaking twelve, beating the batsman and yet missing the wicket.

I have seen Spofforth, time after time, vary his break from three to twelve inches the same over, and every time the ball got past the batsman it hit the wicket. No greater compliment can be paid to any bowler, for his ability to do it shows that he has perfect command of the ball. If the bowler be right-handed, he breaks, as a rule, from the off; if left-handed, generally from leg. Here and there you may find a phenomenon who can do it both ways; but then he is a phenomenon, and one does not write for that class of bowler.

The state of the wicket has much to do with the amount of break to be obtained. When it is dry and hard you must be content with very little indeed; but after heavy rains, with a strong sun drying it, you may be able to perform wonders. A. G. Steel and Spofforth amongst the amateurs, Peate, Alfred Shaw and J. C. Shaw amongst the professionals, used to perform great things then, the amount of curl they got on being simply astonishing. Mr. D. Buchanan, Jimmy Southerton and Barratt belonged to that school; and Messrs. Turner and Ferris, and Peel and Briggs, of our own time, are very effective also.

The next point to be considered is: learn something about the nature and condition of the wicket on which you are bowling. Nothing shows the experienced captain so much as the thought he exercises before a match. Before he has tossed for choice of innings, he has examined the wicket carefully, taken into consideration the changes which are likely to occur during the next hour or two, and deliberated whether they will be in favour of the batsman or the bowler. Surely it is not too much to expect the bowler, upon whom so much depends, to give the same thought.

Remember it is a very old saying that "a match well made is half won." There are very few grounds on which a bowler may not find one end more helpful than the other. Perhaps there is a slight slope which will enable him to get a great deal of twist on the ball, or a spot that will cause it to kick and rise quickly off the pitch. Not to find that out before the match begins means that the bowler has failed to do his duty to his side, and lacks one of the characteristics of a first-class player.

Old Nyren says in his treatise of the game: "Contrive, if fortune so favour you, that your bowler shall bowl his first ball *when a cloud is passing over.*" I have never been able to have the cloud passing when I bowled my first ball—indeed, I have rarely noticed the cloud passing at all—but on more than one occasion I have observed a distracting glare or leafy tree behind one of the wickets, and I always took particular care to put my most deadly bowler on at that end. Now, if a captain can notice these amongst the multitude of things he has to consider, surely a bowler ought to. Then there are some grounds on which the ball bounds higher than others, and a short-pitched one cannot be pulled very easily. That is something to know when you put in a faster one occasionally and cannot be so sure of your length. Lord's ground was of that nature not so many years ago, and Wootton and Grundy, who knew every foot of it, never hesitated to bowl a little bit short. There are many other points of detail which a bowler ought to know, but I need not enumerate them. I have said sufficient to make the bowler think for himself, if he possess the thinking faculties; if he does not, he may as well give up the hope of ever becoming first-class.

And that brings me to my last point—seek for the weak spot in the batsman's defence. There are very few batsmen without one, and the sooner you find it out the better for your side and yourself. No one plays the first over or two with the same confidence he shows after he has been batting for a quarter of an hour, and if you can only spot his weakness and lay siege to it, then you have an excellent chance of getting him out. It used to be considered a very good plan to bowl a yorker to a batsman immediately he came in, on the assumption, I believe, that he would not be ready for it. A straight half-volley was also thought likely to find him half-hearted in hitting, and a catch sure to follow. Now most batsmen have made up their minds to get either of those balls early in their innings, and you must not be disappointed if you fail to succeed with it. One thing I can tell you: it is a huge mistake to give him a short one. It is the one ball which he can see best of all, and he rarely fails to play it. Repeat it, and you have given him a favourable start, and will have some difficulty in finding his weak spot and getting him out.

It is better a thousand times to bowl an over-pitched ball than a short one at any time of his innings. You cannot do better than begin in your usual way, aiming at a good-length straight ball, and not attempting too much. If you find that he is playing confidently, then you may change your tactics and tempt him to hit. You need not be disheartened because your good balls have been played so easily, for there are more ways of getting a batsman out than bowling him. The mistake is too often made of pegging straight at the wicket to keep down the runs, trusting that the batsman will sooner or later allow one to pass him. Maiden overs are useful in their way, and serve a good purpose when they are bowled by a change bowler to give the principal bowler of his side a rest, but a really first-class bowler has something else to think about. He is played to get men out, and by hook or crook he means to do it.

Messrs. Spofforth, Boyle and Ferris, of the Australians, and Mr. A. G. Steel, Freeman, A. Shaw, Southerton, and Tom Emmett, were a treat to witness in that respect. They gave the batsman no rest, and tried him with every conceivable kind of ball until he made a mistake. If he had a particular hit they humoured him, but they took care to have a safe pair of hands waiting for it: if they failed to beat him with a break-back, they tried a simple straight one, or tossed a full-pitch at him; in short, did everything to prevent him from feeling at home. I remember once at Cheltenham, when playing for Gloucestershire *v.* Nottinghamshire, placing an extra man at long-leg and bowling entirely for catches, and it was amusing to find how one after another fell into the trap and were caught out. Of course I could depend on my fieldsmen, and that is a point slow and medium-pace bowlers must always consider.

Fast bowlers depend on their pace and length to beat the batsmen, slow bowlers depend principally on their fieldsmen. I am sorry to say there are exceptions here and there. More than once I have seen a medium-pace bowler deliver a goodly number of balls, all of them a good length, who thought he had done particularly well because no runs had been scored. He felt slightly hurt when it was pointed out to him that there were ten men in the field who would not mind attempting a catch and be glad to have a little more exercise than the mere promenade at the end of each over. Most big hitters lift the ball occasionally when they are given a straight half-volley, or one slightly to leg. And remember that though the old trap of bowling outside the off-stump and causing the ball to break away from the batsman is well known, very few can resist having a smack at it some time in their innings.

An article on bowling would not be complete without some reference to slow underhand, or, to use the familiar word, "lobs." Fast underhand and daisy-cutters are seldom seen now-a-days, and would have little chance on our perfect wickets; but lobs are still as effective as ever, and there are two or three first-class batsmen who, after playing all kinds of round-arm bowling with confidence, lose their heads entirely at the sight of lobs.

The lob bowler, like the slow round-arm bowler, must depend on his field, especially on his wicket-keeper, and not mind being hit. Good men have been and will continue to be clean bowled by a ball of that kind, but for one clean bowled the lob bowler may expect half-a-dozen caught out or stumped. The bowler should guard against being too slow, or a quick-footed batsman will hit him full pitch; but whatever mistake he makes, he must not bowl too short. And the elevation should not be too high, or he will get hit all over the ground; although there are some batsmen who spoon a ball which is bowled straight at them before touching the ground. Of course the more break a lob bowler can get on the better, and he must be very accurate in his length. That was the great characteristic of old Clarke's lobs, the finest lob bowler we have ever had; but he also possessed the gift of making the ball come quickly off the pitch. I have it on good authority that at his best he could pitch a ball half-a-dozen times in succession on a spot not more than three inches in diameter; and I firmly believe that if we had a lob bowler of his quality at the present time, he would get good batsmen out even on our perfect wickets.

From what I have said the young player will gather that there is a large amount of thought required to make a first-class bowler, and that he must not expect to do brilliant things at first, even if he possess the perfection of style. Style is the foundation of a good bowler; but hard thought and constant practice are necessary to make him first-class.

CHAPTER X.

FIELDING.

IT has been said that any one can field well if he looks out for every ball and tries his hardest. I do not altogether agree with that, for I have seen more than one cricketer do his very best and yet fall short of what is considered first-class form; but I am strongly of opinion that perseverance and attention are the essential points which every young fieldsman must keep in mind. In fielding, as in batting and bowling, success can only be achieved after long practice and experience. I sometimes think that our representative teams are chosen without sufficient consideration of the fitness of some of the players for the positions in the field where they are almost sure to be placed; for more than once I have noticed a man who was known to be good close in compelled to go out to the long-field, because there was no one else who could do better. Not being accustomed to that position, he could not do himself justice.

It may be safely taken for granted, then, that for one player who can go anywhere in the field with credit to himself there are a dozen, if not more, who are only fit for one position. Messrs. V. E. Walker, A. N. Hornby, Geo. Strachan, and Ulyett in their best days, and Messrs. A. E. Stoddart, S. M. J. Woods, and Peel and Maurice Read at the present time, may be quoted as fine illustrations of first-class all-round fieldsmen. Activity, dash and throwing-in are the qualities which are indispensable to enable a fieldsman to go anywhere.

Speed and being able to throw-in well are, more or less, gifts which belong to the few; but dash and certainty are the fruits of long practice, which most players can acquire if they give their mind to them. The most of those I have named are always on the look-out and seem to know when the ball is coming their way, and pick it up and return in one action.

A lazy or indifferent fieldsman has a demoralising effect on the rest of the eleven, and is an eyesore to every lover of the game: a very bad one will, probably, lose more runs than he makes, and is better out of the team altogether. A good man may not always bat or bowl up to his best form; but, if he tries, can always save runs in the field. The young player should keep that before him, if he desires to play in good matches; for every Committee and Captain know and consider it in the selection of a team.

Before touching upon the different positions in the field, I shall mention a few points which every beginner should carry in his mind:

I. Always be on the look-out; and use two hands, if possible.

II. Keep your legs together when the ball is hit straight to you.

III. Do not dash in too quickly.

IV. Pick up the ball and throw it in with one action.

V. Throw at the wicket-keeper's head, or so that the ball will bound to the bails.

VI. Always back up when the ball is thrown in; but do not go too near to the wicket-keeper or bowler, or you will miss it: about eight yards is the best distance to be from each other in backing up.

VII. Always try for a catch. Impossible things are not expected of you; but you never know what you can reach until you try.

VIII. Keep your hands out of your pockets, and never wear a jacket or coat in the field. A sweater will interfere very little with your movements and keep you warm enough under all circumstances.

IX. Do not go iuto the field with a cigarette or a pipe in your mouth.

X. Go cheerfully and promptly to whatever position the bowler or captain sends you.

XI. If you make a mistake, do your best to rectify it.

These are golden maxims, which every player should consider carefully; but the whole secret of success lies in his trying all he can. My brother Fred and Jupp used to go after everything and try for every catch, as if the match depended on their individual efforts; and the extraordinary results which followed surprised themselves as well as others. There is no finer sight in the cricket field than a brilliant fieldsman doing his utmost; and every feat he performs meets with quick and hearty recognition by the spectators. Grounds generally are now as near as can be to perfection, and fine fielding has become comparatively easy.

The grounds of the past were not to be compared with those of to-day. The best pitches were, as a rule, treacherous and kicked a good deal. I do not know what might not be said of the out-fielding. It is told of Clarke's All-England Eleven that, on one occasion when they played in Cornwall, one of the players flushed a covey of partridges in the long-field, so excellent was the cover. As a contrast to this it might to-day be said of every important ground that a wicket could be pitched on any part of it, and that a false bound in the field is the exception rather than the rule.

I shall now refer to the different positions in the field, and begin with the

WICKET-KEEPER.

He is worthy of the first place; for there is little doubt that his is the most important and responsible position of all. He should stand so that he can take the ball immediately it passes the wicket, and at once knock the bails off if necessary.

I would refer my readers to the illustration of G. McGregor on page 197. He (as well as Blackham, the prince of wicket-keepers) stands so close that the fingers almost touch the bails. Their hands are touching each other unless the ball is wide of the wicket, and catching or stumping is done without any show or fuss. They always stand with a full front to the bowler, and seldom move the feet unless the ball is very wide.

The wicket-keeper should be always on the alert, and if he has a doubt as to whether the foot is over the crease should whip off the bails, especially when the ball is on the leg side; for he cannot always see with certainty. But should he knock the bails off when he knows the batsman is in his ground, he should replace them quietly without appealing. Nothing looks so bad in a wicket-keeper as fussiness and appealing without reason.

Until late years our amateur wicket-keepers have never been up to the form of the professional; and by good judges it has been considered owing to their habit of standing too far back, and snapping at the ball instead of taking it quietly.

The wicket-keeper should be quick to go after a ball when it is near the wicket, or when it is played to leg where there is no fieldsman, and try to save the run. He should always be behind the wicket when the ball is thrown in to him. He must not mind hard

"HOW'S THAT?"

(From Drawing by N. FELIX, 1853.)

knocks; and ought to accustom himself to all kinds of bowling.

As far as hard knocks go, wicket-keepers to-day have reason to be thankful for improved grounds; and perhaps that may, in a degree, account for the better form shown by them.

The best amateur wicket-keepers I have met were J. Round, E. F. S. Tylecote, J. A. Bush, G. A. B. Leatham, A. Lyttelton, H. Philipson, J. McC. Blackham, G. McGregor, and A. T. Kemble. The best professionals were Lockyer, Biddulph, Pinder, Plumb, Pooley, Phillips, Pilling, and Sherwin. Some took slow bowling best, some fast. Blackham, McGregor, and Lyttelton might be placed as the best of the amateurs; while Pilling was, undoubtedly, the best of the professionals. With the exception of Blackham and McGregor no amateur has been up to the form of the professionals.

LONG-STOP.

Long-stopping is fast becoming a thing of the past; owing to the improvement in grounds and in wicket-keeping, and bowling. A good man was wanted for that post to such fast bowlers as Sir Frederick Bathurst and Messrs. Mynn, Marcon and Fellowes, especially on rough, bumpy wickets, when most of the balls kept kicking and twisting; but to-day the bowling is straighter, and a ball rarely gets past both batsman and wicket-keeper. I am speaking of first-class cricket: in second-class matches the wicket-keeper is not always efficient and a long-stop may be necessary. He should stand rather deep, but close enough to save a bye; and he must be a quick and accurate thrower, and never get bustled or lose his head when a sharp run is attempted. He must be quick to decide at which wicket to throw. The Rev. C. H. Ridding, Mr. H.

Perkins, Mr. H. M. Marshall and Mortlock, were the most expert long-stoppers at the time when long-stop was even of more importance than the wicket-keeper. The first-named had a wonderfully good return, and knew, as if by instinct, at which end there was the greater chance of a run-out. He stood rather on the leg side, and was very quick to back up sharp returns to the wicket-keeper.

SHORT-SLIP.

The qualities required to make a good short-slip are judgment, quickness and a safe pair of hands. He must have sound judgment to know how far to stand from the wicket according to the pace of the bowling, for the bowler does not always know. He must be quiek to get to a ball coming low down, or going over his head at lightning pace; and he must have a safe pair of hands, and be able to hold the ball even if he loses his balance and stumbles in reaching it. He should stand slightly stooping, with his eyes on the ball and the batsman; but not so near that he cannot see the ball properly, or he will miss all the quick snicks. The state of the wicket will always be a guide to a great extent, and he must be on the look-out for every change in the pace and flight of the ball.

The position used to be filled by the bowler when not bowling, to save him from running and over-exertion; but now-a-days the post is one which gives plenty of exercise, as he has to run after most of the snicks which pass the wicket-keeper. He must back up the wicket-keeper to save overthrows, take his place when he leaves the wicket, and be able to throw smartly and accurately.

Alfred Shaw was very successful in that position, and Watson and Abel are exceptionally good at it to-day. Lohmann is a marvel: he seems to be able to get to everything within six feet of him; and anything he

FIELD PLACED FOR SLOW ROUND-ARM BOWLING.

can reach, he can hold. Time after time I have seen him go head over heels in trying for an almost impossible catch; but rarely, if ever, did he lose hold of the ball. The young player should watch him; for he is a fine illustration of quickness and safety, and is continually bringing off remarkable catches.

THIRD MAN.

This position can only be filled by a really good man, for it is one in which temper and judgment will be tried to the utmost. He is expected to stop everything that comes to him, for, if he miss it, it may mean a boundary hit, and if he is too far away, the batsman will steal a sharp run. Whatever the state of the ground, but particularly if at all rough, the ball, after it pitches, comes twisting and kicking; and if he is standing too square, he will have to try for it with his left hand. The slightest mistake, and the batsman is off; and the fraction of a second makes all the difference between a run and a run-out. The fieldsman must never get flurried, must be quick to decide the wicket to be thrown at, and not forget to throw the ball straight at the wicket-keeper or bowler's head, or so that it will fall into his hands about the height of his chest after first bound.

Sharp runs have a most demoralising effect on some fieldsmen; and I remember, on more than one occasion, in an important match third man losing his head completely and mistakes and overthrows were the result.

Third man must ask the bowler whether he should stand rather fine or square; he should also find out whether the batsmen are quick or slow in running, so that he may go close in or deep as the case may be. Four of the best men in this position at the present time are Messrs. A. E. Stoddart, P. J. de Paravicini, and Gunn and Maurice Read.

POINT.

A good point must have perfect eyesight, a pair of very safe hands, and the activity of a cat; but even with these it will take many years before he becomes first-class. It is essential for him to know something of the style of every batsman; for upon that depends whether he will do brilliant things, or simply stop the balls that come straight to him. It is a matter of opinion whether he should watch the ball or the batsman, but everyone is agreed that he should not stand perfectly still in one position. His original position should be in a line with the wicket, or a little in front of it, according to the pace of the bowling and condition of the ground. The left foot should be a little in advance, the body slightly stooping, and the hands ready to receive the ball.

Nerve goes a great length in that position; and those who have it most perform the greatest feats. My brother E. M., was the finest point I have ever seen; for not only did he bring off some extraordinary catches that came at a terrific pace straight to him, but he could tell, almost by intuition, where the batsman meant to put the ball; and no matter how close he stood, never failed to hold it. With a poky batsman he took the most outrageous liberties, and times without number he has taken the ball within an inch or two of the bat. He exercised a magnetic influence upon certain batsmen. No matter how hard they tried they could not keep the ball away from him, and Jupp in his later days got fairly stuck up by his restless activity and catlike quickness. He was equally certain with either hand whether the ball was hit at his feet or a foot or two above his head.

V. E. Walker, T. S. Pearson and Carpenter were excellent points also, and W. W. Read and Shrewsbury are quite as good. All of them stand much further back than my brother. Mr. Walker was the quickest of the five, and was very good at finding out in an over or so the batsman's strength and weakness.

COVER-POINT.

Cover-point affords plenty of opportunities for a brilliant fieldsman to distinguish himself. He gets plenty of work; for if he is unable to get to the ball when it is hit anywhere near to him, he has to go after it at his best pace, in the hope of stopping it before it reaches the boundary. Pick-up and return must be one action, or the batsman will steal a sharp run; and he must be quick and accurate in his return, or overthrows will occur pretty often. To fast bowling he may stand rather deep and wait for the ball, but to medium pace and slow he must dart in if he wants to save the run. He has to gauge to a yard the exact position to stand, and he must be constantly on the look-out; for, as a rule, he gets twice as much work as any two other fieldsmen. He must be prepared for an occasional curly one breaking away from him, which he will do well to stop. If, when dashing in to save the run, he cannot get into position to throw in his usual way, an underhand return can be utilised.

Messrs. Halifax Wyatt, G. Strachan, W. W. Read, Rev. Vernon Royle, and John Smith, of Cambridge, were brilliant in that position, and worked untiringly. Messrs. Gregory and J. Shuter, Briggs, and Peel, are just as good to-day. Mr. Gregory's fine exhibition was one of the features of the fielding of the 1890 Australian team.

SHORT-LEG.

It is not so very many years ago that the weakest fieldsman in the eleven was invariably placed at short-leg. A complete change has taken place with respect to that position, and a quick eye and a safe pair of hands are now as much needed there as in any part of the field. Leg-hitting is very little resorted to now, for the reason that a first-class bowler rarely bowls one on that side ; but the batsman tries hard to play away to leg everything bowled on the leg-stumps and pads, and the fieldsman has to be as nimble as a cat to save the run. He has also to go as close in as he can with safety, so as to get hold of a catch. Very often when it comes to him there is a fair amount of spin on it, and if he is not very careful he will miss it altogether.

Short-leg must keep his wits about him, for the ball is on him instantly; and should it pass, will most probably travel for two or three runs. He must be quick to detect the intention of the batsman, whether he means to play it fine, square, or more in the direction of mid-on; but he must be guided by the wish of the bowler as to where he should stand. He should stand slightly stooping, with his hands ready for the ball to drop into them; and be quick to save overthrows from cover-point and mid-off. Against a poky batsman, on a sticky wicket, he has often as many opportunities as point of bringing off a smart catch. He must keep his head under all circumstances, but especially when a sharp run is attempted: the slightest indecision then, and the run-out is lost. A bad thrower should never be placed there, or overthrows will be of common occurrence, and many a run out lost.

LONG-LEG.

Owing to the accuracy of the bowling, very few balls are now hit to long-leg. Fast bowling without length in the old days was not uncommon, and one never was surprised to see a ball hit to leg as often as anywhere else; but I have seen many a long innings played in the last year or two with only a few hits to leg in it. To medium-pace bowling so accurate as we have now, there is no need for a long-leg, and a man can be better utilised on the off-side; indeed, most bowlers would rather have an extra man there, and take the chance of an occasional one being pulled or hit to leg.

My brother Fred. and J. Smith of Cambridgeshire were the best in that position of all the cricketers I have known. They had the four things required to fill it: a safe pair of hands, dash, speed, and good throwing. Rarely did they fail to bring off a catch they could get to, and I have seen batsman after batsman afraid to hit out when either was in that part of the field. They could tell to a yard whether they had to move forward or go back, and never thought anything out of their reach; but it was in their dash they shone conspicuously over others. They did not expect to save the first run, but they considered it bad fielding if a second were obtained. Immediately the batsman hit they were on move, and they covered the first ten yards at top speed, and had the ball into the wicket-keepers' hands almost as soon as the first run was finished. If they could use both hands, they invariably did it; but if time did not permit, they were equally certain with right or left, and they did not forget to allow for the spin which is more or less on every ball hit to leg. Their throw-in was as straight as an arrow, and invariably fell into the wicket-keeper's hands first-bound a foot above the wicket. They rarely stopped a ball with their foot; for they were strongly of opinion that a good fieldsman in that position could stop anything possible more effectually with his hand, and that upon the quick pick-up and return depended the saving of the second run.

Another good quality of theirs was their judgment in knowing whether to stand fine or square. Very rarely do you meet two batsmen who hit exactly alike to leg. My brother and Smith generally thought of that, and could tell exactly where to go without being told to nearly every batsman they played against.

MID-ON.

Mid-on is one of the easiest places in the field; for there is no twist on the ball, and the fieldsman has plenty of time to see it coming to him. His position depends entirely on the bowling, and he is placed close in or deep according to the wish of the bowler. Boyle fielding close in to Spofforth's bowling was a fine illustration of what can be done against certain batsmen when fieldsman and bowler have perfect faith in each other; but the fact of it not being generally adopted shows that it will not do for every-day use. On a line with the bowler's wicket is the position usually taken, but a great deal will depend on the activity of the batsmen. If they are very quick runners, the fieldsman should go as near as he can with safety, and he should practise picking-up and throwing-in under-hand. The state of the ground must always be remembered: when it is dry and fast, he should not be too near; but when it is soft and slow, he should go closer in.

MID-OFF.

The position of mid-off is rather more difficult to fill than that of mid-on, especially to a slow left-hand bowler. The ball has a slight twist on it; and often when it is hit, it rises at a peculiar and trying angle. It is just the distance when the ball is at its greatest velocity, and a catch that, at first sight, looks as if it could be taken breast-high has often to be taken above the head. There is rather a peculiar sensation for a second when the ball comes that way, and it requires a good man to catch it.

Messrs. I. D. Walker, A. J. Webbe, and F. Townsend are very good in that position. I have seen them bring off catch after catch at all conceivable altitudes—sometimes with one hand, sometimes with both. Now it would be at a foot from the ground, then breast-high, and occasionally with hand fully extended over the head. Messrs. W. J. Ford and A. N. Hornby used to be difficult men to field to in that position, their hitting being exceptionally hard and low. The ball came like a flash of lightning—sometimes actually humming—and required a very quick eye and hand to stop it. More than once the fieldsman has been seen to draw away from it altogether. Against good batsmen who play hard from the wicket and place the ball, mid-off has plenty of work to save the run. He must be constantly on the watch, and dash in immediately the ball leaves the bat; in fact, he should be able to tell from the nature of the ball bowled whether it is likely to come his way, and should be on the move as soon as it is hit. If the bowling is round the wicket, he should not go quite so far out as he would when it is over; for the bowler cannot cover so much ground on his side when bowling that way.

LONG-FIELD.

No one who is not accustomed to the position of long-field should be placed there, whether it be on the on-side, the off-side, or over the bowler's head. Close in, remarkable catches are brought off, but no one is surprised when one is missed now and then. In the long-field the fieldsman has plenty of time to see the ball coming; but a lofty catch, and one that has to be waited for, is more difficult to bring off than one that comes quickly and is all over in a second or two. While the ball is travelling to long-field there is time for many thoughts to flash through his mind: chief of which are, that the players and spectators have all turned their

FIELD PLACED FOR FAST ROUND-ARM BOWLING.

eyes upon him, and that he will get no sympathy should he fail to bring off the catch.

I question if there is any position in the field that the beginner should practice so much as that of long-field. He should begin with having the ball thrown low and straight at him at a distance of forty yards; afterwards he should go back further, and have it thrown higher into the air; and then at a distance away from him that he can reach at full speed. He will find that in each case making the catch is slightly different, but waiting for and bringing off a very lofty one most difficult of all. When the ball is dropping into his hands, he should allow them to give a little to it, or it will rebound out of them. A brilliant out-fieldsman is worth his place in any eleven for the work he can do there alone. Upon him will depend whether the hit is to count one, two, or four runs: a mistake there means, in most cases, a boundary hit.

One sterling cricketer comes to my mind who is a grand example of what I mean: Mr. P. J. de Paravicini. From the time Mr. Paravicini captained the Eton XI. in '80 and '81 down to the present time, no player has shown more clearly what a quick pair of legs, a safe pair of hands, and a sound head can do in the long-field. He is dashing and safe, equally good with both hands, and does not know what an impossible catch means. Some of his feats for Middlesex have been quite phenomenal.

Many a match has been lost by bad generalship; so it may be safely said that an eleven in the field is of little use without a good captain at the head of it. The ideal captain should possess sound judgment, enthusiasm, firmness and good temper, and have plenty of patience; for his duties are numerous, and he is certain to have these qualities severely tried during a long or close match. I have said elsewhere that an experienced captain before tossing takes into consideration the light and state of the ground. There are other things as well that make or mar a match: the time for drawing stumps and interval allowed for luncheon. These, though seemingly small points, should always be decided before tossing, or unpleasantness may follow.

If the toss falls in his favour, the captain should, as a rule, decide for his side to bat first; for the wicket is generally better, and every batsman is more likely to score when he is fresh than when tired: besides, the light is invariably better in the morning than in the evening, and it is easier to save runs than make them at a pinch.

It used to be thought bad judgment to put two quick scorers in together, the reason given being that they would run each other off his legs in consequence. I do not think it matters much to-day when nearly every hit of any force goes to the boundary and there is little occasion to run more than one run. Twenty-five years ago it was different; for a hit for six one ball, and seven the next, occurred now and then, and, as there were no boundaries, two free-hitters very soon tired themselves out.

A captain, once he has decided upon the order of his men going in, should stick to it, unless exceptional circumstances arise which, according to his judgment, demand a change—such as keeping back a good man a few minutes before time for drawing stumps, or a sudden change in the light. He should also impress on his men the importance of going promptly to the wicket when their turn comes. Carelessness in that respect shows ignorance of the laws, is annoying to the other side, and not likely to improve the form of the batsman who is waiting.

If his bowlers are fair bats he should not put them down very low on the list; for it is now pretty well known that if a bowler makes runs, he cannot bowl well without a short rest. Lohmann never bowls up to his proper form if he has made a score just before he begins. The hitting has cramped his fingers, and he cannot feel the ball properly for an over or two. His is not a solitary case.

A captain has now the power of closing his innings any time on the last day of a match ; but great judgment is required to do it at the right moment. If he be half-hearted or timid, he will decide to do so when it is absolutely certain that he cannot lose; but it is just as likely that his delay of half-an-hour, or even a quarter, has made it impossible for him to win. If he have pluck and dash, and does not mind risking a little, he may snatch a brilliant victory a few minutes before time. Personally I side with a forward policy, and would rather any day have an exciting finish than one in which players and spectators have lost all interest.

Between the innings, and on each morning when his side is going to bat, the captain should see that the pitch is carefully and thoroughly rolled. I am glad to say that there is little need of this on our leading and best county grounds; still, it should not be neglected.

A captain has greater responsibility on his shoulders when his eleven is in the field. His hardest task is to make the best use of the bowling under his command. Occasionally when the wicket is difficult the first two bowlers may get the batsmen out without a change being necessary; and the captain may have little to do but see that his fieldsmen are always in their proper places. But when the wicket is an easy one a long innings is oftener the case, and he is sure to have his skill and resources tried to the utmost. He should always begin with what he considers his two best bowlers, and never forget that a difference in pace and style is likely to prove most effective. A fast right-hand bowler at one end and a slow left-hand at the other is a powerful combination.

Should these fail to come off, the captain should

not hesitate to make a change, if only for a few overs. Any change is better than none. A very good plan is to make it after 20 runs have been scored, if no wicket has fallen. A change should also be made after a series of maiden-overs without a wicket falling. Of course, there are times when a bowler is out of luck. He keeps beating the batsman ball after ball, but the wicket does not fall, or perhaps catches are missed off him. In that case, the captain will do right to keep him on a little longer.

The bowler should be allowed to place his own field. At the same time, the captain should make suggestions now and again about having another man in the long-field, an extra short-leg or cover-point; anything, in fact, that would tend to get the batsmen out. The captain should keep his eye on all the field, and notice at the beginning of each over whether they are in their right places. Some fieldsmen cannot stand in the same place two overs in succession, and it is very annoying to the bowler to see runs scored off him on account of it. The captain should also notice whether the field back up properly, and set them a good example in that respect. He should also field, if possible, somewhere near the wicket, so that he may be able to watch the bowling. In that position, he will have better command of the team than anywhere in the long-field. When a ball is skied and two men go for it, he should immediately shout the name of the fieldsman who has the better chance of bringing off the catch. Quick decision then will save them from colliding, and often prevent an easy catch from being missed.

In conclusion, let me say that, whether in the field or out of it, the captain should not openly reprimand any of his eleven for a mistake. A word or two spoken quietly will have more effect; and he should remember, above all things, to set a good example and always practise what he preaches.

CHAPTER XI.

CRICKETERS I HAVE MET.

IN order to facilitate reference, I have adopted the plan of placing "Cricketers I have Met" in alphabetical order.

ROBERT ABEL was born at Rotherhithe, Surrey, November 30th, 1859. His height is 5 ft. 5 in.; weight, 10 st. He played his first match for Surrey in 1881; but showed very little promise with either bat or ball until a year or two later. In the year 1885 he came to the front very quickly, and, with the exception of 1887, has been well up in the first-class batting averages ever since. His bowling has not improved to the same extent; but then his county has been so well off in that respect the last two or three years, that he has rarely been called upon to bowl for it.

As a batsman he is in the first flight, having exceptionally strong defence and patience, and for his size he hits very freely all round. His pluck and cheerfulness are really first-rate, whether they are required in fighting an uphill game with the bat or in the field. He has played many fine innings in first-class company, but the best I have witnessed was his 105 in the second innings of the South *v.* North at Scarborough on the 7th September, 1889. He went in first, and with myself, in three hours and three-quarters, put on 226 runs before we were parted; and his defence and hitting were as fine as any cricketer could wish to see. He is a brilliant fieldsman, very certain with plenty of dash, and has been one of the mainstays of the Surrey Eleven for half-a-dozen years.

His best years with the bat have been:

	Completed Innings.	Runs.	Most in an Innings.	Average.
1885	39	966	92	24.30
1886	42	1221	144	29. 3
1888	42	1323	160	31.21
1889	38	1095	138	28.31
1890	30	914	151*	30.14

Mr. Charles Alfred Absolom was born at Blackheath, 7th June, 1846. His height was 5 ft. 10 in.; weight, 13 st. As a batsman he had a peculiar style of his own. He held the bat very high up in the handle, and did not pay much attention to the pitch of the ball. Balls bowled to the off he hit to long-on—in fact, anywhere but where the bowler intended and hoped they would be hit to. It will be easily inferred that he did not trouble much about keeping up his wicket: all the same, he made some very good scores against the best bowling of his time; and more than once, like my brother E. M., I have seen him upset bowlers who had been bowling accurately against good players before he went in. He always played bareheaded, and without pads or gloves.

He bowled slow medium-pace round-arm, with a high delivery, varying it with an occasional fast one; and would go on for a whole day without any appreciable diminution of strength or accuracy. He could not be tired, either in bowling or fielding, and he was worthy of his place in any eleven for the excellent and stimulating example he showed of working heart and soul from beginning to end of a match, whether he was on the winning or losing side. A good illustration of it occurred in the M.C.C. *v.* Kent match at Canterbury on August 10th, 11th and 12th, 1876. He was never happier than when bowling, he said, and it was strikingly enforced on that occasion. Kent batted first, scoring 473. M.C.C. made 144 first innings, and followed on at five o'clock of the second day. "Let me begin the bowling," said Absolom; "I'm in rare form, and strong enough for anything." After six hours' fielding next day, when I had scored 300 runs, and every one of the Kent Eleven showed the effects of the long outing, he was as eager as ever and kept beseeching to be allowed to have another trial!

Rarely have I seen a man of such excellent physique and staying powers. In the Inter-University contests, in 1867, he won the broad jump for Cambridge, clearing 22 ft. 2 in.; and on another occasion he cleared 21 ft. 2 in. More than once he "put" the 16-lb. shot 32 feet, and he is said to have thrown the cricket-ball over 100 yards; he was also successful on the running path.

He did excellent work for his county, and we can also all recall the just and touching acknowledgment of it made by Lord Harris when the news arrived of his untimely death on board the steamer *Muriel* on the 27th July, 1889. He said: "A generation of cricketers is short-lived: but though it is ten years since 'Bos' played his last match for the county, there must be thousands of onlookers who can remember what a safe pair of hands were his; what a successful, if not very difficult, bowler he was occasionally; what good service he did many a time in his own peculiar but vigorous style with the bat; and last, but not least, how he always played up for his side. At any rate, there are many lovers of the game in Kent who will gratefully remember the yeoman service he rendered the county from 1875 to 1879. I had the good fortune to be able to induce him to play for the county. It brought me more than a right sturdy comrade in the cricket-field: it brought me a sincere, true-hearted friend, whose early death I, and all who knew him, deeply deplore."

Mr. C. W. ALCOCK was born at Sunderland, 2nd December, 1842. His height is 5 ft. 11 ins.; weight, about 14 st. He played for M.C.C. *v.* Middlesex at Lord's, 28th, 29th July, 1862. Mr. Alcock is one of the workers; he succeeded Mr. W. Burrup as secretary of the Surrey County Club in 1872, and an excellent secretary he has made. He has also been an indefatigable worker outside of his club. Most of the teams that came to us from Australia and America have been indebted to him for smoothing their way in the arrangement of fixtures and other matters. Very few possess his knowledge of the game, its players, and its literature; and, like all true and energetic secretaries, he has desired the success of his club, and his desires have been more than fulfilled. Surrey has been great in the past, and it is great to-day; and it has been pretty much owing to Mr. Alcock's efforts that the list of members reached the high figure of 3291 in 1890. While it has for its secretary so able a gentleman it need have little doubt about the future.

The total size of the ground at Kennington Oval is 11 acres, the playing part about 8 acres.

GEORGE ANDERSON was born in Yorkshire, 20th January, 1826. His height was 6 ft.; weight, 14½ st. He was an excellent field, and as a batsman possessed rare hitting powers. He stood well up, played freely and confidently; and when he hit, the ball travelled at a great pace. He was one of the English Eleven which visited Australia in 1864. He was superior to the average professional player in manner and education, and was a great favourite wherever he played.

Mr. ARTHUR APPLEBY was born at Enfield, Accrington, Lancashire, 22nd July, 1843. His height was 6 ft.; weight, 13 st. Lancashire has reason to be proud of him; for he did good work with both bat and ball for it, and he was just as successful in the Gentlemen *v.* Players and other matches. Few bowlers had so easy and beautiful an action, or could keep up their end for so long a time without going to pieces. He bowled fast round, left-hand, took a deliberate and long run, was very straight, and kept a good length. He very rarely bowled a loose ball: now and then you might get one a little bit short, but it rose quickly off the pitch, and required a very quick eye and flexible wrist to do anything with it. The general opinion is that he was one of the best of our amateur bowlers.

He had a wonderful break from the off for a left-hand bowler. The ball came with his hand, and I remember he bowled Daft with such a ball in the Gentlemen *v.* Players' match at Lord's in 1872, when he had scored 102 runs. The ball was so wide of the wicket that Daft did not attempt to play it. For Mr. Fitzgerald's team, in Canada and America, he bowled very successfully, and came out second in the batting averages.

William Attewell was born at Keyworth, Nottinghamshire, on the 12th June, 1861. His height is 5 ft. 10 ins.; weight, 11 st. 12 lbs. He had barely completed his twentieth year when he was asked to represent his county, and it may be safely said of him that he has been the mainstay of the team in bowling since 1884. The year 1889 was a great year with him, and to-day his hand has lost none of its cunning. He has been equally successful for the M.C.C., for the Players *v.* Gentlemen, for English elevens in Austialia, and against Australian elevens in England.

He bowls right-hand, round-arm, medium-pace, is very straight, and keeps a wonderfully good length; in fact his length is so good and accurate, that he can depend on it alone to get wickets on an indifferent ground. When the wicket is at all sticky, his break from the off is very effective. He is a fair bat, but has not come up to his early promise; however, he hits very hard, and makes good scores occasionally: his fielding is excellent. His best years with the ball so far have been:

	Overs.	Maidens.	Runs.	Wickets.	Average.
1884	1150	659	1217	101	12. 5
1885	1301	767	1218	87	14
1886	1295	736	1272	97	13.11
1887	1330	810	1238	89	13.81
1888	1393	848	1235	91	13.52
1889	1314	654	1555	140	11.15
1890	1581	820	1874	151	12.62

His proportion of maiden overs is larger than that of any bowler since Alfred Shaw.

Mr. ALEXANDER CHARLES BANNERMAN was born at Sydney, New South Wales, on the 21st March, 1859. He was a member of the first Australian team in 1878, and has been here on four occasions since. Very few have shown better all-round cricket; for he was a good batsman, a brilliant field at mid-off and cover-point, and a fair change, medium-pace, round-arm bowler. His strong defence and great patience were his best points; but it must not be thought that he was lacking in hitting. Against loose bowling he was fairly effective, and he rarely allowed a ball to pass that was off the wicket. I believe that he possessed the best defence of all the Australian batsmen, and many a match he saved by it. His pick-up and smart return in the field were really brilliant, as many an English batsman found to his cost. Batting performances in England, in eleven-a-side matches:

	Completed Innings.	Runs.	Most in an Innings.	Average.
1878	23	260	71*	11. 7
1880	12	196	38	16. 4
1882	54	1196	120*	22. 8
1884	50	961	94	19.11
1888	56	943	93*	16.47

RICHARD GORTON BARLOW was born at Bolton, Lancashire, on May 28th, 1850. His connection with the county began about 1872; and he has done good work for it with bat and ball. Until late years, he invariably batted first with Mr. A. N. Hornby, and as a rule scored ten runs or thereabouts while Mr. Hornby made a hundred. He has the patience of Job, and takes rank with the Scotton and L. Hall type of batsmen; but I do not know which holds the record for slowness. I know on one occasion Barlow batted 80 minutes without scoring, and took 2½ hours to make 5 runs! He has been an exceedingly useful all-round player for his county, and has both batted and bowled with success for the Players *v.* Gentlemen. He bowls above medium-pace, keeps a good length, and is very seldom off the wicket.

WILLIAM BARNES was born at Sutton-in-Ashfield, Nottinghamshire, on the 27th May, 1852. He has been a host in himself for his county, since he first played for it in 1875. He has also done excellent work for the M.C.C., the Players *v.* Gentlemen, and England *v.* Australia. His highest score so far is 266 for M.C.C. *v.* Leicestershire at Lord's in 1882, when Midwinter and he scored 473 runs in the remarkably quick time of 5½ hours before they were parted. He has also exceeded 100 in an innings on twenty-six occasions: twelve times for the M.C.C., eleven times for his county, once for the Players, once for England *v.* Australia, and once for England *v.* Eighteen of Bendigo. His batting average in first-class matches in 1889 was a very fine one:

36 completed innings, 1249 runs, average 34.25.

He is not a graceful batsman; but he has excellent defence, and watches the ball very carefully. He scores faster than the average professional, his hitting to the off and cutting being exceptionally good; and he keeps the ball well down.

As a bowler he has also been very successful, and at times unplayable. He bowls round-arm, faster than medium pace, with a high delivery, and breaks slightly from the off. Repeatedly when the wicket was in a crumbling condition he has done exceptionally good performances. Two of these were for the Players *v.* Gentlemen in 1887 at Lord's. In the first innings he took six wickets for 23 runs; in the second, four for 35. Another was his two wickets for 18 runs for England *v.* Australia in the first innings at the Oval in 1888, and five for 32 in the second.

He is an excellent fieldsman anywhere, and a safe catch.

EDWARD BARRATT was born at Stockton-on-Tees, 21st April, 1844. His height was 5 ft. 8½ in.; weight, 11 st. 4 lbs. He was a very good left-hand slow round-arm bowler, and was the bowling mainstay of Surrey for years. He could break a great deal from leg, and against batsmen who were timid about running out invariably got wickets. Like most slow bowlers, he sent in a fast straight one now and then; but his pet ball was one a little bit up, about a foot to the off, which he caused to break away a few inches, and an impatient or thoughtless batsman "spooned" in trying to hit. I have seen good batsmen hit wildly at that kind of ball, although Barratt had placed extra fieldsmen on the off for the chance of a catch. It was all owing to the eagerness of the batsman, who could not resist the temptation to hit out at everything off the wicket. A little thought would have shown that stepping back and cutting it, instead of hitting it on the rise, was the right way to treat it; or that quickness in running out and hitting before it pitched would have been equally effective.

But Barratt seemed to divine this inherent weakness of young players, and rarely failed to profit by it. Against my brother E.M. and myself he seldom bowled that ball. We played against him at Swindon in local matches before he appeared at Lord's and the Oval, and knew his trap; and as he said repeatedly, when bowling against us for Surrey *v.* Gloucestershire, "It's no use now; my little game is over. Help yourselves, gentlemen!"—which E.M. promptly did. He ran yards out of his ground, and pulled him to the boundary so often that Barratt was frightened to bowl a good length against him, and his short ones were just as mercilessly thrashed.

It was rather hard luck on Barratt that when he represented Surrey the eleven was not only weak, but had very little fast bowling. In many matches he was kept on too long because there was no one good enough to relieve him, and the consequence was that the batsmen got set and hit him. Nothing disheartens a bowler so much; and these circumstances must be taken into consideration in forming an estimate of the good work he did for his county. He represented the Players in 1877, and might have been chosen oftener; but Alfred Shaw and Southerton were in great form at that time, and naturally were chosen first. Barratt has many fine performances to his credit; but his best was for an Eleven of Players *v.* Australians, at the Oval, on the 2nd and 3rd Sept., 1878, when he took all ten wickets first innings for 43 runs. Like most left-hand batsmen he could hit, but his defence was weak. I took more than common interest in his progress, for I was the first to find out his powers when he played at Swindon, and recommended him to the M.C.C., where he was engaged in 1872. The year after he moved to Prince's; and in 1874 he was on the staff of the Surrey Club at the Oval, where he remained for many years.

William Bates was born at Lascelles Hall, near Huddersfield, on 19th November, 1855. He first played for his county in 1877; but it was in 1878 that he proved himself to be a first-class bat and bowler. For years Peate and he ran a close race for first place in the Yorkshire bowling averages, and there can be very little doubt the pair did much to give that county the high position which it held for some years. Bates bowled slow medium-pace, and on his day was very successful. He got a fair amount of break from the off, and made the ball come rather quickly off the pitch.

But he was even more successful with the bat than the ball. Some of his batting performances were really brilliant, and on a good fast wicket he scored at a rate which few could surpass. He hit very hard all round, and one or two of his performances against time will stand out conspicuously. His big scores were all made in a free, dashing style, and if he could have fielded with more certainty he might have been classed as the best all-round player of his time. He represented the Players in 1880, and rarely missed doing so until 1886. He was also a member of Daft's team which visited Canada in 1879; and he was one of the sixth English team which went to Australia in 1881-82: for the latter he came out first in the batting averages and fourth in the bowling. Afterwards he accompanied most of the English teams to Australia, doing well with both bat and ball. Out there he did a most brilliant performance for the Hon. Ivo Bligh's team against Murdoch's Australian Eleven, on the 19th of January, 1883. He scored fifty-five runs in the only innings of Mr. Bligh's team, and bowled:

First innings: 26 overs, 14 maidens, 28 runs for 7 wickets; three of the wickets were with successive balls. Second innings: 33 overs, 14 maidens, 74 runs, 6 wickets.

He met with an unhappy accident while practising as a member of Mr. Vernon's team in Australia in 1887-8, and has not been able to play in first-class cricket since.

His best batting years were:

	Completed Innings.	Runs.	Most in an Innings.	Average.
1883	44	1024	79	23.12
1884	42	1000	133	23.34
1885	46	1161	98	25.11
1886	43	1018	136	23.29
1887	40	996	103	24.36

His best bowling years were:

	Overs.	Maidens.	Runs.	Wickets.	Average.
1878	901	337	1160	99	11.71
1879	690	309	815	78	10.35
1881	1279	540	1883	114	16.59

Mr. John McCarthy Blackham was born at Fitzroy, Melbourne, on the 11th of May, 1855. His height is 5 ft. 9½ in.; weight, 11 st. 3 lbs. It can be said of him as of no other Australian, that he is without a rival in his own particular branch of the game. Blackham has a genius for wicket-keeping, but it is a genius that has been built up by stern hard work and pluck. He has been a member of every Australian team which has come to us. Before he had been a month in England in 1878 his quickness with the gloves was the admiration of all cricketers; to-day he has still no equal behind the wickets.

Above all other wicket-keepers he is noted for standing close to the wicket; and taking the ball and knocking off the bails may be described as one action. He is marvellously quick, taking shooters and yorkers between the wicket and the pads with comparative ease. The quality of the bowling makes no difference to him, for he is equally at home with fast and slow. I believe he was the first to teach us to do without a long-stop against fast bowling; but it must be remembered

MR. JOHN McCARTHY BLACKHAM.

that he has always been used to good bowling, and has had no occasion to look out for erratic balls. He never funks, and seems partial to hard knocks; but it is his stamina that has elicited our admiration most. The wear and tear he has gone through in the last twelve years are without parallel. I have no need to say that he has kept wicket more than once in a fairly long innings without giving a single extra.

His batting has been characterised more by hard hitting than finished style; but he can keep up his wicket when necessary, and play a plucky uphill game. He has been very useful with the bat, as may be seen from some of his results in England:—

	Completed Innings.	Runs.	Most in an Innings.	Average.
1878	14	256	53	18. 4
1880	15	205	42*	13.10
1882	36	612	62	17
1884	40	690	69	17.10
1886	45	731	71	16.11

Mr. George John Bonnor was born at Bathurst, New South Wales, on the 25th February, 1855. His height is 6 ft. 6 ins.; weight 17 st. He was the hitter of the Australian teams, and when he made up his mind to play that game he was really a dangerous batsman on all kinds of wickets; but the last time he visited us he indulged now and then in what some called a "sweetly pretty" game, and came sadly to grief. As a hitter he has no superior in the world, although Mr. C. I. Thornton has been considered quite as good by English judges.

Mr. Bonnor was a magnificent field in the country; for not only did he catch well, but he could throw in at a great pace. Repeatedly he has thrown over 120 yards, and he is credited with having once exceeded 130.

He was a great favourite on English grounds,

for he was undoubtedly a model of physical beauty, and "looked so very amiable," as a lady once remarked.

Batting averages in England, in eleven-a-side matches:

	Completed Innings.	Runs.	Most in an Innings.	Average.
1880	16	145	35	9. 1
1882	40	815	122*	20.15
1884	49	937	95*	19. 6
1886	32	581	49	18. 5
1888	61	1204	119	19.45

Mr. Henry Frederick Boyle was born at Sydney, New South Wales, on the 10th December, 1847. His height is 6 ft.; weight, 11 st. 7 lbs. He came to England with the first Australian team, and ran a very close race with Spofforth for first place in bowling honours. He bowled right-arm, medium pace, generally round the wicket, and broke slightly both ways. His length was good, and he kept altering pitch and pace with excellent judgment; in fact, at his best he had a rare head on his shoulders, and was successful in getting batsmen out when other bowlers equally good had tried and completely failed. He was a magnificent field to his own or anybody's bowling; and was the first man to stand at short mid-on, where he brought off some remarkable catches. Once or twice I thought him a little bit foolhardy there; and I know he had two or three remarkable escapes when my brother E.M. was batting. He was a fair bat.

Bowling performances in England, in eleven-a-side matches:

	Overs.	Maidens.	Runs.	Wickets.	Average.
1878	409	168	569	54	10.29
1880	516	239	616	39	15.31
1882	1200	525	1680	144	11.96
1884	727	291	1143	67	17. 4

John Briggs was born at Sutton-in-Ashfield, Nottinghamshire, on October 13th, 1862. His height is 5 ft. 5 in.; weight, 11 st. 3 lbs. He is the most prominent player

JOHN BRIGGS.

in the Lancashire Eleven at the present time, and may be described as an exceptionally good little one. In batting, bowling, and fielding he is quite first-class, and no English representative eleven would be complete without him. His bowling is above medium pace, round-arm, left-hand, and he breaks both ways; but he is most destructive with his leg-breaks. He fields his own bowling and everybody else's with the quickness of a cat, and he has had no superior at cover-point for years. He bats right-hand, and plays in a free style; and, for a player of his size, he hits very hard. As he is only in his 29th year, he may be expected to shine for some years to come.

He represented Lancashire in his seventeenth year, and made his mark as a batsman and field; but it was not until 1884 that he bowled so well and took his position amongst first-class players, and played in representative matches against the Australians and the Gentlemen. He has been to Australia on several occasions; and his most successful years with bat and ball so far have been:

BATTING.

	Completed Innings.	Runs.	Most in an Innings.	Average.
1885	31	857	186	27.20
1887	29	819	68	28. 7
1888	41	872	126*	21.11
1890	38	708	129*	18.24

BOWLING.

	Overs.	Maidens.	Runs.	Wickets.	Average.
1885	657	326	921	67	13.50
1886	1176	612	1471	92	15.91
1887	1592	831	2018	114	17.80
1888	1450	763	1679	160	10.79
1889	1040	447	1646	140	11.106
1890	1113	456	1950	158	12.54

Mr. David Buchanan was a first-class player almost before I was born, and had not lost much of his power as a bowler when I met him in some of the big matches in 1866. He was born in Scotland, 16th January, 1830, and was educated at Rugby and Cambridge. His height was 5 ft. 5 in.; weight, 12 st. At first he bowled fast round-arm, left-hand, and was very successful for his School and University; but it was after he moderated his pace that I met him, and that he did his finest performances. He had a wonderful command of the ball, and could break both ways; and when he found a batsman too eager to hit, had little difficulty in getting him caught out. The ball he was most successful with was one well up, about a foot on the off, which he caused to break slightly away from the batsman when he hit at it. It was sure to touch the edge of the bat, and an easy catch followed. He placed extra fieldsmen to the off for this particular ball, and I have seen many good players walk into the trap with their eyes open, and then come away from the wicket railing at their simplicity and stupidity.

Mr. R. F. Miles, of Gloucestershire, and Barratt, of Surrey, were fairly successful with the same kind of delivery; but after a time batsmen became wary and left it alone, and it is one rarely bowled to-day, unless to a novice. But I remember Messrs. Buchanan and Miles, who were carrying everything before them against right-hand batsmen, being completely knocked all over the ground more than once by a left-hand player. The break which had done so much mischief in one case was useless in the other. Mr. Buchanan was very closely connected with the Free Foresters' Club, and was their principal bowling mainstay for years. He bowled splendidly for the Gentlemen *v.* Players in 1868, when he was 38 years old, taking nine wickets for 82 runs in the second innings. He bowled with success in the same matches for four or five years afterwards; and if he could only have fielded his own bowling as well as some of our brilliant amateurs, he would have taken a higher position among our great bowlers. He has lived at Rugby for many years, and takes great interest in the school cricket there.

Mr. FREDERIC BURBIDGE was born at Champion Hill, Camberwell, Surrey, 23rd November, 1832. His height was 5 ft. 8 in.; weight, 11½ st. He batted in a very correct style, had sound defence, and hit with great freedom all round; but his distinguishing feature was the way in which he played an uphill game. He was also a brilliant fieldsman, and brought off many a remarkable catch in the Gentlemen *v.* Players matches and for his county. The year 1857 saw him representing the Gentlemen, and he played for them several years afterwards, and as late as 1865. When he gave up playing, he did not give up his interest in the game; for he was continually thinking of his county's interests, and was ever on the alert for promising colts. He is a constant spectator at the Oval of all important matches.

Mr. JAMES ARTHUR BUSH was born at Cawnpore, India, 28th July, 1850. His height is 6 ft. 2 in.; weight, 15½ st. He has been closely associated with Gloucestershire, having played every year but one since its formation. It will be news to a great many that he was first played for his batting and fielding. The year 1877 was his best batting performance for the county, when he averaged 22.75, but he did not keep it up afterwards; though, fortunately, he tried his hands with the gloves, and soon proved himself to be one of the best amateur wicket-keepers of his day. I have little hesitation in saying that at his best he was the safest amateur wicket-keeper for a catch, no matter how fast the bowling, and I have heard outside opinions expressed to the same effect. He kept wicket for the eleven I took out to Australia in 1873-4, and it was the general opinion of the team that no wicket-keeper alive could have done better, or stood the wear and tear of the task so well. He represented the Gentlemen in 1874 and 1875.

As a batsman he used to have good defence, and could hit; but he is about the most casual player I know. At the Oval, when Gloucestershire met Surrey in 1876, he played at a ball on the leg side, and missed it. Without looking to see if Pooley had stopped the ball, he quietly stepped out of his ground, and was stumped. He had got into his head that such a ball ought to go to the boundary. We chaffed him over it, but he did not mind, and when he telegraphed the score home that evening, he coolly added: "I was magnificently stumped off a leg-shooter!"

In a match at Kadina, South Australia, he was bowled first ball; but he quietly put on the bail again, and said, "he never could play a 'trial ball,' and wished the cricket authorities would put their foot down and expunge it from the rules." He gained his point, and resumed batting.

But on another occasion, at Castlemaine, the laugh went against him. We had only a few runs to get to win, and I sent him in first on a bumpy wicket. He insisted on having the first ball, and told his partner he was going to run everything. The first ball was a shooter, and just grazed the leg stump, the bail falling quietly down. His partner, not noticing it, yelled, "Come on, Frizzy!" But after they had run three, the wicket-keeper and bowler, to his disgust, pointed to the wicket, and asked "if it was a running match." In the same match he kept wicket splendidly; but the umpire, not quite sympathising with his display, declined to give a man out, on the ground that the tip of his nose was just over the wicket, and that it was an infringement of the laws.

Julius Cæsar was born at Godalming, Surrey, 25th March, 1830. His height was 5 ft. 7½ in.; weight,

11 st. 7 lb. He appeared at Lord's for his county in 1850. He was a good fieldsman at point and at long-stop; and he was also a very free batsman. He was one of the famous eleven of Surrey which a few years later more than held its own against the other counties. He was also a member of the first English Eleven which visited Australia in 1862.

William Caffyn was born at Reigate, Surrey, 2nd February, 1828. His height was 5 ft. 7½ in.; weight, 11 st. He was the Surrey crack for a good many years, and one of the best all-round players of his time. As a batsman, his cutting was exceptionally good and his scores very large. Repeatedly he scored over 100 runs in an innings. He was a good field anywhere, and worth playing in any team for his bowling alone. He was a member of the first team that visited Australia in 1862, and he created so favourable an impression in the Colonies that he was engaged to remain for some years at a very high salary. I played against him on his return; and though he was not the man he had been, yet the style was there, and we had occasional glimpses of his old form.

Robert Carpenter was born at Millroad, Cambridge, 18th November, 1830. His height was 5 ft. 8½ in.; weight, 11 st. 7 lbs. He may be safely placed as one of the finest of our great batsmen; his defence, considering he did not play forward, being perfect. I have rarely seen a batsman who watched the ball so carefully, and his back play and patience were exceptionally good. The bowler had all his work cut out to get Carpenter's wicket, whatever the state of the ground—shooting or bumping balls being confidently met. Batsman after batsman was beaten on a kicking wicket in some of the matches Carpenter played; but there he remained, keeping the straight ones down, punishing the loose ones, and breaking the hearts of many a twenty-two, who saw victory slipping out of their grasp owing to his patience and coolness. He was not of the stone wall type of batsman. Often he carried out his bat, but rarely without a good score to his credit. He could hit to every part of the field, but excelled in leg-hitting; he was also a first-rate fieldsman at point, but no bowler.

I remember an amusing remark of Carpenter's in 1872, when I was scoring heavily. It was made at the end of the Gentlemen *v.* Players match at the Oval on the 5th of July. The Gentlemen had won the first match two days before at Lord's by seven wickets, and my share of the runs was 77 first innings, 112 second. On this occasion the Gentlemen won by nine wickets, and my score was 117.

"I have had about enough of fielding out to Mr. Grace this week; but thank goodness I shall be on his side the next match," said Carpenter.

My next match was at Lord's on the 8th, when Carpenter and I played for England *v.* Nottinghamshire and Yorkshire. I batted first, and two wickets were down for 77 when Carpenter joined me. I was scoring as rapidly then as I ever scored in my life, and there were no boundary hits. Nearly every ball was hit away, and at the end of an hour, when Carpenter was caught at the wicket, we had put on exactly a hundred runs, of which he had made 36. He was over forty years of age at the time, had played splendidly, and was warmly cheered when he walked from the wicket.

"Well, Carpenter," said one of the players, "you ought to feel happy to-day!"

"Feel happy! If I had been in much longer I should have died. It is a deal harder work to be in with him than fielding against him. When you are fielding you do get a rest now and again, but when batting you never do!"

I believe it was the first time that we played on the same side.

I had played four innings in succession in seven days, and had scored 77, 112, 117, and 170 not out.

Mr. JAMES STEWART CARRICK was born at Glasgow, 4th September, 1855. His height is 5 ft. 10 ins.; weight, 13 st. 5 lbs. He is one of the best all-round cricketers in Scotland, and has done good work with both bat and ball for close upon twenty years. I met him first at Glasgow when I was playing for the United South in 1872, and was rather struck with his bowling form for a youth of sixteen years of age. He bowls slow round-arm, left-hand, and varies his pace and pitch. He belonged to the old Caledonian Club, and when it gave up attached himself to the West of Scotland, for which he has done excellent work most years. His sensational score of 419 not out for the West of Scotland against Priory Park at Chichester in 1885, though not made against first-class bowling, was a very fine display of good defence and vigorous hitting. He was batting two days, and made as many as thirty 4's.

Since that time he has scored over 100 in an innings two or three times; but his best was, undoubtedly, 112 for an Eleven of Scotland against Nottinghamshire, on the West of Scotland ground, 1888. It was rather a noteworthy performance, from the fact that it was the only century scored against Nottinghamshire that year. He bats left-hand, and is one of the few cricketers who has raised the standard of Scottish batting to the level of English. He was a first-class Rugby football player, and represented Scotland *v.* England in 1876 and 1877.

Scotland had, however, even a finer batsman before he appeared in the person of his brother-in-law, Thomas Chalmers, who was born at Glasgow, 19th March, 1850.

His height was 5 ft. 10 in.; weight, 11 st. 7 lbs. From 1870 to 1880 Mr. Chalmers was, without doubt, the premier batsman of Scotland, and rarely failed to score against the All-England and United South of England Elevens when they played in Glasgow. He also belonged to the Caledonian and West of Scotland clubs. His defence was good, and he hit low and hard to all parts of the ground. But it was his power to play the ball hard away from him, whatever the quality of the bowling, that gave him his high position amongst Scottish cricketers. He was also a very fair wicket-keeper and a first-class long-field, and has thrown the cricket-ball repeatedly over 100 yards.

Another eminent Scottish cricketer to be included with such good men as Messrs. Chalmers and Carrick is Mr. Leslie Melville Balfour. He was born in 1854, and from 1876 until the present time no one has done more for the game in his own country. He has been closely indentified with the Grange Club, Edinburgh, one of the oldest, strongest, and most influential in Scotland. The string of centuries to his credit in club matches is an exceptionally long one, and he has invariably scored in the inter-city contests between Edinburgh and Glasgow.

He is a very fast scorer, his late cutting and leg-hitting being quite first-class. In the field he is very quick, especially at cover-point, and he can keep wicket in very fair style; and he makes an excellent captain. As an all-round athlete he has few equals in his own country, being quite at the top of the tree at golf, and not far short of it at football and lawn-tennis.

A Scottish cricketer better known in England than either of the three I have just mentioned is Mr. James George Walker. He was born at Glasgow, October 9th, 1859, but received his cricket education at Loretto School, Edinburgh. He entered Trinity

College, Oxford, in 1879, and secured a place in the eleven in 1882. Of late years he has played for Middlesex, M.C.C., Gentlemen of England, Free Foresters, and I Zingari, and has done very good work for all of them. He was seen at his best in 1883 and 1886, when he could show the fine batting averages of 29.9 and 27.9 in first-class cricket.

His defence is sound and his cutting very good, and he has scored well against all kinds of bowling. He is a fair field anywhere, but he usually stands point and fields in that position very well; and he is also one of the willing players and goes cheerfully to any part of the field he is asked to.

HENRY RUPERT JAMES CHARLWOOD was born at Horsham, Sussex, 19th December, 1847. His height was 5 ft. 7 in.; weight, 10½ st. For a player of his height and weight, he hit very hard. At the early age of 17 he played for his county, and he was a member of the United South Eleven the year after. A good many times he was at the head of the averages for his county, 1876 in particular being a brilliant season for him. Against Kent and Surrey he scored over 100 runs in an innings that year, and few players have done so well for Sussex. He was a very fine field and safe catch, and was in the Players' Eleven on several occasions, but he did not come off so successfully as he did for his county. The best hit I saw him make was for the United South *v.* I Zingari at Enville Hall (Lord Stamford's). It was a straight drive over the bowler's head, and the ball travelled low and at a tremendous pace. We were in together, and had run six for the hit; but in turning for the seventh he slipped, put his knee out, and had to stop. We could easily have run three more, for I remember I had time to run up to his end to see what was the matter and get back in time to my own before the ball was thrown in. Afterwards his knee interfered with his jumping out to hit, and it was only occasionally he gave us a glimpse of the form which at one time earned him the title of "The Hope of Sussex."

Mr. Bransby Beauchamp Cooper was born in India, 15th March, 1844. His height was 5 ft. 10½ in.; weight, 10½ st. He was a very fine batsman, with splendid defence, and took part in a great many important matches in England between 1864 and 1870. His driving powers were good, and he could cut very prettily, but it was his patience and defence which made him so valuable. He played for Kent and Middlesex, and represented the Gentlemen *v.* Players in 1865, 1867, 1868 and 1869, batting with fair success and keeping wicket as well. But his finest effort was for the Gentlemen of the South *v.* Players of the South, at the Oval, in 1869, against Willsher, Lillywhite, Southerton and Silcock. Batting together, he and I made 283 for first wicket—a record in a first-class match which holds good to-day. One hundred runs were hit in two hours, 200 runs in three, and 283 in three hours and forty minutes. Mr. Cooper's share was 101, and his hitting comprised one 6, two 5's, six 4's and singles.

He was a moderately good wicket-keeper; but never, to my recollection, bowled in first-class matches; although he was fairly successful against second-class batsmen. I met him again at Melbourne in 1873, when he played for Eighteen of Victoria against England, and showed that he had lost little of his skill as a batsman. He scored 84 against us, and helped Victoria very materially to win the match.

Mr. Joseph Montagu Cotterill was born at Brighton, 23rd November, 1851. His height was 5 ft. 10¾ ins.; weight, 11½ st. He was one of the brilliant lights of Sussex, representing that county when he was only 18 years of age, and at once taking a very high position as a splendid batsman and fine field. The season of 1875 was his best for the county; he scored 191 in a single innings against Kent, and averaged 61 for the whole season. When the bowling was at all off the spot, Mr. Cotterill was in his element, and spectators had a rare display of scientific and all-round hitting; or, if the boundaries were small, he adapted himself to the situation, and, instead of going in for low hitting all along the ground, he put additional force into the stroke and hit right over the ropes. The match, United South *v*. Twenty-two of Edinburgh, at Edinburgh, in 1872, was played on a rather small ground, and I remember how he ran out at every favourable opportunity and hit the ball time after time among the spectators for his 95, second innings. He did not play for the Gentlemen so often as his performances entitled him to, but after his removal to Edinburgh he doubtless found his medical work prevented him from travelling so far south.

Few players have been so successful in throwing the cricket-ball, his performances that way being exceptionally good.

I competed against him at Eastbourne Sports in 1870, and a very good contest we had. The cricketers present took sides, and we were heartily cheered in the final throw, which was considered excellent at the time. My last effort, when measured, was 116 yds.; his, as well as I can remember, half-dozen yards less. But it will be seen from the following results that he exceeded that five years later:

In June, 1872, at the Edinburgh University Sports, he threw 116 yds. 1 ft. 4 ins.

In September, 1874, at Lewes Priory Sports, Sussex, he threw 111 yds.

In March, 1875, at Edinburgh University Trial Sports, he threw 113 yds.

On March 27th, 1875, in the Scottish Inter-University Sports, at Edinburgh, he threw 121 yds.

Mr. JAMES CRANSTON was born at Birmingham on the 9th January, 1859. His height is 5 ft. 11 ins.; weight, 14 st. 6 lbs. He is, in my opinion, the finest left-hand batsman in England. As long ago as 1876, when he was but seventeen years of age, he played for Gloucestershire, and met with fair success. Gradually he built up his reputation, and in 1881 he was acknowledged to be quite first-class in county contests as a batsman and field. In the year 1883 he was very successful with the bat for his county, and could show the very good average of 28 for eleven completed innings; a brilliant 127 against Lancashire at Clifton being his highest score. A break then occurred in his cricketing career, owing to his removal to Warwickshire, and he did not appear in the eleven again until 1889. Very quickly he showed that he had lost none of his powers, for that season revealed that he still possessed his old hitting form and had improved his defence and placing, while his fielding was as accurate and safe as ever. The year 1890 was his best batting year. He displayed grand form for Gloucestershire, and came out fourth in the first-class averages.

He played for Warwickshire once or twice in 1886 and 1887, but did not come off; and the committee of that county have been censured more than once for not having played him oftener. Many amusing things have been written concerning this since his subsequent success for Gloucestershire; but I think the following, which appeared in a Birmingham paper, is really the most laughable:

"A batsman named Cranston made a promising *debut* last week down in the West Country. He was playing for a local club named Gloucestershire, captained by a Mr. Grace who has some reputation in the district, and he began his season by making over a hundred against an eleven from Yorkshire, which has some grand bowlers. We wonder if Cranston is the same man who was tried for Warwickshire a few seasons ago and rejected. But, of course, ability to make a hundred in such cricket as he is now playing is no criterion of his capacity to make runs for Warwickshire."

Now that is very funny, and very sarcastic; but I am sure Mr. Cranston will agree with me when I say that he was living in the country at the time, where he could get very little, and no good practice, and was consequently not in his best form.

Mr. Cranston plays with a very straight bat, and comes down on the ball very firmly. He drives and cuts well, and rarely allows a ball to pass. He is very good in the long-field, and, though not so brilliant as he was ten years ago, can always be relied on for a catch. He represented the Gentlemen against the Players in 1889-90, and England *v.* Australia in 1890. His best batting years have been:

	Completed Innings.	Runs.	Most in an Innings.	Average.
1881	12 ...	317 ...	63 ...	26. 5
1889	23 ...	709 ...	130 ...	30.19
1890	34 ...	978 ...	152 ...	28.26

Mr. RICHARD DAFT was born at Nottingham, 2nd November, 1835. His height was 5 ft. 9¼ in.; weight, 11 st. He was the most finished and graceful batsman in England for a great many years. It seems but the other day that I was playing against him; and I can hardly believe that he belonged to the great players when I was in my ninth year and quite unknown. He originally played as an amateur, but joined the ranks of the professionals in 1859. From that year until 1876 he was the most scientific batsman amongst the professionals, delighting everyone by his upright, manly style of defence and exceptional wrist-power. The

MR. R. DAFT

quality of the bowling made little difference to him; he played all sorts from fast round to underhand lobs with consummate ease and confidence, and never seemed to tire.

Many a weary day he gave us in the Gentlemen *v.* Players matches, and I was just as thankful to see his back to the wicket as he was mine. He was a fine field at long-leg, and that too at a time of rough kicking grounds, when it required both skill and nerve to pick up a ball smartly and accurately. He made an excellent captain, and led the Players and Nottinghamshire to many a victory. He returned to his first love, the Amateurs, before giving up first-class play. His best batting years were:

	Completed Innings.	Runs.	Most in an Innings.	Average.
1867	7	377	72*	53. 6
1869	10	494	105	49. 4
1870	11	565	117	51. 4
1871	15	565	92	37.10
1872	17	589	102	34.11
1873	11	416	161	37. 9
1876	26	886	99	34. 2

Mr. Ludford Charles Docker was born at Smethwick, in Staffordshire, 26th November, 1860. His height is 6 ft. 2 in.; weight, 12 st. 12 lbs. His brilliant batting and fielding capabilities at a very early age, in connection with the Smethwick Club, attracted the attention of the Derbyshire Committee, and he was asked to play for that county when he was in his twenty-first year.

I question if any young player has ever done better for his county the first year of his appearance. From the beginning right to the end of the season of 1881 Mr. Docker batted in exceptionally fine form, and one week in particular towards the end of the season was a veritable triumph for him. Against Sussex, at Brighton, he scored 52 and 80, and in the next match, against Kent at Maidstone, 107 and 35 not out. For the whole of the season he could show in County matches the fine average of 36 for 12 completed innings. He continued to play for Derbyshire until 1886, and captained the eleven in 1884-5. In 1887 he transferred his services to Warwickshire, and for that county he has since played. For both counties he has, with one or two exceptions, been at the top of the batting averages every year. He was a member of Shrewsbury's team which visited Australia in 1887-8, and it is said of him that he never missed a catch in the long field throughout the tour.

As a batsman he has good defence, and is one of the quickest of scorers, his cutting and off-driving being exceptionally fine. In the field he is very safe and quick, especially in the long-field; and he is a cheerful, willing worker, whether the match is going in his favour or against him.

THOMAS EMMETT was born at Halifax, Yorkshire, September 3rd, 1841. His height was 5 ft. 8 ins.; weight, 11½ st. No finer professional cricketer has ever appeared, and to give his great bowling performances would take up twenty pages of a goodly-sized book. He bowled fast round-arm left hand, with a high and puzzling delivery and a fair amount of break from the leg, and on his day was unplayable. I have had more wide balls from him than I can remember; but I have had occasional balls from him that would have beaten any batsman, and, with the exception of Freeman, I had to watch him more than any bowler. When they were on together, I realised that a hundred runs against them was something to be proud of. His best ball was one pitching between the legs and the wicket, with sufficient break and rise to hit the off bail. More than once he bowled me with that ball when I was well set

T. EMMETT.

and had scored heavily, and I left the wicket believing a similar ball would always beat me or anyone. He had another ball which was sometimes effective. It was bowled a little outside the off stump, and broke away slightly, often touching the edge of the bat and going to long-slip: but he overdid it occasionally, and was hit to the boundary. It will not do to reveal the number of wide balls he has bowled; but he had not much occasion to grumble at the umpires on that score, for many a glaring one was passed over, the umpire excusing it on the ground of it being "only Tom's preliminary canter."

I might give a dozen of his great bowling performances, but shall content myself with three. For Twenty-two of Dudley against the United England Eleven, in 1867, he took eight wickets first innings and eight second; ten of them clean-bowled, and Carpenter's among them. For Yorkshire *v.* Nottinghamshire, in 1868, he took nine wickets for 34 runs (the other was run out), Daft, Parr, and Wild's among them, and Freeman bowling at the other end. For Yorkshire *v.* Cambridgeshire, in 1869, he took seven wickets for 16 runs first innings, and nine for 23 second (he caught the tenth), Hayward and Carpenter's among them and Freeman bowling at the other end. He appeared for the Players in 1869, and as late as 1884, in his 43rd year, and bowled and batted in good form.

He batted in much better style than most left-hand batsmen, pulling less and possessing sounder defence, and his driving was both clean and hard. He rarely failed to score against Gloucestershire, and played against that county in 1887, when he was in his 46th year. As captain of Yorkshire he was modest about his own abilities, and ought to have bowled more; and I am of opinion that, though advanced in years, that county might have played him a year or two longer with advantage. At the beginning of his innings he was sometimes rather excited, and started off for a run as soon as he touched the ball, without looking where it had gone. Once at Lord's he touched one which came straight to me at short-slip; but as usual he was off, and I had thrown the wicket down before he thought of looking round. I can remember now the expression that stole over his face when he realised how impetuous he had been.

He had a keen sense of the ludicrous, and could laugh as heartily, when he had blundered, as anyone. On a certain occasion, after having passed my medical examination, I had travelled all night from Edinburgh to London, and was making my way from the railway-station to Lord's, when I overtook Tom. He knew where I had been and my purpose, and was anxious to know the result. "Is it all right, sir?" "All right, Tom," I replied, "I have got my diploma," pointing to the case containing it which I had in my hand. It had rained during the night, and the ground at Lord's was very wet. We batted first, and Tom was fielding at cover-point. In trying to stop a hard hit of mine, he slipped and fell heavily backward, and did not get up for a little. "Are you hurt, Tom?" I asked. He pulled himself together, got up and, pointing to a lovely mud-mark on his trousers, replied, "No, sir; but I have got my diploma!"

Gloucestershire played England in 1878, and Emmett was batting to F. Townsend's curly underhand slows. Rather than run the risk of hitting into cover-point's hands one or two that were a foot or more off the wicket, he allowed them to pass. Townsend persevered, and Emmett, to show his contempt for the bowling, shouldered his bat and smiled as the ball passed him. But the bowler got rather more break than usual on one ball, and the batsman, with uplifted bat, had the mortification of seeing it curl in and hit the off stump. "A little over-confident, were you not, Tom?" we shouted as he left the wicket; but he took no notice of our remarks. Quite a storm of voices greeted him as reached the pavilion: "What was the matter, Tom?" "Don't Tom me!" he replied. "Well, Emmett, then." "Don't Emmett me!" "Would you like to be called Mr. Emmett?" "Look you," he said, "call me a—fool, for I feel like one!"

There was no brighter spirit in the field, and there was none more willing. He worked heart and soul in every department of the game, and was always ready to do a spell of fielding to oblige anyone. He had a bumper benefit in the Yorkshire *v.* Gloucestershire match at Sheffield in 1878, and every player in both elevens worked with a will to testify to the merits of one of the ablest and best-hearted cricketers that ever played. His best bowling years were:

	Overs.	Maidens.	Runs.	Wickets.	Average.
1867	166	69	236	40	5.36
1868	407	205	529	59	8.57
1869	558	285	721	59	12.13
1870	437	177	753	55	13.38
1874	856	308	1171	99	11.82
1877	617	260	1004	72	13.68
1878	982	464	1278	112	11.46
1879	435	161	566	54	10.26
1882	730	350	1044	95	10.94
1884	1031	557	1250	107	11.73
1886	1339	677	1675	132	12.91

Mr. John James Ferris was born at Sydney on the 21st of May, 1867. His height is 5 ft. 8 ins.; weight, 11 st. 3 lbs. He may be safely considered the best left-hand bowler that has ever come from Australia; the only one likely to question his right to it being Mr. Frank Allan, who accompanied the first team in 1878. Ferris bowls medium-pace, keeps a splendid length, and as a rule breaks from leg; but occasionally he puts in a beauty which comes with his arm. Like Turner, he alters his pace with good judgment; but he is more reliable on a perfect wicket, not caring a bit about being hit, and he can keep up his end as pluckily as any one. As he has only completed his 24th year, he may be expected to improve for some years to come. He is a safe field, and can make runs when they are badly wanted. His bowling performances in England in 1888 and 1890 were something remarkable for so young a player:

	Overs.	Maidens.	Runs.	Wickets.	Average.
1888	2222	998	3103	220	14.23.
1890	1685	688	2838	215	13.43.

Mr. CHARLES KING FRANCIS was born at Upminster, Essex, 3rd February, 1851. His height was 5 ft. 10 ins; weight, 11 st. 8 lbs. He was a good all-round man, batting freely and in good style, and bowling with great success in good matches. For Rugby he bowled with great effect against Marlborough, at Lord's, in June, 1869, taking seven wickets first innings and all ten second. He played for the Gentlemen when he was 19 years of age, and for some years afterwards; but was more successful with the ball than the bat. He bowled very straight and very fast round-arm, and occasionally gave a short, bumpy ball that was difficult to get away from. He was one of Mr. Fitzgerald's team which visited Canada in 1872, and he did good work for it.

GEORGE FREEMAN was born at Boroughbridge, Yorkshire, 28th July, 1844. His height was 5 ft. 10½ in.; weight, about 14 st. He was the finest fast bowler I ever played against: not, perhaps, the fastest; but his bowling came quickly off the pitch, and the spin he got on it troubled me more than any bowler I can remember. His delivery was easy, and he could keep it up for a very long time; and when the ball hit you, you felt as

GEORGE FREEMAN

if you had been cut with a knife or a piece of the skin had been snipped off. The first time I met him was in the South *v.* North match at Sheffield in 1869, when I had just completed my twenty-first year, and was batting in my best form. In the first innings I made 122 out of a total of 169, and Freeman was the only bowler who gave me trouble; in the second innings he beat me with a shooter, and after the ball hit the wicket it kept spinning for a few seconds between the stumps, and then lay perfectly dead at the bottom of them.

As a bat he was a fine hitter, and scored largely at times, as witness his 123 for Malton *v.* All-England Eleven in 1868, against Tarrant, Tinley, J. C. Shaw and Alfred Shaw. Owing to pressure of business, he played very little first-class cricket after 1872. I sometimes think if a bowler of the quality of Freeman were to appear to-day, he would astonish the majority of good batsmen who think it a first-rate performance to keep up their wickets against medium-pace bowlers because they can break a little both ways. Freeman was a good fieldsman as well, and a real good fellow also. His best bowling years were:

	Overs.	Maidens.	Runs.	Wickets.	Average.
1867 ...	564 ...	310 ...	553 ...	66 ...	8,25
1868 ...	392 ...	197 ...	454 ...	46 ...	9.40
1869 ...	540 ...	300 ...	577 ...	50 ..	11.27
1870 ...	433 ...	216 ...	417 ...	55 ...	7.32
1871 ...	255 ...	122 ...	331 ...	29 ...	11.12

Mr. Thomas William Garrett was born at Wollongong, near Sydney, New South Wales, on the 26th July, 1858. His height is 5 ft. 11 ins.; weight, 12 st. He came to England with the first Australian Eleven, and was very successful as a bowler. He bowls right-hand, fast round-arm, mostly over the wicket, and has a beautifully easy action. The ball comes very quickly off the pitch, and he can break both ways. I have little hesitation in saying that he was at that time the best of the Australian bowlers on a good wicket; for he kept pegging away with a good length, and required a great deal of watching. His particular ball was one that pitched on the off stump and broke slightly away, and he was a lucky batsman who did not touch it either into short-slip or the wicket-keeper's hands. Like all of the Australian bowlers, he is very fond of a yorker. He is a good field and a fair bat, hitting out well and occasionally running up good scores; in fact, he is a good all-round cricketer, and a good fellow as well. His best bowling performances for the Australian Elevens in England, in eleven-a-side matches, were:

	Overs.	Maidens.	Runs.	Wickets.	Average.
1878	... 296	... 144	... 394	... 38	... 10.14
1882	... 1206	... 488	... 1759	... 128	... 13.95
1886	... 1650	... 778	... 2221	... 123	... 18. 7

Mr. GEORGE GIFFEN was born at Adelaide, South Australia, on the 27th March, 1852. His height is 5 ft. 9½ in.; weight, 12 st. 7 lb. He has the reputation of being the best all-round cricketer in Australia: he has certainly proved himself to be the best that has yet visited England. In bowling he was not up to Spofforth's form or one or two others; nor was he so successful with the bat as Murdoch; but there can be little doubt that he combined both in a way no other Australian has yet done.

He first came to us in 1882, but 1886 was his great year, when he headed the averages with both bat and ball, and was the backbone of the team. I know that he has done even better in Australia than in England, but I have not his doings on the other side by me, and can only give what I know and what I have seen. One feat on the other side I must make room for: his bowling for the Anglo-Australian Eleven *v.* Combined Australia on the 16th February, 1884, when he took all 10 wickets for 66 runs.

As a batsman Giffen never gave me the impression of being troubled with nerves. He was perfectly cool and collected on all occasions, and it made little difference whether he went in first man or later in the innings. He had great patience as well, and watched the ball very closely; and his hitting was good all round. His bowling was medium-pace, right-hand, with a good break from the off, varied with a fast one; and he altered both pitch and pace with great effect. He had a very high delivery and a peculiar swing of the arm, which distracted the attention of the batsman. In the field he was very good also. Batting and bowling averages in England, in eleven-a-side matches:

BATTING.

	Completed Innings.	Runs.	Most in an Innings.	Average.
1882	48	873	81	18. 9
1884	50	1052	113	21. 2
1886	54	1453	119	26.49

BOWLING.

	Overs.	Maidens.	Runs.	Wickets.	Average.
1882	386	122	728	32	22.24
1884	827	285	1619	82	19.61
1886	1693	722	2711	159	17. 8

Mr. CHARLES ERNEST GREEN was born at Walthamstow, Essex, 26th August, 1846. His height was 6 ft.; weight, 13 st. He was a rare good batsman, and one of the pluckiest. When we were in together the runs came at a great pace, and it was a treat to watch him punish the bowling. Very few of our best batsmen played in so free a style against all kinds of bowling, and he did not always require a perfect wicket to do it. I can recall one match at Lord's, M.C.C. and Ground *v.* Yorkshire, in 1870, when he stood up to Emmett and Freeman, on one of the roughest, bumpiest wickets we had now and then on that ground twenty years ago. About every third or fourth ball kicked badly, and we were hit all over the body and had to dodge an occasional one with our heads. Shooters were pretty common on the same wicket, and what with playing one ball and dodging another we had a lively and unenviable time of it. But not once did Mr. Green shirk the work, and his 51 against such bowling was, to my mind, a wonderful performance. On another occasion, for the Gentlemen of the South *v.* Players of the South, at the Oval, on a good wicket, he rattled up 50 in a very short time in a way that I have rarely seen equalled; and his 57 not out for the Gentlemen *v.* Players, at the Oval in 1871, was one of the finest bits of hitting I can remember, and enabled the Gentlemen to win the match three minutes before time.

He was a splendid fieldsman also, and at long-leg, or long-stopping, could hold his own with our finest exponents. He bowled round-arm, very fast, and took wickets when better bowlers had failed. At his best he played in most of the great matches, the Gentlemen *v.* Players included, and invariably accompanied the Uppingham Rovers on their annual tour. He also played for Sussex in his younger days; but his native county, Essex, has had the best of his time and manhood, and may be said to owe its existence to-day to his unwearied and unselfish efforts. In 1867 he was one of the secretaries of the Cambridge University Cricket Club, and was elected President the year after. As an all-round athlete he was much above the average, and represented his university in 1867 and 1868. He threw the cricket-ball 103 yards; in a long jump cleared 18 ft. 9 in., and in the high jump 5 ft. 7½ in.; and held his own against good competitors in the 100 yards, one mile, and hurdle races.

WILLIAM GUNN was born at Nottingham on December 4th, 1858. His height is 6 ft. 3 in.; weight 14 st. 4 lbs. He did not represent his county at so early an age as some players; but he very soon showed that he possessed batting powers of no mean order. So pleased were the authorities of the M.C.C. with his first display at Lord's, that they made him the offer of a place as one of the ground-bowlers, which he promptly accepted. But he very soon gave evidence that it was as a batsman, and not as a bowler, that he was going to attract attention. The year 1881 saw him exceeding 100 more than once for the old club, though he did not score so successfully for his county.

In the year 1884 he made distinct improvement, and every year since he has been a most prominent figure with the bat in county and representative matches. His great height enables him to get well over the ball, and of late years his defence has much improved. He hits very hard and clean; but he has not scored so fast the last two or three years as he used to.

His highest score for his county is 205, made against Sussex in 1887; but he exceeded that by 14 runs two years later, and was not out, in the memorable match M.C.C. and Ground *v.* Northumberland. He has proved himself to be a magnificent field in the country; and his displays for the Players *v.* Gentlemen at the Oval and Lord's the last two or three years have been magnificent. The year 1889 saw him at the top of the batting averages in first-class cricket; and he took second place in 1890. His grand score of 228 for the Players against the Australians at Lord's on the 19th and 20th June, 1890, will be remembered as one of the finest bits of batting that has ever been witnessed against first-class bowling. There was not the shadow of a chance in it, and the last 28 runs were made in the same careful and scientific manner as the first hundred. Altogether he batted nine and a half hours, and it was the highest score ever made by professional or amateur against an Australian eleven in England. He has been moderately successful as a bowler.

His best batting averages in first-class matches:

	Completed Innings.	Runs.	Most in an Innings.	Average.
1884	25	647	138	25.22
1885	40	1451	203	36.11
1886	28	752	83	26.24
1887	27	958	205*	35.13
1888	45	920	91	20.20
1889	34	1299	118	38. 7
1890	47	1621	228	34.23

Mr. E. Maitland Hadow was born at Sudbury, Middlesex, March 13th, 1863. His height is 5 ft. 10 in.; weight, 12 stone. He is the youngest brother of a well-known family, of which more than one member has played a prominent part in first-class cricket. The year 1880 saw him representing Harrow *v.* Eton; and in 1881, in the same match, he played two very fine innings, and enabled his school to win very easily. Two years later he played for Middlesex; but from various causes he has not been able to play much for that county until the last three years. Since 1888, however, he has been a most active player, playing for Middlesex, M.C.C., I Zingari, Free Foresters, and Harrow Wanderers, and doing fine work for all of them. He is a good batsman, his off-driving being exceptionally fine; an excellent change fast round-arm bowler and a brilliant fieldsman; and if he continues playing will take a still higher position amongst first-class cricketers.

Mr. Walter Henry Hadow was born in London, 25th September, 1849. His height was 6 ft. 0½ in.; weight, 13½ st. He was a very fine batsman, with a free style, and could hit all round. For Harrow he was very successful, scoring 181 not out against the Household Brigade when he was only 16 years of age. His finest performance was 217 for Middlesex *v.* M.C.C. in 1871, when he scored very freely and rapidly. Owing to an injured leg, he had a man to run for him the greater part of the innings; but, considering the quality of the bowling, it was a very fine display, and created a great impression at the time. He accompanied Mr. Fitzgerald's team to Canada; but hurting his knee before the tour commenced, he did not do himself justice; although I remember he batted very pluckily at a critical moment in the close and exciting match against Philadelphia, which enabled us to pluck it out of the fire. He was very successful for Middlesex in 1875; and in 1871, for the Gentlemen *v.* Players, at the Oval, he batted very finely for 97 against the bowling of Alfred Shaw, J. C. Shaw, and Southerton. He was one of the racquet champions for Oxford in 1871-72, and excelled at tennis also.

LOUIS HALL was born at Batley, Yorkshire, on November 1st, 1852. His height is 5 ft. 10 in.; weight, about 11 st. He first played for his county on the 22nd May, 1873, when he scored 37 runs, after he had batted for an hour and 40 minutes. It was a promising start for him, and as his defence was excellent, the Yorkshire Committee naturally thought they had secured a valuable recruit for the eleven; however, he did not do much during the remainder of the season, and he was left out of county contests until 1878. From that year he improved quickly; and to-day, although in his 39th year, there is no more dependable bat in the Yorkshire eleven. He invariably goes in first, and the spectators are never surprised when he comes out last, or carries his bat throughout the innings. I believe that he has carried his bat through the Yorkshire innings on thirteen different occasions. His patience and coolness are quite equal to Scotton's, and his scoring pace not much faster. From 10 to 15 runs an hour is a fair average for him. But he can hit when he makes up his mind to; these occurrences, however, are few and far between.

I remember one of them. It was some years ago, when the United South played Eighteen of Batley. I was bowling to him, and had tried to tempt him to hit out for some overs, but failed. Suddenly he woke up, and, to my surprise, hit me to square-leg clean out of the ground: and he kept it up for some time.

In the same match I had rather a peculiar experience. I was fairly well set, when a bowler whom I had never seen before was commissioned to have a try at me. The very first ball was a deliberate throw, and it hit my wicket, and I had to go out, every one of the opposite side alleging that as the umpire had not "no-balled" him, the ball must be considered to have been fairly delivered. The joke of the thing lay in the fact that the bowler had been engaged to play entirely owing to his throwing powers, and was only to be allowed to bowl one over at me. They still tell that story against me in the North.

Hall can drive fairly well, and is good on the leg-side; but it is his unwearied patience and strong defence which make him so valuable a bat. He is a good field close in, and can bowl lobs or slow round. He has scored over 100 runs in an innings on several occasions, and has represented the Players against the Gentlemen for many years. He captained the Yorkshire eleven for some time. Hall is a strict teetotaller. His best batting years have been:

	Completed Innings.	Runs.	Most in an innings.	Average.
1883	35	1180	127	33.25
1887	32	1240	160	38.24

The Hon. GEORGE ROBERT CANNING HARRIS, now Lord Harris, was born at St. Anne's, Trinidad, West Indies, 3rd February, 1851. His height is 5 ft. 11½ ins.; weight, 11 st. 12 lbs. He has proved himself to be a distinguished cricketer and a distinguished politician; an upright, true-hearted English gentleman, and the best of friends. No one has had the game more at heart, or done more for it; and every cricketer in England felt it had lost one of its greatest supporters when, in taking farewell of the County Cricket Council, at Lord's, in December, 1889, he said: "My cricket book is closed; but it contains nothing but the pleasantest of recollections."

Eton, Oxford, and Kent have had occasion to be proud of him: his county in particular; for he displayed good form as a batsman and field, and bowled occasionally with success during the many years he represented it. There are few better judges of what constitutes a first-class cricketer, and as captain of an eleven no one can spot the weakness or strength of an opponent better. He has a very free, correct style of batting; keeps up his wicket with great patience when the bowling is good, and hits freely when it is loose. Repeatedly he has scored over 100 runs in an innings for his county, and he played in the Gentlemen's Eleven for many years. He was Secretary, Captain, and President of Kent County Club, and executed the duties pertaining to these offices with great success for the county and marked credit to himself; and it was entirely owing to his personal efforts that his county has again come to the front. In his younger days he was a most brilliant outfield, covering a large amount of ground, picking up the ball quickly and neatly, and returning it smartly and accurately to the wicket; but in later years he has fielded in closer, chiefly at short-slip,

LORD HARRIS.

and is just as successful in that position. No safer pair of hands can be desired, and no more willing worker ever played in an eleven. He bowls round-arm, medium-pace.

We have played side by side in more matches than I can remember: first for Mr. Fitzgerald's team in Canada and America; then for Gentlemen *v.* Players, Kent and Gloucestershire *v.* England, England *v.* Australia and other representative matches. He was the heart and soul of the Canadian trip, and we were the closest of friends from beginning to end of it; for we had two things in common—our sailing and speaking capabilities. We never sailed but we were ill together, and we never got on our legs to attempt a speech without wishing we had never been born! When I listened to his eloquent remarks at Canterbury at the end of 1889 season, I could not help recalling certain efforts in the Canadian trip, and feeling keenly how I had neglected my opportunities, while he had cultivated his. But he has had many long innings at it since, and gone forward; while mine have been short, and I very much fear I have gone back.

No cricketer is quicker to congratulate a comrade on a fine performance. In the Kent *v.* Gloucestershire match at Clifton, in 1887, when I scored 100 twice in a match, the second time in my career, he was the first to applaud. A little before the time for drawing stumps on the third day, when I was about twenty runs short of the number to complete the feat, and the regular Kent bowlers had failed to dislodge me, he put on underhand bowling. That had no effect; and, knowing the match could not be lost, he kindly allowed the bowler to continue an over or two longer so that I might accomplish my end. He could easily have made another change, which might have prevented me from doing it before time expired.

His best batting years were:

	Completed Innings.	Runs.	Most in an Innings.	Average.
1874	8	234	58	29. 2
1875	19	631	92	33. 4
1876	29	916	154	31.17
1880	22	722	123	32.18
1882	24	787	176	32.19
1883	30	919	118	30.19
1884	42	1417	112*	33.31
1886	20	644	76	32. 4

The Hon. Martin Bladen Hawke, now Lord Hawke, was born on the 10th August, 1860. He has taken a very prominent part in Yorkshire County Cricket, and the game has no warmer supporter. He first represented his county in 1881, and was chosen captain of the team in 1883, a position which he has filled most satisfactorily. Always a hard worker, he has the power of stimulating his team to do their best, and he has fought pluckily for years to give Yorkshire a better position amongst the counties. His style of batting is excellent, as he plays both forward and back with equal confidence, and comes down on the ball clean and hard. Few batsmen hit more freely, his driving being particularly good; and he always plays the game, whether it be a winning or losing one. And when he is in for one of his long scores no one can bat in better style. As one or two critics have remarked, "When he makes runs, he gets them as well as anybody."

He represented Cambridge University in 1882 and 1883, and was captain of the eleven in 1885; and he also played in Mr. Vernon's Australian team in 1887-8, and Indian team in 1890.

Thomas Hayward was born at Chatteris, Cambridgeshire, 21st March, 1835. His height was 5 ft. 8 in.; weight, 9 st. 10 lbs. For years Carpenter and he ran a close race for batting honours, and it is difficult to say

LORD HAWKE.

which was the better batsman. Hayward had a freer, more graceful style of play, and did not hesitate to go out of his ground to hit; but Carpenter's was the more difficult wicket to get. Hayward was also a good bowler —medium-pace, round-arm, with a break from the off —and owing to that was considered the best all-round cricketer of his day. More than once he scored over 100 runs in the Gentlemen *v.* Players match, and he is one of the few credited with a 200 score in a single innings. The 200 was made for the Gentlemen of Cambridgeshire *v.* Undergraduates in 1859, when he was playing as a given man. The bowling was not first-class by any means, but good enough to make the score noteworthy.

THOMAS HEARNE was born at Chalfont St. Peter's, Buckinghamshire, Sept. 4th, 1826. His height was 5 ft. 10½ in.; weight 11⅓ st. He was a fine batsman, possessing good sound defence, and hit to all parts of the field. His leg hitting and driving were exceptionally good, and his runs were made very quickly; and he was one of the few I can call to mind who played the old-fashioned draw with great certainty and effect, That stroke may be said to have died with him and one or two other batsmen of his time, for it has been little used of late; indeed it would be dangerous against bowlers who get much break on the ball, and I have always thought there was more likelihood of playing on or being bowled off the pads in attempting it than playing the ball firmly in front. Hearne did not appear at Lord's until late in life, and he was 36 years of age before he represented the Players. He also played for Middlesex and M.C.C., and was very successful for both. When the Eleven was being chosen to represent the Players, in 1866, the opinion of the majority was dead against Hearne, but one or two pressed for another chance, as it was likely to be his last opportunity, he then being in his 40th year. He scored 16 first innings, 122 not out second, and he never batted better in his life, playing his pet stroke—the draw—repeatedly and well.

As a bowler he was above medium-pace, but not fast; but he bowled very straight and kept a fair length. Like Grundy and one or two others belonging to the ground bowlers at Lord's, he was more inclined to bowl too short than too far up, a habit they had got into owing to the nature of the ground. The pitch was very lively, and short balls bounded rather high, which made them difficult to hit with safety—a point which Hearne and Grundy made use of. I know when they tried a similar length ball on a slower wicket elsewhere they got punished rather severely. Hearne was a very good fieldsman close in, and could keep wicket. He succeeded Grundy as head bowler at Lord's in 1872, which position he still holds.

ALLEN HILL was born at Kirkheaton, near Huddersfield, Yorkshire, 14th November, 1845. His height was 5 ft. 11 ins.; weight, 12½ st. He was one of our very best fast round-arm bowlers, particularly between 1870 and 1875. For Yorkshire he did good work in conjunction with Emmett, after Freeman gave up playing. In pace he was not quite so fast as Freeman or Tarrant; but he had a very easy delivery and beautiful style. He did not put much work on the ball, although now and then he would break from the off; but he bowled very straight and kept a good length, and I have had occasional balls from him that required all my skill to get my bat in front of, and one or two that completely beat me. I forget the exact distance he took before delivering the ball; but I know it was much shorter than the average run of fast bowlers. For his county he was very successful during the years I have mentioned, and in 1874 his form with the ball enabled the Players to win their match against the Gentlemen at Lord's on the 6th and 7th July. He clean-bowled Messrs. A. N. Hornby, C. F. Buller, G. F. Grace and myself in the first innings. The Players had not won a match since 1866, and Hill had reason to be pleased with his performance. He was very keen, and tried all he knew to get wickets, no matter the quality of the batsmen against him: but after I got well set I have seen him decline to bowl a third or fourth time.

He was not much of a bat, being more inclined to hit than keep up his wicket; but he was a good field at short-slip, and one of the quietest and most unassuming players it has been my pleasure to meet. But that has been characteristic of Yorkshire county players generally, ever since I played against them.

His best bowling years were:

	Overs.	Maidens.	Runs.	Wickets.	Average.
1873	741	299	1064	81	13.11
1874	668	266	983	89	11. 4
1875	1265	577	1738	109	15.103
1876	1208	504	1861	109	17. 8
1881	337	154	435	43	10. 5

Mr. ALBERT NEILSON HORNBY is another of our brilliant amateurs. He was born at Blackburn, Lancashire, 10th February, 1847. His height is 5 ft. 9½ ins.; weight, at his best, 11½ st. I have been associated very closely with him, for we made the trip together to Canada in 1872, and have fought side by side or against each other at home every year in the last twenty. Harrow boasts of him as one of her greatest sons; for he was in the school eleven at an early age, and has since done wonders at both cricket and football. Very few cricketers have so attractive a style, and it has always been a treat to watch his dashing play. Perhaps he is a little too anxious to score at times; but when he makes up his mind to defend his

MR. A. N. HORNBY.

wicket, the bowling, whatever the quality of it, has a heavy problem to solve. And when he begins hitting there is no stopping him: it means hitting to all parts of the ground at a terrific pace, and the batsman at the other end is dwarfed by comparison.

I should say Mr. Hornby, with the exception of myself, has gone in to bat first man oftener than any man in England or out of it, and his record for first wicket down in the matches he has played—Lancashire county matches in particular—should be exceptionally high. He has a wonderful eye, and at his best was very quick on his legs for a short run, at times accomplishing extraordinary things which electrified his opponents and the spectators. I know he used to be the terror of some batsmen who were in with him, and one or two have said they never knew whether they were on their head or their legs while the partnership continued; but I never had any difficulty with him. If I said "No," he was prompt to respond; and no matter how far up the wicket he might be, he could always get back in time.

On one occasion, at Prince's, when we were in together, instead of trying to punish the bowling and make as many runs as we could, we played tip and run for half an hour, and completely demoralised the bowlers and fieldsmen. Each tried to outdo the other in desperate endeavour, and I should say that that half-hour was about the liveliest seen on a cricket-field. One run was a curiosity. I played a ball in front of me, and without looking where it was going yelled "Come on, Hornby!" I had no need to say "Come on" to him; for he was up like a flash of lightning, and had crossed before the words were out of my mouth. The ball travelled straight up the pitch to Willsher, the bowler, who ran up a yard or so to meet it, and I thought it was all over with me; for I was not more than half-way when he picked it up. I had the sense to keep running, and Willsher hearing my feet thundering behind him lost his head, and instead of putting the wicket down quietly, as he might have done, let fly with all his force and missed it by yards! I believe that was the culminating point of our temporary insanity; for Mr. Hornby and I were so tickled at the absurdity of the run attempted that we settled down and played correctly.

Mr. Hornby's scores have been very large. He has exceeded 100 as many as eight times in one year, and more than once has scored over 200 runs in an innings. He scored 104 in the Gentlemen *v.* Players match in 1873, against the bowling of J. C. Shaw, Alfred Shaw, Emmett, Willsher and James Lillywhite; and 144 in the same match, against Mycroft, Morley, Emmett, Ulyett and Barratt, in 1877; and at the end of the season of 1881 took first place in batting honours, being well ahead of both amateurs and professionals. Three times in 1881 he scored over a hundred in an innings for his county, the highest being 188, against Derbyshire.

No finer fieldsman ever donned flannels: in his best days he was most brilliant at coverpoint or longleg, and never seemed to tire. He has captained the Lancashire Eleven to many a glorious victory, and he is almost idolised by them.

His best batting years:

	Completed Innings.	Runs.	Most in an Innings.	Average.
1870	8	338	132	42. 2
1872	10	314	80	31. 4
1873	17	586	64	34. 8
1877	26	764	144	29.10
1879	20	606	64*	30. 6
1881	37	1531	188	41.14
1882	49	1383	131	28.11
1890	30	672	75	22.12

GEORGE HOWITT was born at Old Lenton, Nottinghamshire, 14th March, 1843. His height was 5 ft. 8½ in.; weight, 10½ st. He was a very successful fast left-hand, round-arm bowler, with a good break from the leg. Now and then he would put in a real beauty which would test any batsman's defence. In 1868, he got me out for a brace of "ducks" at Neath, in the match United South *v.* Twenty-two of Cadoxton Club, when he was playing for the Twenty-two. He moved to London about 1860, and afterwards played for both Middlesex and Nottinghamshire. He was an indifferent batsman; but he has the credit of winning a very exciting match by one wicket for Middlesex and Surrey *v.* England at the Oval in 1868, which was played for the benefit of Julius Cæsar. He was last man in, and skied a ball very high to Charlwood at long-on, which everyone expected that player would hold; but for once about the safest pair of hands in England failed, and the ball fell to the ground.

THOMAS HUMPHREY was born at Mitcham, Surrey, 16th January, 1839. His height was 5 ft. 5 ins.; weight, about 10 st. Humphrey's style was very free, and he could play forward as well as back. He had great patience, and his cutting was equal to Caffyn's in his best days. As a fieldsman he was first-class anywhere, especially at long-leg or long-on, and he was always a willing worker; 1,000 runs during the season was a common thing with him. I remember my father and a clergyman friend travelling up to Swindon solely to see Humphrey and Jupp batting. When they arrived on the ground the pair were in together, and they kept together until my father and his friend were compelled to return home. "What do you think of them?" I asked my father before he left. "Wonderful!" said he; "but, do you know, I should like to see someone else before I go."

About the last time I played with Humphrey was in the Grimsby match in 1876. He had gone off in his play then, and generally batted late in the innings; but as two or three of the eleven had not turned up when we were ready to begin, I said, "Put on your pads, Tom; you may as well come in with me." We were not out at luncheon time; and an hour or so afterwards the absent members were seen making their way to the ground, running at top speed. They had seen Humphrey batting from a distance, and concluded he must be last man in, and they did not want to lose their innings. When they got into the field and saw 80 runs for no wicket, they sat down and laughed heartily. And one or two of them laughed even more heartily next day, for it was well on in the third and last day before their turn came! It was the match in which I scored 400 not out.

Roger Iddison was born at Bedale, Yorkshire, 15th September, 1834. His height was 5 ft. 8 ins.; weight, 12 st. He played his first match at Lord's, 9th, 10th, 11th June, 1862, for The United All-England Eleven *v.* The All-England Eleven. He was a first-rate batsman, and met with great success as a lob-bowler; and he was a good fieldsman at point. G. Freeman and he were the founders of the United North of England Eleven in 1869.

John Jackson was born at Bungay, Suffolk, 21st May, 1833, but his parents soon after removed to Nottinghamshire. His height was 6 ft. 0¼ in.; weight, 15 st. He was one of our great bowlers, and by some thought superior to Wisden and Willsher. He was much faster, and change of weather or wicket made little difference to him. He bowled like a machine, well within his strength, and had a beautiful delivery. His batting was above the average, but not first-class. He belonged to the All-England Eleven, played for the North and Nottinghamshire, and was at his best between 1856 and 1866.

HENRY JUPP, the Surrey crack and mainstay for so many years, was born at Dorking, 19th November, 1841. His height was 5 ft. 6½ in.; weight, about 11 st. Very few profesionals have so good a batting and fielding record. Between the years 1865 and 1876, he scored over 100 in an innings a great many times, and an aggregate of 1,000 runs during the season was of common occurrence with him. He had wonderful defence and patience; but if anything he was a little too steady, blocking balls six inches off the wicket rather than risk his wicket by hitting. His 216 for Players of South *v.* Fourteen Gentlemen of South, in 1865, though not against first-class bowling, was a very fine performance; for he was in a whole day, and did not give the slighest semblance of a chance from beginning to end. There were 78 singles in it. The year 1869, when he scored over 100 runs in an innings five times, was one of his best. In 1874 he did a very fine and exceptional performance for Surrey *v.* Yorkshire at the Oval: going in first in both innings, and being not out at the end of each; his scores being 43 and 109.

He was about the safest catch in the long field I ever saw, and in his younger days covered an immense amount of ground. When we played together for the United South, I could always depend on him for a catch, and I bowled many a ball for that purpose when I knew he was in the long field. What I liked about his fielding was his pluck. No catch seemed impossible to him, and trying for everything, he brought off now and then some of the most remarkable catches ever seen on a cricket-field. He could keep wicket at a pinch, and bowl also. His services were invaluable to me in my Australian tour; but we never could depend on him if we had to travel by water, for he was a wretched sailor.

It is an old story, but will bear repetition, how Jupp and Southerton tried to get me in a fix when the ball bounded into an opening of my shirt while I was running in the Gloucestershire *v.* Surrey match at Clifton College in 1878. Townsend and I were batting, and had run three when the ball lodged there, and after we had run three more, Jupp and Southerton collared me. "We don't know how many runs you mean to run, sir; but you might give us the ball." "No, thank you; take it out for yourself, Jupp," I said, laughing. "You don't get me out in that way!"

He had rather a liking for a glass of champagne, but objected to dilution. When the United South played Walsall on a certain occasion, I was the guest of Mr. Russell, a great supporter of the game. He invited the professionals of the team to look in upon him in the morning, when he would crack a bottle or two before they began the day's play. Jupp turned up with the others, and when asked to have seltzer with it said, "No, thank you, sir; I have always found champagne good enough by itself!"

His best batting years were:

	Completed Innings.	Runs.	Most in an Innings.	Average.
1866	64	1557	165	24.21
1869	37	1299	170	35. 4
1874	35	1275	154	36.15
1876	39	983	92*	25. 8

Rev. CHARLTON GEORGE LANE was born at the Parsonage, Kennington, Surrey, 11th June, 1836. His height was 6 ft.; weight, 12½ st. He was one of the most brilliant amateur batsmen of his time, playing in a fine free style, and possessing great hitting powers. He might be called a "model" batsman for correctness of style. In 1860 he played in the First Eleven of

England *v.* Next Fourteen, and he represented the Gentlemen *v.* Players in 1857, 1858, 1859, 1860, and 1861; and he was one of the veteran players in the Centenary match of the M.C.C. in 1887. He was a very fine field anywhere. He pulled in the Oxford Eight *v.* Cambridge in 1858 and 1859.

JAMES LILLYWHITE, jun., was born at West Hampnett, Sussex, 23rd February, 1842. His height was 5 ft. 7 ins.; weight, at his best, 11 st. 7 lbs. He was in his twenty-first year when he appeared at Lord's, playing for Sussex *v.* the M.C.C., and he improved every year afterwards, and very soon was acknowledged to be one of the best bowlers of the day. He was a nephew of William Lillywhite, the great bowler, and a worthy successor in accuracy of pitch, straightness, and ease of delivery. He bowled left-hand, medium-pace, and never seemed to tire; and earned the title of "The Young Nonpareil." He was a fair left-hand batsman, and scored the century once or twice for his county. He was a member of the team I took to Australia, and has been there several times since.

His best bowling years were:

	Overs.	Maidens.	Runs.	Wickets.	Average.
1866	841	463	894	73	12.18
1872	936	442	1244	94	13.22
1873	1010	441	1377	101	13.64
1875	833	339	1209	88	13.65
1876	990	547	1315	91	14.41

JOHN LILLYWHITE, a son of William Lillywhite the great bowler, was born at Hove, Brighton, 10th Nov., 1826. His height was 5 ft. 5 in.; weight, 11 st. His powers were worthy of the tuition his father bestowed on him, and he became a good all-round player. As a batsman his hitting was very good, and he was an excellent field also. At first he bowled fast round; but afterwards he changed to medium-pace, and became more effective.

Ephraim Lockwood was born at Lascelles Hall, near Huddersfield, Yorkshire, 4th April, 1845. He was one of the best all-round players of his time; batting with success, and fielding with great certainty. He was not a brilliant batsman, nor particularly free in his style; but what he lacked in that respect he made up in patience and carefulness. His bat was always in the way of the ball, and he had few superiors in watching and timing all kinds of bowling on a rough and kicking wicket. He could hit anywhere, his cutting being particularly fine; and he had one peculiar stroke which I used to consider a mis-hit for a long time. Off slow bowling, he made what seemed a half-hearted hit just over the bowler's or mid-off's head, but which did not go far enough for long-field to reach. Time after time a catch seemed likely to come off; but the fieldsman was always a yard or two short, which was very tantalizing, and I was compelled to conclude that the hit, though not pretty to look at, was intentional, especially as he scored by it every time. On a wet or dead wicket he was seen at his best; then he could watch the ball for any length of time; keeping up his wicket with a very straight bat, and putting on the runs at a fair pace when others failed to score.

He bowled round-arm, with a high delivery, varying from medium-pace to slow, and when the ground was heavy got a fair amount of spin on the ball. He batted well for the Players for many years; but particularly in 1874, 1875, 1876, and 1877. In 1874 he scored 67 not out and 48 at the Oval, and 70 in the first innings at Lord's. In 1875 he scored 67 in the second innings at Lord's; in 1876 he scored 70 at Prince's; and in 1877 he scored 97 and 20 at the Oval; and on each occasion he went in first. But I remember we got him out for a brace of ducks at the Oval in 1873.

He captained the Yorkshire Eleven for some years;

but he lacked firmness in that position, pretty much owing to his desire to please everyone. Occasionally bowlers presumed on it, and more than once a member of the eleven refused to bowl when the wicket was not suitable, or the batsman had got set. The Yorkshire *v.* Gloucestershire match at Cheltenham, in 1876, was a case in point. On the second day, when I had scored close upon 300 runs, Lockwood had some difficulty in getting one or two of his bowlers to have a third or fourth trial. His pleadings were responded to with "I don't feel up to it," and his good-nature caused him to give way. Tom Emmett was a bright exception, and blurted out, "Why don't you make 'em? Aint you captain?" "Why don't you, yourself?" said the offending bowler. "You 're as much afraid of the big 'un as I am!" Tom snatched up the ball rather impetuously. "Get out of the way!" said he; "and look out in the long-field. I'm going to finish his innings!" Tom's heart was bigger than his head, or rather his heart was truer than his arm; for he favoured me with three monstrous wides to begin with, and laughing was general all over the ground.

Lockwood's best batting years were:

	Completed innings.	Runs.	Most in an Innings.	Average.
1871	21	612	89	29. 3
1876	40	1261	108	31.21
1881	38	1060	109	27.34

Tom Lockyer was born at Croydon, Nov. 1, 1828, and made his first appearance at Lord's in 1850, playing for Surrey *v.* M.C.C. His height was 5 ft. 10½ in.; weight, 12 st. He was a valuable addition to Surrey, and scored largely at times. He earned a great reputation as a wicket-keeper; taking the ball with equal ease and certainty on both sides of the wicket. When he visited Australia he astonished everyone there, and it was generally admitted that he was the best wicket-keeper of his day.

GEORGE LOHMANN was born at Kensington on the 5th June, 1865. His height is 5ft. 10½in.; weight, 12st. 6lbs. I have little hesitation in saying that no cricketer has attracted more attention in cricket circles during the last two or three years than Lohmann, and that Surrey is mainly indebted to his exceptional performance with the ball for its very high position among the counties any time in the last four years. His rapid success has been almost phenomenal; and to-day he has no superior as a bowler. Since he first represented his county, in 1884, his bowling has been the theme of admiration in England; and very good judges in Australia have said he is the best bowler that ever visited them. He has the enviable and exceptional power of rising to the occasion; and the better the company, the better he performs. He is rapidly developing into a first-class batsman. In the field he is good anywhere, his quickness being almost electrical; and the amount of ground he covers, especially at short-slip, is something remarkable. He rarely allows anything to pass him, and nearly everything possible in the way of a catch he brings off.

He bowls right-hand, round-arm, above medium pace—indeed he might almost be classed as fast—has a beautiful action, and keeps a splendid length; and he alters his pace without altering his action, which is one of the strongest characteristics of a first-class bowler. His command of the ball is half the secret of his success. To a right-hand batsman he bowls on or just outside the off-stump, and breaks back very quickly, but now and then he puts in a very fast one with a break from leg. Should a left-hand batsman follow, especially if he can hit well on the leg-side, he pitches everything on the wicket or off-stump,

GEORGE LOHMANN.

varying it with a faster one, breaking slightly from the off to leg. But the ball he has been as successful with as any is a simple straight good-length one without any break. The batsman expects something exceptional from him every ball, and never thinks that he will treat him with such an easy one, and so while he is looking for the break his wicket is bowled down.

He has a brilliant future before him, possessing good health, strength, and stamina. His greatest performances in first-class cricket so far have been :

BOWLING.

	Overs.	Maidens.	Runs.	Wickets.	Average.
1885	1264	592	2030	142	14.42
1886	1715	809	2425	160	15.25
1887	1634	737	2404	154	15.94
1888	1649	783	2280	209	10.190
1889	1614	646	2714	202	13.90
1890	1759	737	2998	220	13.138

BATTING.

	Completed Innings.	Runs.	Most in an Innings.	Average.
1887	33	843	115	25.18
1890	43	832	57	19.15

Mr. Alfred Percy Lucas was born in London, February 20th, 1857. He is indebted to H. H. Stephenson for his early coaching at Uppingham and the foundation of a batting style that has been the admiration of every first-class player. At school, in 1874, he had the exceptionally fine average of 50.1 for 14 innings. He represented Cambridge against Oxford in 1875, and continued to do so until 1878; and, by right of residence, he played for Surrey in 1874 and most years down to 1882. The year after saw him playing for Middlesex, the county of his birth, and his form that season in county matches and for the Gentlemen *v.* Players was equal to anything he had shown previously. Of late years he has played for Essex. He has also represented England against

Australia, and was a member of Lord Harris's team which visited Australia in 1878–79.

His batting was free and correct, and he had great patience. He made the most of his height, and came down on the ball with great force; and he was particularly strong in driving. We invariably went in first together, and had many a long and profitable partnership. In the field he was very quick, and brought off many a grand catch in the long-field: one in particular for England *v.* Australia, which Bonnor hit tremendously hard and low, was as fine as anything I have ever seen. He was a good change bowler, medium-pace round-arm, and when he had a wicket to suit him did good work.

His best batting years were:

	Completed Innings.	Runs.	Most in an Innings.	Average.
1876	27	816	105	30.6
1877	24	832	115	34.16
1879	17	423	70	24.15
1881	25	612	142	24.12
1882	22	707	145	32.3
1883	20	664	97	33.4

The Hon. ALFRED LYTTELTON was born in London on the 7th February, 1857. He is the youngest member of a distinguished family of eight brothers who have all more or less made their mark in the cricket world, and in the world of sport generally. The Hon. C. G., the eldest, was considered second to none of his time; the Hon. Edward, the seventh, born in 1855, was equally good; and the subject of my sketch, though last, was certainly not least; indeed, he had few superiors with the bat, and he was one of our best amateur wicket-keepers. I say was, for, unfortunately, though he is many years my junior, and still possesses all his old skill, professional duties have kept him out of the cricket field for years. He was very successful for Cambridge

University, the Gentlemen *v.* Players, England *v.* Australia, and for Middlesex.

As a batsman he had a most commanding and beautiful style, and scored at a very fast pace against all kinds of bowling. I remember hearing some one remark that his style was the champagne of cricket, and I thought it hit the nail full on the head. He has done many fine performances with the bat—chief of them, to my mind, being his 181 in the memorable partnership with Mr. I. D. Walker for Middlesex *v.* Gloucestershire, at Clifton in 1883. His wicket-keeping was always first-class. There was no fuss or show about it, and I have rarely seen him knock the bails off unless there was a possible chance of stumping. He was very quick, and took the ball on both sides with equal ease and certainty. His best batting years were :—

	Completed Innings.	Runs.	Most in an Innings.	Average.
1876	15	383	83	25. 8
1877	21	611	101	29. 2
1878	19	476	72	25. 1
1879	24	688	102	28.16
1880	13	378	47*	29. 1
1883	8	555	181	69. 3
1884	16	417	103	26. 1

The Hon. CHARLES GEORGE LYTTELTON, now Lord Cobham, was born at Hagley Park, Stourbridge, on 27th October, 1842. His height was 6 ft. 2 ins.; weight, about 13 st. He was at his best when I appeared in first-class cricket, and I was delighted with his free, hard-hitting style. His cutting in particular was most brilliant, and the ball travelled with startling rapidity after it left the bat. There were no boundaries at the Oval in those days, and the sound of the ball hitting the palings was heard all over the ground with a clearness and distinctness that told of the force and skill put into the hit. He is senior member of a distinguished family which has been a power in the cricket world. At Cambridge he was very successful with bat and ball, and he represented his University in the single and double contests at tennis, winning both. He threw the cricket-ball repeatedly over 100 yards, and was fairly successful as a bowler, bowling round-arm, medium-pace, and lobs; and he was above the average as a wicket-keeper. He was chosen to represent the Gentlemen in his 18th year, and played for them for six years, bowling, batting, fielding and wicket-keeping with great success. The M.C.C. elected him on their Committee in 1874, and he was chosen President in 1888.

Mr. PERCY STANISLAUS McDONNELL was born at Kensington, London, on the 13th November, 1860. He made his first appearance in England with Murdoch's team in 1880, and created a great impression as a batsman and field, which he fully maintained in subsequent visits. As a dashing batsman he has had no equal in any Australian Eleven, and it is not too much to say of him that on a bad wicket he might win any match by the wonderful way in which he can force the game. In the early part of his innings he is rather too eager to score, but once he gets set all kinds of bowling are treated alike. His fine score of 103 out of the first 158 runs for Australia *v.* England at the Oval in 1884 was a very dashing effort on a good wicket; but his 82 out of 86 against the North of England at Manchester in 1888, on a slow treacherous wicket, which enabled his side to win the match, was one of the grandest efforts ever witnessed. He hits hard all round and keeps the ball low, and his driving is particularly fine. In the field he is exceptionally smart, and has a good return. He captained the sixth Australian team in 1888, and managed the eleven with excellent judgment.

His batting averages in England, in eleven-a-side matches, were:—

	Completed Innings.	Runs.	Most in an Innings.	Average.
1880	18	418	79	23. 4
1882	52	900	82	17.16
1884	52	1225	103	23.29
1888	61	1393	105	22.51

MARTIN MCINTYRE was born at Eastwood, Nottinghamshire, 15th August, 1847. His height was 5 ft. 11 ins.; weight 12½ st. Nottinghamshire, like Yorkshire, has been singularly fortunate in nearly always having first-class bowlers; and in 1871, when McIntyre was at his best, it had occasion to be proud of him. He bowled fast round-arm, with a very high delivery, and when he had a wicket to suit him was quite unplayable, and frightened timid batsmen as much as ever Tarrant did. If the wicket were at all fast, and a little bit fiery or rough, his cart-wheel delivery caused the ball to get up with startling quickness, and the batsman's fingers and body were visited as often as the wicket. An occasional shooter came along, and altogether it was a lively time while it lasted. McIntyre beamed and smiled at the results; though he was always ready to apologise when an exceptionally hard knock came.

He first represented the Players in 1871. Very few first-class bowlers paid much attention to batting twenty years ago, but McIntyre was one of the exceptions; for he had good defence, and his hitting was clean, hard, and low.

He was very good-tempered, too; and whenever he committed a slight mistake it was a very difficult thing to reprove him. Once, if not twice, during my Australian tour, the hospitality of our friends on the other side was too much for him, and he stayed up later than he should have; although I had given strict orders that every one should retire early, so that we might win our match next day. I learned one morning that he had been out late, and made up my mind to speak sharply. He appeared on the ground in good time, smiling as usual, although he had got a hint of the storm brewing. "Good-morning, sir!" said he, before I could get a word out, "McIntyre has just been talking to himself, and won't let it occur again." What could I say after that? I certainly could not improve upon it. However, it was a very hot day, and the wicket suited him, and he both batted and bowled well.

Mr. JOSEPH MAKINSON was born at High Broughton, Manchester, 25th August, 1836. His height was 5 ft. 6¾ ins.; weight, at his best, about 10½ st. My first experience of his powers was in the South Wales match against Surrey in 1864, and a hot one it was. In the first innings he scored 86 run out; in the second, 36 not out; and when Mr. John Walker was batting with him we had a most lively time of it. He was in his 28th year at the time, and was very quick on his legs, running up the pitch and converting a good-length ball into a half-volley; and he seemed to be able to hit to every part of the field. He was a magnificent field anywhere, and a very fast bowler. I met him a great deal in the United South matches at Broughton, and in later years at Manchester in connection with the Gloucestershire and Lancashire matches—in fact, scarcely a year has passed in which I have not met him; for he is an enthusiastic lover of the game, and is just as happy playing the part of spectator now as he was when he took an active part in the game twenty years ago.

In his 21st year, playing for the Undergraduates at Cambridge against the Gentlemen of Cambridge with Arnold and Reynolds, two professional bowlers, he scored 126 out of a total of 311; his cutting, driving, and leg-hitting being most severe and accurate. In the same match he captured eight of the Gentlemen's wickets first innings, and three out of the five taken in the second, when the Gentlemen gave up the match. The year after, for the same team, against the Professionals of Cambridge, he scored 136 out of a total of 364, against the bowling of Buttress and Reynolds; and in June, 1860, playing for the Broughton Club, Manchester, he gave the All-England Eleven an illustration of what the best of our amateurs could do against their crack bowlers—Jackson, Willsher, Tarrant, and Hayward—scoring 104 out of a total of 180; and bowling successfully as well. Another fine performance was his 64 not out for the Gentlemen against the Players at the Oval in 1864; his bowling being fairly successful in the same match.

He identified himself very closely with the Broughton Club, and worked heart and soul in its interest. The members appreciated it, and presented him with a gold watch and chain, with the following inscription: "Presented to Joseph Makinson by his fellow-members of the Broughton Club, as a mark of their pride in him as a cricketer and their affection for him as a friend." That occurred some thirty years ago, and he is still very proud of it; for when I saw him last I said, "Let me have a look at the watch I have heard so much about, Makinson;" and out it came, and the interesting story in connection with it. The members of the Broughton Club were certainly the gainers by his enthusiasm; but first-class cricket suffered by his enforced absence, for he did not play so often as lovers of the game desired.

Mr. Frederic Peel Miller was born at Clapham, Surrey, 29th July, 1828. His height was 5 ft. 6½ in.; weight, 11 st. He was a most brilliant hitter, and scored largely; and he was one of the finest fieldsmen at long-leg or cover-point of his time. And he could bowl also; round-arm and slow underhand. In the Gentlemen *v.*

Players' matches he was very successful, and he was an ardent supporter of the game after he gave up playing. His figure at the Oval in all important matches was very well known, and many a chat I had with him about the rise and progress of the game.

We are mainly indebted to him for Vols. I. to IV. of Fred. Lillywhite's *Scores and Biographies*. He spent a very large sum of money collecting materials for them; but in publishing them did not get the support his unselfish efforts so richly deserved.

Mr. RICHARD ARTHUR HENRY MITCHELL was born at Enderby Hall, near Leicester, on 22nd January, 1843. His height was 6 ft. 2 ins.; weight, about 13 st. His tall, commanding figure was well known in the cricket-field, and his vigorous hitting and scientific defence were well worth copying. He was a good change fast round-arm bowler, and an excellent fieldsman at point. At school, college, Lord's and the Oval, he did very well, and was paid the compliment of being asked to play for the Gentlemen in his 19th year. He did not play for them, however, until 1862. In 1863, in one of those matches, he scored 76 and bowled also; in 1865 he scored 53 and 33 in the first match, and not out 44 in the second. I met him often then at Lord's and the Oval, and occasionally at Canterbury, but not so frequently after he was appointed to a mastership at Eton.

Mr. WILLIAM OCTAVIUS MOBERLY was born at Shoreham, in Sussex, 14th November, 1850. His height was 5 ft. 10 in.; weight, 12 st. 7 lbs. From 1876 to 1881 he was one of the most brilliant batsmen in England, his large scores for Gloucestershire against first-class bowling being made in perfect style. For that county he had an average of 40 runs in 1876, 39 in 1880, and 39 in 1881, and scored over 100 runs in an innings two or three times. He was a splendid hitter all round, and always kept the ball well down; his late cutting in particular being equal to anything I have ever seen. He reminded me of the Hon. C. G. Lyttelton in his best days when he made that hit. You saw the flash of the bat when he made it, and a second or two afterwards the ball had reached the boundary.

Undoubtedly he was the finest batsman I can remember at any University who was unfortunate enough not to be chosen to play in the great match of the year; but the Oxford Eleven of his time had so many good men that it was difficult to know whom to leave out, and of course he did not display the fine form then which made him so valuable to Gloucestershire.

He was a magnificent field and safe catch, and was always ready to go anywhere. In the absence of our regular wicket-keeper, he put on the pads and gloves cheerfully, and did good work at it, although I knew he had no great liking for the post. When the bell rang he was one of the first to appear in the field, and he was always ready when it was his turn to bat. He was appointed one of the masters at Clifton College in 1876, which prevented him from playing much until the latter part of the season, or representing the Gentlemen against the Players. He was also a very fine football player.

FRED. MORLEY was born at Sutton-in-Ashfield, Nottinghamshire, 16th December, 1850. His height was 5 ft. 9 in; weight, 10½ st. For years the names of Morley and Alfred Shaw were before the public as the renowned Nottinghamshire pair, and there can be little doubt that they were a wonderful and effective combination. Morley bowled very fast left round-arm, had a fair break both ways, and generally kept a good length. On his day, on an indifferent wicket, his ball on the leg-stump, breaking to the off, was a difficult one to play, and I had to cry beaten to him more than once. His county had the best of his services, and he served it well. The

Players also were much strengthened by his bowling, and in more than one match he and Shaw were their mainstay. That memorable match in which the Australians made their first appearance at Lord's, on the 27th May, 1878, will come to the minds of cricketers how Spofforth and Boyle, on the treacherous wicket, slaughtered the M.C.C. batsmen, and Shaw and Morley retaliated on the Australians.

He was a very poor bat, and a very indifferent fieldsman. His name was invariably last on the batting list, and when he made a run the crowd cheered him heartily. In the field he was anything but a safe catch; but give him a chance of running a man out when he had the ball in his hand and was about forty or fifty yards from the wicket, and he rarely failed to do it, so accurate and fast was his throwing.

He accompanied the seventh English team to Australia in 1882-3, but was unfortunate enough to meet with an injury to his side when the steamer which took them out collided with another. It turned out to be a more serious injury than was at first thought, and he was never the same man afterwards, and both Nottinghamshire and England lost one of the very best fast bowlers of his time.

His best bowling years were:

	Overs.	Maidens.	Runs.	Wickets.	Average.
1874	977	437	1493	111	13.50
1875	1257	608	1676	114	14.80
1877	1726	839	2021	148	13.97
1878	1953	654	2311	191	12.19
1879	1361	676	1551	146	10.91
1880	1717	867	2077	174	11.163
1882	1051	541	1297	115	11 32

Mr. William Lloyd Murdoch was born at Sandhurst, Victoria, 18th October, 1855. His height is 5 ft. 10 ins.; weight, 13½ st. Without doubt he is the best batsman that ever represented Australia, and we can all remember his fine innings of 153 not out in 1880, at the Oval, against the finest bowling of England. When he first came to us he had not the command of the bat he showed in after years, nor did he possess the free, scientific style which we like to associate with him at his best. He always possessed good and sound defence, and could hit well all round; but his particular hit was stepping out and driving hard and low to the off, a stroke which yielded him many a boundary figure. Like many of us, he is getting on in years and has lost the dash of ten years ago, but he is still a good bat, a safe field, a good wicket-keeper, and one of the best captains that ever led an Australian eleven into the field.

His highest scores in first-class matches have been:

Feb.	1882.	For New South Wales *v.* Melbourne	321
May	„	For Australian XI. *v.* Sussex	286*
Jan.	1884.	For Australian XI. *v.* Combined Australia	279*
Aug.	„	For Australian XI. *v.* England	211
Dec.	1883.	For New South Wales *v.* Victoria	158
July	1890.	For Australian XI. *v.* Sussex	158*
Sept.	1880.	For Australian XI. *v.* England	153*
Dec.	1878.	For Australian XI. *v.* Eighteen of Victoria	153
June	1884.	For Australian XI. *v.* Cambridge University	132
Aug.	1890.	For Australian XI. *v.* Cambridge Past and Present	129
May	1882.	For Australian XI. *v.* Orleans Club	107*

And his batting averages for the Australian Elevens in England, in eleven-a-side matches:

	Completed Innings.	Runs.	Most in an Innings.	Average.
1878	24	319	49	13. 7
1880	18	465	153*	25.15
1882	56	1711	286*	30.31
1884	45	1378	211	30.28
1890	62	1459	158*	23.33

Mr. CHARLES A. NEWHALL, of Philadelphia, was a long way the best fast right-hand bowler who has yet appeared in America, and is a member of the family of that name which has given the Gentlemen of Philadelphia a good position in the cricket world. I met him at Philadelphia in 1872, and was much impressed with his pace, length, and break from the off. He was quite as fast as Freeman, and made the ball come quickly off the pitch. On a good wicket many of his balls kept low, and on a bumpy one he was most dangerous and very successful.

In the match, Gentlemen of England *v.* Twenty-two of Philadelphia, played at Philadelphia in September, 1872, he bowled grandly, and with Mr. Meade, a fast left-hand bowler, at the other end, gave us the closest and most exciting match of the whole trip. Mr. Meade and he made a strong combination and required a lot of playing, and on their form that day would have puzzled the finest batting eleven in England. Mr. Newhall took 10 wickets for 69 runs; Meade, 6 for 52; and they bowled unchanged in both innings. Mr. Newhall was just as successful against Parr's team in 1859, and Willsher's in 1868.

He was a fair bat, but not up to the form of his younger brother Dan, who was quite first-class. Dan had fine defence and could hit well all round, and was a splendid field.

Mr. Timothy Carew O'Brien was born at Dublin on November 5th, 1861, but received his cricket education in England. He played for Middlesex in 1881, but it was not until 1884 that he began to make the fine reputation he has since earned as a first-class batsman. In the latter year he played for Oxford University, and had an average of 25 runs for 15 completed innings; but he failed sadly against Cambridge University, at Lord's, the match in which he hoped, and everyone expected, he would do something out of the common. He certainly did something out of the common, for he gained his spectacles, much to his chagrin. The year after, however, he scored 44 and 28 in the same match, and had the fine average of 27.16 for 42 completed innings in first-class cricket. He had even a finer average in 1889—31.11 for 25 innings—and to-day he is as good as he ever was.

His defence is good, but it is his free, dashing style that has made him so great a favourite. He is a poor beginner, and looks anything but at home the first over or two; but once he gets set, he is irresistible against all kinds of bowling. A half-volley, long-hop, or good-length gives him no trouble then, and there is no stopping him. His grand scores of 92 and 100 not out for Middlesex *v.* Yorkshire, at Lord's, in 1889, will never be forgotten, especially the latter. It was equal to anything ever hit on that ground, and was made in one hour and 20 minutes. The Yorkshire bowlers were all treated alike, and the spectators could hardly sit still for excitement and admiration of the grand display, which enabled Middlesex to win the match a few minutes before time.

He is a good field and safe catch, and always ready to go anywhere and everywhere. So far, he has not had much opportunity of showing the bowling skill he possesses, although he can bowl both right-hand and left, and is always practising when a wicket goes down. He thinks it rather hard luck that he cannot get the Middlesex captain to believe in his powers, but consoles himself with the thought that a prophet has little honour in his own country; and with having got me out on one occasion at Cheltenham when the regular bowlers had failed. He has played for the Gentlemen *v.* Players, and was one of Mr. Vernon's Australian team in 1887–88.

Mr. Cuthbert John Ottaway was born at Dover, Kent, 20th July, 1850. His height was 6 ft.; weight, 12½ st. He was a brilliant batsman at school, scoring repeatedly for Eton over 100 runs in an innings, and having an average of 70 for it in 1869. And he was just as successful for Middlesex in 1876, scoring over 100 in an innings against Surrey and Nottinghamshire that year, and averaging 89 for the whole season. He was one of Mr. Fitzgerald's Eleven which went to America in 1872; and though he did not score heavily, yet he was very successful in his wicket-keeping. He rarely played forward; but his back play was almost perfect, and he had great patience. Nothing would tempt him to hit out if cautious and safe play were necessary, and few batsmen could play an uphill fight or a defensive innings more perfectly. He represented the Gentlemen first in 1870, and for two or three years afterwards, but was not so successful for them as in other matches.

As an all-round athlete he had few equals, taking first honours in racquets, tennis, and football.

Mr. GEORGE EUGENE PALMER was born at Albury, New South Wales, on 22nd February, 1860. His height was 5 ft. 10 ins.; weight, 12 st. He bowled rather above medium pace—might be called fast—and had a very easy action. He was very straight, kept a good length, and did most damage with his break from the off; but now and then he put in a beautiful leg-twister which was very difficult to play. The leg-break was rather a pet weakness of his, and he got hit severely at times by overdoing it. If he had stuck to his off-break he would have shown better results; for he had a rare command of the ball on that side. He was as good a batsman as anyone in the 1886 team. His best bowling performances in England, in eleven-a-side matches, were:

	Overs.	Maidens.	Runs.	Wickets.	Average.
1880	710	342	892	80	11.12
1882	1185	511	1731	138	12.75
1884	1241	466	2131	132	16.19
1886	1416	564	2328	106	21.102

BATTING.

	Completed Innings.	Runs.	Most in an Innings.	Average.
1886	52	1028	94	19.40

Mr. William Harry Patterson was born at the Royal Military College, Sandhurst, March 11th, 1859. He was in the Harrow Eleven in 1877, represented Oxford University in the 1880 Inter-University match, and has played for Kent from 1880 to the present time; he has also represented the Gentlemen against the Players.

The year 1881 saw him in his very best form, doing good work for his county, and carrying his bat right through the innings for 107 for Oxford *v.* Cambridge. Altogether he was batting five hours for his score, and it was owing to his fine defence and great patience that Oxford won the match when it was regarded as a certainty for Cambridge.

For Kent he has saved and won more than one match by the same patience and sound defence, and there is no more reliable bat in the eleven. When Mr. Patterson has made up his mind to save a match nothing will tempt him to risk anything. The years 1884 and 1885 were notable ones for him in that respect, and on two or three occasions he and that fine and enthusiastic player the Rev. Richard Thornton Thornton staved off defeat and gained an unexpected victory. Last year (1890) he was very successful, and had the very fine average of 50.2 for 8 innings. His 123 not out against Nottinghamshire, at Trent Bridge, was his principal score, and it was a wonderful performance, considering that he had only two or three night's practice before the day of the match.

He bats in very correct style, but his strong characteristics are patience and fine judgment in accommodating himself to every kind of wicket. On a sticky wicket he is almost as safe as on a fast, true wicket. He is also a very reliable field anywhere, but more especially in the long-field; and he can bowl medium-pace with fair success at times.

Mr. THOMAS SHERWIN PEARSON was born at Barwell, Leicestershire, 20th June, 1851. His height is 6 ft. 2 in.; weight, 13½ st. For a player who did so well for Middlesex he was very unfortunate in not being chosen to represent Oxford *v.* Cambridge, and the same reason may be given for it that was given in Mr. Moberly's case—an exceptionally good lot were in residence at the time, and some one had to stand out. However, he had the satisfaction of representing his University in tennis contests, being one of the champions in 1875.

He is a good batsman, and makes some good scores by sound, free hitting. He is also a fair change slow round-arm bowler, with a very high action; and on more than one occasion he did good work for Middlesex when the regular bowlers had failed; and he has brought off some remarkably good catches, fielding at point.

EDMUND PEATE was born at Holbeck, near Leeds, 2nd March, 1856. He was, undoubtedly, one of the very best slow bowlers of his time. That is the opinion held by very good judges in Australia and England, and we have only to look at his results with the ball to see the truth of it. He bowled left-hand, round-arm, had a very easy action, kept a beautiful length, and varied his pace with good judgment. When the wicket was at all difficult, he was quite as puzzling as anyone; and he had a fair amount of break from leg: but now and then he put in a very nasty ball which came with his arm, and it was all the more difficult because it was unexpected.

He first played for his county in 1879, and before the season was over he had taken rank with the very best bowlers in England. Every year added to his fine reputation; and no matter the company he played in he came through the ordeal most successfully. In England and Australia he was the wonder of English slow bowlers for years, as his splendid results will show:

	Overs.	Maidens.	Runs.	Wickets.	Average.
1880	1312	580	1668	138	12.12
1881	1638	731	2088	162	12.144
1882	1853	868	2466	214	11.112
1883	1376	665	1753	120	14.73
1884	1575	777	1868	137	13.87
1885	1699	903	1945	115	16.105
1886	980	542	1027	70	14.47

He was not a good field, and he did not trouble himself much about his batting average; but he made rather an amusing remark in the memorable and sensational match England *v.* Australia, at the Oval, in 1882, when Spofforth and Boyle bowled with such extraordinary results in the second innings of England. Mr. C. T. Studd, rather strangely, was down on the list as tenth man, and Peate was eleventh. Ten runs were wanted to win, and it was not considered an impossible task if Peate could only keep up his wicket or allow Mr. Studd to have the bowling. However, Peate hit out at the first or second ball and made two runs off it; then tried it again off the next ball, and was clean bowled. On being remonstrated with for his rashness and want of judgment, he said: "Very sorry, gentlemen, but I could not trust Mr. Studd." Not a bad remark, considering that Mr. Studd had made a hundred runs against the same bowling a month or so before!

ROBERT PEEL was born at Charwell, Yorkshire, on the 12th February, 1857. His height is 5 ft. 6 ins.; weight, 11 st. He first played for his county in 1882, when he was in his 25th year. Peate and Bates were at their best then, and Emmett was still a power in the eleven, or Peel would have represented Yorkshire even before that date, for it was well known that his bowling abilities only required development to become first-class. The year after he showed considerable improvement, and at the end of the season he took a good position amongst first-class bowlers. Four years later he was admitted to be one of the best all-round players in the Yorkshire Eleven, and, indeed, was considered worthy of a place in any eleven. To-day he is still well to the front, and has lost none of his skill with bat or ball. He played with great success in Australia, and has been even more successful against the Australians in England.

What I like about Peel is his plucky, willing, cheerful way, and on that account I would as soon have him on my side as any man in England. Never a grumble comes from him, and he is ready at a moment's notice to go anywhere in the field. Now and then a bowler begs to be let off, alleging that he is either a little bit tired or that the end does not suit him. Peel is never tired, at least he never admits it, and he does not care whether he bowls up-hill, down-hill, with the wind or against it. He bowls left-hand, round-arm, slow medium, keeps a very good length, and breaks principally from leg, but occasionally he puts in a very fast one which comes with his arm. And he is not afraid of sending up a lofty toss to the off to tempt the batsman to hit. Of late years he has been very successful; and he is undoubtedly the best professional left-hand batsman in England at the present time.

His best years in first-class cricket so far have been:

BOWLING.

	Overs.	Maidens.	Runs.	Wickets.	Average.
1888	1648	830	2091	171	12.39
1889	1229	479	2054	118	17.48
1890	1552	714	2239	172	13. 3

BATTING.

	Completed Innings.	Runs.	Most in an Innnings.	Average.
1887	33	835	91	25.10
1890	44	817	83	18.25

Mr. HENRY PERKINS, the secretary of the Marylebone C.C., was born at Sawston, Cambridgeshire, December 10th, 1832. His height was 5 ft. 8½ ins.; weight, 11 st. 7 lbs. He played for Cambridge University *v.* Oxford in 1854, and was captain and manager of the Cambridge County Eleven from 1858 to 1864. As an all-round player he performed very well for years, but 1859 was his best, when he was in his 27th year, his results being exceptionally good. At the end of that season he could show the very fine batting average of 33.25 for 51 completed innings; total number of runs scored, 1,708. Average and aggregate number of runs were thought highly of then, for grounds were far from perfect, and the ball had to be very carefully watched. He was just as successful with the ball that year, and in one match, against a strong University eleven, on Fenner's ground, carried everything before him, taking 9 wickets for 35 runs.

His defence was good and he could hit very hard, driving particularly well to the off and on. He bowled fast underhand lobs, and fielded his own bowling smartly. But he could field well anywhere, and earned a good reputation at mid-off and in long-stopping.

He was elected secretary of the M.C.C. in 1877, and the old club has flourished greatly under his charge. When he took office the number of matches played annually did not exceed 60; last year as many as 160 were played.

HENRY PHILLIPS was born at Hastings, Sussex, on the 14th of October, 1844. His height was 5 ft. 4 ins.; weight, 9 st. 7 lbs. To the best of my recollection, he is the smallest first-class wicket-keeper who has yet appeared. In many respects height is a decided advantage in that post; but Phillips has proved that in wicket-keeping, as in batting and bowling, height is not everything. His cat-like activity and quickness quite made up for his short reach, and his performances compared favourably with the very best of our wicket-keepers. I have seen him fail to touch a ball that such players as Mr. Bush, Pinder and Lockyer could have reached with ease; but then I have seen him sprint from the wicket to short-leg, and bring off a catch which I very much question if either of those players could have got to.

He was as plucky as he was quick, and faced fast bowling with a cheerful face and a stout heart; but it was against slow bowling that he did his remarkable performances, and created his reputation as long ago as 1872. For Sussex *v.* Surrey on the 20th June of that year, he stumped 5 and caught 5; for Sussex *v.* Yorkshire, 20th August, 1874, he stumped 3 and caught 4; and for the United South in 1875 he stumped 3 and caught 7 against Twenty-two of Chelmsford; G. F. Grace, Lillywhite and myself the bowlers. He did good work for his county a great many years, and he was fairly successful for the Players *v.* Gentlemen in 1871 and 1873.

As a batsman he was very steady, but did not hit much or score heavily; although he rather astonished the Australian Eleven in 1884, when he scored 111 against them for his county—off the bowling of Spofforth, Palmer and Giffen,—and with Mr. Wyatt, who scored 112, put on 182 runs for the eighth wicket.

RICHARD PILLING was born at Bedford, on July 5th, 1855, and made his first appearance for Lancashire in 1877. He very quickly showed that he had no superior as a wicket-keeper in England, and gained hosts of admirers for his quick, neat, and quiet style. Very few stand so close to the wicket as he does, and he is equally effective on both sides. For his county, the Players *v.* Gentlemen, and English teams in Australia, he has done excellent work; but after 1883 ill-health prevented him from appearing so often as the cricketing public desired, and of late years he has played very little at all. He will take rank with our great wicket-keepers as being equally good against all kinds of bowling. He bats in very good style, and once or twice has made runs for his county when they were badly wanted.

George Pinder was born at Ecclesfield, near Sheffield, 15th July, 1841. His height was 5 ft. 11½ ins.; weight, 12½ st. He was one of the best of our professional wicket-keepers, with a quiet, neat style; and on the leg side against fast bowling exceptionally good. Freeman and Emmett were at their best when he kept wicket for Yorkshire, and the work he did was quite enough to have ruined most hands; but he never flinched: and I question if any one can show a finer record to the bowling of these two bowlers. It should be remembered that Yorkshire has never been without good fast bowlers, and I am at a loss to understand how his hands served him so long and well. In the year 1866, for the All-England Eleven *v.* Eighteen of Birkenhead, he stumped one and caught eight off the bowling of J. C. Shaw and Luke Greenwood: and he was just as good against slow bowling; for the year after, for the same Eleven *v.* Twenty-two of Arnold, he caught one and stumped ten, nine of them off Tinley's lobs. He was a fair bat, with good hitting powers, but weak defence; and he could bowl lobs at a pinch, and used to do it with the pads on. I suppose he had got so used to the pads, that wearing them had become second nature to him! He appeared for the Players once or twice, but did the best of his cricket for his county and the All-England Eleven.

Thomas Plumb was born at Aylesbury, Buckinghamshire, 26th July, 1833. His height was 5 ft. 10 in.; weight, 12 st. As a wicket-keeper he was not considered quite up to Lockyer or Pooley's form, although I cannot account for it; possibly it was owing to his connection with Buckinghamshire, whose position as a county was not first-class. I am inclined to believe if he had had greater opportunities for displaying his powers, or if he had been connected with a crack county, he would have taken quite as high a position as either of the famous pair I have just mentioned. Anyhow, I am convinced that he was a great deal better than he was thought, and about the best wicket-keeper of his time against fast bowling. His style was quick and neat, without the slightest show; and while as keen as anyone, he never kept knocking off the bails uselessly as I have seen others do. He stood up to Freeman and Howitt without flinching, and his certainty in taking their bowling, especially on the leg side, was a treat of its kind. And if evidence were wanting of his proficiency against slow bowling, it can be found in the United All-England Eleven matches *v.* Twenty-two of St. Helen's and Twenty-two of Yeadon, in August, 1867. In the former he stumped seven and caught four; in the latter he stumped seven and caught one, principally off Iddison's underhand slows; and I remember what an excellent catch he made off Silcock's bowling, when he got me out in the second innings of the Gentlemen *v.* Players' match at Lord's in 1869. He was a very fair batsman as well, and made many a good score for the United Eleven, and in other matches.

EDWARD POOLEY was born at Richmond, Surrey, 13th February, 1843. His height was 5 ft. 6 in.; weight, about 10½ st. He was a brilliant wicket-keeper, and did splendid work for Surrey. He was worth his position in the eleven for his batting and fielding, but after Lockyer retired he became indispensable to them for his wicket-keeping alone. As a batsman he was a fine free hitter, and many a time made a good score when it was badly wanted. He could bowl lobs at a pinch, but they could not be considered first-rate, and I know on several occasions they were very severely handled. When Southerton was bowling and he wicket-keeping they were an effective combination, and he brought off some remarkable catches.

His best stumping records were also made with that bowler, although, rather strangely, one of the, if not the finest, was when they were opposed to each other in 1868—he playing for Surrey, Southerton for Sussex. In that match he stumped four and caught eight! For the United South Eleven he was just as successful, keeping up his wonderful form until his hands gave way. Afterwards he rather shied at fast bowling, although, when compelled to, he would face it as pluckily as any man living.

It was intensely amusing to watch him go out to inspect the wicket in later days, and then return and say: "First-rate wicket, sir; slow bowling is sure to come off to-day." After he had done it two or three times it became rather a standing joke in the eleven, and no matter how slight the inspection of the wicket before a match, someone was sure to remark: "A slow-bowler's wicket to-day, Pooley."

Once or twice he was thought to have been too eager in appealing to the umpire for a decision, and was accused of trying to entrap the batsman. My experience of him never showed that; and if he had exceeded the laws I should have certainly put it down more to keenness to win than a desire to overreach. He was always on the alert to stump or run out a batsman if he moved his foot before the ball was dead, but the batsman had only himself to blame if it came off; and if a mistake had been made, the umpire was more to blame than Pooley.

Mr. Octavius Goldney Radcliffe was born at North Newnton Rectory, Wiltshire, on the 20th of

October, 1860. His height is 5 ft. 8½ ins.; weight, 11 st. 7 lbs. He has the entire credit of having taught himself, and in the full sense of the word may be called a self-made player. Until he was 17 years of age he played little or no cricket, but after that he cultivated the game with great perseverance, and he is now one of the most punishing and dangerous bats in England. His defence is excellent, and he can play all the correct strokes characteristic of a good batsman; but he has two strokes of his own which have puzzled many a bowler. A ball well up on the off-side and breaking away from him, he drives over cover-point's head; if it is breaking into him, he pulls it perfectly square to leg. How on earth he makes the latter I know not. He scores very rapidly, and made sad havoc of my brother E.M.'s lobs on one occasion at Thornbury, actually scoring 53 in three overs—four balls to the over.

He is a good change bowler, with a big break from the off, and only wants practicc to become first-class; and he is a very good field and safe catch. So far his fine performances have been made for Gloucestershire, which he has represented since 1886; but he has represented the Gentlemen against the Players, and performed brilliantly once or twice against the Australians. He played for Somersetshire in 1885.

For Gloucestershire his best years have been:

	Completed Innings.	Runs.	Most in an Innings.	Average.
1886	22	590	104*	26.18
1889	24	568	101*	23.16

Mr. Walter William Read was born at Reigate, Surrey, on the 23rd November, 1855. His height is 5 ft. 11½ in.; weight, 14st. 5 lbs. He will stand out as one of the great batsmen of the age. For excellent defence and vigorous hitting he has had few equals; and to-day, though in his 36th year, his form is almost up to his best years. As far as I can learn, he had no special training, but his innate love for the game and unwearied perseverance brought him rapidly to the front. He was tried by the Surrey Committee at the early age of 17. His defence was excellent then; and great things were predicted of him when he reached the years of manhood. He always played with a straight bat, and, as the years went on and strength came, his hitting powers improved rapidly. For quick scoring he has few equals, and there is no one the cricket-loving public watches with greater delight.

The very first over he is on the alert for a loose ball, and I do not envy the bowler when he has got well set. Like most of our great batsmen, he has his pet hits. A long hop on the off-side is his especial delight. He makes no attempt to pull it to the on, as one or two powerful hitters do, but steps back with his right foot, and smites terrifically hard between point and mid-off. He plays every ball clean and hard, however good the length of it, and on the leg-side he is exceptionally strong in placing. Of late years he has fielded close in, but he is also good in the long-field; and it is an open secret that he can keep wicket fairly well, and bowl lobs at a pinch. In 1881, for Surrey *v.* Yorkshire, at Huddersfield, he kept wicket while Yorkshire scored 388 and did not give a single extra.

He first represented his county in 1873, and was at the head of the averages in 1875. The year 1877 saw him representing the Gentlemen against the Players, and, with the exception of 1878 and 1879, not a year has passed in which he has not played a great part in all matches of importance.

To give every three-figure innings he has made would take too much space, so I confine myself to those scored from 1884 to 1890, when he was undoubtedly seen at his best:—

May 26, 1884.	For Surrey *v.* Leicester	162
Aug. 11, ,,	For England *v.* Australia	117
Aug. 25, ,,	For Surrey *v.* Gloucestershire	135
May 11, 1885.	For Surrey *v.* Essex	143
May 28, ,,	For Surrey *v.* Derbyshire	123
June 15, ,,	For Surrey *v.* Essex	214
June 29, ,,	For Surrey *v.* Sussex	163
July 2, ,,	For Gentlemen *v.* Players	159
July 13, ,,	For Surrey *v.* Sussex	101
Aug. 3, ,,	For Surrey *v.* Nottinghamshire	135
Aug. 6, ,,	For Surrey *v.* Derbyshire	109
June 24, 1886.	For Surrey *v.* Cambridge University	114
Aug. 5, ,,	For Surrey *v.* Derbyshire	115
Aug. 23, ,,	For Surrey *v.* Gloucestershire	120
Aug. 26, ,,	For Surrey *v.* Leicestershire...	157*
Sept. ,,	For South of England *v.* Australians	102*
June 9, 1887.	For Surrey *v.* Oxford University...	118
June 16, ,,	For Surrey *v.* Lancashire	247
June 20, ,,	For Surrey *v.* Cambridge University	244*
July 28, ,,	For Surrey *v.* Derbyshire	145
Aug. 22, ,,	For Surrey *v.* Kent	100
May 28, 1888.	For Gentlemen of England *v.* Australians...	109
June 4, ,,	For Surrey *v.* Essex	129
June 7, ,,	For Surrey *v.* Yorkshire...	103
June 22, ,,	For Gentlemen of Surrey *v.* Parsees	132
June 25, ,,	For Surrey *v.* Oxford University...	338
Aug. 9, ,,	For Surrey *v.* Sussex	171
July 18,&c.,1889.	For Gentlemen of Surrey *v.* Gentlemen of Philadelphia...	105, 130
Aug. 8, ,,	For Surrey *v.* Middlesex	115

Batting Averages, from 1875 *to* 1890.

	Completed Innings.	Runs.	Most in an Innings.	Average.
1875	8	247	98	30. 7
1876	14	588	106	42
1877	11	399	140	36. 3
1878	12	278	80	23. 2
1879	6	123	53	20. 3
1880	12	306	93	25. 6
1881	29	931	160	32. 3
1882	34	884	117	26
1883	33	1573	168	47.22
1884	43	1256	135	29. 9
1885	42	1880	163	44.32
1886	43	1825	120	42.19
1887	34	1615	247	47.17
1888	39	1414	338	36.10
1889	32	805	115	25. 5
1890	46	1169	94	25.19

In 1883, 1886, and 1888, Mr. Read was at the top of the first-class averages.

JOHN MAURICE READ was born at Thames Ditton, February 9th, 1859. His height is 5 ft. 11 in.; weight, 11 st. 8 lbs. He first played for Surrey in 1880, when he was twenty-one years of age, and it is safe to say that no member of that famous eleven has done better service for his county in the last ten years. In county matches, for The Players *v.* The Gentlemen, for England *v.* Australia, and for English Elevens in Australia, he has done grand work with the bat and as a fieldsman; and he is as good to-day as he ever was. Nor is he to be despised as a change-bowler.

His batting is free and vigorous, and once he gets set he is a most difficult man to get out. His style is slightly marred by a tendency to pull occasional balls; but his pluck is equal to any emergency, and in more than one representative match, for England *v.* Australia in particular, he has stopped what looked like disaster. I cannot praise his fielding too highly. He has no superior and few equals in the long-field to-day, and he will stand comparison with most of the giants of the past; in fact, he is fit to go anywhere and in any company, and has about the safest pair of hands in England.

His best batting years have been:

	Completed Innings.	Runs.	Most in an Innings.	Averages.
1885	33	1137	186*	34.15
1886	39	1364	186	34 38
1887	38	908	71	23.24
1888	31	786	109	25.11
1889	25	847	136	33.22
1890	40	829	135	20.29

MR. HENRY WAUGH RENNY-TAILYOUR was born at Missouri, in India, 9th October, 1849. His height was 5 ft. 10 in.; weight, 12½ st. For years he was one of the finest batsmen in England against second-class bowling, and he still retains much of his old skill. His hitting was magnificent, and he scored very rapidly.

He was tried several times in first-class matches, but rarely came off. Why he should have failed there, is a mystery to me; for he must have had occasional good balls to play in his long scores against second-class bowling; and it has always been a theory of mine that a player who can score over 100 runs in an innings as often as he has done, whatever the quality of the bowling, is good enough to play in any eleven. I should have liked to have seen him play oftener in first-class matches than he did. He played a good innings once or twice for Kent; but his finest performances were for the Royal Engineers. A score of 100 was not unusual with him; and in one match in 1875 he scored 285 not out. His average for his regiment in 1875 was a very fine one indeed: 21 innings played, average 50.

He was a fine field either at long-leg or cover-point, covering a great amount of ground, and picking up and returning the ball very quickly and accurately. He played for the Gentlemen in 1873 and for a year or two afterwards.

Mr. Arthur William Ridley was born at Hollington, Newbury, in Berkshire, 11th September, 1852. His height was 6 ft. 4 in.; weight, 13 st. He was a good all-round man, and worth his place in any eleven, either for batting, slow underhand bowling, or fielding. For Eton *v.* Harrow he scored 117 runs in a single innings; and he was very successful at Oxford also, representing that University against Cambridge in 1872, 1873, and 1874, and bowling on each occasion with great success. He also played for Hampshire, Middlesex, and in the Gentlemen *v.* Players' matches. For the Gentlemen he scored consistently well, especially in 1876 at Lord's, when he made 103, against A. Shaw, Morley, and Emmett, in a free, sound style. His driving was particularly good; and he played forward with great freedom, his height and reach enabling him to get well over the ball. His slow lobs were about the finest of their kind; and as he was exceptionally smart in the field, he brought off now and then a very smart catch when he was bowling. He threw his heart into every department of the game, and his play all round was characterised by dash and brilliancy.

Mr. ALEXANDER BUTLER ROWLEY was born at Manchester, 3rd October, 1837. His height was 5 ft. 11 ins; weight, 11½ st. He was a very fine batsman, with a free style, hitting severely to all parts of the ground; and some of his scores were made very rapidly and against the best professional bowlers of the day. Business engagements, unfortunately, interfered with his cricket; and although he appeared for the North *v.* South, his county, and other important matches, he was seen very little in the south after 1861. He bowled left-hand, slow round-arm, with a good break, and now and then met with great success. I have met him a great deal at Old Trafford and at the Oval, and occasionally at Hastings, but more as a personal friend than a cricketer; and his geniality and hospitality have always been worthy of the reputation which Lancashire county gentlemen have so well and deservedly earned.

He is the third member of a family of seven brothers who created a position in the cricket world very little short of the Walkers and Lyttletons. As joint Hon. Secretary of the Lancashire County Club with Mr. Swire, the year of its formation, he did excellent work, and he was elected President some years later.

Mr. EDMUND BUTLER ROWLEY, the fourth brother, was almost as good, and represented Lancashire for many years. He was a fine batsman and a good field. His batting was characterised by vigorous hitting, and against second-class bowling he scored very rapidly. He played for the Gentlemen *v.* Players in 1862: and for the Gentlemen of Lancashire *v.* Gentlemen of Yorkshire in 1867 he ran up a fine score of 219.

H.H. PRINCE CHRISTIAN VICTOR OF SCHLESWIG-HOLSTEIN was born at Windsor Castle, April 14th, 1867. He is the only member of the Royal Family who has yet shown anything approaching first-class cricket form, although H.R.H. the Prince of Wales and other members have always taken great interest in our national game.

Prince Christian Victor was in the Wellington College Eleven in 1883, '84 and '85, and was captain the last year. He repeatedly made large scores there, and on one occasion got 230 not out in a school match. He went to Magdalen College, Oxford, in January, 1886, and was the reserve man on the list to represent his University against Cambridge. He was at Sandhurst in September, 1887; and entered the King's Royal Rifles in 1888. After he left school and college, he played a great deal and scored the century several times; but last year his form for the Royal Rifles was superior to anything he has yet shown. He is a good wicket-keeper, and shows great pluck in that position.

WILLIAM H. SCOTTON was born at Nottingham, 15th January, 1856. He first represented his county in 1874; but it was not until 1879 that he began to play regularly in the eleven. At that time he had the reputation of being a good left-hand batsman, with strong defence and fair hitting powers. To-day he would be described as a good batsman, with strong defence and no hitting powers. Many a batsman has longed to make 100 runs in an innings, and one or two can boast of having done it within the hour. Scotton has a record of a different kind; he can boast of having made 123 runs in eight hours and a quarter, and of having batted for an hour, on more than one occasion, without scoring at all.

He has been a very useful man with the bat for his county, and has broken the heart of many a bowler. I must confess to siding with a freer style; but once or twice, when a rot had set in, and runs were wanted badly, I wished from the bottom of my heart that Scotton, or a batsman of his type, had been opposite me. When England played Australia at the Oval in 1886, he and I batted first, and put on 170 runs before we were parted. We had been batting three hours and three-quarters, and Scotton's share was 34. At one stage of the innings he was in *an hour and seven minutes without scoring*. One cannot imagine what the crowd would have done if *two* Scottons had been batting at the same time.

Whatever may be said about Scotton's style of batting, there cannot be two opinions about his being worth a place in the Nottinghamshire or any eleven. The fact of his having been chosen to represent England proves it. Besides, he has scored 100 in an innings oftener than most players imagine, and on two occasions has exceeded 200 runs for the M.C.C.; and he has also shown well up in the first-class averages for years. He has been to Australia on three occasions; and represented the Players against the Gentlemen as long ago as 1880. For a left-hand batsman, he plays very straight; but he has no particular hit. He is an excellent field and safe catch anywhere; and a fair left-hand, round-arm, medium pace practice bowler.

ALFRED SHAW was born at Burton Joyce, Nottinghamshire, 29th August, 1842. His height was 5 ft. 6½ in.; weight, at his best, about 12 st. He has proved himself to be one of the very best round-arm bowlers of the present century. Rather strangely, he was played at first for his batting, and he performed very well: but after 1870, when he began to bowl about medium pace, his success was so great that his batting excellence was

ALFRED SHAW.

lost sight of by the general public. The great power of his bowling lay in its good length and unvaried precision. He could break both ways, but got more work on the ball from the off; and he was one of the few bowlers who could very quickly cause a batsman to make a mistake if he was too eager to hit. An impatient batsman might make two spanking hits in succession off him, but he would not make a third. Shaw was sure to take his measure and get him in a difficulty.

On a good wicket, when batting against him, I did not find it difficult to play the ball; but I had to watch him carefully, and wait patiently before I could score. Some days he was irresistible; and there can be little doubt that for the M.C.C. and his county few bowlers have done such good service. He had wonderful stamina, in some seasons bowling as many as 8,000 to 10,000 balls; and he was a very fine fieldsman as well. He was on the bowling staff of the M.C.C. in 1865, '66, and in '67, and again from 1870 until he gave up first-class play; and he captured 10 wickets in an innings for that club against the North in 1874.

His best bowling years were:

	Overs.	Maidens.	Runs.	Wickets.	Average.
1867	885	435	957	96	9.93
1870	1171	645	1289	103	12.53
1871	1404	755	1467	98	14.95
1872	1006	498	1109	92	12.5
1873	1317	630	1638	128	12.102
1874	1461	722	1729	131	13.26
1875	1741	1022	1499	161	9.50
1876	2546	1470	2515	178	14.23
1878	2522	1512	2084	196	10.124
1879	1575	924	1259	134	9.53
1880	1994	1231	1525	177	8.109

JAMES COUPE SHAW was born at Sutton-in-Ashfield, Nottinghamshire, 11th April, 1837. His height was 5 ft. 9 in.; weight, 12 st. Very few bowlers have a better record. In first-class matches, he was most successful, doing good work between 1865 and 1875. The year 1867 was one of his best, when he took 450 wickets in all matches, and delivered very little short of 10,000 balls. He bowled fast left-hand, with a high delivery, and at times was very difficult to play. There was not the spin in his bowling that made Freeman's so difficult, but he brought his arm from behind with a very quick action, making it difficult to see; and if you were at all careless, the ball was on you before you expected it. More than once he beat me in that way; and one year in particular, 1871, he got me out first ball or first over in the first innings of two important matches. He used to tell of them with glee in after years, although he was compelled to put in—"But I had it hot the second." The first time was at the Oval, July 31st and August 1st and 2nd, 1871. I was out l.b.w. to him first ball in the first innings; in the second I scored 268. The second time was at Brighton, 14th, 15th, and 16th August, in the Gentlemen *v.* Players' match, for John Lillywhite's benefit, the same year. He bowled me third ball in the first innings with a lovely break from the off; in the second I scored 217. My experience of him was that at first he tried all he knew to get me out, but that after I got set he repeatedly gave me a ball to hit, for no other purpose than to get me to the other end "so that he might have a try at somebody else." And over after over he bowled a ball rather wide on the off-side, in the hope of getting me caught; giving as his reason for doing it, "It ain't a bit of use my bowling good 'uns to him now; it is a case of I puts the ball where I please, and *he* puts it where he pleases."

He was a very poor bat, although more than once he kept up his wicket when runs were badly wanted and allowed others to score. An instance of it occurred in the year 1872, for Nottinghamshire *v.* Gloucestershire, when I was in Canada with Mr. Fitzgerald's team. Gloucestershire scored 317 first innings, my brother Fred making 115 not out and E. M. 108. There were nine of the Notts men out for a little over 200 runs, and Daft was playing an uphill game to save the "follow" as steadily and pluckily as he ever played in his life. Very little faith was put in Shaw's batting powers; but for once he rose to the occasion—although it was well known he had not gone to bed at orthodox hours the night before—and kept his bat in front of everything until Daft made the requisite number. I should say J. C. Shaw holds the record in England for going in last man. He was in the Players' Eleven *v.* Gentlemen in 1871 and a year or two afterwards, and bowled with effect every time he played for them. He has also taken all ten wickets in an innings.

Mordecai Sherwin was born at Kimberley, Nottinghamshire, 26th February, 1851. His height is 5 ft. 9½ in.; weight 17 st. 4 lbs. He is one of the best wicket-keepers in England at the present time. His pluck has been tried against all kinds of bowling, and it has never failed him. Hard work he likes, and hard work seems to like him; for his big, burly figure has been seen behind the stumps in first-class cricket for fifteen years, and his powers to-day show no abatement. For so heavy a man he is surprisingly active, and the player who thinks he can steal a short run on account of it is hugely mistaken. He can sprint from the wicket as quickly as a more slenderly-built man, and he is always on the alert for any attempt of the kind. He takes the ball as well on the leg-side as on the off; and he has a wonderfully safe pair of hands for a catch.

From 1876 to the end of 1889 he has a very fine record for his county, having caught 254 and stumped

93; his most successful year being 1887, when he caught 39 and stumped 11. When it is remembered that he captained his county that season, the record becomes all the more remarkable, for few players can take that responsibility on their shoulders and play up to their best form. I need hardly say that he has represented the Players *v.* Gentlemen and England *v.* Australia, and that in these matches he has been very successful.

He is not a good bat, but when runs are wanted at a pinch, he sometimes makes them. He was one of the English team that visited Australia in 1886-7.

ARTHUR SHREWSBURY was born on the 11th April, 1856, at New Lenton, near Nottingham. His height is 5 ft. 8 in.; weight, 12 st. 2 lbs. It used to be said of Shrewsbury that he was a worthy successor of R. Daft, who helped materially with the bat to gain Nottinghamshire its very high position amongst the counties between 1860 and 1879. By his doings in later years, Shrewsbury has more than confirmed it. Daft's fine performances have been equalled, and it may be safely said of Shrewsbury that no professional has ever wielded a bat with such excellent results.

It is a great many years since he first appeared for his county. As far back as 1875 he represented it, and captivated the critics by his admirable style of play and great coolness. Greater things were expected of him yearly, but somehow they did not come. Bit by bit he built up his great reputation; but it was not until 1885, when he was in his thirtieth year, that he was seen at his best. Two or three years previously he scored over 200 runs in an innings (twice for his county), batting in a way that was worthy of the highest praise; but in 1885, from the beginning to the end of the season, his form was consistently good, and he could show the fine average of 54.7 for fifteen completed innings. He continued his successful career in 1886; and in 1887 his results with the bat far outshone every professional display since the game began.

The year 1888 was a blank one for him in English cricket, owing to his absence in Australia; but 1889 saw him well to the front again. To-day he has lost none of his skill.

He has represented the Players against the Gentlemen since 1876, and his batting has been a tower of strength for them. In conjunction with Alfred Shaw and Jas. Lillywhite, he has taken a team to Australia four times, and on every occasion batted splendidly. On his return from Australia, in December, 1888, a very handsome testimonial was presented to him by the noblemen, gentlemen, and residents of the town and county of Nottingham, in acknowledgment of his great ability as a cricketer, and manly, straightforward bearing in private life.

His style is too well known to demand a lengthy description. Great patience and coolness are his chief characteristics. You can never tell by his manner or play whether he has just scored his first run or his hundredth. Good balls are carefully watched by him to the end of his innings, however long it may be; and loose ones are freely punished. His defence is admirable, and his fine wrist-play enables him to play the ball firmly away from his wicket, and he rarely allows a ball to pass. His hitting is as safe and scientific as his defence. He times the ball most accurately, gets well over it, and risks nothing in the way of lofty hitting. On good or bad wickets he is equally at home, and more than once he has shone conspicuously when the rest of the team had collapsed. Of late years he has fielded chiefly at point; but it is not so very long ago since he could have been placed anywhere. His best years with the bat have been:

	Completed Innings.	Runs.	Most in an Innings.	Average.
1876	25	593	118	23.18
1882	20	533	207	26.13
1883	38	1117	98	29.15
1884	32	908	209	28.12
1885	20	1130	224*	56.10
1886	33	1404	227*	42.18
1887	21	1653	267	78.15
1889	14	522	104	37. 4
1890	38	1568	267	41.10

His Three-figure Innings in First-class Matches.

June, 1876.	For Notts *v.* Yorkshire, at Trent Bridge	118
May, 1877.	For Players of the North *v.* Gentlemen of the South, at Oval	119
August, 1882.	For Notts *v.* Surrey, at Oval	207
June, 1884.	For Notts *v.* Sussex, at Brighton	209
August, ,,	For Notts *v.* Surrey, at Oval	127
March, 1885.	For England, *v.* Australia, at Melbourne	105*
July, ,,	For Notts *v.* Middlesex, at Lord's	224*
July, ,,	For Notts *v.* Gloucestershire, at Trent Bridge	137
July, ,,	For North *v.* South, at Manchester	101
August, ,,	For Notts *v.* Derbyshire, at Derby	118
June, 1886.	For Notts *v.* Gloucestershire, at Moreton-in-Marsh	227*
July, ,,	For England *v.* Australia, at Lord's	164
July, ,,	For Players *v.* Gentlemen, at Oval	127
Oct., ,,	For England, *v.* Fifteen of South Australia, at Adelaide	100
March, 1887.	For England *v.* Victoria, at Melbourne	144
March, ,,	For Non-Smokers *v.* Smokers, at Melbourne	236
June, ,,	For Notts *v.* Middlesex, at Lord's	119
June, ,,	For England *v.* M.C.C. and Ground, at Lord's	152
June, ,,	For Notts *v.* Lancashire, at Trent Bridge	130
July, ,,	For Players *v.* Gentlemen, at Lord's	111
July, ,,	For Notts *v.* Sussex, at Brighton	101
August, ,,	For Notts *v.* Gloucestershire, at Clifton	119*
August, ,,	For Notts *v.* Middlesex, at Trent Bridge	267
August, ,,	For Notts *v.* Sussex, at Trent Bridge	135
Dec., ,,	For England *v.* Victoria, at Melbourne	232
March, 1888.	For England *v.* Sixth Australian Team	206
May, 1889.	For Notts *v.* Sussex, at Trent Bridge	104
May, 1890.	For Notts *v.* Sussex, at Trent Bridge	267
June, 1890.	For Notts *v.* Lancashire, at Trent Bridge	117

Mr. JOHN SHUTER was born at Thornton Heath, Surrey, on the 9th February, 1855. His height is 5 ft. 6 in.; weight, 11 st. As a public school boy he acquired a great reputation, and before he had completed his twentieth year he had played for Kent by right of residence. But it was in 1877 that he identified himself with the county of his birth. Surrey has had no warmer supporter, and few more brilliant batsmen and fieldsmen. He is a safe field anywhere; and can get runs in any company, and makes them in a way that delights the spectators. His hitting is brilliant all round, and in forcing the game he has few equals. His defence is good and sound, but it is his dashing, rapid scoring that charms every one; and he is a rare good man at a pinch. Every one who has had to do with the captaining of a team knows how difficult it is to get some players to hit out and risk their wickets in the hope of achieving a win. I have never had to ask Mr. Shuter twice to make a bid for victory. He can grasp the situation as quickly as any one, and is invariably equal to it.

Surrey has done wonders under his leadership. Matters were not too rosy when he undertook the captaincy, but it did not take long to prove to the Surrey Committee that they had got the right man in the right place. He has the eleven well under his command, and he has the gratification of knowing that Surrey has to thank him to a great extent for its high position to-day. He played for the South *v.* North in 1878, for the Gentlemen *v.* Players in 1879, and most years since. His best years with the bat have been:

	Completed Innings.	Runs.	Most in an Innings.	Average.
1882	32	832	93	26
1883	32	805	108*	25. 5
1884	36	968	125	26.32
1885	34	841	135	24.25
1887	27	871	111	32. 7
1888	33	834	95	25. 9

MR. J. SHUTER.

JAMES SOUTHERTON, the man of many counties, was born at Petworth, Sussex, November 16th, 1827. His height was 5 ft. 6 ins.; weight, at his best, about 11 st. Like one or two bowlers I have mentioned, he did almost better after his 40th year than before it. In turn, he played for Surrey, Sussex, and Hampshire; but it was not until he went back to his first love in his 39th year that he became one of the most successful bowlers of his time. His bowling was slow round-arm, with a rather peculiar delivery, and by many players it was considered doubtful. On a sticky wicket he could get a great deal of work on the ball, and he was very clever in altering his pace and pitch. A careless batsman, or one playing against him for the first time, was very often taken in by it, and Southerton used to chuckle when he gained a wicket in that way. Another trick of his was to deliver three balls, causing them to break six inches or more, and then to put in a fast straight one—a trick which was often successful. He had to be watched very closely: for he had a good head on his shoulders, and was continually seeking for a weak spot; and more than once I have seen him deliver the ball before he reached the crease. He did good work for the United South Eleven; but his best performances were for Surrey. In 1872, in his 45th year, he is said to have captured 340 wickets in good matches; and the year after, for his county alone, he obtained 147 wickets, and had a batting average of 22. He represented the Players in 1870, '71, and '72, and did fairly well with both bat and ball.

His batting was characterised more by hard hitting than sound defence, and occasionally he shut his eyes when he hit. He strenuously denied it; but we caught him napping beautifully in one match—M.C.C. *v.* Surrey. I was fielding at point when he hit a ball very hard that struck the ground a yard or two in front of me, which I caught on the bound. I tossed it up, and said, "That's a hot 'un, Jim!" then chucked it to the bowler. To my surprise, Southerton walked away, and was indignant when long-slip said, "You 're not out, Jim!" Pooley whistled to him to return. "Keep quiet, Pooley," I said, "and we'll have the laugh at him." The match was a foregone conclusion, or we should not have carried the joke out; but to his dying day Southerton would not admit that it was other than a genuine catch.

His umpiring powers were rather hazy also. He was umpiring in the Castlemaine match of our Australian tour, when I hit a ball which the fieldsman caught, but fell over the ropes with it. It was four under and five over. "How's that, umpire?" "Not out," said he: "it was out of bounds when he caught it." "Then I must have five runs for it," I said; but he would not allow more than the single we had run, and for the life of him he could not see it must either be out or five runs. I did not say much at the time; for I should not have been surprised if he had changed his mind and given me out. All the same, there were not many better-hearted players than Jimmy Southerton.

His best bowling years in first-class cricket were:

	Overs.	Maidens.	Runs.	Wickets.	Average.
1867	996	361	1522	112	13.66
1868	1039	328	1976	151	13.13
1869	1371	505	2081	133	15.86
1870	1863	696	3069	210	14.129
1871	1612	636	2358	151	15.93
1872	1458	487	2019	167	12.15
1873	1386	671	1833	132	13.117
1874	1200	583	1523	127	11.126
1875	1522	737	1810	137	13.29

Mr. Frederick Robert Spofforth was born at Balmain, near Sydney, on the 9th September, 1855. His height is 6 ft. 3 ins.; weight, 12 st. 2 lbs. First-class bowlers have come and gone with the Australian Elevens, but to my mind not one of them has come up to the standard of Spofforth, who visited England with the first team in 1878. I first met him when I took a team out to Australia in 1874, but I little thought then that he was to stir the whole cricket world some four years later. We can all remember the impression he made in the memorable match against the M.C.C. and Ground the first year he came to us, and how before the season was over he challenged the best of our English players for first place. Right well he proved his title to the name of "demon" bowler which had been given him on the other side. He came with every team down to 1886, and maintained his great reputation in all of them.

His style has been described many times: right-hand, round-arm, a high delivery and fairly fast, with a break from both sides, but chiefly from the off. He was most successful with his medium-pace balls, which, when he was in form, he could pitch where he liked. Whether he broke six inches or two feet, so wonderful was his command of the ball that if it beat the batsman it invariably hit the wicket. His very fast ones were generally yorkers, which were delivered without any apparent alteration of pace. Length and accuracy were his great characteristics, and it used to be said of him that, if he were allowed to pour water on a space six inches square on a dry and hard wicket, he would bowl out the best eleven in England for a very small score. Though he has not played much of late years, I believe with practice he would prove as effective as ever. His performances must speak for themselves. The following are confined to eleven-a-side matches played in England for the Australian Elevens:

	Overs.	Maidens.	Runs.	Wickets.	Average.
1878	717	264	1198	108	11.10
1880	240	82	396	46	8.28
1882	1592	700	2282	188	12.26
1884	1544	649	2642	216	12.50
1886	925	372	1528	89	17.15

Mr. ALLAN GIBSON STEEL was born at Liverpool on the 24th September, 1858. His height is 5 ft. 8 in.; weight, about 11 st. 7 lbs. It is very difficult to arrive at a proper estimate of his abilities as a cricketer. Before he had completed his sixteenth year he had played well enough to warrant the prediction that he would do as well as any one since the game began. Unfortunately, professional and other duties have interfered very much with his cricketing career; for while he has performed most brilliantly with bat and ball, he has not been able to develop his powers to the extent everyone sincerely wished he would. For weeks and months he would be unable to play in first-class cricket; and then suddenly he would appear in some great match, and astonish everyone by his brilliant form.

From the time he first represented Cambridge University in 1878, his form was indeed remarkable. He was in residence there until 1881, and it may be safely said of him that no more brilliant player ever represented either eleven in the Inter-University matches since they were first instituted. During the four years he represented Cambridge *v.* Oxford he played 6 completed innings, scored 182 runs; average, 30.2; and bowled 317 overs for 342 runs, 38 wickets; average, 9.

He played for the Gentlemen *v.* Players when he was but nineteen years of age, and nearly every time he appeared afterwards he was very successful. Lancashire, too, was strengthened by his fine play; but that eleven has also had to bear with his occasional presence. For England *v.* Australia he has come off on more than one occasion. He was eminently successful for the Hon. Ivo Bligh's team which visited Australia in 1882-3. In all matches he played 18 completed innings, scored 551 runs; average, 30.11; and bowled 800 overs, 390 maidens, 999 runs, 152 wickets; average, 6.87.

He bowls slow medium pace, round-arm, breaks both

ways, and varies his pace and length with excellent judgment. In fact, you rarely get two balls alike from him; and if there is a weak spot in your batting, he seems to find it out before he has finished the first over. He does not in the least mind being hit; but he is a very clever or lucky batsman who can do it more than once in the same over without giving a chance.

His batting is also first-class. He hits very clean everywhere; balls the slightest bit loose being hit to the boundary. I do not believe he has ever been troubled with nervousness at any period of his innings; anyhow, I shall not readily forget the unceremonious way in which he treated the Australian bowling at Lord's for the M.C.C. and Ground in 1884 immediately he took guard. He lost no time in getting well set that innings, and Spofforth, Giffen, Palmer and Cooper had a most unenviable time of it.

His best batting years have been:

	Completed Innings.	Runs.	Most in an Innings.	Average.
1879	20	553	93	27.13
1880	22	496	118	22.12
1881	28	834	106*	29.22
1882	26	739	171	28.11
1883	12	370	68	30.10
1884	25	967	148	38.17
1886	10	418	83	41. 8

His best bowling years have been:

	Overs.	Maidens.	Runs.	Wickets.	Average.
1878	1223	447	1542	164	9.66
1879	943	432	1120	93	12. 4
1880	925	400	1205	92	13. 9
1881	1257	537	1683	125	13.58

H. H. STEPHENSON was born at Esher, Surrey, 3rd May, 1833. His height was 6 ft.; weight, 11 st. 12 lbs. He was a first-rate bat, good wicket-keeper, and very successful fast round-arm bowler—a combination of qualities rarely met with in the cricket field, and to it Stephenson owed a great deal of his success. The power of his bowling lay in making the ball break back from the off. He belonged to the All-England Eleven, and was captain of the first team that went out to Australia in 1862. After he gave up playing he proved to be one of the best coaches of young players, and since he went to Uppingham he has brought out a great many first-class cricketers.

Mr. ANDREW ERNEST STODDART was born at South Shields on the 11th of March, 1864. His height is 5 ft. 10½ in.; weight, 12 st. 4 lbs. He was very little known in the cricket world until 1885, and then only in connection with the Hampstead Club. However, before that season was over he was chosen to represent Middlesex, and his progress since has been phenomenally rapid. He is one of the most brilliant amateurs we have at the present time, his batting, bowling and fielding being first-class. As a rule he scores very rapidly, and already he holds the record for the highest individual score in an innings: 485, for the Hampstead Club *v.* Stoics, at Hampstead on the 4th August, 1886. It was not a first-class match by any means, but it was a wonderful bit of scoring. His 151 for England *v.* M.C.C. in the Centenary Match in 1887 was a finer effort, and was made against Barnes and Flowers.

He is a brilliant out-field and a very safe catch. I take credit for having introduced him as a bowler, but I have been rather amused by his remarks when he gets hit: "All right, hit away," said he; "but it's all your fault, W. G., and I wish I had never bowled a ball in my life!"

So far his batting results in first-class matches show:

	Completed Innings.	Runs.	Most in an Innings.	Average.
1886	23	640	116	27.19
1887	28	799	151	28.15
1889	33	817	78*	24.25
1890	44	845	115	19. 9

Mr. GEORGE STRACHAN was born at Prestbury, near Cheltenham, 21st November, 1850. His height was 6 ft. 1 in.; weight, 13 st. He was a good bowler and batsman: but it was by his brilliant fielding that he made his reputation; and there can be little doubt that at long-leg or cover-point he had few equals in his own time. Good judges have said that no one has excelled him since at those positions, and I am inclined to agree with them. For a man of his height he was about the quickest starter I ever saw, and the way he got over the ground was a lesson to lazy fieldsmen. Many a batsman, having hit a ball in the direction of cover-point, started to run, being ignorant of his wonderful quickness and great reach, and feeling certain he could never get to it; but not only did he get to it, but picking it up with surprising quickness, he had it into the wicket-keeper's or bowler's hands like a flash and seconds before the batsman had reached his crease! At Cheltenham College, where he was educated, they tell of a smart bit of fielding which he did when the M.C.C. played the College Eleven one year. He was bowling to George Hearne, who stepped back and pulled him twice between the wicket and mid-on. The third ball was bowled in the same place, and Hearne pulled it again; but Mr. Strachan moved a yard or two when he saw him make up his mind to hit in the same way, and brought off a remarkable catch yards from the wicket.

As a batsman he had sound defence, and hit freely. He represented Gloucestershire, Middlesex, and Surrey. For the Gentlemen *v.* Players in 1872 he met with marked success as a bowler, and in the same match at the Oval in 1875 he took five wickets in 21 balls, off which no runs were scored; but he never came off for them in batting, although his fielding was always brilliant.

Mr. CHARLES THOMAS STUDD was the most brilliant member of a well-known cricketing family, and from 1881 to 1884 had few superiors as an all-round player. His batting and bowling were very good, and for Cambridge University, Middlesex, Gentlemen *v.* Players, and England *v.* Australia he was successful with both. He gave up playing at an early age, and was a great loss to the game; for he was one of the finest of our young players.

His style of batting was free and correct, and he scored largely and rapidly against all the best bowlers of his time. He bowled medium-pace, round-arm, with a machine-like delivery, and had a fair break from the off.

His best years were:—

BATTING.

	Completed Innings.	Runs.	Most in an Innings.	Average.
1881	25 ...	799 ...	113 ...	31.24
1882	38 ...	1249 ...	126* ...	32.33
1883	29 ...	1193 ...	175* ...	41. 4
1884	15 ...	398 ...	141* ...	26. 8

BOWLING.

	Overs.	Maidens.	Runs.	Wickets.	Average.
1881 ...	957 ...	426 ...	1284 ...	79 ...	16.20
1882 ...	1564 ...	768 ...	2027 ...	128 ...	15.107
1883 ...	1445 ...	651 ...	1957 ...	112 ...	17 53
1884 ...	714 ...	297 ...	1120 ...	54 ...	20.40

GEORGE TARRANT was born at Cambridge, 7th December, 1838. His height was 5 ft. 7 in.; weight, 9 st. 7 lbs. He was not much of a batsman; but he was a very fast round-arm bowler, and, for so little a man, astonishingly strong. There was no measured, stately walk to the crease in his delivery. He was all over the place like a flash of lightning, never sparing himself, and frightening timid batsmen. He was the terror of twenty-twos when he played for the All-

England Eleven, some of his long-hops bounding over their heads, causing them to change colour and funk at the next straight one. He died at the early age of 31.

Mr. Charles Inglis Thornton was born at Llanwarne, Herefordshire, 20th March, 1850. His height is 6 ft.; weight, 13 st. No more sensational hitter or enthusiastic lover of the game has ever appeared on a cricket-ground. He played for Eton *v.* Harrow in 1866, 1867, and 1868; scoring 46 not out and 7 first year, 35 and 47 second, 44 and 13 third. In the first innings of the 1868 match he commenced his hitting by sending a ball over the bowler's head and over the old pavilion at Lord's into the garden beyond.

At Cambridge, where he was much esteemed, he did a wonderful bit of hitting for his University in June, 1871, his most successful year for the eleven. Playing against the Gentlemen of England, he scored 74 at a great pace. Mr. D. Buchanan, one of the best amateur bowlers of that time, bowled the first over to him, and a hot one it was. The first ball was hit for 6, the second and third for 4 each, and the fourth for 6. I was playing in that match, and not being the bowler, could afford to laugh heartily.

The same year, at the Oval, playing for the Gentlemen of South *v.* Players of South, he scored 31 in 16 minutes first innings, and 61 in 47 minutes second. One hit of the 61, off Southerton's bowling, travelled a great distance, right over the old racquet-court, which used to be situated by the present entrance gate, and into the road beyond. An uncommon and amusing incident occurred in the same match. In the first innings of the Players, Thornton was put on to bowl at the beginning of it—a compliment, I should think, never paid him before or since. Of course it was underhand grubs he bowled, and he obtained three or four wickets for a very small number of runs. The captain of the Players, not to be outdone in originality, put on H. H. Stephenson to bowl grubs when the Gentlemen commenced batting; but the result was sadly different. The same year for Gentlemen *v.* Players at Brighton, John Lillywhite's benefit, he had only eight balls bowled to him, off which he scored 34—7 fours and 1 six. But his finest performance was at Scarborough, fifteen years later, for Gentlemen of England *v.* I Zingari, when he scored 107 not out, Mr. A. G. Steel being the bowler most punished. There were 8 sixes, 12 fours, 2 twos, and 7 singles in his score; one of the sixes off Steel went right out of the ground, over the high houses, and into the square beyond. Unfortunately this hit could not be measured; but it was thought by those who witnessed it to be the largest he ever made. There is no waiting to get set in his batting. The first over is invariably as sensational as the last, and right sorry are spectators and players alike when he leaves the wicket.

He was chosen President of Cambridge University Cricket Club in 1872, and was closely identified with the old Orleans Club. Of late years he has taken a very prominent part in arranging matches in connection with the Scarborough Festival, and no one is more heartily welcomed there.

It is difficult to find out the exact distance of his greatest hits, but the following can be relied on: In 1878, in a minor match, in which he scored 188 not out, two of the hits travelled 140 yards before they touched the ground. At Brighton he hit a ball which travelled 168 yards before it pitched, the distance being measured by the Rev. J. Pycroft. At Canterbury, in a North *v.* South match, he hit one off W. M. Rose 152 yards, which was measured by W. de Chair Baker; and at the Orleans Club, off Boyle, the Australian, he hit one the same distance, which was measured by Rylott and

Wild. But he must not be judged in the light of a sensational hitter only; for he has scored over 100 runs in an innings repeatedly, some of them against first-class bowling. He is also very good in the outfield, and has thrown a cricket-ball 106 yards.

R. C. TINLEY was born at Southwell, Nottinghamshire, 25th October, 1830. His height was 5 ft. 8 ins.; weight, 10 st. He will be best remembered as the successor of Clarke as a slow underhand bowler to the All-England Eleven. He used to bowl fast round with indifferent success, but was more successful with his slows. He was an excellent fieldsman at point; but as a batsman he was given to slogging, and had very little defence.

Mr. FRANK TOWNSEND was born at Clifton, Bristol, 17th October, 1847. His height is 6 ft.; weight, 12 st. Very few cricketers have done so well for their county. He represented Gloucestershire the first match it played in 1870, and he has continued to do so for twenty years.

From 1870 to 1874 he batted in 25 innings for his county, and averaged 27; in 1876 he played 10 innings, and averaged 30; in 1880 he played 12 innings, and averaged 25; in 1885 he played 18 innings, and averaged 23; and in 1889 he played 21 innings, and averaged 17. Three times he has scored over 100 runs in an innings for his county, and in the twenty years I have mentioned he batted in 236 innings and scored 4,261 runs.

He represented the Gentlemen *v.* Players in 1874 and 1875; but school duties prevented him from continuing in these matches, and he did not appear in them so often as his undoubted abilities entitled him to. In local matches, for the Clifton Club he has scored over 200 runs in an innings more times than I can remember, and he has always taken great interest in the success of the County Club.

As a batsman he is a magnificent hitter, especially in driving and leg-hitting, and he always contrives to keep the ball well down. His defence is sound, and he plays the ball with firmness. He has a peculiar habit of flourishing his bat; but he plays very straight, and comes down on shooters with surprising quickness.

He was a good lob-bowler for years, and his right hand has lost little of its cunning to-day. As a rule he bowls slow, with a good curl from leg; but now and then he puts in a fast yorker, which often proves effective. Half his success has been owing to the smart fielding of his own bowling; and now, as years ago, he is a magnificent field and safe catch anywhere. He has a springy, elastic action in the field; and he goes after the ball in leaps and bounds. He was fielding at long-leg when Gloucestershire played Yorkshire, at Sheffield, on a certain occasion. Yorkshire spectators are invariably free and outspoken, and in this match they kept applauding the way he got over the ground and saved the runs. One extraordinary effort, in which he had to run a long distance, and brought off a magnificent, and what seemed an impossible, catch, roused their enthusiasm, and they unanimously dubbed him the "india rubber gentleman!"

No more genial or popular cricketer has ever played; and he has been ever ready to express an opinion on the game, or listen to one. All classes of cricketers have been tempted by his pleasant face to ask questions of him. But he had a curious experience on one occasion, when we played Lancashire. He was standing outside the hotel—in cricket costume, I believe—having a quiet cigar before starting for the ground for the day's play, when he was accosted by a seedy-looking individual.

"Good-morning! governor, be you an Australian?" asked the seedy one.

"Not quite that," replied Mr. Townsend.

"Well now, be you a Canadian?"

"Try again," said he.

"You ar'n't one of them foreigners they call Aboriginals, be you?"

"Not even that," he replied, laughing.

"Now I knows what you be, governor; you're what I've been often called—a nondescript!"

Mr. CHARLES THOMAS BIASS TURNER was born at Bathurst, New South Wales, on November 16th, 1862. He is 5 ft. 9½ ins. in height; weight, 12 st. 3lbs. He takes rank with Spofforth; indeed, very good judges consider that it is a toss-up between them for first place amongst Australian bowlers. Anyhow, he was nicknamed the "terror"; and against certain batsmen he richly deserves it. His pace is above medium, but not very fast; but, with the exception of Freeman, his ball comes quicker off the pitch than any bowler's I have met. That peculiarity, added to his break from the off, makes him a most dangerous bowler. He alters his pace without showing it, is very fond of a yorker or fast straight one, and on a sticky wicket is unplayable. He is a really good fieldsman, full of pluck, and never seems to tire; and he is fast becoming a dangerous batsman. His doings in 1888 and 1890 were first-class, and it is safe to predict that he has a great future before him.

Bowling performances in eleven-a-side matches in England:

	Overs.	Maidens.	Runs.	Wickets.	Average.
1888 ...	2589 ...	1222 ...	3492 ...	314 ...	11.38
1890 ...	1651 ...	724 ...	2725 ...	215 ...	12.145

Mr. EDWARD FERDINANDO SUTTON TYLECOTE was born at Marston Rectory, Ampthill, Bedfordshire, 23rd June, 1849. His height was 5 ft. 10½ in.; weight, 11 st. He was one of the finest amateur wicket-keepers for many years: equally good at stumping and catching,

MR. J. J. FERRIS, MR. C. T. B. TURNER.

and he stood up pluckily against all kinds of bowling. He did many smart things with the gloves; one of the best, if not the very best, was his two stumped and five caught for the Gentlemen *v.* Players at the Oval in 1876.

But he will be remembered best for his great score of 404 not out, in a School contest at Clifton College in 1868, made in six hours on three successive afternoons. It was the first time 400 runs in an innings had ever been scored by any cricketer, and it was thought wonderful and phenomenal at the time, though against very moderate bowling. He was in great batting form for his college all that year, scoring over 100 runs three times; and at the end of the season showed an average of 70 for nineteen innings. For five seasons he played for his college; but his last, 1868, when he captained them, was his best, and no more popular captain ever led a college eleven to victory.

At Oxford he was successful also, playing for Oxford *v.* Cambridge in 1869, 1870, 1871, and 1872, and captaining the eleven the last two. He represented the Gentlemen first in 1871, and most years down to 1886. The year 1883 was his best in these matches, when he scored 107 against Peate, Barlow, Barnes, and Ulyett. His batting was characterised by great steadiness and patience; but immediately the bowling got loose, he hit very hard, his driving of an over-pitched ball in particular being a treat to witness. He was one of the Hon. Ivo Bligh's team which visited Australia in 1882-3.

George Ulyett was born at Pitsmoor, near Sheffield, 21st October, 1851. His height is 5 ft. 10½ in.; weight, 14 st. With the exception of Emmett, Ulyett has been the most prominent player in the Yorkshire eleven any time during the last fifteen years. He was one of the best all-round professional cricketers in 1875, and he is one of the best to-day. Whether as a batsman, bowler, or fieldsman, he has been worthy of a place in any eleven, and very few players have so fine a record. He was at the head of the batting averages of his county some years in succession. He was almost as successful with the ball; and he is still a brilliant fieldsman anywhere.

He represented the Players *v.* Gentlemen in 1876, and he represents them still. Indeed, it would be difficult, even to-day, to choose a representative eleven of any kind without including him. And I should think he has played oftener out of the United Kingdom than any player. He first visited Australia in 1876 with Lillywhite's team; went out again with Lord Harris's eleven in 1878; and was also a member of Shaw's team in 1881-2. On each occasion he was at the head of the batting averages in eleven-a-side matches, and showed the very fine results of: 1876, average 48.6; 1878, average 34; 1881, average 39.2.

He is very popular with all followers of the game; and his clean and vigorous hitting commands the admiration of everyone. He hits well all round, and scores at a great pace, and invariably bats first man; and when he has got well set, the quality of the bowling makes little difference to him.

As a bowler he has been very successful at times, and on a kicking wicket almost unplayable. He bowls fast round with a high delivery, and gets a good deal of break from the off. Now and then he makes the ball rise very quickly, and he has to be very carefully watched. His performance with the ball for England *v.* Australia, in the 2nd innings at Lord's, July 22nd and 23rd, 1884, was a very fine one: 39 overs, 23 maidens, 36 runs, 7 wickets; and the way he caught Bonnor off his own bowling in that innings has never been surpassed. The year 1890 showed that he had lost little of his form—a very exceptional thing, considering that he is now in his 40th year.

His best years with the bat have been:

	Completed Innings.	Runs.	Most in an innings.	Average.
1878	46	1347	109	29.13
1881	36	1197	112	33. 9
1882	56	1542	138	27.30
1883	51	1572	84	30.42
1884	45	1334	146*	29.29
1885	46	1337	91	29. 3
1887	39	1487	199*	38. 5
1890	53	1093	107	20.33

Mr. GEORGE FREDERICK VERNON was born in London, 20th June, 1856. He was educated at Rugby, and was captain of the eleven in 1875. After he left school he became a prominent member of Middlesex and the M.C.C., and continued to do grand work for both with the bat and in the field until last year, when, to the great regret of everyone, he gave up first-class cricket. The 100 he has scored repeatedly for both, and in a dashing way that has often astonished the best bowlers of the present time. He has also done well for the Gentlemen against the Players, and has been chosen in these matches as much for his magnificent fielding as his batting.

He is one of the quick scorers, and for low, clean, hard hitting has few equals: in fact, like McDonnell, the famous Australian, he might win a match by himself at any time, whatever the condition of the ground. Against weak bowling he has made some fine scores, and he holds the record, in conjunction with Mr. A. H. Trevor, for longest partnership—605—made for Orleans Club *v.* Rickling Green, in 1882. He has no superior in the out-field for quickness and certainty, and he has brought off many a fine catch.

He was a member of the seventh team which visited

Australia in 1882–83, and took out a team of his own in 1887-88. He also took out a team of amateurs to India in October, 1889.

Mr. ISAAC DONNITHORNE WALKER was born at Southgate, 8th January, 1844. His height was 5 ft. 11½ ins.; weight, at his best, about 13 st. He was, without doubt, one of the finest amateur batsmen I ever played with or against, and an earnest and most enthusiastic supporter of the game. It looks rather strange to me to write of him in the past tense, for it seems only the other day that he was playing in first-class cricket with all the dash and brilliancy of his youth, though the years had silvered his head. His batting style was a model of ease and power. He stood very erect, played with a straight bat, and his hitting was clean and vigorous. One hit of his always came off, and puzzled his opponents sadly. A half volley on the off he drove over coverpoint's head, and it invariably travelled to the boundary. I can only remember three other players who hit in that peculiar way—Mr. Massie, of Australia; Mr. A. J. Webbe, of Middlesex; and Mr. Radcliffe, of Gloucestershire; but neither does it so successfully as Mr. Walker did. Another peculiarity of his was batting without pads. I know he is about as plucky an athlete as you will find in a day's journey, and I daresay he thinks, with one or two other players I know, that if a player cannot protect his legs with his bat he does not know how to use it; but, all the same, I have seen him put on pads to Freeman's bowling.

It would require more room than I can spare to recount half of his great innings. Repeatedly he has scored over 100 in an innings, and more than once over 1,000 runs during the season in first-class matches. His 165 in the Gentlemen *v.* Players' match at the Oval in 1868, in his 25th year, will undoubtedly be considered his finest performance; for it was made against Willsher, James Lillywhite, jun., and Silcock, and was one of the most brilliant innings he ever played. The quality of his batting will be understood when I say there were 2 sixes, 3 fives, 17 fours, and 10 threes in it. It was a rare display, and he was in consistently good form all that year; for in first-class matches he played 19 innings and had an average of 34.

If evidence were wanting of the power of his play in later years, no better illustration can be had than his fine display for Middlesex *v.* Gloucestershire in the return match at Clifton, in August, 1883, when he was in his 40th year. The Hon. Alfred Lyttelton and he scored 226 in an hour and three-quarters, and while they were together put on 324 runs; Mr. Walker scoring 145, Mr. Lyttelton, 181. I have rarely witnessed a better exhibition of batting. True, after they had both scored 100, we bowled them balls to hit, and placed the field accordingly; but the remarkable part of the display was, that neither made a mistake until the finish, and their hitting at the end of the innings was as clean and hard as at the beginning—certainly a remarkable show of strength and condition for a veteran.

Mr. Walker was also a very good lob bowler, and as captain of Middlesex was much esteemed by his fellow-members. He is a great supporter of the game, and has always taken special interest in the doings of his old school, Harrow. Indeed, it is no secret that since he gave up first-class cricket, and for some time before, he has been in the habit of going down once or twice a week to coach the Harrow boys. He was also a good racquet player, and champion of his school. I might say a great deal more about this, the youngest, and not the least remarkable member of this famous family; for he has been a power in the cricket world, and no finer or truer cricketer ever breathed.

His best batting years were:

	Completed innings.	Runs.	Most in an innings.	Average.
1868	19	651	165	34. 5
1869	18	540	90	30
1870	22	820	179	37. 6
1873	17	586	64	34. 8
1876	28	796	94	28.12
1877	27	787	95	29. 4
1883	23	750	145	32.14
1884	24	674	83	28. 2

Mr. JOHN WALKER, the eldest brother of this celebrated cricketing family, was born at Palmer's Green, Middlesex, 15th September, 1826. His height was 6 ft. 2 ins.; weight, about 15½ st. The first time I met him was at the Oval in 1864, when he played for the Surrey Club against South Wales Club. I can remember now the impression his tall, strongly-built figure made upon me as I watched him make his 44 by vigorous hitting. He was then in his 38th year. My brothers Henry and E. M. had often talked to me about the family reputation, and I was pleased when he hit our bowling all over the field, as I desired to see him score. He was just as successful with the ball on that occasion, for he took six wickets for 39 runs with his slow bowling in the first innings, and we were defeated by 7 wickets. I was fortunate enough to score 38 in the second innings, and was greatly pleased when he uttered a word or two of praise, although I had to thank him for getting me out in both innings.

But, of course, he had made his reputation as a player and generous supporter of the game long before that. His first appearance at Lord's was in June, 1846, for his University. In 1852 he scored 58 in the Gentlemen *v.* Players' match, the highest score on the Gentlemen's side, and bowled also. In 1861, against the Players he scored 48 and 22, and was again the highest scorer for his side; and in 1862, in the same match, he scored 98 and 10, the former score being the highest made on either side. At Southgate, where he lived for many years, he formed the Southgate Club, which became a very strong one, owing to the all-round proficiency of himself and his younger brothers. Mr. Walker has been closely identified with the Marylebone and Surrey Clubs for years.

Mr. RUSSELL DONNITHORNE WALKER, another member of the famous family, was born at Southgate, Middlesex, 13th February, 1842. His height was 5 ft. 8½ ins.; weight, 13 st. He possessed the family hitting powers, and could play steadily when wanted. His quickness of eye and wrist-power were remarkable, and one hit was unique and exceptional; indeed, I cannot remember anyone but himself attempting it. If he were bowled a long-hop to leg, and it bounded high, with indescribable quickness he would hit it over his shoulder sufficiently hard to make it go over long-stop's head. I used to think it a fancy stroke, but changed my mind when I saw how repeatedly and effectively he brought it off. Where he got the quickness to do it, I do not know: possibly his racquet training at Oxford may account for it. He was champion at that there in 1861-2-3-4. In later years he showed the same quickness at tennis, and I have watched him with infinite pleasure in the court at Lord's, when he gave some of his fine displays against very much younger players, who fancied they had rather an easy undertaking before them. He had the power of being able to disguise his play, and you might look for a very long time into his eyes before you could find out where he meant to place the ball.

As a batsman, he met with great success in important matches; but his finest effort, to my mind, was his 92 in the second innings of the Gentlemen *v.* Players at the Oval in 1865, when I made my first appearance in the same match. It was a splendidly hit innings, the highest in the match; and as he took four of the Players' wickets for 55 runs in the first innings, two for 47 second, and caught out two others as well, the performance may be considered an exceptionally good one. He was a good slow round-arm bowler, and one of the best changes I ever met, frequently obtaining wickets when others had failed.

Mr. VYELL EDWARD WALKER was born at Southgate, Middlesex, 20th April, 1837. His height was 5 ft. 11 in.; weight, 13½ st. He represented the Gentlemen *v.* Players when he was but 19 years of age, and was chosen to represent England when he was 21, and took all ten wickets in the first innings; and scored 20 not out first, and 108 second, for England *v.* Surrey, when he was 22. In the year 1860 he was paid the compliment of being chosen in the First Eleven of England *v.* Next Fourteen. He was one of the most brilliant fieldsmen of his day, his fielding at point being very fine. He bowled underhand lobs, not quite so accurately as Clarke; but what he lacked in accuracy, he almost made up by his wonderful fielding. His sprinting powers up the pitch, or to mid-on and mid-off were exceptional, and he seemed to divine where the batsman meant to place the ball. As a batsman he possessed good defence and fine hitting powers, and scored at a great rate.

He played quite up to his best batting form in 1866, when I began first-class cricket; for he could show that year the fine average of 42 for 18 completed innings; but his best bowling years were rather before that. All ten wickets in an innings is considered a remarkable feat: reference to the records in Chapter XII. will show that he is the only player, amateur or professional,

MR. V. E. WALKER.

who has done it more than once in first-class cricket; in fact, he has done it thrice.

Six out of the seven brothers have played for Gentlemen *v.* Players from 1852 to 1877, the exception being Mr. Alfred Walker, the second brother, who was born in 1827. He was a very fast underhand bowler of the old school, with a good curl from leg, and as good a bowler of that style as has been seen. On the rough wickets, which were very common in those days, he did great execution, and probably one of his performances is unique; for he obtained all the wickets except one in both innings, and he himself threw down that batsman's wicket from his own bowling!

The Southgate Club first played regularly in 1855; down to 1877 it played 192 matches, of which Southgate won 133, lost 27, and 32 were unfinished: one-day matches were decided first innings. All the seven brothers took part in three matches, and would have done in several more had not illness or accident prevented.

ALEXANDER WATSON was born at Coatbridge, Lanarkshire, 4th November, 1846. His height is 5 ft. 6½ in.; weight, 10 st. 10 lbs. Scotland has reason to be proud of him as a cricketer, and it was a fortunate day for Lancashire when he crossed the border to accept an engagement with the Rusholme Club. He learned his cricket as a member of the Drumpellier Club, well known as Colonel Buchanan's team, and was even more successful with the bat than the ball. His first good match was against the All-England Eleven at Glasgow, when he was about 18 years of age. At that time he bowled fast round, with little or no break. Mr. D. Buchanan, who was in the habit of taking an eleven of the Free Foresters to Scotland, was the first to notice his exceptional abilities, and advised him to moderate his pace and cultivate break, which he promptly did. A two years' engagement with the Edinburgh Caledonian Club enabled him to develop his bowling powers. Two years later he took up his residence in Manchester, and from 1872 down to the present Lancashire has had no harder worker or more conspicuous bowler.

He has rarely been far from the top of the first-class bowling averages, and the amount of wear and tear he has gone through has been something remarkable. When he bowled first for the county his pace was slower than it is to-day, and very often the batsmen ran out and hit him. He quickly put an end to that by increasing the pace without sacrificing much of his break from the off. He keeps a very good length, and the ball travels very low after it pitches; and he can go on like a machine for hours. Very few bowlers have the knack of delivering shooters so often, and he is very quick in finding out a batsman's weakness. Unfortunately, his reputation has suffered by a slight suspicion in his delivery. He is an excellent field at short-slip, rarely allowing anything to pass that he can touch, and he used to keep wicket in a very efficient way; and he can bat too. His best bowling performances have been, for the North of England *v.* Australians on May 31st, June 1st, 1886, when he bowled 27 overs, 18 maidens, 12 runs, 6 wickets; and for Lancashire *v.* Sussex, at Manchester on the 3rd of July, 1890, when he took 5 wickets for 7 runs first innings, and 4 wickets for 6 runs second.

His best bowling years have been:

	Overs.	Maidens.	Runs.	Wickets.	Average.
1873	279	92	446	48	9.14
1876	534	248	650	51	12.38
1877	1089	548	1233	96	12.81
1878	535	280	586	49	11.47
1880	881	455	946	84	11.22
1881	879	512	812	69	11.53
1882	924	495	953	76	12.41
1883	940	463	1135	96	11.79
1886	1188	701	1109	99	11.20
1887	1532	937	1482	100	14.82
1889	850	438	1139	90	12.59
1890	1041	561	1331	81	16.35

Mr. ALEXANDER JOSIAH WEBBE was born in London on the 16th January, 1855. His height is 5 ft. 8 in.; weight, about 11½ st. He might almost be called a veteran; for he has been before the public as a first-class player for more than 17 years. He earned a great school reputation at Harrow, strengthened it by his doings at Oxford, and in 1875, when he first represented the Gentlemen, he played most brilliantly. His fine score in the second innings, against the Players, at Lord's that year will not readily be forgotten for the sound defence and great patience he exercised in compiling it. I have had the pleasure of an enjoyable and profitable partnership with him on two or three occasions since; but I do not believe he has ever played more brilliantly than he did then, when he was in his 21st year, and was almost a stranger to first-class professional bowling. Morley, A. Shaw, and Hill were at their best, but we put on 203 runs before we were parted; his 65, as well as I can remember, being faultless.

Very few know how successful he has been with the bat. Year after year he has been well up in the averages, and to-day, though he is in his 37th year, he is as sure and effective as ever. The year 1887 was far and away his finest. On the 5th of August that season he scored 192 not out against Kent, and a week later 243 not out against Yorkshire. In the second match the wicket was very fiery, and Hunter, the wicket-keeper, had to stand back to the fast bowlers. Ball after ball went over Mr. Webbe's head, but his nerve and patience never deserted him.

When Mr. I. D. Walker gave up the captaincy of the Middlesex Eleven, Mr. Webbe took up the responsibility, and ever since he has worked with hands and head to speed its interests. That he has succeeded everyone will admit, just as freely as it will be admitted that he is still one of the most dangerous batsmen in England.

His style cannot be called graceful, for his position at the wicket is more crouching than upright, but that does not prevent him playing with a straight bat, or scoring at a great pace. No one watches the ball more carefully, and his quiet way of placing it without any show is a striking contrast to the vigour of his hitting. Rarely does he allow the ball to pass the bat. With a quick turn of the wrist he places it without seeming effort, and as he gets well over it, it travels low and safely. The quality of the wicket makes little difference to him, for he is nearly as safe and effective when it is wet and sticky as when it is dry and fast. He is an excellent field close in, but has done many brilliant things in the long-field also.

His best batting years so far have been:

	Completed Innings.	Runs.	Most in an Innings.	Average.
1875	26	696	120	26.20
1876	23	723	109	31.10
1877	25	651	100	26. 1
1878	24	588	118	24.12
1879	23	532	122	23. 3
1880	21	660	132	31. 9
1882	22	660	108*	30
1885	24	667	82	27.19
1887	26	1244	243	47.22
1890	35	995	134	28.15

Frederic Wild was born at Eastwood, Nottinghamshire, 28th August, 1847. His height is 5 ft. 9 in.; weight, 12 st. He was a good all-round player. When he made his first appearance at Lord's in 1869, for Nottinghamshire *v.* M.C.C., he clean-bowled me middle stump when I had made over 120 runs and was well set, and Alfred Shaw, J. C. Shaw, and Wootton had almost given up hope of getting my wicket; and he scored 13 and 54 in the same match. For Nottinghamshire he batted well for many seasons, particularly in 1875, when he was at the head of the averages. In 1872, against Gloucestershire, at Trent Bridge, he scored 104—an innings freely hit and correctly played. His hands could not stand very well the hard work of wicket-keeping, or he would have done better for his county in that position: at long-leg or cover-point he was very quick. He represented the Players on one or two occasions, played for the All-England Eleven, and was on the staff of the M.C.C. for many years.

EDGAR WILLSHER was, without doubt, one of the greatest bowlers we have had. He was born at Rolvenden, in Kent, 22nd November, 1828. His height was 5 ft. 10½ in.; weight, about 11 st. He learned to bowl at a very early age, played for his county in his 19th year, and appeared at Lord's in 1852. He batted and bowled left-hand, and helped considerably to spread the reputation of the All-England Eleven. His bowling was fast roundarm, twisting in from the leg, and he has been known to bowl as many as 20 maiden overs in succession. Like A. Mynn and one or two others he walked quietly up to the crease when delivering the ball, and yet was able to bowl fast.

Willsher was past his best when I began playing; but his results for some years afterwards, when he was over forty years of age, will show what a grand bowler he must have been some years previous:

	Overs.	Maidens.	Runs.	Wickets.	Average.
1866	551	263	653	50	13. 3
1868	1003	529	1123	114	9.97
1869	811	409	920	68	13.40
1870	941	495	1083	84	12.75
1871	752	420	938	73	12.62

JOHN WISDEN was born at Brighton, Sept. 5th, 1826. His height was 5 ft. 4½ in., and his weight for some time after he commenced to play did not exceed 7 st. However, like the majority of first-class cricketers I have known, or read of, improvement in play is invariably accompanied by increase of weight and strength, and he was at his best in 1850, in his twenty-fifth year, when he weighed about 11 st. He bowled very fast when he began, but was slower in 1850, and more successful. The 15th and 16th of July of that year were memorable days for him. Playing for the North *v.* South, he *clean-bowled* all ten wickets in the second innings. It was a first-class match, which made the feat all the more remarkable. A very good authority who witnessed the performance told me that he kept up his break from the off from one to two feet right through the innings. He was infected with the success of Clarke's slows, and not unfrequently took to that kind of bowling when his round-arm failed. As a batsman he played very straight and was most patient.

WI LIAM ALFRED WOOF was born at Gloucester, July 9th, 1859. He was tried for the Gloucestershire Colts in 1878, and bowled so well that he was chosen to play for his county in one or two of the matches the same season. The year after he was engaged on the Old Trafford Ground at Manchester; but securing an engagement at Cheltenham College in 1880, he again played for Gloucestershire, and has done so every year since. He showed great improvement the next year or two, and I obtained him a position on the staff of ground-bowlers at Lord's in 1882, where he continued for some years. He returned to Cheltenham College as their coach, and is there still.

Without doubt he is one of the best slow left-hand bowlers at the present time, and on a sticky wicket as good as anyone. He has great command of the ball, and has a good break from leg; and now and then, without a change of action, he can put in a puzzling one which comes with his arm and gets quickly off the pitch. For Gloucestershire he has been invaluable for years, and, with myself, has had to bear the brunt of the bowling. He has also played for the South *v.* North. He is a very good field close in, and makes runs occasionally.

Mr. William Yardley was born at Bombay, 10th June, 1849. His height was 5 ft. 11½ ins.; weight, 12½ st. He was, without doubt, one of the most brilliant amateurs of his or any time, batting in excellent style, and scoring freely and quickly against all kinds of bowling. For his University, Cambridge, he was very successful, scoring 100 in the second innings against Oxford, at Lord's, in 1870, and 130 in 1872. He was the first to score 100 runs in University contests, and he is the only player who has done it twice in these matches. Altogether, in the three years he played for Cambridge *v.* Oxford, he scored 259 runs for 5 innings, average 51.4; and for the Gentlemen *v.* Players, considering the quality of the bowling against him, he was quite as successful, scoring 435 runs for 12 innings, average 36. He played for Kent in 1868, and occasionally for some years afterwards. He was not a good bowler; but he could bowl fast round-arm with his right and lobs with his left; and fielded with great dash and certainty at cover-point. He won the Racquet Championship for Cambridge *v.* Oxford in 1871.

CHAPTER XII.

RECORDS AND CURIOSITIES.

COUNTY CRICKET FROM 1870 TO 1890.

1870.

	Yorks.		Glos.		Lanc.		Notts.		Sussex		Midd.		Kent		Surrey		*Won.*	*Lost.*	*Dwn.*
Yorkshire	...	...	...	...	...	...	W	D	...	...	...	...	W	W	W	W	5	–	1
Gloucestershire ..	...	...	...	...	...	...	...	...	...	...	...	...	...	...	W	W	2	–	–
Lancashire ...	...	...	...	...	...	...	...	...	...	...	...	...	...	...	W	L	1	1	–
Nottinghamshire	L	D	...	...	...	...	...	...	...	...	...	...	W	W	W	L	3	2	1
Sussex	...	...	...	...	...	...	...	...	...	...	...	...	W	L	W	L	2	2	–
Middlesex	...	...	...	...	...	...	...	...	...	...	...	...	...	...	W	L	1	1	–
Kent	L	L	...	...	...	...	L	L	L	W	...	...	...	...	W	L	2	6	–
Surrey	L	L	L	L	L	W	L	W	L	W	L	W	L	W	...	...	5	9	–

1871.

	Sussex		Notts.		Midd.		Glos.		Yorks.		Lanc.		Kent		Surrey		*Won.*	*Lost.*	*Dwn.*
Sussex	...	...	...	...	...	...	...	...	...	...	...	...	W	W	W	W	4	–	–
Nottinghamshire	...	...	...	...	...	...	D	W	W	L	...	...	...	...	W	W	4	1	1
Middlesex	...	...	...	...	...	...	...	...	...	...	...	...	...	...	D	W	1	–	1
Gloucestershire ..	...	...	D	L	...	...	...	...	...	...	...	...	...	...	W	W	2	1	1
Yorkshire	...	...	L	W	...	...	...	...	...	...	W	L	...	...	D	W	3	2	1
Lancashire ...	...	...	...	...	...	...	...	...	L	W	...	...	L	W	...	...	2	2	–
Kent	L	L	...	...	...	...	...	...	...	...	W	L	...	...	W	D	2	3	1
Surrey	L	L	L	L	D	L	L	L	D	L	...	...	L	D	...	...	–	9	3

1872.

	Surrey		Notts		Glos.		Lanc.		Sussex		Yorks.		Midd.		Kent		*Won.*	*Lost.*	*Dwn.*
Surrey	...	...	D	D	W	L	...	...	L	W	W	L	W	W	W	W	7	3	2
Nottinghamshire	D	D	...	...	D	D	...	...	...	...	W	WD	...	...	...	...	2	–	5
Gloucestershire ..	L	W	D	D	...	...	...	...	D	W	W	...	...	...	...	...	3	1	3
Lancashire ...	...	...	...	...	...	...	...	...	...	...	W	W	...	...	...	...	2	–	–
Sussex	W	L	...	...	D	L	...	...	...	...	...	...	...	...	W	W	3	2	1
Yorkshire	L	W	L	LD	L	...	L	L	...	...	...	...	W	...	...	...	2	6	1
Middlesex	L	L	...	...	...	...	...	...	...	...	L	...	...	...	..	..	–	3	–
Kent	L	L	...	...	...	...	...	..	L	L	...	...	...	...	...	...	–	4	–

1873.

	Notts.		Glos.		Yorks.		Kent		Midd.		Lanc.		Sussex		Surrey		Won.	Lost.	Dwn.
Nottinghamshire	...	...	...	...	W	D	...	...	...	...	...	...	W	W	W	W	5	–	1
Gloucestershire ..	...	...	...	...	W	W	...	...	...	...	...	...	W	D	W	D	4	–	2
Yorkshire	L	D	L	L	...	...	...	...	L	...	W	W	W	W	W	W	6	4	1
Kent	...	...	...	...	...	...	...	...	...	...	W	...	W	L	W	L	3	2	–
Middlesex	...	...	...	...	W	...	...	...	...	...	...	...	...	...	L	W	2	1	–
Lancashire ...	...	...	...	...	L	L	L	...	...	...	...	...	...	...	W	W	2	3	–
Sussex	L	L	L	D	L	L	L	W	...	...	...	...	...	...	W	D	2	6	2
Surrey	L	L	L	D	L	L	L	W	W	L	L	L	L	D	...	...	2	10	2

1874.

	Yorks.		Glos.		Notts.		Kent		Lanc.		Midd.		Surrey		Sussex		Won.	Lost.	Dwn.
Yorkshire	...	...	L	L	W	W	...	...	W	L	W	D	W	W	W	W	8	3	1
Gloucestershire ..	W	W	...	...	...	...	...	...	...	...	...	...	L	W	W	D	4	1	1
Nottinghamshire	L	L	...	...	...	...	...	...	...	...	W	W	W	W	W	L	5	3	–
Kent	...	...	...	...	...	...	...	...	D	W	...	...	...	...	...	...	1	–	1
Lancashire ...	L	W	...	...	...	...	D	L	...	...	...	...	...	...	...	...	1	2	1
Middlesex	L	D	...	...	L	L	...	...	...	...	...	...	L	W	...	...	1	4	1
Surrey	L	L	W	L	L	L	...	...	...	...	W	L	...	...	D	W	3	6	1
Sussex	L	L	L	D	L	W	...	...	...	...	...	...	D	L	...	...	1	8	2

1875.

	Notts.		Sussex		Yorks		Lanc.		Glos.		Surrey		Kent		Midd.		Won.	Lost.	Dwn.
Nottinghamshire	...	...	...	...	W	L	...	...	W	D	D	W	...	...	D	W	4	1	3
Sussex	...	...	...	...	...	...	...	...	W	L	D	W	W	W	...	...	4	1	1
Yorkshire	L	W	...	...	...	...	L	W	W	L	W	W	...	...	D	W	6	3	1
Lancashire ...	...	...	...	...	W	L	...	...	...	...	...	...	W	W	...	...	3	1	–
Gloucestershire ..	L	D	L	W	L	W	...	...	...	...	L	W	...	...	...	...	3	4	1
Surrey	D	L	D	L	L	L	...	...	W	L	...	...	...	...	W	W	3	5	2
Kent	...	...	L	L	...	...	L	L	...	...	...	...	...	...	...	...	–	4	–
Middlesex	D	L	...	...	D	L	...	...	...	...	L	L	...	...	...	...	–	4	2

1876.

	Glos.		Yorks.		Notts.		Kent		Midd.		Sussex		Lanc.		Surrey		Won.	Lost.	Dwn.
Gloucestershire ..	...	...	W	D	W	W	...	...	...	...	W	D	...	...	W	D	5	–	3
Yorkshire	L	D	...	...	D	L	...	...	W	D	...	...	W	W	W	W	5	2	3
Nottinghamshire	L	L	D	W	...	...	...	...	D	D	...	...	L	W	W	W	4	3	3
Kent	...	...	...	...	...	...	...	...	...	...	L	W	L	W	W	L	3	3	–
Middlesex	...	...	L	D	D	D	...	...	...	...	...	...	...	...	W	Tie	1	1	4
Sussex	L	D	...	...	...	...	W	L	...	...	...	...	W	L	L	W	3	4	1
Lancashire ...	...	...	L	L	W	L	W	L	...	...	L	W	...	...	...	...	3	5	–
Surrey	L	D	L	L	L	L	L	W	L	Tie	W	L	...	...	...	...	2	8	2

1877.

	Glos.		Surrey		Kent		Lanc.		Notts.		Yorks.		Midd.		Sussex		Won.	Lost.	Dwn.
Gloucestershire ..	...	...	W	W	...	...	...	...	W	W	D	W	...	...	W	W	7	–	1
Surrey	L	L	...	...	W	D	...	...	L	W	W	D	W	W	D	W	6	3	3
Kent	...	...	L	D	...	...	W	W	L	W	...	...	...	...	W	W	5	2	1
Lancashire ...	...	...	...	...	L	L	...	...	L	W	W	W	...	...	W	W	5	3	–
Nottinghamshire	L	L	W	L	W	L	W	L	...	...	W	D	W	D	...	...	5	5	2
Yorkshire	D	L	L	D	...	...	L	L	L	D	...	...	W	D	...	...	1	5	4
Middlesex	...	...	L	L	...	...	...	...	L	D	L	D	...	...	...	...	–	4	2
Sussex	L	L	D	L	L	L	L	L	...	...	...	...	...	...	...	...	–	7	1

1878.

	Midd.		Glos.		Lanc.		Notts.		Yorks.		Kent		Surrey		Sussex		Won.	Lost.	Dwn.
Middlesex	...	...	...	...	...	...	D	D	W	W	...	...	W	D	...	...	3	–	3
Gloucestershire .	...	...	...	...	D	W	D	W	L	D	...	...	L	D	W	W	4	2	4
Lancashire ...	...	...	D	L	...	...	L	W	W	D	W	W	...	...	...	...	4	2	2
Nottinghamshire	D	D	D	L	W	L	...	...	L	W	W	D	W	W	...	...	5	3	4
Yorkshire	L	L	W	D	L	D	W	L	...	...	...	...	W	W	W	W	6	4	2
Kent	...	...	...	...	L	L	L	D	...	...	...	...	W	D	L	W	2	4	2
Surrey	L	D	W	D	...	...	L	L	L	L	L	D	...	...	W	W	3	6	3
Sussex	...	...	L	L	...	...	...	...	L	L	W	L	L	L	...	...	1	7	–

1879.

	Yorks.		Notts.		Lanc.		Midd.		Surrey		Sussex		Glos.		Kent		Won.	Lost.	Dwn.
Yorkshire	...	...	D	W	L	W	W	W	W	D	...	...	W	D	W	L	7	2	3
Nottinghamshire	D	L	...	...	D	D	D	D	...	...	...	...	D	W	W	W	3	1	6
Lancashire ..	W	L	D	D	...	...	...	...	...	...	...	...	W	D	W	D	3	1	4
Middlesex	L	L	D	D	...	...	...	...	W	W	...	...	D	D	...	...	2	2	4
Surrey	L	D	...	...	...	...	L	L	...	...	W	D	L	D	W	W	3	4	3
Sussex	...	...	...	...	...	...	...	...	L	D	...	...	...	...	L	W	1	2	1
Gloucestershire ..	L	D	D	L	L	D	D	D	W	D	...	...	...	...	...	...	1	3	6
Kent	L	W	L	L	L	D	...	...	L	L	W	L	...	...	...	...	2	7	1

1880.

	Notts		Glos.		Kent		Lanc.		Yorks.		Midd.		Surrey		Sussex		Won.	Lost.	Dwn.
Nottinghamshire	...	...	D	D	...	...	W	W	W	L	W	W	D	W	...	...	6	1	3
Gloucestershire ..	D	D	...	...	...	...	D	W	D	W	D	W	L	W	...	...	4	1	5
Kent	...	...	...	...	...	...	L	L	D	W	...	...	W	D	W	W	4	2	2
Lancashire ...	L	L	D	L	W	W	...	...	D	D	...	...	W	W	...	...	4	3	3
Yorkshire	L	W	D	L	D	L	D	D	...	...	W	L	D	W	...	...	3	4	5
Middlesex	L	L	D	L	...	...	...	...	L	W	...	...	D	W	...	...	2	4	2
Surrey	D	L	W	L	L	D	L	L	D	L	D	L	...	...	W	D	2	7	5
Sussex	...	...	...	...	L	L	...	...	...	...	...	...	L	D	...	...	–	3	1

1881.

	Lanc.		Yorks.		Glos.		Notts.		Midd.		Kent		Surrey		Sussex		Won.	Lost	Dwn.
Lancashire ...	...	...	W	W	W	D	W	D	...	D	W	W	W	W	...	...	8	–	3
Yorkshire	L	L	...	...	L	D	W	D	W	W	W	W	W	W	W	W	9	3	2
Gloucestershire ..	L	D	W	D	...	...	D	L	W	D	...	...	W	W	...	...	4	2	4
Nottinghamshire	L	D	L	D	D	W	...	...	L	D	...	...	W	L	W	W	4	4	4
Middlesex	...	D	L	L	L	D	W	D	...	...	...	...	W	W	...	...	3	3	3
Kent	L	L	L	L	...	...	...	...	...	...	...	...	L	L	W	W	2	6	–
Surrey	L	L	L	L	L	L	L	W	L	L	W	W	...	...	W	D	4	9	1
Sussex	...	...	L	L	...	...	L	L	...	...	L	L	L	D	...	...	–	7	1

1882.

	Lanc.		Notts.		Yorks.		Midd.		Surrey		Glos.		Kent		Sussex		Won.	Lost.	Dwn.
Lancashire ...	...	...	L	D	D	W	W	W	D	W	W	W	W	W	...	...	8	1	3
Nottinghamshire	W	D	...	...	W	L	W	D	W	W	W	D	...	...	W	W	8	1	3
Yorkshire	D	L	L	W	...	...	L	W	D	W	W	L	W	L	W	W	7	5	2
Middlesex	L	L	L	D	W	L	...	...	L	W	W	W	W	...	...	...	5	5	1
Surrey	D	L	L	L	D	L	W	L	...	...	D	L	W	W	W	L	4	7	3
Gloucestershire ..	L	L	L	D	L	W	L	L	D	W	...	...	...	...	...	...	2	6	2
Kent	L	L	...	...	L	W	L	...	L	L	...	...	...	...	W	D	2	6	1
Sussex	...	...	L	L	L	L	...	...	L	W	...	...	L	D	...	...	1	6	1

1883.

	Yorks.		Notts.		Surrey		Midd.		Lanc.		Sussex		Kent		Glos.		Won.	Lost.	Dwn.
Yorkshire	...	...	D	L	W	D	W	D	W	W	L	W	W	W	D	W	8	2	4
Nottinghamshire	D	W	...	...	W	D	D	D	L	D	W	D	...	...	W	D	4	1	7
Surrey	L	D	L	D	...	...	W	L	L	W	W	W	D	D	W	W	6	4	4
Middlesex	L	D	D	D	L	W	...	...	...	...	...	...	W	W	W	D	4	2	4
Lancashire ...	L	L	W	D	W	L	...	...	...	...	...	...	W	L	W	L	4	5	1
Sussex	W	L	L	D	L	L	...	...	...	...	...	...	W	L	...	...	2	5	1
Kent	L	L	...	...	D	D	L	L	L	W	L	W	...	...	...	...	2	6	2
Gloucestershire ..	D	L	L	D	L	L	L	D	L	W	...	...	...	...	...	...	1	6	3

1884.

	Notts.		Yorks.		Surrey		Midd.		Lanc.		Sussex		Kent		Glos.		Won.	Lost.	Dwn.
Nottinghamshire	...	...	W	W	W	D	W	W	...	...	W	W	...	...	W	W	9	–	1
Yorkshire	L	L	...	...	D	D	D	D	W	L	W	L	W	W	W	W	6	4	4
Surrey	L	D	D	D	...	...	L	W	W	L	W	W	L	D	W	D	5	4	5
Middlesex	L	L	D	D	W	L	...	...	...	...	...	...	W	W	W	D	4	3	3
Lancashire ...	...	...	L	W	L	W	...	...	...	...	...	...	L	W	D	L	3	4	1
Sussex	L	L	L	W	L	L	...	...	...	...	...	...	D	W	W	W	4	5	1
Kent	...	...	L	L	W	D	L	L	W	L	D	L	...	...	...	...	2	6	2
Gloucestershire ..	L	L	L	L	L	D	L	D	D	W	L	L	...	...	...	...	1	8	3

1885.

	Notts.		Yorks.		Lanc.		Surrey		Kent		Glos.		Midd.		Sussex		*Won.*	*Lost.*	*Dwn.*
Nottinghamshire	...	...	D	L	...	...	D	D	...	...	W	W	W	D	W	W	5	1	4
Yorkshire	D	W	...	...	D	W	W	W	L	D	W	D	W	L	D	D	6	2	6
Lancashire	...	...	D	L	...	...	D	L	W	...	W	W	...	...	W	W	5	2	2
Surrey	D	D	L	L	D	W	...	...	W	D	L	L	W	W	W	W	6	4	4
Kent	...	...	W	D	L	...	L	D	...	...	...	...	L	W	W	W	4	3	2
Gloucestershire ..	L	L	L	D	L	L	W	W	...	...	...	...	W	W	L	L	4	7	1
Middlesex	L	D	L	W	...	...	L	L	W	L	L	L	...	...	...	...	2	7	1
Sussex	L	L	D	D	L	L	L	L	L	L	W	W	...	...	...	...	2	8	2

1886.

	Notts.		Surrey		Lanc.		Midd.		Sussex		Yorks.		Kent		Glos.		*Won.*	*Lost.*	*Dwn.*
Nottinghamshire	...	...	D	W	W	D	W	D	W	W	W	D	W	D	D	D	7	–	7
Surrey	D	L	...	...	W	L	W	W	W	L	W	W	W	W	W	W	10	3	1
Lancashire ...	L	D	L	W	...	...	...	...	W	L	W	D	W	L	D	L	4	5	3
Middlesex	L	D	L	L	...	...	...	...	...	...	D	L	W	D	W	W	3	4	3
Sussex	L	L	L	W	L	W	...	...	...	...	D	D	L	W	W	L	4	6	2
Yorkshire	L	D	L	L	L	D	D	W	D	D	...	...	D	L	D	W	2	5	7
Kent	L	D	L	L	L	W	L	D	W	L	D	W	...	...	...	...	3	6	3
Gloucestershire ..	D	D	L	L	D	W	L	L	L	W	D	L	...	...	...	...	2	6	4

1887.

	Surrey		Lanc.		Notts.		Midd.		Yorks.		Sussex		Kent		Glos.		*Won.*	*Lost.*	*Dwn.*
Surrey	...	...	W	L	W	W	W	L	W	W	W	D	W	D	W	W	10	2	2
Lancashire	L	W	...	...	L	W	...	...	D	L	W	W	W	W	W	W	8	3	1
Nottinghamshire	L	L	W	L	...	...	W	D	D	D	W	W	W	W	W	W	8	3	3
Middlesex	L	W	...	...	L	D	...	...	W	D	...	...	W	D	D	W	4	2	4
Yorkshire	L	L	D	W	D	D	L	D	...	...	W	D	W	D	D	W	4	3	7
Sussex	L	D	L	L	L	L	...	...	L	D	...	...	W	L	W	L	2	6	2
Kent	L	D	L	L	L	L	L	D	L	D	L	W	...	...	D	D	1	8	5
Gloncestershire ..	L	L	L	L	L	L	D	L	D	L	L	W	D	D	...	...	1	9	4

1888.

	Surrey		Kent		Yorks.		Glos.		Lanc.		Notts.		Midd.		Sussex		*Won.*	*Lost.*	*Dwn.*
Surrey	...	...	W	W	W	W	W	D	W	L	W	W	W	W	W	W	12	1	1
Kent	L	L	...	...	D	L	L	L	W	W	W	D	W	W	W	W	7	5	2
Yorkshire	L	L	D	W	...	...	W	D	D	W	D	W	L	L	W	W	6	4	4
Gloucestershire ..	L	D	W	W	L	D	...	...	D	L	L	W	W	L	D	W	5	5	4
Lancashire ...	L	W	L	L	D	L	D	W	...	...	D	D	W	W	D	L	4	5	5
Nottinghamshire	L	L	L	D	D	L	W	L	D	D	...	...	L	D	W	W	3	6	5
Middlesex	L	L	L	L	W	W	L	W	L	L	W	D	...	...	...	...	4	7	1
Sussex	L	L	L	L	L	L	D	L	D	W	L	L	...	...	...	...	1	9	2

1889.

	Notts		Lanc.		Surrey		Kent		Midd.		Glos.		Yorks.		Sussex		*Won.*	*Lost.*	*Dwn.*
Nottinghamshire	...	...	W	D	W	L	W	L	W	D	W	W	W	D	W	W	9	2	3
Lancashire ...	L	D	...	...	W	W	W	W	L	W	W	L	W	W	W	W	10	3	1
Surrey	L	W	L	L	...	...	W	W	W	W	W	D	W	W	W	W	10	3	1
Kent	L	W	L	L	L	L	...	...	W	...	D	W	W	W	W	W	7	5	1
Middlesex	L	D	W	L	L	L	L	...	...	...	W	D	W	D	...	...	3	5	3
Gloucestershire ..	L	L	L	W	L	D	D	L	L	D	...	...	W	L	D	W	3	7	4
Yorkshire	L	D	L	L	L	L	L	L	L	D	L	W	...	...	L	W	2	10	2
Sussex	L	L	L	L	L	L	L	L	...	...	D	L	W	L	...	...	1	10	1

1890.

	Surrey		Lanc.		Kent.		Yorks.		Notts.		Glos.		Midd.		Sussex		*Won.*	*Lost.*	*Dwn.*
Surrey	...	...	W	W	D	L	D	L	L	W	W	W	W	W	W	W	9	3	2
Lancashire ..	L	L	...	...	W	W	D	W	D	W	D	D	L	W	W	W	7	3	4
Kent	D	W	L	L	...	...	L	D	D	D	W	D	W	W	W	W	6	3	5
Yorkshire	D	W	D	L	W	D	...	...	L	D	W	L	W	D	W	W	6	3	5
Nottinghamshire	W	L	D	L	D	D	W	D	...	...	L	L	L	W	W	W	5	5	4
Gloucestershire ..	L	L	D	D	L	D	L	W	W	W	...	...	L	W	L	W	5	6	3
Middlesex	L	L	W	L	L	L	L	D	W	L	W	L	...	...	...	...	3	8	1
Sussex	L	L	L	L	L	L	L	L	L	L	W	L	...	...	...	...	1	11	-

Nottinghamshire has been top county 7 times
Surrey " " " 4 "
Yorkshire " " " 4 "
Gloucestershire " " " 2 "
Lancashire " " " 2 "
Middlesex " " " 1 "
Sussex " " " 1 "

Sussex has been at the bottom 10 times
Surrey " " " 4 "
Gloucestershire " " 4 "
Kent " " " 2 "
Middlesex " " " 1 "

TOTAL NUMBER OF MATCHES PLAYED.

	Won.	*Lost.*	*Drawn.*		*Total.*	
Nottinghamshire	108	43	70	=	221	+65
Lancashire	91	54	34	=	179	+37
Yorkshire	108	76	66	=	250	+32
Surrey	112	110	50	=	272	+ 2
Gloucestershire	67	75	59	=	201	- 8
Middlesex	48	70	43	=	161	-22
Kent	60	91	31	=	182	-31
Sussex	39	114	23	=	176	-75
	633	633	376		1642	

GENTLEMEN AND PLAYERS' MATCHES.

AT LORD'S AND THE OVAL.

1806 Lord's... Gentlemen won by an innings and 14 runs. Beldham and Lambert played for the Gentlemen.

1806 Lord's... Gentlemen won by 82 runs. Lambert played for the Gentlemen.

1819 Lord's... Players won by 6 wickets.

1820 Lord's... Gentlemen won by 70 runs. Howard played for the Gentlemen.

1821 Lord's... Players, 278 runs for 6 wickets: Gentlemen, 60 runs for one innings. Gentlemen gave up the match.

1822 Lord's... Gentlemen won by 6 wickets.

1823 Lord's... Players won by 345 runs.

1824 Lord's... Players won by 101 runs.

1825 Lord's... Gentlemen won by 72 runs. The Gentlemen played 16 men.

1827 Lord's... Gentlemen won by 29 runs. The Gentlemen played 17 men.

1827 Lord's... Players won by an innings and 42 runs. The Gentlemen played 17 men.

1829 Lord's... Gentlemen won by 193 runs. Lillywhite and Broadbridge played for the Gentlemen.

1830 Lord's... Drawn. Pilch and Lillywhite played for the Gentlemen.

1831 Lord's... Players won by 5 wickets. The Players played 9 men; the Gentlemen, 11.

1832 Lord's... Players won by an innings and 34 runs. The size of the Players' wickets was 27 in. by 8 in.; the Gentlemen's, 22 in. by 6 in.

1833 Lord's... Players won by 9 wickets. The Gentlemen played 16 men.

1834 Lord's... Players won by an innings and 21 runs.

1835 Lord's... Players won by 6 wickets. Cobbett and Redgate played for the Gentlemen.

1836 Lord's... Gentlemen won by 35 runs. The Gentlemen played 18 men.

1837 Lord's ... Players won by an innings and 10 runs. Size of Players' wickets, 36 ins. by 12 ins.; Gentlemen's, 27 ins. by 8 ins. The Barn Door Match.
1837 Lord's ... Players won by an innings and 38 runs. Gentlemen played 16 men.
1838 Lord's ... Players won by 40 runs. Pilch, Cobbett, and Wenman played for the Gentlemen.
1839 Lord's ... Drawn.
1840 Lord's ... Players won by 9 wickets.
1841 Lord's ... Players won by 3 wickets.
1842 Lord's ... Gentlemen won by 95 runs.
1843 Lord's ... Gentlemen won by an innings and 20 runs.
1844 Lord's .. Players won by 38 runs.
1845 Lord's ... Players won by 67 runs.
1846 Lord's ... Gentlemen won by 1 wicket.
1847 Lord's ... Players won by 147 runs.
1848 Lord's ... Gentlemen won by 27 runs.
1849 Lord's ... Gentlemen won by an innings and 40 runs.
1850 Lord's ... Players won by an innings and 48 runs.
1851 Lord's ... Players won by an innings and 14 runs.
1852 Lord's ... Players won by 5 wickets.
1853 Lord's ... Gentlemen won by 60 runs.
1854 Lord's ... Players won by 9 wickets.
1855 Lord's ... Players won by 7 wickets.
1856 Lord's ... Players won by 2 wickets.
1857 Oval ... Players won by 10 wickets. First match at the Oval.
1857 Lord's ... Players won by 13 runs.
1858 Oval ... Players won by 3 wickets.
1858 Lord's ... Players won by 285 runs.
1859 Oval ... Players won by an innings and 25 runs.
1859 Lord's .. Players won by 169 runs.
1860 Oval ... Players won by 8 wickets.
1860 Lord's ... Players won by an innings and 181 runs.
1861 Lord's ... Players won by an innings and 60 runs.
1861 Oval ... Players won by an innings and 68 runs.
1862 Oval ... Drawn.
1862 Lord's ... Players won by an innings and 157 runs. This match was Gentlemen under thirty years of age *v.* Players under thirty.
1863 Lord's ... Players won by 8 wickets.
1863 Oval ... Players won by 9 wickets.
1864 Oval ... Players won by 205 runs.
1864 Lord's ... Players won by an innings and 68 runs.

1865 Oval ... Players won by 118 runs. W. G. Grace's first match for the Gentlemen.
1865 Lord's ... Gentlemen won by 8 wickets. The Gentlemen had not won a match since 1853.
1866 Lord's ... Players won by 38 runs.
1866 Oval ... Gentlemen won by 98 runs. First win for the Gentlemen at the Oval.
1867 Lord's ... Gentlemen won by 8 wickets.
1867 Oval ... Drawn.
1868 Lord's .. Gentlemen won by 8 wickets.
1868 Oval ... Gentlemen won by an innings and 87 runs.
1869 Oval ... Gentlemen won by 17 runs.
1869 Lord's ... Gentlemen won by 3 wickets.
1870 Oval ... Drawn.
1870 Lord's ... Gentlemen won by 4 runs.
1871 Lord's ... Drawn.
1871 Oval ... Gentlemen won by 5 wickets.
1872 Lord's ... Gentlemen won by 7 wickets.
1872 Oval ... Gentlemen won by 9 wickets.
1873 Oval ... Gentlemen won by an innings and 19 runs.
1873 Lord's ... Gentlemen won by an innings and 55 runs.
1874 Oval ... Gentlemen won by 48 runs.
1874 Lord's ... Players won by 2 wickets. The Players had not won a match since 1866.
1875 Oval ... Drawn.
1875 Lord's ... Gentlemen won by 262 runs.
1876 Oval ... Drawn.
1876 Lord's ... Gentlemen won by an innings and 93 runs. Shrewsbury's first match for the Players.
1877 Oval ... Drawn.
1877 Lord's ... Gentlemen won by 1 wicket.
1878 Oval ... Gentlemen won by 55 runs.
1878 Lord's ... Gentlemen won by 206 runs.
1879 Oval ... Gentlemen won by an innings and 126 runs.
1879 Lord's ... Drawn.
1880 Oval ... Players won by 37 runs.
1880 Lord's .. Gentlemen won by 5 wickets.
1881 Oval ... Gentlemen won by 2 wickets.
1881 Lord's ... Gentlemen won by 4 wickets.
1882 Lord's ... Gentlemen won by 8 wickets.
1882 Oval ... Players won by 87 runs.
1883 Lord's ... Gentlemen won by 7 wickets.
1883 Oval ... A tie match. Players—1st innings, 203; 2nd, 131. Gentlemen—1st innings, 235; 2nd, 149.

1884 Oval ... Players won by 9 wickets.
1884 Lord's... Gentlemen won by 6 wickets.
1885 Oval ... Drawn.
1885 Lord's... Players won by 4 wickets.
1886 Lord's... Players won by 5 wickets.
1886 Oval ... Drawn.
1887 Lord's ... Players won by an innings and 123 runs.
1887 Oval ... Players won by an innings and 16 runs.
1888 Lord's... Gentlemen won by 5 runs.
1888 Oval ... Players won by an innings and 139 runs.
1889 Oval ... Players won by 8 wickets.
1889 Lord's... Players won by 10 wickets.
1890 Oval ... Players won by 9 wickets.
1890 Lord's... Drawn.

AT PRINCE'S.

1873 Gentlemen won by an innings and 54 runs.
1874 Gentlemen won by 61 runs.
1875 Players won by 43 runs.
1876 Gentlemen won by 5 wickets.
1877 Gentlemen won by 9 wickets.

Matches played, 113: Players won 54; Gentlemen won 45; drawn, 13; tied, 1.

Other matches have been played at Brighton, Scarborough, Hastings, and elsewhere.

BATTING AVERAGES OF SOME OF THE LEADING BATSMEN IN THE GENTLEMEN *v.* PLAYERS' MATCHES.

GENTLEMEN.

	Completed Innings.	Runs.	Average.
Mr. W. G. Grace	96	4243	44 19
Mr. W. Yardley	12	435	36. 3
Mr. C. T. Studd	9	313	34. 7
Mr. A. Lubbock	11	355	32. 3
Mr. G. F. Grace	33	927	28. 3
Mr. W. W. Read	23	601	26. 3
Mr. T. C. O'Brien	9	236	26. 2
Mr. A. G. Steel	22	572	26
Mr. G. H. Longman	12	293	24. 5
Mr. A. E. Stoddart	11	265	24. 1
Mr. A. N. Hornby	47	1101	23.20
Mr. A. W. Ridley	21	491	23. 8
Mr. R. A. H. Mitchell	10	235	23. 5
Mr. I. D. Walker	29	639	22. 1
Mr. A. P. Lucas	32	704	22
Mr. R. D. Walker	17	362	21. 5
Mr. F. Penn	12	253	21. 1

PLAYERS.

	Completed Innings.	Runs.	Average.
T. Hayward	15	552	36.12
T. Hearne	14	474	33.12
W. Barnes	33	1055	32. 1
A. Shrewsbury	31	972	31.11
G. Ulyett	53	1637	30.47
W. Bates	22	632	28.16
W. Gunn	20	573	28.13
G. Parr	22	618	28. 2
R. Daft	35	925	26.15
W. Mortlock	15	398	26. 8
R. Carpenter	25	599	24. 9
J. Wisden	17	390	22.16
Jno. Lillywhite	15	338	22. 8
J. M. Read	12	265	22. 1
E. Lockwood	54	1179	21.45
H. Jupp	62	1321	21.19

THREE-FIGURE INNINGS SCORED IN THE GENTLEMEN *v.* PLAYERS' MATCHES.

1821 Beagley, 113*
1825 Mr. W. Ward, 102
1827 Saunders, 100
1860 T. Hayward, 132
1860 R. Carpenter, 119
1861 R. Carpenter, 106
1863 T. Hayward, 112*
1864 H. H. Stephenson, 117
1866 T. Hearne, 122*
1867 Mr. A. Lubbock, 107*
1868 Mr. W. G. Grace, 134*
1868 Mr. I. D. Walker, 165
1870 Mr. W. G. Grace, 109
1870 Mr. W. G. Grace, 215
1870 Mr. W. B. Money, 109*
1871 Mr. W. G. Grace, 217
1872 Mr. W. G. Grace, 112
1872 Mr. W. G. Grace, 117
1872 R. Daft, 102
1873 Mr. W. G. Grace, 163
1873 Mr. W. G. Grace, 158
1873 Mr. A. N. Hornby, 104
1874 Mr. W. G. Grace, 110
1875 Mr. W. G. Grace, 152
1876 Mr. W. G. Grace, 169
1876 Mr. A. W. Ridley, 103
1877 Mr. A. N. Hornby, 144
1877 Mr. G. F. Grace, 134
1877 G. Ulyett, 118
1881 Mr. W. G. Grace, 100
1882 Mr. A. P. Lucas, 107
1882 Mr. C. T. Studd, 100
1883 Mr. E. F. S. Tylecote, 107
1884 G. Ulyett, 134
1885 Mr. W. W. Read, 159
1886 A. Shrewsbury, 127
1887 A. Shrewsbury, 111
1889 W. Barnes, 130*

* Not out.

Mr. W. G. Grace	has	scored it	12	times.
Mr. A. N. Hornby	,,	,,	2	,,
R. Carpenter	,,	,,	2	,,
T. Hayward	,,	,,	2	,,
G. Ulyett	,,	,,	2	,,
A. Shrewsbury	,,	,,	2	,,

PUBLIC SCHOOL MATCHES.

ETON *v.* HARROW — AT LORD'S.

Year	*Winner.*	*Won by*
1805	Eton	Ins. and 2 runs
1818	Harrow	13 runs
1822	„	87 runs
1823	Eton	Ins. and 33 runs
1824	„	9 wickets
1825	„	7 wickets
1827	„	6 wickets
1828	„	6 wickets
1832	„	Ins. and 156 runs
1833	Harrow	8 wickets
1834	„	13 runs
1835	Eton	165 runs
1836	Harrow	9 wickets
1837	Eton	8 wickets
1838	„	Ins. and 30 runs
1839	„	8 wickets
1840	„	31 runs
1841	„	Ins. and 175 runs
1842	Harrow	65 runs
1843	„	20 runs
1844	Eton	Ins. and 69 runs
1845	„	Ins. and 174 runs
1846	„	Ins. and 135 runs
1847	„	9 wickets
1848	Harrow	41 runs
1849	„	77 runs
1850	Eton	7 wickets
1851	Harrow	8 wickets
1852	„	71 runs
1853	„	3 wickets
1854	„	98 runs
1855	„	Ins. and 66 runs
1857	„	10 wickets*
1858	Harrow	Ins. and 7 runs
1859	„	Ins. and 48 runs
1860		Drawn
1861		Drawn
1862	Eton	54 runs
1863		Drawn
1864	Harrow	Ins. and 67 runs
1865	„	Ins. and 51 runs
1866	„	Ins. and 136 runs
1867		Drawn
1868	Harrow	7 wickets
1869	Eton	Ins. and 19 runs
1870	„	20 runs
1871	„	Ins. and 77 runs
1872	„	6 wickets
1873	Harrow	5 wickets
1874	Eton	5 wickets
1875		Drawn
1876	Eton	Ins. and 24 runs
1877		Drawn
1878	Harrow	20 runs
1879		Drawn
1880	Harrow	95 runs
1881	„	112 runs
1882		Drawn
1883		Drawn
1884		Drawn
1885	Harrow	3 wickets
1886	Eton	6 wickets
1887	„	5 wickets
1888	Harrow	150 runs
1889	„	9 wickets
1890		Drawn

* *This match was Etonians v. Harrovians under 20.*

Matches played, 66: Harrow won 28; Eton won 27; drawn, 11.

ETON *v.* WINCHESTER.

	Winner.	*Won by*	*Where*
1826	Winchester	53 runs	Lord's
1829	Eton	4 wickets	"
1830	Winchester	8 wickets	"
1832	Eton	Ins. and 10 runs	"
1833	"	14 runs	"
1834	"	13 runs	"
1835	"	5 wickets	"
1836	"	2 wickets	"
1838	Winchester	Ins. and 34 runs	"
1839	Eton	108 runs	"
1840	Winchester	43 runs	"
1841	"	109 runs	"
1842	Eton	7 wickets	"
1843	Winchester	8 wickets	"
1844	Eton	27 runs	"
1845	A tie match—		
	Winchester	111 and 52	"
	Eton	66 and 97	"
1846	Eton	Ins. and 55 runs	"
1847	"	Ins. and 78 runs	"
1848	"	65 runs	"
1849	"	Ins. and 27 runs	"
1850	"	5 wickets	"
1851	Winchester	26 runs	"
1852	"	30 runs	"
1853	"	35 runs	"
1854	"	3 wickets	"
1855	Eton	46 runs	Eton
1856	"	Ins. and 4 runs	Winc.
1857	"	Ins. and 31 runs	Eton
1858	Winchester	1 wicket	Winc.
1859	"	3 wickets	Eton
1860	Eton	10 runs	Winc.
1861	"	9 wickets	Eton
1862	"	1 wicket	Winc.
1863	"	Ins. and 194 runs	Eton
1864	"	9 wickets	Winc.
1865		Drawn	Eton
1866	Eton	10 wickets	Winc.
1867	"	Ins. and 10 runs	Eton
1868	"	8 wickets	Winc.
1869	"	Ins. and 36 runs	Eton
1870	Winchester	1 wicket	Winc.
1871	"	8 runs	Eton
1872	Eton	Ins. and 125 runs	Winc.
1873	"	5 wickets	Eton
1874	"	Ins. and 202 runs	Winc.
1875	"	5 wickets	Eton
1876	"	Ins. and 99 runs	Winc.
1877	"	Ins. and 121 runs	Eton
1878	Winchester	6 wickets	Winc.
1879	Eton	45 runs	Eton
1880	"	9 runs	Winc.
1881	"	6 wickets	Eton
1882	Winchester	Ins. and 20 runs	Winc.
1883	"	224 runs	Eton
1884	Eton	5 wickets	Winc.
1885		Drawn	Eton
1886	Eton	8 wickets	Winc.
1887	"	9 wickets	Eton
1888		Drawn	Winc.
1889	Winchester	114 runs	Eton
1890		Drawn	Winc.

Matches played, 61: Eton won 38; Winchester won 18; drawn, 4; tied, 1.

RUGBY *v.* MARLBOROUGH.

	Winner.	*Won by*	*Where*
1855	Rugby	10 wickets	Lord's
1856	"	5 wickets	"
1857	"	Ins. and 83 runs	Oval
1860	"	Ins. and 50 runs	Lord's
1862	Marlbro'	Ins. and 17 runs	"
1863	Rugby	83 runs	Oval
1864	"	Ins. and 33 runs	Islgtn.
1865	"	9 wickets	Lord's
1866		Drawn	"
1867	Rugby	6 wickets	Oval
1868	"	Ins. and 133 runs	Rugby
1869	"	179 runs	Lord's
1870	"	5 wickets	Marl.
1871	Marlbro'	68 runs	Lord's
1872	"	9 wickets	"
1873	Rugby	8 wickets	"
1874	"	5 wickets	"
1875	Rugby	Ins. and 35 runs	Lord's
1876	Marlbro'	5 wickets	"
1877	"	196 runs	"
1878	Rugby	Ins. and 24 runs	"
1879	"	97 runs	"
1880	"	Ins. and 120 runs	"
1881	"	2 wickets	"
1882	Marlbro'	5 wickets	"
1883		Drawn	"
1884	Marlbro'	8 wickets	"
1885		Drawn	"
1886	Rugby	37 runs	"
1887	Marlbro'	217 runs	"
1888	No play, owing to rain		
1889	Marlbro'	6 wickets	"
1890	"	145 runs	"

Matches played, 32: Rugby won 19; Marlborough won 10; drawn, 3.

CHELTENHAM *v.* MARLBOROUGH.

Date.		*Where Played.*		*Winner.*		*Won by*
1856	...	Cheltenham	...	Cheltenham	...	77 runs.
1857	...	Marlborough	...	Cheltenham	...	4 wickets.
1858	...	Cheltenham	...	Cheltenham	...	6 wickets.
1859	...	Marlborough	...	Marlborough	...	32 runs.
1860	...	Cheltenham	...		...	Drawn.
1861	...	Marlborough	...	Cheltenham	...	7 wickets.
1862	...	Cheltenham	...		...	Drawn.
1863	...	Marlborough	...	Cheltenham	...	36 runs.
1864	...	Cheltenham	...		...	Drawn.
1865	...	Marlborough	...	Marlborough	...	10 wickets.
1866	...	Cheltenham	...		...	Drawn.
1867	...	Marlborough	...		...	Drawn.
1868	...	Cheltenham	...	Cheltenham	...	10 wickets.
1869	...	Marlborough	...	Marlborough	...	Innings and 12 runs.
1870	...	Cheltenham	...	Cheltenham	...	6 wickets.
1871	...	Marlborough	...	Cheltenham	...	7 wickets.
1872	...	Cheltenham	...	Marlborough	...	7 wickets.
1873	...	Marlborough	...	Marlborough	...	84 runs.
1874	...	Cheltenham	...	Cheltenham	...	233 runs.
1875	...	Marlborough	...		...	Drawn.
1876	...	Cheltenham	...	Marlborough	...	6 wickets.
1877	...	Marlborough	...	Marlborough	...	Innings and 170 runs.
1878	...	Cheltenham	...	Marlborough	...	6 wickets.
1879	...	Marlborough	...	Marlborough	...	15 runs.
1880	...	Cheltenham	...		...	Drawn.
1881	...	Marlborough	...	Cheltenham	...	4 wickets.
1882	...	Cheltenham	...	Marlborough	...	70 runs.
1883	...	Marlborough	...	Marlborough	...	Innings and 102 runs.
1884	...	Cheltenham	...		...	Drawn.
1885	...	Marlborough	...		...	Drawn.
1886	...	Cheltenham	...	Cheltenham	...	5 wickets.
1887	...	Marlborough	...	Cheltenham	...	7 wickets.
1888	...	Cheltenham	...	Cheltenham	...	Innings and 71 runs.
1889	...	Marlborough	...	Marlborough	...	9 wickets.
1890	...	Cheltenham	...	Marlborough	...	39 runs.

Matches played 35: Cheltenham won 13; Marlborough won 13; drawn, 9.

CLIFTON *v.* CHELTENHAM.

Date.		*Where Played.*		*Winner.*		*Won by*
1872	...	Clifton ...	...	Clifton ...	...	6 wickets.
1873	...	Cheltenham	...	Clifton ...	...	Innings and 44 runs.
1874	...	Clifton ...	...		...	Drawn.
1875	...	Cheltenham	...	Clifton ...	...	Innings and 107 runs.
1876	...	Clifton ...	...		...	Drawn.
1877	...	Cheltenham	...	Clifton ...	...	Innings and 209 runs.
1878	...	Clifton ...	...	Clifton ...	...	9 wickets.
1879	...	Cheltenham	...	Cheltenham	...	19 runs.
1880	...	Clifton ...	...		...	Drawn.
1881	...	Cheltenham	...	Cheltenham	...	8 wickets.
1882	...	Clifton ...	...	Cheltenham	...	99 runs.
1883	...	Cheltenham	...	Clifton ...	...	4 wickets.
1884	...	Clifton ...	...		...	Drawn.
1885	...	Cheltenham	...	Clifton ...	...	5 wickets.
1886	...	Clifton ...	...	Clifton ...	...	10 wickets.
1887	...	Cheltenham	...	Cheltenham	...	9 wickets.
1888	...	Clifton ...	...	Cheltenham	...	10 wickets.
1889	...	Cheltenham	...		...	Drawn.
1890	...	Clifton ...	...	Clifton ...	...	Innings and 53 runs.

Matches played, 19: Clifton won 9; Cheltenham won 5; drawn, 5.

ENGLISH TEAMS IN AUSTRALIA.

First Team—1862.

H. H. Stephenson (Capt.), Surrey.
W. Caffyn, Surrey.
G. Griffith, Surrey.
W. Mortlock, Surrey.
W. Mudie, Surrey.
T. Sewell, Surrey.
C. Lawrence, Surrey.
G. Bennett, Kent.
T. Hearne, Middlesex.
G. Wells, Sussex.
R. Iddison, Yorkshire.
E. Stephenson, Yorkshire.

Matches played, 12—against Eighteen, 1; against Twenty-two, 11.
England won 6; lost 2; drawn 4.

Second Team—1864.

Geo. Parr (Capt.), Notts.
A. Clarke, Notts.
J. Jackson, Notts.
R. C. Tinley, Notts.
W. Caffyn, Surrey.
J. Cæsar, Surrey.
T. Lockyer, Surrey.
R. Carpenter, Cambridgeshire.
T. Hayward, Cambridgeshire.
G. Tarrant, Cambridgeshire.
Mr. E. M. Grace, Glo'stershire.
G. Anderson, Yorkshire.

Matches played, 16—all against Twenty-two.
England won 10; lost *none;* drawn 6.

Third Team—1873-74.

Mr. W. G. Grace (Capt.), Glos.
Mr. G. F. Grace, Glo'stershire.
Mr. J. A. Bush, Glo'stershire.
Mr. W. R. Gilbert, Glo'stershire.
R. Humphrey, Surrey.
H. Jupp, Surrey.
Mr. F. H. Boult, Surrey.
J. Southerton, Surrey.
M. McIntyre, Notts.
W. Oscroft, Notts.
A. Greenwood, Yorkshire.
Jas. Lillywhite, Sussex.

Matches played, 15—against Fifteen, 2; against Eighteen, 3; against Twenty-two, 10.
England won 10; lost 3; drawn 2.

Fourth Team—1876-77.

Jas. Lillywhite (Capt.), Sussex.
H. Charlwood, Sussex.
A. Greenwood, Yorkshire.
T. Armytage, Yorkshire.
T. Emmett, Yorkshire.
A. Hill, Yorkshire.
G. Ulyett, Yorkshire.
H. Jupp, Surrey.
J. Southerton, Surrey.
E. Pooley, Surrey.
A. Shaw, Notts.
J. Selby, Notts.

Matches played, 23.
Eleven-a-side, 3: England won 1; lost 1; drawn 1.
Against odds, 20: England won 10; lost 3; drawn 7.

BATTING IN ELEVEN-A-SIDE MATCHES.

	Innings.	Not out.	Highest.	Total.	Average.
Ulyett	5	0	94	243	48.3
Hill	5	2	35*	103	34.1
Emmett	5	0	48	91	18.1

* Not out.

BOWLING IN ELEVEN-A-SIDE MATCHES.

	Overs.	Maidens.	Runs.	Wickets.	Average.
A. Shaw	260	133	200	16	12.8
Hill	135	63	190	11	17.3
Lillywhite	125	50	176	10	17.6

Fifth Team.—1878-79.

Lord Harris (Capt.), Kent.
Mr. C. A. Absolom, Kent.
Mr. F. A. Mackinnon, Kent.
Mr. F. Penn, Kent.
Mr. A. N. Hornby, Lancashire.
Mr. V. F. Royle, Lancashire.
Mr. S. S. Schultz, Lancashire
Mr. A. P. Lucas, Surrey.
Mr. A. J. Webbe, Middlesex.
Mr. H. C. Maul, Warwickshire
Mr. L. Hone, Ireland.
T. Emmett, Yorkshire.
G. Ulyett, Yorkshire.

Matches played, 13.
Eleven-a-side, 5: England won 2; lost 3.
Against odds, 8: England won 3; lost *none*; drawn 5.

BATTING IN ELEVEN-A-SIDE MATCHES.

	Innings.	Not out.	Highest.	Total.	Average.
Ulyett	9	0	71	306	34
Lord Harris	9	0	67	289	32.1
Mr. V. F. Royle	8	0	75	213	26.5

BOWLING IN ELEVEN-A-SIDE MATCHES.

	Overs.	Maidens.	Runs.	Wickets.	Average.
Emmett	482	255	521	45	11.26

Sixth Team—1881-82.

A. Shaw (Capt.), Notts.
Shrewsbury, Notts.
Selby, Notts.
Scotton, Notts.
Bates, Yorkshire.
Peate, Yorkshire.
Emmett, Yorkshire.
Ulyett, Yorkshire.
Barlow, Lancashire.
Pilling, Lancashire.
Midwinter, Gloucestershire.
Lillywhite, Sussex.

Matches played, 25.

Eleven a-side, 7: England won 3; lost 2; drawn 2.

Against odds, 18: England won 10; lost 1; drawn 7.

BATTING IN ELEVEN-A-SIDE MATCHES.

	Innings.	Not out.	Highest.	Total.	Average.
Ulyett	14	0	149	549	39.3
Shrewsbury	12	2	82	382	38.2
Barlow	14	1	75	391	30.1

BOWLING IN ELEVEN-A-SIDE MATCHES.

	Overs.	Maidens.	Runs.	Wickets.	Average.
Bates	401	205	520	30	17.10
Peate	494	234	552	30	18.12

Seventh Team—1882-83.

Hon. Ivo Bligh (Capt.), Kent.
Mr. E. F. S. Tylecote, Kent.
Mr. C. T. Studd, Middlesex.
Mr. C. F. H. Leslie, Middlesex.
Mr. G. B. Studd, Middlesex.
Mr. G. F. Vernon, Middlesex.
Mr. W. W. Read, Surrey.
Mr. A. G. Steel, Lancashire.
Barnes, Notts.
Morley, Notts.
Bates, Yorkshire.
Barlow, Lancashire.

Matches played, 17.

Eleven-a-side, 7: England won 4; lost 3.

Against odds, 10: England won 5; lost *none*; drawn 5.

BATTING IN ELEVEN-A-SIDE MATCHES.

	Innings.	Not out.	Highest.	Total.	Average.
Mr. A. G. Steel	11	1	135*	415	41.5
Mr. C. F. H. Leslie	11	1	144	310	31
Barlow	12	2	80	281	28.1

* Not out.

BOWLING IN ELEVEN-A-SIDE MATCHES.

	Overs.	Maidens.	Runs.	Wickets.	Average.
Mr. A. G. Steel	283	113	401	24	16.17
Bates	311	150	429	23	18.15
Barlow	375	203	473	24	19.17

Eighth Team—1884-85.

A. Shaw (Capt.), Notts.	Peel, Yorkshire.
Barnes, Notts.	Hunter, Yorkshire
Scotton, Notts.	Ulyett, Yorkshire.
Attewell, Notts.	Bates, Yorkshire.
Flowers, Notts.	Lillywhite, Sussex.
Shrewsbury, Notts.	J. M. Read, Surrey.

Briggs, Lancashire.

Matches played, 33.
Eleven-a-side, 8: England won 6; lost 2.
Against odds, 25: England won 10; lost *none;* drawn 15.

BATTING IN ELEVEN-A-SIDE MATCHES.

	Innings.	Not out.	Highest.	Total.	Average.
Barnes	13	1	134	520	43.4
Shrewsbury	14	3	105*	440	40
Bates	12	0	68	363	30.3

* Not out.

BOWLING IN ELEVEN-A-SIDE MATCHES.

	Overs.	Maidens.	Runs.	Wickets.	Average.
Barnes	280	148	344	26	13.6
Flowers	297	158	332	22	15.2
Attewell	527	332	428	28	15.8

Ninth Team—1886-87.

A. Shrewsbury (Capt.), Notts.	Sherwin, Notts.
Barnes, Notts.	Lohmann, Surrey.
Gunn, Notts.	J. M. Read, Surrey.
Scotton, Notts.	Briggs, Lancashire.
A. Shaw, Notts.	Barlow, Lancashire.
Flowers, Notts.	Lillywhite, Sussex.

Bates, Yorkshire.

Matches played, 29.
Eleven-a-side, 10: England won 6.; lost 2; drawn 2.
Against odds, 19: England won 6; lost *none*; drawn 13.

BATTING IN ELEVEN-A-SIDE MATCHES.

	Innings.	Not out.	Highest.	Total.	Average.
Shrewsbury	18	4	144	485	34.9
Barnes	12	1	109	319	29
Bates	17	0	86	379	22.5

BOWLING IN ELEVEN-A-SIDE MATCHES.

	Overs.	Maidens.	Runs.	Wickets.	Average.
Barnes	374	225	338	25	13.13
Flowers	365	195	345	24	14.9
Lohmann	763	372	915	59	15.30

Tenth Team (Mr. Vernon's)—1887-88.

Hon. M. B. Hawke (Capt.), Yorks.
Bates, Yorkshire.
Peel, Yorkshire.
Rawlin, Yorkshire.
Attewell, Notts.
Mr. A. E. Newton, Somerset.
Mr. G. F. Vernon, Middlesex.
Mr. A. E. Stoddart, Middlesex.
Mr. T. C. O'Brien, Middlesex.
Mr. W. W. Read, Surrey.
Mr. M. P. Bowden, Surrey.
Beaumont, Surrey.
Abel, Surrey.

Matches played, 26.
Eleven-a-side, 8: England won 6; lost 1; drawn 1.
Against odds, 18: England won 5; lost *none;* drawn 13.

BATTING IN ELEVEN-A-SIDE MATCHES.

	Innings.	Not out.	Highest.	Total.	Average.
Mr. W. W. Read	11	2	183	592	65.7
Peel	13	2	55	437	39.8
Mr. A. E. Stoddart	13	0	94	417	32.1

BOWLING IN ELEVEN-A-SIDE MATCHES.

	Overs.	Maidens.	Runs.	Wickets.	Average.
Attewell	740	463	586	53	11.3
Peel	695	348	764	40	19.4

Eleventh Team (Shrewsbury's)—1887-88.

Mr. C. A. Smith (Capt.), Sussex.
Mr. W. Newham, Sussex.
Mr. G. Brann, Sussex.
J. Lillywhite, Sussex.
Lohmann, Surrey.
J. M. Read, Surrey.
Briggs, Lancashire.
Pilling, Lancashire.
Ulyett, Yorkshire.
Preston, Yorkshire.
Shrewsbury, Notts.
Pougher, Leicestershire.
Mr. L. C. Docker, Warwickshire.

Matches played, 25.
Eleven-a-side, 7: England won 5; lost 2.
Against odds, 18: England won 9; lost *none;* drawn 9.

BATTING IN ELEVEN-A-SIDE MATCHES.

	Innings.	Not out.	Highest.	Total.	Average.
Shrewsbury	14	1	232	764	58.10
Mr. G. Brann	8	2	118	158	26.2
Mr. C. A. Smith	8	0	69	198	24.6

BOWLING IN ELEVEN-A-SIDE MATCHES.

	Overs.	Maidens.	Runs.	Wickets.	Average.
Lohmann	659	354	755	63	11.62
Briggs	371	215	434	30	14.14

Eleven-a-side matches played by the Eleven teams, 55.
England won 33; lost 16; drawn 6.
Against odds, 179: England won 84; lost 9; drawn 86.

REPRESENTATIVE MATCHES, ENGLAND *v.* AUSTRALIA, PLAYED IN AUSTRALIA.

Date.	Played at	Result.
1877	Melbourne ...	Lillywhite's Team *v.* Australia. Australia won by 45 runs.
1877	Melbourne ...	Lillywhite's Team *v.* Australia. Lillywhite's Team won by 4 wickets.
1882	Melbourne ...	Shaw's Team *v.* Australia. Drawn.
1882	Sydney ...	Shaw's Team *v.* Australia. Australia won by 5 wickets.
1883	Sydney ...	Hon. Ivo Bligh's Team *v.* Australia. Australia won by 4 wickets.
1885	Melbourne ...	Shaw's Team *v.* Australia. Shaw's Team won by 10 wickets.
1885	Sydney ...	Shaw's Team *v.* Australia. Australia won by 6 runs.
1885	Sydney ...	Shaw's Team *v.* Australia. Australia won by 8 wickets.
1885	Melbourne ...	Shaw's Team *v.* Australia. Shaw's Team won by an innings and 98 runs.
1887	Sydney ...	Shaw's Team *v.* Australia. Shaw's Team won by 13 runs.
1887	Sydney ...	Shaw's Team *v.* Australia. Shaw's Team won by 71 runs.
1888	Melbourne ...	Mr. Vernon's Team *v.* Australia. Mr. Vernon's Team won by an innings and 78 runs.
1888	Sydney ...	Shrewsbury's Team *v.* Australia. Shrewsbury's Team won by 5 wickets.
1888	Sydney ...	Combined English Team *v.* Australia. Combined Team won by 126 runs.

England won 8; lost 5; drawn 1.

AUSTRALIAN TEAMS IN ENGLAND.

First Team—1878.

D. W. Gregory (Capt.), N.S.W.
F. R. Spofforth, N.S.W.
T. W. Garrett, N.S.W.
W. L. Murdoch, N.S.W.
C. Bannerman, N.S.W.
A. C. Bannerman, N.S.W.
H. F. Boyle, Victoria.
T. Horan, Victoria.
F. E. Allan, Victoria.
J. M. Blackham, Victoria.
W. Midwinter, Victoria.
G. H. Bailey, Tasmania.

Matches played, 37.
Eleven-a-side, 17: Australia won 9; lost 4; drawn 4.
Against odds, 20: Australia won 9; lost 3; drawn 8.

BATTING IN ELEVEN-A-SIDE MATCHES.

	Innings.	Not out.	Highest.	Total.	Average.
C. Bannerman	31 ...	1 ...	133 ...	723 ...	24.3
J. M. Blackham	22 ...	8 ...	53 ...	256 ...	18.4

BOWLING IN ELEVEN-A-SIDE MATCHES.

	Overs.	Maidens.	Runs.	Wickets.	Average.
T. W. Garrett ...	296 ...	144 ...	394 ...	38 ...	10.14
H. F. Boyle ...	409 ...	168 ...	569 ...	54 ...	10.29
F. R. Spofforth ...	717 ...	264 ...	1198 ...	108 ...	11.10

Second Team—1880.

W. L. Murdoch (Capt.), N.S.W.
F. R. Spofforth, N.S.W.
A. C. Bannerman, N.S.W.
J. M. Blackham, Victoria.
H. F. Boyle, Victoria.
W. H. Moule, Victoria.
J. Slight, Victoria.
G. J. Bonnor, Victoria.
T. U. Groube, Victoria.
P. S. McDonnell, Victoria.
G. E. Palmer, Victoria.
G. Alexander, Victoria.
A. H. Jarvis, South Australia.

Matches played, 37.
Eleven-a-side, 11: Australia won 5; lost 2; drawn 4.
Against odds, 26: Australia won 16; lost 2; drawn 8.

BATTING IN ELEVEN-A-SIDE MATCHES

	Innings.	Not out.	Highest.	Total.	Average.
W. L. Murdoch ...	19 ...	1 ...	153* ...	465 ...	25.15
P. S. McDonnell ...	19 ...	1 ...	79 ...	418 ...	23.4
F. R. Spofforth ...	9 ...	1 ...	44 ...	169 ...	21.1

* Not out.

BOWLING IN ELEVEN-A-SIDE MATCHES.

	Overs.	Maidens.	Runs.	Wickets.	Average.
F. R. Spofforth ...	240 ...	82 ...	396 ...	46 ...	8.28
G. E. Palmer ...	710 ...	342 ...	892 ...	80 ...	11.12
H. F. Boyle	516 ...	239 ...	616 ...	39 ...	15.31

Third Team—1882.

W. L. Murdoch (Capt.), N.S.W.
T. W. Garrett, N.S.W.
S. P. Jones, N.S.W.
H. H. Massie, N.S.W.
F. R. Spofforth, N.S.W.
A. C. Bannerman, N.S.W.
J. M. Blackham, Victoria.
G. J. Bonnor, Victoria.
H. F. Boyle, Victoria.
T. Horan, Victoria.
P. S. McDonnell, Victoria.
G. E. Palmer, Victoria.
G. Giffen, South Australia.

Matches played, 38—all against Eleven-a-side.
Australia won 23; lost 4; drawn 11.

BATTING.

	Innings.	Not out.	Highest.	Total.	Average.
W. L. Murdoch	61	5	286*	1711	30.31
T. Horan	52	5	141*	1175	25
H. H. Massie	61	4	206	1405	24.37

* Not out.

BOWLING.

	Overs.	Maidens.	Runs.	Wickets.	Average.
H. F. Boyle	1200	525	1680	144	11.96
F. R. Spofforth	1592	700	2282	188	12.26
G. E. Palmer	1185	511	1731	138	12.75
T. W. Garrett	1206	488	1759	128	13.95

Fourth Team—1884.

W. L. Murdoch (Capt.), N.S.W.
F. R. Spofforth, N.S.W.
A. C. Bannerman, N.S.W.
J. M. Blackham, Victoria.
H. F. Boyle, Victoria.
G. E. Palmer, Victoria.
G. Alexander, Victoria.
G. J. Bonnor, Victoria.
W. H. Cooper, Victoria.
P. S. McDonnell, Victoria.
H. J. H. Scott, Victoria.
W. Midwinter, Victoria.
G. Giffen, South Australia.

Matches played, 32—all against Eleven-a-side.
Australia won 18; lost 7; drawn 7.

BATTING.

	Innings.	Not out.	Highest.	Total.	Average.
W. L. Murdoch	50	5	211	1378	30.28
P. S. McDonnell	54	2	103	1225	23.29
H. J. H. Scott	51	8	102	973	22.27
G. Giffen	51	1	113	1052	21.2

BOWLING.

	Overs.	Maidens.	Runs.	Wickets.	Average.
F. R. Spofforth	1544	649	2642	216	12.50
G. E. Palmer	1241	466	2131	132	16.19
H. F. Boyle	727	291	1143	67	17.4
G. Giffen	827	285	1613	82	19.55

Fifth Team—1886.

H. J. H. Scott (Capt.), Victoria.
G. J. Bonnor, Victoria.
G. E. Palmer, Victoria.
J. M. Blackham, Victoria.
W. Bruce, Victoria.
J. McIlwraith, Victoria.
J. W. Trumble, Victoria.
E. Evans, N.S.W.
S. P. Jones, N.S.W.
T. W. Garrett, N.S.W.
F. R. Spofforth, N.S.W.
A. H. Jarvis, South Australia.
G. Giffen, South Australia.

Matches played, 39.
Eleven-a-side, 38: Australia won 9; lost 7; drawn 22.
Against odds, 1: Australia lost by 9 wickets.

BATTING.

	Innings.	Not out	Highest.	Total.	Average.
G. Giffen	63	9	119	1453	26.49
S. P. Jones	64	2	151	1498	24.10
H. J. H. Scott	64	5	123	1289	21.50

BOWLING.

	Overs.	Maidens.	Runs.	Wickets.	Average.
G. Giffen	1693	722	2711	159	17.8
F. R. Spofforth	925	372	1528	89	17.15
T. W. Garrett	1650	778	2221	123	18.7
G. E. Palmer	1416	564	2328	106	21.102

Sixth Team—1888.

P. S. McDonnell (Capt.), N.S.W.
C. T. B. Turner, N.S.W.
J. J. Ferris, N.S.W.
A. C. Bannerman, N.S.W.
S. P. Jones, N.S.W.
S. M. J. Woods, Camb. Univ.
J. D. Edwards, Victoria
G. J. Bonnor, Victoria.
H. Trott, Victoria.
J. M. Blackham, Victoria.
H. F. Boyle, Victoria.
J. Worrall, Victoria.
J. J. Lyons, South Australia.
A. H. Jarvis, South Australia.

Matches played 40: all against Eleven a-side.
Australia won 19; lost 14; drawn 7.

BATTING.

	Innings.	Not out.	Highest.	Total.	Average.
P. S. McDonnell	62	1	105	1393	22.51
G. J. Bonnor	64	3	119	1204	19.45
H. Trott	65	2	83	1212	19.15

BOWLING.

	Overs.	Maidens.	Runs.	Wickets.	Average.
C. T. B. Turner	2589	1222	3492	314	11.38
J. J. Ferris	2222	998	3103	220	14.23

Seventh Team—1890.

W. L. Murdoch (Capt.), N.S.W.	J. E. Barrett, Victoria.
C. T. B. Turner, N.S.W.	H. Trott, Victoria.
J. J. Ferris, N.S.W.	J. M. Blackham, Victoria.
P. C. Charlton, N.S.W.	F. H. Walters, Victoria.
S. E. Gregory, N.S.W.	H. Trumble, Victoria.
S. P. Jones, N.S.W.	J. J. Lyons, South Australia.

K. E. Burn, Tasmania.

Matches played, 38—all against Eleven-a-side.
Australia won 13; lost 16: drawn 9.

BATTING.

	Innings.	Not out.	Highest.	Total.	Average.
W. L. Murdoch	64	2	158	1459	23.33
J. E. Barrett	64	7	97	1305	22.51
H. Trott	65	1	186	1273	19.57

BOWLING.

	Overs.	Maidens.	Runs.	Wickets.	Average.
C. T. B. Turner	1651	724	2725	215	12.145
J. J. Ferris	1685	688	2838	215	13.43

Eleven-a-side matches played by the Seven teams, 214.
Australia won 96; lost 54; drawn 64.

Against odds, 47: Australia won 25; lost 6; drawn 16.

REPRESENTATIVE MATCHES PLAYED IN ENGLAND —ENGLAND v. AUSTRALIA.

Date.	Played at	Result.
1880	Oval	England won by 5 wickets.
1882	Oval	Australia won by 7 runs.
1884	Manchester	Drawn.
1884	Lord's	England won by an innings and 5 runs.
1884	Oval	Drawn.
1886	Manchester	England won by 4 wickets.
1886	Lord's	England won by an innings and 106 runs.
1886	Oval	England won by an innings and 217 runs.
1888	Lord's	Australia won by 61 runs.
1888	Oval	England won by an innings and 137 runs.
1888	Manchester	England won by an innings and 21 runs.
1890	Lord's	England won by 7 wickets.
1890	Oval	England won by 2 wickets.

England won 9; lost 2; drawn 2.

BATTING AVERAGES OF THE LEADING ENGLISH BATSMEN AGAINST THE AUSTRALIANS

IN ELEVEN-A-SIDE MATCHES TO THE END OF 1890.

	Innings.	Not out.	Highest Innings.	Runs.	Aver.
Mr. W. G. Grace	95	5	170	3035	33.65
Shrewsbury	112	15	232	3244	33.43
Mr. A. G. Steel	61	4	148	1779	31.12
Mr. W. W. Read	90	4	183	2593	30.13

CENTURIES SCORED.

Mr. W. G. Grace, eight	170	165	152	148	116*	110	107	101
Mr. W. W. Read, six	183*a*	142*a**	119*a*	117	109	102*		
Shrewsbury, five	232*a*	206*a*	164	144*a*	105*a**			
Mr. A. G. Steel, three	148	135*a**	134					

a Signifies made in Australia. * Not out.

ENGLISH TEAMS IN AMERICA AND CANADA.

First Team (Parr's).—1859.

G. Parr.	R. Carpenter.
John Lillywhite.	J. Wisden.
A. Diver.	J. Jackson.
W Caffyn.	J. Grundy.
T. Lockyer.	Julius Cæsar.
T. Hayward.	H. H. Stephenson.

Matches played, 5; all against odds. Parr's Team won 5.

Second Team (Willsher's).—1868.

E. Willsher.	H. Charlwood.
G. Griffith.	J. Rowbotham.
T. Humphrey.	Jno. Smith (C.)
H. Jupp.	A. Shaw.
E. Pooley.	G. Tarrant.
Jas. Lillywhite, jun.	G. Freeman.

Matches played, 6; all against odds.
Willsher's Team won 5; drawn 1.

Third Team (Mr. Fitzgerald's).—1872.

Mr. R. A. Fitzgerald.	Mr. C. J. Ottaway.
Mr. A. Lubbock.	Mr. C. K. Francis.
Mr. E. Lubbock.	Mr. A. N. Hornby.
Mr. A. Appleby.	Mr. F. P. U. Pickering.
Hon. G.(now Lord) Harris.	Mr. W. M. Rose.
Mr. W. H. Hadow.	Mr. W. G. Grace.

Matches played, 8; all against odds.
Mr. Fitzgerald's Team won 7; drawn 1.

Fourth Team (Daft's).—1879.

R. Daft.	F. Morley.
A. Shaw.	T. Emmett.
J. Selby.	G. Ulyett.
A. Shrewsbury.	E. Lockwood.
W. Oscroft.	W. Bates.
W. Barnes.	G. Pinder.

Matches played, 12. Eleven-a-side, 1: Daft's Team won 1.
Against odds, 11: Daft's Team won 8; drawn 3.

Fifth Team (Gentlemen of Ireland).—1879.

Mr. W. Hone, sen.
Mr. W. Hone, jun.
Mr. N. Hone.
Sir G. Colthurst.
Mr. D. N. Trotter.
Mr. H. W. Brougham.
Mr. J. H. Nunn.
Mr. G. D. Casey.
Mr. G. Hone.
Mr. H. Hamilton.
Mr. A. G. Exham.
Mr. R. A. Miller.
Mr. H. Gore.

Matches played, 12.

Eleven-a-side, 4: Gentlemen of Ireland won 3; lost 1.

Against odds, 8: Gentlemen of Ireland won 6; drawn 2.

Sixth Team (Mr. Sanders').—1885.

Mr. E. J. Sanders.
Mr. W. E. Roller.
Mr. C. E. Horner.
Mr. J. A. Turner.
Mr. T. R. Hine Haycock.
Mr. A. R. Cobb.
Mr. A. E. Newton.
Mr. H. O. Whitby.
Mr. W. E. Bolitho.
Mr. H. Bruen.
Mr. A. J. Thornton.
Rev. R. T. Thornton.

Matches played, 8.

Eleven-a-side, 5: Mr. Sanders' Team won 3; lost 1; drawn 1.

Against odds, 3: Mr. Sanders' Team won 3.

Seventh Team (Mr. Sanders').—1886.

Mr. E. J. Sanders.
Mr. W. E. Roller.
Mr. J. A. Turner.
Mr. A. R. Cobb.
Mr. T. R. Hine Haycock.
Mr. H. W. Bainbridge.
Mr. C. E. Cotterill.
Mr. H. Rotherham.
Mr. F. T. Welman.
Mr. E. H. Buckland.
Mr. K. J. Key.
Rev. A. T. Fortescue.

Matches played, 9.

Eleven-a-side, 5: Mr. Sanders' Team won 5.

Against odds, 4; Mr. Sanders' Team won 3; drawn 1.

Eighth Team (Gentlemen of Ireland).—1888.

Mr. J. Dunn.
Mr. J. M. Meldon.
Mr. D. Gillman.
Mr. W. Synnott.
Mr. J. W. Hynes.
Mr. J. P. Fitzgerald.
Mr. W. Johnston.
Mr. T. Tobin.
Mr. J. P. Maxwell.
Mr. E. Fitzgerald.
Mr. D. Cronin.
Mr. F. Kennedy.

Matches played, 13.
Eleven-a-side, 5: Gentlemen of Ireland won 2; lost 2; drawn 1.
Against odds, 8: Gentlemen of Ireland won 3; drawn 5.

Eleven-a-side matches played by the Eight teams, 20.
English Elevens won 14; lost 4; drawn 2.

Against odds, 53: English Elevens won 40; lost *none;* drawn 13.

AMERICAN AND CANADIAN TEAMS IN ENGLAND.

Gentlemen of Philadelphia.—1884.

Mr. R. S. Newhall.
Mr. C. A. Newhall.
Mr. F. E. Brewster.
Mr. Wm. Brockie, jun.
Mr. H. Brown
Mr. E. W. Clark, jun.
Mr. J. M. Fox.
Mr. S. Law.
Mr. Wm. C. Lowry.
Mr. H. McNutt.
Mr. W. C. Morgan, jun.
Mr. J. A. Scott.
Mr. D. P. Stoever.
Mr. J. B. Thayer, jun.

Matches played, 18—all against Eleven-a-side.
Gentlemen of Philadelphia won 8; lost 5; drawn 5.

Gentlemen of Canada.—1887.

Mr. W. A. Henry.
Mr. D. W. Saunders.
Mr. A. C. Allan.
Mr. G. W. Jones.
Mr. W. J. Fleury.
Mr. W. C. Little.
Mr. A. Gillespie.
Mr. W. W. Jones.
Mr. C. J. Annand.
Mr. W. W. Vickers.
Mr. G. G. S. Lindsay.
Mr. R. B. Ferrie.
Dr. E. R. Ogden.

Matches played, 19—all against Eleven-a-side.
Gentlemen of Canada won 5; lost 5; drawn 9.

Gentlemen of Philadelphia.—1889.

Mr. D. S. Newhall.
Mr. G. S. Patterson.
Mr. Wr. Scott.
Mr. E. W. Clark, jun.
Mr. F. E. Brewster.
Mr. H. J. Brown.
Mr. R. D. Brown.
Mr. N. Etting.
Mr. W. C. Morgan, jun.
Mr. C. R. Palmer.
Mr. J. W. Sharp.
Mr. D. P. Stoever.
Mr. A. G. Thomson.
Mr. H. P. Baily.

Matches played, 12—all against Eleven-a-side.
Gentlemen of Philadelphia won 4; lost 3; drawn 5.

Matches played by the Three teams, 49.
America and Canada won 17; lost 13; drawn 19.

MAJOR WARTON'S TEAM IN SOUTH AFRICA.

1888-9.

Mr. C. A. Smith (Captain).
Mr. M. P. Bowden.
Mr. B. A. F. Grieve.
Mr. E. McMaster.
Mr. R. Skinner.
Hon. C. Coventry.
Abel, Surrey.
Wood, Surrey.
J. M. Read, Surrey.
F. Hearne, Kent.
Ulyett, Yorkshire.
Fothergill, Somersetshire.
Briggs, Lancashire.

Total matches played, 19.
Against odds, 17: won 11; lost 4; drawn 2. Eleven-a-side, 2: won 2.

MR. G. F. VERNON'S TEAM IN INDIA AND CEYLON.

1889-90.

Mr. G. F. Vernon (Capt.).
Lord Hawke.
Mr. J. G. Walker.
Mr. A. E. Gibson.
Mr. E. M. Lawson Smith.
Mr. H. Philipson.
Mr. E. R. de Little.
Mr. F. L. Shand.
Mr. J. H. J. Hornsby.
Mr. A. E. Leatham.
Mr. T. K. Tapling.
Hon. A. M. Carson.
Mr. G. H. Goldney.

Total matches played (all Eleven-a-side), 13: Won 10; lost 1; drawn 2.

BATTING RECORDS.

Highest Aggregate Scores:

920 by Orleans Club *v.* Rickling Green, at Rickling Green, 4th August 1882
813 for 9 wickets by Hampstead *v.* Stoics, at Hampstead (the greatest number of runs made in one day), 4th August 1886
745 for 4 wickets by West of Scotland *v.* Priory Park, at Chichester, 13th July 1885

Highest Aggregate Scores in a First-class Match:

803 by Non-Smokers *v.* Smokers, at East Melbourne, 17th March 1887
775 by New South Wales *v.* Victoria, at Sydney, 10th February 1882
703 for 9 wickets by Cambridge University *v.* Sussex, at Brighton, 19th June 1890
698 by Surrey *v.* Sussex (highest in a County Match), at Oval, 9th August 1888
643 by Australians *v.* Sussex, at Brighton, 18th May ... 1882

Highest Aggregate Score at Lord's:

735 by M.C.C. and Ground *v.* Wiltshire, 13th August ... 1888

Highest in Gentlemen v. *Players' Matches:*

513 by the Gentlemen, at Oval, 15th and 16th July ... 1870

Lowest Aggregate Scores in a First-class Match:

6 by Kent *v.* Bexley with Lord F. Beauclerk and Hammond, at Dartford, 25th August 1805
12 by Oxford University *v.* M.C.C. and Ground, at Oxford, 24th May 1877
16 by Surrey *v.* Nottinghamshire, at Oval, 26th July ... 1880
19 by M.C.C. and Ground *v.* Australians, at Lord's, 27th May 1878

Highest Individual Scores:

485, Mr. A. E. Stoddart, for Hampstead *v.* Stoics, at Hampstead, 4th August 1886

419 not out, Mr. J. S. Carrick, for West of Scotland *v.* Priory Park, Chichester, 13th July 1885

415 not out, Mr. W. N. Roe, for Emmanuel College L.V.C. *v.* Caius College L.V.C., at Cambridge, 12th July ... 1881

404 not out, Mr. E. F. S. Tylecote, Classicals *v.* Moderns, Clifton College, May 1868

400 not out, Mr. W. G. Grace, for U.S.E.E. *v.* Twenty-two of Grimsby and District, 10th July 1876

328 not out, Mr. W. Bruce, for Melbourne C.C. *v.* Hotham (highest in Australia), January 1884

323 not out, Mr. F. E. Lacey, for Hampshire *v.* Norfolk, at Southampton, 30th May 1887

Highest in a First-Class Match:

344, Mr. W. G. Grace, for M.C.C. *v.* Kent, at Canterbury, 11th August 1876

338, Mr. W. W. Read, for Surrey *v.* Oxford University, at Oval, 28th June 1888

321, Mr. W. L. Murdoch, for New South Wales *v.* Victoria, at Sydney, 10th February 1882

318 not out, Mr. W. G. Grace, for Gloucestershire *v.* Yorkshire, at Cheltenham, 17th August (highest in a County Match) 1876

Highest at Lord's:

278, Mr. W. Ward, for Marylebone *v.* Norfolk, 24th July... 1820

266, Barnes, for M.C.C. and Ground *v.* Leicestershire, 1st June 1882

228, Gunn, for Players of England *v.* Australians, 19th June 1890

Total Aggregate of Runs in a First-class Match:

1411 for 30 wickets, Victoria *v.* New South Wales, at Sydney, 10th February 1882

1339 for 39 wickets, Cambridge University *v.* Sussex, at Brighton, 19th June 1890

1295 for 36 wickets, Middlesex *v.* Yorkshire, at Lord's, 20th June 1889

1145 for 31 wickets, Gentlemen *v.* Players, at the Oval, 4th July 1889

Highest Scores for First Wicket:

470 no wicket, Mr. L. Wilson, 246 not out, and Mr. W. G. Wyld, 203 not out, for Beckenham *v.* Bexley, at Beckenham, 1st August 1885

404, Viscount Throwley and Mr. W. F. Forbes, for Mr. A. E. Fellowes' XI. *v.* Huntingdonshire, at Huntingdon, 13th July 1881

402, Mr. J. Shuter (304 not out) and Mr. T. Ashdown, for Bexley *v.* Emeriti, 14th June 1884

Highest for First Wicket in a First-class Match:

283, Mr. W. G. Grace (180) and Mr. B. B. Cooper (101), for Gentlemen of the South *v.* Players of the South, at the Oval, 15th July 1869

266, Shrewsbury (152) and Mr. A. E. Stoddart (151), for England *v.* M.C.C. and Ground, Centenary Festival, at Lord's, 13th June 1887

243, Mr. W. Rashleigh (107) and Mr. K. J. Key (143), for Oxford *v.* Cambridge, at Lord's 1886

238, Mr. W. G. Grace and Mr. T. G. Matthews, for Gloucestershire *v.* Yorkshire (highest in a County Match), at Sheffield, 29th July 1872

226, Mr. W. G. Grace and Abel, for South *v.* North, at Scarborough, 19th September 1889

Highest Scores for Last Wicket:

194, by Mr. W. H. Edgar and Mr. J. M. Swayne, for Oxford Perambulators *v.* Etceteras, 1st June ... 1885

173, by Briggs and Pilling, for Lancashire *v.* Surrey, at Liverpool, 16th July 1885

157, by Parnham and White, for XI. of North *v.* XI. of South, at Lord's, 14th June 1886

149, by Lohmann and Sharpe, for Surrey *v.* Essex, at Oval, 20th May 1889

Longest Partnerships:

603 for second wicket by Mr. G. F. Vernon and Mr. A. H. Trevor, for Orleans Club *v.* Rickling Green, 4th and 5th August 1882

454 for third wicket, by Barnes and Midwinter, for M.C.C. and Ground *v.* Leicestershire, at Lord's, 1st June ... 1882

398 for second wicket, Shrewsbury and Gunn, for Nottinghamshire *v.* Sussex, at Nottingham (highest in a first-class match), 15th May 1890

Centuries and over in First-class Matches:

Mr. W. G. Grace, from 1866 to 1890, 93 (19 of them not out).
Mr. W. W. Read, from 1876 to 1890, 25.
Shrewsbury, from 1875 to 1890, 28.

Two Centuries in a First-class Match:

Mr. W. G. Grace, 130 and 102 not out, for South *v.* North of the Thames, at Canterbury, 3rd August 1868
Mr. W. G. Grace, 101 and 103 not out, for Gloucestershire *v.* Kent, at Clifton, 25th August 1887
Mr. W. G. Grace, 148 and 153, for Gloucestershire *v.* Yorkshire, at Clifton, 16th August 1888
W. Lambert, 107 not out and 157, for Sussex *v.* Epsom, at Lord's, 2nd July 1817

Two Centuries in a Minor Match:

Mr. W. Townshend, at Rossall; Mr. D. G. Spiro, at Cambridge; Mr. F. W. Maude, at Lord's; Mr. R. A. A. Beresford, at Oundle; Mr. W. W. Read, at Oval; Mr. A. Bannerman, in Australia; and Mr. W. D. Llewellyn, at Oxford.

Biggest Hits:

175 yards, by Mr. H. W. Fellows, Christ Church Ground, Oxford, 1856.
168 yards, by Mr. C. I. Thornton.
152 yards, by Mr. C. I. Thornton.
149 yards, by Mr. G. J. Bonnor.
140 yards, by Mr. W. G. Grace.

BOWLING RECORDS.

All Ten Wickets in an Innings in First-class Matches:

Mr. G. H. Kirwan, for Eton *v.* M.C.C. (all bowled), 9th July, 1835.

E. Hinkly, for Kent *v.* England, 11th July, 1848—no analysis.

J. Wisden, for North *v.* South, 15th July, 1850—no analysis (all bowled).

Mr. V. E. Walker, for England *v.* Surrey, 21st July, 1859, for 74 runs.

Mr. E. M. Grace, for M.C.C. *v.* Kent, 14th August, 1862—no analysis.

Mr. V. E. Walker, for Gentlemen of Middlesex *v.* Gentlemen of Kent, 16th June, 1864, for 37 runs.

G. Wootton, for All-England *v.* Yorkshire, 19th July, 1865—no analysis.

Mr. V. E. Walker, for Middlesex *v.* Lancashire, 22nd July, 1865, for 104 runs.

W. Hickton, for Lancashire *v.* Hants, 21st July, 1870, for 46 runs.

J. C. Shaw, for Notts *v.* England, 15th Sept., 1870, for 20 runs.

Mr. S. E. Butler, for Oxford *v.* Cambridge, 26th June, 1871, for 38 runs.

J. Lillywhite, for South *v.* North, 7th August, 1872, for 129 runs.

A. Shaw, for M.C.C. and Ground *v.* North, 1st June, 1874, for 73 runs.

E. Barratt, for Players *v.* Australians, 2nd Sept., 1878, for 43 runs.

Mr. G. Giffen, for Anglo-Australian XI. *v.* Combined Australia, 16th February, 1884, for 66 runs.

Mr. W. G. Grace, for M.C.C. *v.* Oxford University, 22nd June, 1886, for 49 runs.

G. Burton, for Middlesex *v.* Surrey, 19th July, 1888, for 59 runs.

Mr. S. M. J. Woods, for Cambridge University *v.* Mr. C. I. Thornton's XI., 12th May, 1890, for 69 runs.

It will be thus seen that Mr. V. E. Walker has done it thrice; no other bowler has done it more than once.

FIELDING RECORDS.

Throwing the Cricket Ball:

140 yards, by Billy the Aboriginal, Australia, 19th Dec. 1872

137 yards, by G. Brown (doubtful), Wolverton Common 1819

132 yards, by Mr. W. F. Forbes (18 years old), Eton College Sports, 16th March 1876

130 yards, by Mr. G. J. Bonnor, Australia ... ...

128 yards 10½ inches, by Crane (Baseball player), Melbourne, 5th January 1889

127 yards 1 foot 3 inches, by Mr. W. H. Game, Oxford University Sports, 13th March 1873

AVERAGES.

1866.

BATTING IN FIRST-CLASS MATCHES.

	Completed Innings.	Runs.	Average.
Mr. W. G. Grace	15	640	42.10
Mr. V. E. Walker	18	756	42
Hon. C. G. Lyttelton	10	371	37. 1
Mr. A. H. Winter	16	540	33.12
Mr. R. A. Fitzgerald	22	721	32.17
Mr. C. F. Buller	34	1093	32. 5
Carpenter	35	1096	31.11
Mr. H. A. Richardson	14	442	31. 8
Hon. F. G. Pelham	11	297	27
T. Hearne	48	1254	26. 6
Daft	22	555	25. 5
Jupp	64	1557	24.21
Mr. R. D. Walker	36	880	24.16
Mr. C. Warren	15	356	23.11
Mr. M. A. Troughton	14	324	23. 2
Mr. C. Lucas	12	271	22. 7
Mr. E. Davenport	12	274	22.10
Mr. W. F. Maitland	23	479	20.19
Mr. E. L. Fellowes	13	267	20. 7

The list comprises 15 amateurs and 4 professionals.

BOWLING IN FIRST-CLASS MATCHES.

	Overs.	Maidens.	Runs.	Wickets.	Average.
Emmett	28	13	65	6	10. 5
J. C. Shaw	330	157	385	36	10.25
A. Shaw	341	161	479	43	11. 6
Mr. E. L. Fellowes	176	84	238	20	11.18
James Lillywhite	841	463	894	73	12.18
Wootton	1385	611	1898	150	12.98
Willsher	551	263	653	50	13. 3
Mr. W. G. Grace	283	109	415	31	13.12
Tarrant	544	225	809	61	13.16
Howitt	383	155	612	43	14.10
Mr. E. M. Grace	246	95	346	24	14.10
Mr. R. D. Walker	673	294	954	66	14.30
Grundy	1101	549	1226	85	14.36
T. Hearne	448	234	630	39	16. 6
Bennett	532	189	927	58	15.57
Southerton	385	79	828	48	17.12
Griffith	632	196	1080	58	18.36

The list comprises 13 professionals and 4 amateurs.

1867.

BATTING IN FIRST-CLASS MATCHES.

For not less than Five Innings.

	Completed Innings.	Runs.	Average.
Mr. A. Lubbock	5	364	72. 4
Daft	7	377	53. 6
Charlwood	10	371	37. 1
Iddison	14	460	32.12
Mr. B. B. Cooper	9	288	32. 0
Mr. W. G. Grace	5	154	30. 4
T. Hayward	10	301	30. 1
Mr. V. E. Walker	15	444	29. 9
Mr. R. A. H. Mitchell	6	167	27. 5
Mr. E. B. Rowley	8	218	27. 2
Hon. G. S. Lyttelton	10	267	26. 7
Mr. E. M. Grace	15	401	26.11
Payne	24	615	25.15
T. Humphrey	34	882	25.32
Mr. R. D. Balfour	8	207	25. 7
Mr. C. E. Green	7	180	25. 5

The list comprises 10 amateurs and 6 professionals.

BOWLING IN FIRST-CLASS MATCHES.

	Overs.	Maidens.	Runs.	Wickets.	Average.
Emmett	166	69	236	40	5.36
Mr. W. G. Grace	200	96	255	39	6.21
Freeman	564	310	553	66	8.25
Tarrant	344	181	382	44	8.30
A. Shaw	885	435	957	96	9.93
Wootton	1207	582	1469	151	9.110
Southerton	996	361	1522	112	13.66
Grundy	604	313	697	46	15. 7

The list comprises 7 professionals and 1 amateur.

1868.

BATTING IN FIRST-CLASS MATCHES.

For not less than Five Innings.

	Completed Innings.	Runs.	Most in an Innings.	Average.
Mr. W. G. Grace	9	588	134*	65. 3
Mr. R. A. H. Mitchell	5	205	92	41
T. Hayward	7	270	84	38. 4
Mr. I. D. Walker	19	651	165	34. 5
Mr. T. Case	6	198	75*	33
Mr. W. Yardley	5	161	59	32. 1
Jas. Lillywhite	21	631	126*	30. 1
Mr. G. Saville	10	294	105*	29. 4
Mr. H. A. Richardson	15	431	143	28.11
Daft	13	335	94	25.10
Jupp	39	965	134	24.29

* Not out.

The list comprises 7 amateurs and 4 professionals.

BOWLING IN FIRST-CLASS MATCHES.

	Overs.	Maidens.	Runs.	Wickets.	Average.
A. Shaw	121	69	111	13	8. 7
Emmett	407	205	522	59	8.50
Howitt	504	219	648	69	9.27
Freeman	392	197	454	46	9.40
T. Hearne	403	167	540	55	9.45
Willsher	1003	529	1123	114	9.97
Mr. E. L. Fellowes	275	124	392	33	11.29
Iddison	227	62	429	36	11.33
J. C. Shaw	449	222	544	44	12.16
Wootton	912	435	1430	112	12.86
Mr. D. Buchanan	132	54	254	19	13. 7
Southerton	1039	328	1976	151	13.13
Grundy	651	299	850	62	13.44
Mr. W. G. Grace	327	116	639	44	14.23

The list comprises 11 professionals and 3 amateurs.

1869.

BATTING IN FIRST-CLASS MATCHES.

For not less than Five Innings.

	Completed Innings.	Runs.	Most in an Innings.	Average.
Mr. W. G. Grace	23	1320	180	57. 9
Daft	10	494	105*	49. 4
Iddison	10	359	112	35. 9
Jupp	37	1299	170	35. 4
Rev. W. F. Wright	6	185	120*	30. 5
Mr. A. Lubbock	8	243	50	30. 3
Mr. I. D. Walker	18	540	90	30
Mr. F. H. Hill	6	179	73	29. 5
Charlwood	17	480	155	28. 4
Mr. C. I. Thornton	27	716	124	26.14
Mr. R. D. Walker	6	161	92	26. 5
Killick	10	260	76	26
Mr. W. Yardley	13	329	65	25. 4
M. McIntyre	5	127	99	25. 2

The list comprises 8 amateurs and 6 professionals.

BOWLING IN FIRST-CLASS MATCHES.

	Overs.	Maidens.	Runs.	Wickets.	Average.
Crundy	215	123	185	23	8. 1
T. Hearne	352	198	377	46	8. 9
Mr. R. F. Miles	177	64	269	24	11. 5
Hickton	322	126	449	39	11.20
Freeman	540	300	577	50	11.27
Emmett	558	285	721	59	12.13
Howitt	284	152	340	27	12.16
J. C. Shaw	668	354	809	65	12.29
Wootton	1187	969	1517	119	12.89
Mr. A. Appleby	292	126	391	30	13. 1
Willsher	811	409	924	68	13.40
Southerton	1371	505	2081	133	15.86
Mr. W. G. Grace	785	352	1187	74	16. 3

The list comprises 10 professionals and 3 amateurs.

1872.

BATTING IN FIRST-CLASS MATCHES.

For not less than Five Innings.

	Completed Innings.	Runs.	Most in an Innings.	Average.
Mr. W. G. Grace	26	1485	170*	57. 3
Selby	9	377	128*	41. 8
Daft	17	589	102	34.11
Mr. E. M. Grace	7	244	108	34. 6
Mr. W. Yardley	17	552	130	32. 8
Mr. A. N. Hornby	10	314	80	31. 4
Mr. J. M. Mare	7	220	97	31. 3
Mr. S. H. Akroyd	6	165	87	27. 3
Mr. E. K. Browne	5	136	52	27. 1
Mr. F. E. R. Fryer	15	405	91	27
Wild	12	322	104	26.10
Lockwood	34	857	121	25. 7
Oscroft	18	455	68	25. 5
R. Humphrey	45	1071	96	23.36
Jupp	47	1017	82	21.30
Mr. G. F. Grace	21	431	115*	20.11

The list comprises 9 amateurs and 7 professionals.

BOWLING IN FIRST-CLASS MATCHES.

	Overs.	Maidens.	Runs.	Wickets.	Average.
W. Mc Intyre	214	108	232	41	5.27
Watson	144	57	178	21	8.10
Wootton	310	151	361	37	9.28
Mr. A. W. Ridley	210	70	332	32	10.12
Mr. D. Buchanan	302	148	374	36	10.14
Howitt	313	149	424	38	11. 6
A. Shaw	1006	498	1109	92	12. 5
Southerton	1458	487	2019	167	12.15
Mr. W. G. Grace	419	166	688	56	12.16
Mr. A. Appleby	181	99	221	17	13
Barratt	180	53	332	25	13. 7
Jas. Lillywhite	936	442	1244	94	13.22
Mr. W. N. Powys	347	168	514	37	13.33
Willsher	591	256	657	48	13.33
Lockwood	420	150	642	45	14.12
Mr. R. Lipscomb	193	53	389	25	15.14
Emmett	572	228	952	62	15.22
M. Mc Intyre	462	193	682	43	15.37
Freeman	152	72	200	12	16. 8
J. C. Shaw	929	431	1413	66	21.27

The list comprises 14 professionals and 6 amateurs.

30

1873.

BATTING IN FIRST-CLASS MATCHES.

For not less than Five Innings.

	Completed Innings.	Runs.	Most in an Innings.	Average.
Mr. W. G. Grace	30	2139	192*	71. 9
Mr. F. Townsend	5	261	136	52. 1
Mr. J. M. Cotterill	6	248	78	41. 2
Daft	11	416	161	37. 9
Mr. I. D. Walker	17	586	64	34. 8
Mr. A. N. Hornby	10	348	128	34. 8
Mr. C. J. Ottaway	9	304	89	33. 7
Mr. C. I. Thornton	6	190	91	31. 4
Mr. G. F. Grace	17	513	165	30. 3
Mr. E. M. Grace	13	381	76	29. 4
Mr. C. E. Nepean	8	228	50	28. 4
Mr. R. D. Walker	6	160	38	26. 4
Jupp	41	996	94	24.12
Mr. W. Yardley	19	426	51	22. 8
Emmett	28	608	104	21.20

The list comprises 12 amateurs and 3 professionals.

BOWLING IN FIRST-CLASS MATCHES.

	Overs.	Maidens.	Runs.	Wickets.	Average.
W. Mc Intyre	379	162	527	59	8.55
Watson	279	92	446	48	9.14
Rylott	443	217	664	69	9.43
Morley	309	154	376	35	10.26
Mr. D. Buchanan	287	138	394	35	11. 9
A. Shaw	1317	630	1638	128	12.102
Southerton	1386	671	1833	132	13.117
Willsher	296	149	378	30	12.18
Jas. Lillywhite	1010	441	1377	101	13.64
Hill	741	299	1064	81	13.11
Fillery	773	339	1129	72	15.49
Emmett	650	285	1106	68	16.18
Mr. G. F. Grace	562	241	859	52	16.27
Street	725	289	1115	65	17.10
J. C. Shaw	749	276	1011	59	17. 8
Mr. W. G. Grace	496	91	983	55	17.48
M. Mc Intyre	395	139	710	39	18. 8

The list comprises 14 professionals and 3 amateurs.

1874.

BATTING IN FIRST-CLASS MATCHES.

For not less than Five Innings.

	Completed Innings.	Runs.	Most in an Innings.	Average.
Mr. W. G. Grace	31	1658	179	53.15
Jupp	35	1275	154	36.15
Mr. C. S. Gordon	5	183	96	36. 3
Lord Harris	8	234	58	29. 2
Mr. A. N. Hornby	12	349	72	29. 1
Mr. G. F. Grace	22	630	103	28.14
Mr. J. M. Cotterill	9	240	61	26. 6
Charlwood	26	667	100	25.17
Lockwood	40	998	96	24.38
J. Phillips	20	496	58	24.16

The list comprises 6 amateurs and 4 professionals.

BOWLING IN FIRST-CLASS MATCHES.

	Overs.	Maidens.	Runs.	Wkts.	Average.
Mr. W. H. Hadow	127	49	209	23	9. 2
Hill	668	266	983	89	11. 4
Mr. T. W. Lang	332	159	394	35	11. 9
M. McIntyre	278	85	373	33	11.10
Emmett	856	308	1171	99	11.82
Southerton	1200	583	1523	127	11.126
Mr. E. Rutter	289	96	528	44	12
Mr. W. G. Grace	1034	363	1658	129	12.110
Willsher	299	139	434	35	12.14
Watson	224	63	409	32	12.25
J. C. Shaw	553	270	775	61	12.43
A. Shaw	1461	722	1729	131	13.26
Morley	977	437	1493	111	13.50
Ulyett	378	159	626	44	14.10
Mr. G. F. Grace	688	292	791	50	15.41

The list comprises 10 professionals and 5 amateurs.

1875.

BATTING IN FIRST-CLASS MATCHES.

For not less than Five Innings.

	Completed Innings.	Runs.	Most in an Innings.	Average.
Barlow	10	388	87	38. 8
Mr. J. M. Cotterill	12	430	191	35.10
Mr. E. M. Grace	6	214	71	35. 4
A. Greenwood	24	819	93	34. 3
Mr. F. Penn	14	469	101	33. 7
Lord Harris	19	631	92	33. 4
Mr. W. G. Grace	46	1498	152	32.26
Mr. L. Winslow	11	337	124	30. 7
Mr. W. W. Read	8	247	98	30. 7
Mr. A. N. Hornby	24	686	78*	28.14
Mr. W. Blacker	11	315	64*	28. 7
Mr. G. F. Grace	35	978	180*	27.33
Lockwood	33	921	74	27.30
Selby	15	418	66	27.13
Mr. A. J. Webbe	26	696	120	26.20
Mr. F. J. Greenfield	19	501	79	26. 7
Mr. G. H. Longman	17	445	80	26. 3
Mr. E. F. S. Tylecote	5	133	64	26. 3

The list comprises 14 amateurs and 4 professionals.

BOWLING IN FIRST-CLASS MATCHES.

	Overs.	Maidens.	Runs.	Wickets.	Average.
Mycroft	513	278	588	80	7.28
A. Shaw	1741	1022	1499	161	9.50
Watson	262	81	370	32	11.18
Mr. W. G. Grace	1690	698	2470	192	12.166
Mr. R. F. Miles	364	164	431	35	12.11
Mr. A. Appleby	286	106	418	33	12.22
Mr. W. Foord Kelcey	489	204	714	56	12.42
Mr. W. H. Hadow	411	176	525	40	13. 5
W. Mc Intyre	508	188	747	57	13. 6
Clayton	468	204	702	52	13.26
Mr. A. W. Ridley	397	168	521	38	13.27
Southerton	1522	737	1810	137	13.29
Jas. Lillywhite	833	339	1209	88	13.65
Mr. C. M. Sharpe	540	177	928	67	13.57
Fillery	586	258	835	57	14.37
Morley	1257	608	1676	114	14.80
Hill	1265	577	1738	109	15.103
Emmett	563	252	853	52	16.21

The list comprises 11 professionals and 7 amateurs.

1876.

BATTING IN FIRST-CLASS MATCHES.

For not less than Five Innings.

	Completed Innings.	Runs.	Most in an Innings.	Average.
Mr. W. G. Grace	42	2622	344	62.18
Mr. C. J. Ottaway	6	374	112	62. 2
Mr. W. W. Read	14	588	106	42
Mr. W. O. Moberly	6	245	103	40. 5
Mr. W. R. Gilbert	23	870	205*	37.19
Mr. A. W. Ridley	17	585	105*	34. 7
Daft	26	886	99	34. 2
Charlwood	19	645	123	33.18
Mr. W. H. Game	10	336	141	33. 6
Lockwood	40	1261	108	31.21
Lord Harris	29	916	154	31.17
Mr. A. J. Webbe	23	723	109	31.10
Mr. A. P. Lucas	27	816	105	30. 6
Mr. F. Townsend	9	271	88	30. 1
Mr. R. D. Walker	7	209	104	29. 6
Mr. I. D. Walker	28	796	94	28.12
Mr. D. Q. Steel	16	463	82	28.15
Mr. H. R. Webbe	5	141	52	28. 1
Mr. A. N. Hornby	30	826	72	27.16
Mr. G. F. Grace	29	789	95	27. 6
Mr. W. Yardley	15	408	92	27. 3
Mr. J. M. Cotterill	8	217	70	27. 1
Hon. E. Lyttelton	12	316	72	26. 4
Jupp	39	983	92*	25. 8
Hon. A. Lyttelton	15	383	83	25. 8
Mr. C. R. Filgate	6	151	93	25. 1
Shrewsbury	25	593	118	23.18

The list comprises 22 amateurs and 5 professionals.

BOWLING IN FIRST-CLASS MATCHES.

	Overs.	Maidens.	Runs.	Wickets.	Average.
W. Mc Intyre	688	259	1015	89	11.36
Watson	534	248	650	51	12.38
Mr. A. W. Ridley	465	178	673	51	13.10
Mycroft	701	306	1126	85	13.21
A. Shaw	2546	1470	2515	178	14.23
Jas. Lillywhite	990	547	1315	91	14.41
Mr. W. S. Patterson	514	208	775	52	14.47
Mr. R. Henderson	533	199	904	53	17. 3
Hill	1208	504	1861	109	17. 8
Southerton	1331	660	1625	95	17.10
Mr. G. F. Grace	840	369	1240	72	17.16
Mr. W. Foord Kelcey	580	220	962	55	17 27
Mr. W. G. Grace	1550	638	2388	124	19 32
Morley	1267	625	1761	89	19 70
Mr. C. A. Absolom	750	245	1342	62	21.40
Emmett	647	302	997	45	22. 7

The list comprises 9 professionals and 7 amateurs.

1877.

BATTING IN FIRST-CLASS MATCHES.

For not less than Ten Innings.

	Completed Innings.	Runs.	Most in an Innings.	Average.
Mr. W. G. Grace	37	1474	261	39.31
Mr. W. W. Read	11	399	140	36. 3
Mr. A. P. Lucas	24	832	115	34.16
Mr. E. M. Grace	10	327	89	32. 7
Mr. F. Penn	30	927	148	30.27
Mr. C. Booth	11	336	77	30. 6
Mr. A. N. Hornby	26	764	144	29.10
Mr. I. D. Walker	27	787	95	29. 4
Hon. A. Lyttelton	21	611	101	29. 2
Mr. W. Lindsay	11	319	74	29
Mr. J. M. Cotterill	15	428	92	28. 8
Platts	16	432	115	27
Mr. G. F. Grace	32	840	134	26. 8
Mr. A. J. Webbe	25	651	100	26. 1
Lockwood	45	1144	103	25.19
Daft	28	709	96	25. 9
Jupp	32	795	93	24.27

The list comprises 13 amateurs and 4 professionals.

BOWLING IN FIRST-CLASS MATCHES.

	Overs.	Maidens.	Runs.	Wickets.	Average.
W. McIntyre	699	307	948	85	11.13
G. Hearne	848	424	1182	107	11. 5
Watson	1089	548	1233	96	12.81
Mr. W. G. Grace	1788	787	2231	179	12.83
Mycroft	1229	798	2169	171	12.117
Mr. W. S. Patterson	939	473	1065	80	13.25
Mr. R. Henderson	525	238	732	53	13.43
Emmett	617	260	1004	72	13.68
Morley	1726	839	2021	148	13.97
Southerton	688	360	804	55	14.34
Mr. W. R. Gilbert	551	220	941	55	17. 6
Mr. W. Foord Kelcey	605	230	956	54	17.38
Barratt	1080	424	1837	92	19.89

The list comprises 8 professionals and 5 amateurs.

1878.

BATTING IN FIRST-CLASS MATCHES.

For not less than Ten Innings.

	Completed Innings.	Runs.	Most in an Innings.	Average.
Selby	30	909	107	30. 9
Ulyett	46	1347	109	29.13
Mr. W. G. Grace ...	38	1115	116	29.13
Hon. Edward Lyttelton	26	779	113	29.25
Mr. F. Penn	18	523	160	29. 1
Hall	13	351	82*	27
Mr. G. F. Grace... ...	29	779	73*	26.25
Hon. A. Lyttelton ...	19	476	72	25. 1
Mr. A. J. Webbe ...	24	588	118	24.12

The list comprises 6 amateurs and 3 professionals.

BOWLING IN FIRST-CLASS MATCHES.

	Overs.	Maidens.	Runs.	Wickets.	Average.
Mr. A. G. Steel ...	1223	447	1542	164	9.66
Mycroft	1049	567	1182	116	10.22
A. Shaw	2522	1512	2084	196	10.124
Emmett	982	464	1278	112	11.46
Watson	535	280	586	49	11.47
Bates	901	337	1160	99	11.71
Morley	1953	654	2311	191	12.19
Hearne	1169	511	1442	114	12.74
Mr. A. Penn ...	564	242	821	61	13.28
Mr. W. G. Grace...	1641	717	2106	148	14.34
Barratt	1219	513	1752	123	14.30
Ulyett	594	272	918	55	16.38

The list comprises 9 professionals and 3 amateurs.

1879.

BATTING IN FIRST-CLASS MATCHES.

For not less than Ten Innings.

	Completed Innings.	Runs.	Most in an Innings.	Average.
Mr. W. G. Grace	25	880	123	35. 5
Mr. A. N. Hornby	20	606	64*	30. 6
Hon. A. Lyttelton	24	688	102	28.16
Mr. A. G. Steel	20	553	93	27.13
Scotton	16	436	84*	27. 4
Oscroft	29	781	140	26.27
Mr. A. P. Lucas	17	423	70	24.15
Ulyett	36	843	81	23.15
Mr. I. D. Walker	20	476	60*	23.16
Mr. A. J. Webbe	23	532	122	23. 3

The list comprises 7 amateurs and 3 professionals.

BOWLING IN FIRST-CLASS MATCHES.

	Overs.	Maidens.	Runs.	Wickets.	Average.
Mycroft	871	502	878	96	9.14
A. Shaw	1575	924	1259	134	9.53
Emmett	435	161	566	54	10.26
Bates	690	309	815	78	10.35
Morley	1361	676	1551	146	10 91
Mr. A. F. J. Ford	525	265	592	51	11.31
Mr. A. G. Steel	943	432	1120	93	12. 4
G. G. Hearne	523	264	610	50	12.10
Peate	691	293	932	75	12.32
Blamires	591	296	751	58	12.55
Mr. W. G. Grace	1060	438	1414	105	13.49

The list comprises 8 professionals and 3 amateurs.

1880.

BATTING IN FIRST-CLASS MATCHES.

For not less than Ten Innings.

	Completed Innings.	Runs.	Most in an Innings.	Average.
Mr. W. G. Grace	24	951	152	39.15
Mr. R. T. Ellis	17	569	103	33. 8
Lord Harris	22	722	123	32.18
Mr. A. J. Webbe	21	660	132	31. 9
Hon. Ivo Bligh	32	957	105	29.29
Hon. A. Lyttelton	13	378	47*	29. 1
Barnes	41	1163	143	28.15
Mr. R. S. Jones	18	521	124	28.17
Charlwood	15	415	67	27.10
Mr. F. Penn	21	576	88	27. 9
Mr. W. W. Read	12	306	93	25. 6
Ulyett	38	929	141	24.17
Mr. T. S. Pearson	22	545	121	24.17
Mr. A. N. Hornby	33	784	126	23.25
Lockwood	41	952	69	23. 9
Mr. A. G. Steel	22	496	118	22.12

The list comprises 12 amateurs and 4 professionals.

BOWLING IN FIRST-CLASS MATCHES.

	Overs.	Maidens.	Runs.	Wickets.	Average.
A. Shaw	1994	1231	1525	177	8.109
Barlow	611	334	639	61	10.29
Watson	881	455	946	84	11.22
Morley	1717	867	2077	174	11.163
Peate	1312	580	1668	138	12.12
Mycroft	700	372	1007	77	13. 6
Mr. A. G. Steel	925	400	1205	92	13. 9
Mr. A. H. Evans	364	128	662	50	13.12
Mr. C. M. Cunliffe	499	180	806	56	14.22
Bates	1001	467	1390	90	15.40
Midwinter	980	477	1139	73	15.44
Potter	1220	658	1314	78	16.66
Mr. W. G. Grace	1015	402	1470	85	17.25

The list comprises 9 professionals and 4 amateurs—10 of them slow and medium-pace round-arm bowlers, 3 of them fast.

1881.

BATTING IN FIRST-CLASS MATCHES.

For not less than Ten Innings.

	Completed Innings.	Runs.	Most in an Innings.	Average.
Mr. A. N. Hornby	37	1531	188	41.14
Mr. W. G. Grace	21	792	182	37.15
Mr. C. F. H. Leslie	21	742	111*	35. 7
Ulyett	36	1197	112	33. 9
Mr. W. W. Read	29	931	160	32. 3
Mr. C. T. Studd	25	799	113	31.24
Mr. L. C. Docker	14	439	107	31. 5
Mr. G. B. Studd	21	647	106*	30.17
Mr. A. G. Steel	28	834	106*	29.22
Mr. W. A. Bettesworth	15	423	77	28. 3
Mr. W. H. Patterson	25	702	107*	28. 2
Lockwood	38	1060	109	27.34
A. Shaw	11	298	78*	27. 1
Mr. J. Cranston	12	317	63	26. 5
Mr. E. M. Grace	14	353	77	25. 3
Mr. G. F. Vernon	35	856	119	24.16
Mr. A. P. Lucas	25	612	142	24.12

The list comprises 14 amateurs and 3 professionals.

BOWLING IN FIRST-CLASS MATCHES.

	Overs.	Maidens.	Runs.	Wickets.	Average.
Hill	337	154	435	43	10. 5
Nash	456	223	557	52	10.37
Watson	879	512	812	69	11.53
Barlow	747	378	939	79	11.70
Peate	1638	731	2088	162	12.144
Mr. A. G. Steel	1257	537	1683	125	13.58
A. Shaw	911	501	999	72	13.63
Jones	568	311	664	45	14.34
Emmett	569	254	861	60	14.21
Flowers	473	210	686	46	14.42
Mycroft	970	501	1343	90	14.83
Morley	840	368	1227	80	15.27
Mr. C. T. Studd	957	426	1284	79	16.20
Jas. Lillywhite	843	393	1045	62	16.53
Bates	1279	540	1883	114	16.59
G. G. Hearne	771	360	1078	64	16·54
Midwinter	810	265	918	51	18
Mr. W. G. Grace	511	194	879	45	19.24
Barratt	911	332	1607	82	19.49

The list comprises 16 professionals and 3 amateurs.

1882.

BATTING IN FIRST-CLASS MATCHES.

For not less than Ten Innings.

	Completed Innings.	Runs.	Most in an Innings.	Average.
Mr. C. T. Studd	38	1249	126*	32.33
Lord Harris	24	787	176	32.19
Mr. A. P. Lucas	22	707	145	32. 3
Mr. A. J. Webbe	22	660	108*	30
Mr. W. Newham	11	334	101	30. 4
Mr. F. Taylor	10	290	62	29
Mr. A. N. Hornby	49	1383	131	28.11
Mr. A. G. Steel	26	739	171	28.11
Barnes	43	1194	130	27.33
Ulyett	56	1542	138	27.30
Barlow	40	1088	68	27. 8
Midwinter	31	823	137*	26.17
Mr. W. G. Grace	37	975	88	26.13
Shrewsbury	20	533	207	26.13
Mr. E. F. S. Tylecote	21	561	100*	26.15
Mr. W. W. Read	34	884	117	26
Mr. J. Shuter	32	832	93	26
Mr. J. S. Russell	13	335	83	25.10

The list comprises 13 amateurs and 5 professionals.

BOWLING IN FIRST-CLASS MATCHES.

	Overs.	Maidens.	Runs.	Wickets.	Average.
Crossland	749	332	1015	105	9.70
Emmett	730	350	1044	95	10.94
Nash	409	172	656	62	10.36
Barlow	863	461	982	90	10.82
Morley	1051	541	1297	115	11.32
A. Shaw	1216	705	1042	87	11.85
Peate	1853	868	2466	214	11.112
Watson	924	495	953	76	12.41
Flowers	1201	586	1405	98	14.33
Burton	744	368	877	59	14.51
Woof	578	221	962	63	15.17
Ulyett	603	280	962	61	15.47
Midwinter	1052	522	1365	88	15.45
Jones	1025	615	987	62	15.57
Mr. C. T. Studd	1564	768	2027	128	15.107
Barratt	1074	446	1591	94	16.87
Mycroft	903	426	1224	72	17
Mr. W. G. Grace	850	268	1745	101	17.28
Mr. R. C. Ramsay	731	284	1212	69	17.39
Bates	1215	500	1518	82	18.42

The list comprises 17 professionals and 3 amateurs.

1882—*continued.*

AUSTRALIAN BATTING.

	Completed Innings.		Runs.		Most in an Innings.		Average.
Mr. W. L. Murdoch...	56	...	1711	...	286*	...	30.31
Mr. T. Horan	47	...	1175	...	141*	...	25
Mr. H. H. Massie ...	57	...	1405	...	206	...	24.37
Mr. A. C. Bannerman	54	...	1201	...	120*	...	22.13
Mr. G. J. Bonnor ...	40	...	815	...	122*	...	20.15

AUSTRALIAN BOWLING.

	Overs.		Maidens.		Runs.		Wickets.		Average.
Mr. H. F. Boyle...	1208	...	525	...	1680	...	144	...	11.96
Mr. F. R. Spofforth	1594	...	699	...	2282	...	188	...	12.26
Mr. G. E. Palmer.	1192	...	515	...	1731	...	138	...	12.75
Mr. T. W. Garrett	1209	...	489	...	1759	...	128	...	13.95

1883.

BATTING IN FIRST-CLASS MATCHES.

For not less than Ten Innings.

	Completed Innings.		Runs.		Most in an Innings.		Average.
Mr. W. W. Read ...	33	...	1573	...	168	...	47.22
Mr. C. T. Studd	29	...	1193	...	175*	...	41. 4
Mr. W. G. Grace ...	39	...	1352	...	112	...	34.26
Hall	35	...	1180	...	127	...	33.25
Mr. A. P. Lucas	20	...	664	...	97	...	33. 4
Mr. I. D. Walker ...	23	...	750	...	145	...	32.14
Mr. H. Whitfeld	13	...	425	...	74	...	32. 9
Ulyett	51	...	1572	...	84	...	30.42
Lord Harris	30	...	919	...	118	...	30.19
Mr. A. G. Steel	12	...	370	...	68	...	30.10
Shrewsbury	38	...	1117	...	98	...	29.15
Mr. J. G. Walker ...	13	...	386	...	93	...	29. 9
Mr. W. O. Moberly ...	12	...	351	...	121	...	29. 3
Barnes	47	...	1308	...	120	...	27.39
Selby	12	...	328	...	100	...	27. 4
Mr. E. Sainsbury ...	13	...	363	...	116	...	27.12
Hon. J. W. Mansfield...	10	...	264	...	117	...	26. 4
Mr. E. J. Diver	21	...	541	...	98	...	25.16
Mr. W. E. Roller ...	34	...	860	...	142	...	25.10
Mr. A. A. G. Asher ...	11	...	284	...	182	...	25. 9
Mr. J. Shuter	32	...	805	...	108*	...	25. 5
Mr. F. Taylor	12	...	302	...	96	...	25. 2
Mr. E. Lumb	11	...	277	...	70*	...	25. 2
Flowers...	46	...	1144	...	131	...	24.40
Bates	44	...	1024	...	79	...	23.12

The list comprises 18 amateurs and 7 professionals.

1883—*continued.*

BOWLING IN FIRST-CLASS MATCHES.

	Overs.	Maidens.	Runs.	Wickets.	Average.
Watson	940	463	1135	96	11.79
A. Shaw	1062	643	840	67	12.36
Crossland	551	207	929	72	12.65
Harrison	786	328	1326	100	13.26
Emmett	476	220	784	55	14.14
Peate	1376	665	1753	120	14.73
Flowers	1250	561	1692	113	14.110
Nash	401	148	775	51	15.10
Peel	517	225	808	51	15.43
Barlow	1242	595	1669	106	15.79
Barratt	1434	590	2353	146	16.17
Barnes	818	349	1361	79	17.18
Mr. C. T. Studd...	1445	651	1957	112	17.53
Bates	795	348	1169	60	19.29
Burton	807	327	1214	62	19.36
Mr. W. G. Grace..	1104	395	2077	94	22. 9

The list comprises 14 professionals and 2 amateurs.

1884.

BATTING IN FIRST-CLASS MATCHES.

For not less than Fifteen Innings.

	Completed Innings.	Runs.	Most in an Innings.	Average.
Mr. A. G. Steel	25	967	148	38.17
Mr. W. G. Grace ...	40	1361	116*	34. 1
Scotton	26	897	134	34.13
Lord Harris	42	1417	112*	33.31
Mr. W. Newham ...	23	741	137	32. 5
Ulyett	45	1334	146*	29.29
Mr. W. W. Read ...	43	1256	135	29. 9
Shrewsbury	32	908	209	28.12
Mr. W. Blackman ...	16	454	77*	28. 6
Mr. I. D. Walker ...	24	674	83	28. 2
Barnes	39	1092	105*	28
Mr. T. C. O'Brien ...	42	1150	119	27.16
Hall	39	1058	135	27. 5
Mr. J. Shuter	36	968	125	26.32
Mr. C. T. Studd ...	15	398	141*	26. 8
Mr. W. H. Patterson...	18	485	73*	26.17
Hon. A. Lyttelton ...	16	417	103	26. 1
Gunn	25	647	138	25.22
Mr. H. B. Steel	16	412	100	25.12
Bates	42	1000	133	23.34
Mr. J. H. Brain	32	791	143	24.23
Mr. M. P. Bowden ...	31	736	89*	23.23
Mr. A. N. Hornby ...	29	678	94	23.11
Flowers...	35	805	122	23

The list comprises 16 amateurs and 8 professionals.

1884—*continued.*

BOWLING IN FIRST-CLASS MATCHES.

	Overs.	Maidens.	Runs.	Wickets.	Average.
A. Shaw	724	425	712	68	10.32
Emmett	1031	557	1250	107	11.73
Attewell	1150	659	1217	101	12. 5
Crossland	525	198	893	71	12.41
Flowers	916	454	1163	90	12.83
Peate	1575	777	1868	137	13.87
Mr. C. E. Horner.	1001	440	1602	107	14.104
Burton	623	301	877	58	15. 7
Barlow	1428	686	1963	130	15.13
Mr. H. O. Whitby	454	153	941	58	16.13
Watson	1061	537	1443	87	16.51
Wootton	1201	493	1963	118	16.75
Barratt	1163	432	2199	121	18.21
Woof	1335	590	2109	116	18.21
Ulyett	778	364	1267	69	18.25
Barnes	769	390	1074	57	18.48
Humphreys	341	62	1030	55	18.40
Mr. J. Robertson	621	282	1039	50	20.39
Mr. C. T. Studd	714	297	1120	54	20.40
Mr. H. V. Page	664	290	1108	53	20.48
Mr. W. G. Grace	1036	448	1762	82	21.40
Mr. S. Christopherson	1025	407	1936	88	22

The list comprises 15 professionals and 7 amateurs.

AUSTRALIAN BATTING.

	Completed Innings.	Runs.	Most in an Innings.	Average.
Mr. W. L. Murdoch	46	1382	211	30. 2
Mr. P. S. McDonnell	54	1246	103	23. 4
Mr. G. J. Bonnor	50	1061	124	21.11
Mr. G. Giffen	52	1073	113	20.33

AUSTRALIAN BOWLING.

	Overs.	Maidens.	Runs.	Wickets.	Average.
Mr. F. R. Spofforth	1625	672	2732	218	12.116
Mr. G. E. Palmer.	1281	475	2201	134	16.57
Mr. H. F. Boyle	729	291	1135	67	16.63
Mr. G. Giffen	835	287	1641	82	20. 1

1885.

BATTING IN FIRST-CLASS MATCHES.

For not less than Twenty Innings.

	Completed Innings.	Runs.	Most in an Innings.	Average.
Shrewsbury	20	1130	224*	56.10
Mr. W. W. Read	42	1880	163	44.32
Mr. W. G. Grace	39	1688	221*	43.11
Gunn	40	1451	203	36.11
M. Read	33	1137	186*	34.15
Lee	29	901	101	31. 2
Mr. W. E. Roller	24	729	204	30. 9
Ulyett	46	1337	91	29. 3
Barlow	28	816	117	29. 4
Briggs	31	857	186	27.20
Mr. A. J. Webbe	24	667	82*	27.19
Grimshaw	36	946	129*	26.10
Mr. E. J. Diver	36	941	143	26. 5
Bates	46	1161	98	25.11
Abel	39	966	92	24.30
Mr. J. Shuter	34	841	135	24.25
Flowers	35	850	173	24.10
Barnes	39	937	140*	24. 1
Hall	38	900	87	23.26

The list comprises 13 professionals and 6 amateurs.

BOWLING IN FIRST-CLASS MATCHES.

	Overs.	Mdns.	Runs.	Wkts.	Average.
Briggs	657	326	921	67	13.50
Lohmann	1264	592	2030	142	14.42
Attewell	1301	767	1218	87	14
A. Hearne	643	284	928	65	14.18
Flowers	1314	718	1395	94	14.79
Wootton	863	376	1358	90	15. 8
Watson	1237	721	1344	88	15.24
Barnes	1025	497	1508	97	15.53
Beaumont	1466	753	2138	129	16.74
Burton	877	443	1000	62	16. 8
Wright	792	405	980	60	16.20
Peate	1699	903	1945	115	16.105
Barlow	1086	591	1284	74	17.26
Woof	1195	541	1782	100	17.82
Emmett	1103	575	1459	80	18.19
Mr. W. G. Grace	1435	664	2199	118	18.75
Mr. S. Christopherson	697	285	1287	68	18.63
Mr. E. W. Bastard	750	313	1241	62	20. 1
Bates	1085	489	1575	78	20.15
J. Hide	889	400	1365	58	23.31

The list comprises 17 professionals and 3 amateurs.

1886.

BATTING IN FIRST-CLASS MATCHES.

For not less than Twenty Innings.

	Completed Innings.	Runs.	Most in an Innings.	Average.
Mr. W. W. Read ...	43	1825	120	42.19
Shrewsbury	33	1404	227*	42.18
Mr. W. G. Grace ...	52	1846	170	35.26
M. Read	39	1364	186	34.38
Lord Harris	20	644	76	32. 4
Abel	42	1221	144	29. 3
G. G. Hearne	39	1125	126	28.33
Mr. A. E. Stoddart ...	23	640	116	27.19
Mr. J. G. Walker ...	30	819	79	27. 9
Hall	37	1005	92	27. 6
W. Humphreys	27	735	68*	27. 6
Gunn	28	752	83	26.24
Scotton	37	979	110*	26.17
Mr. A. N. Hornby ...	32	842	161	26.10
Mr. G. F. Vernon ...	21	549	160	26. 3
Mr. W. H. Patterson ..	20	517	124	25.17
Bates	43	1018	136	23.29

The list comprises 9 professionals and 8 amateurs.

BOWLING IN FIRST-CLASS MATCHES.

	Overs.	Maidens.	Runs.	Wickets.	Average.
Watson	1188	701	1109	99	11.20
Emmett	1339	677	1675	132	12.91
Attewell	1295	736	1272	97	13.11
Barnes	744	387	936	67	13.65
Bowley	973	497	1219	88	13.75
Peate	980	542	1027	70	14.47
Barlow	1238	653	1525	105	14.55
Lohmann	1715	809	2425	160	15.25
Mr. C. W. Rock ...	975	449	1261	81	15.46
Beaumont	883	441	1165	76	15.25
Briggs	1176	612	1471	92	15.91
Wootton	1618	715	2281	143	15.136
Flowers	1046	556	1137	69	16.33
Bates	826	420	1079	65	16.39
Woof	732	354	945	52	18. 9
J. Hide	1070	516	1435	76	18.67
A. Hearne	879	448	1077	55	19.32
Mr. W. G. Grace ...	1525	648	2439	122	19.121
Burton	1115	494	1620	79	20.40
A. Hide	871	460	1063	51	20.43

The list comprises 18 professionals and 2 amateurs.

1887.

BATTING IN FIRST-CLASS MATCHES.

For not less than Twenty Innings.

	Completed Innings.	Runs.	Most in an Innings.	Average.
Shrewsbury	21	1653	267	78.15
Mr. W. G. Grace	38	2062	183*	54.10
Mr. A. J. Webbe	26	1244	243*	47.22
Mr. W. W. Read	34	1615	247	47.17
Mr. K. J. Key	39	1684	281	43. 7
Hall	32	1240	160	38.24
Ulyett	39	1487	199*	38. 5
Gunn	27	958	205*	35.13
Mr. J. Eccles	20	677	113	33.17
Barnes	29	957	160	33
Mr. J. Shuter	27	871	111	32. 7
Quaife	29	926	111	31.27
Lee	20	591	165	29.11
Mr. A. N. Hornby	25	717	105	28.17
Mr. A. E. Stoddart	28	799	151	28.15
Briggs	29	819	68	28. 7
Mr. W. Rashleigh	29	816	108	28. 4
Mr. F. Marchant	22	586	72	26.14
F. Hearne	36	921	144	25.21
Lohmann	33	843	115	25.18
G. G. Hearne	28	714	91	25.14
Peel	33	835	91	25.10
Bates	40	996	103	24.36

The list comprises 13 professionals and 10 amateurs.

BOWLING IN FIRST-CLASS MATCHES.

	Overs.	Maidens.	Runs.	Wickets.	Average.
Attewell	1330	810	1238	89	13.81
Watson	1532	937	1482	100	14.82
Lohmann	1634	737	2404	154	15.94
Beaumont	684	326	1072	64	16.48
Flowers	885	422	1171	68	17.15
Peel	1097	507	1472	85	17.27
Briggs	1592	831	2018	114	17.80
Mr. E. A. Nepean	476	124	1091	60	18.11
Burton	722	334	1004	55	18.14
Preston	533	233	974	52	18.38
Barlow	727	374	994	53	18.40
Wootton	1373	603	1892	100	18.92
Barnes	1103	518	1712	90	19. 2
Emmett	1030	533	1403	73	19.16
Bowley	957	469	1373	67	20.33
Mr. W. G. Grace	1273	525	2078	97	21.41

The list comprises 14 professionals and 2 amateurs.

1888.

BATTING IN FIRST-CLASS MATCHES.

For not less than Twenty Innings.

	Completed Innings.	Runs.	Most in an Innings.	Average.
Mr. W. W. Read	39	1414	338	36.10
Mr. W. G. Grace	58	1886	215	32.30
Abel	42	1323	160	31.21
M. Read	31	786	109	25.11
Mr. J. Eccles	26	660	184	25.10
Mr. J. Shuter	33	834	95	25. 9
Mr. K. J. Key	35	875	108	25
Mr. M. P. Bowden	22	514	189*	23. 8
Mr. C. J. M. Fox	21	490	93	23. 7
Mr. W. Newham	33	746	138	22.20
Mr. O. G. Radcliffe	34	754	99	22. 6
Mr. J. A. Dixon	24	527	83	21.23
Briggs	41	872	126*	21.11
Gunn	45	920	91	20.20

The list comprises 10 amateurs and 4 professionals.

BOWLING IN FIRST-CLASS MATCHES.

	Overs.	Maidens.	Runs.	Wickets.	Average.
Briggs	1450	763	1679	160	10.79
A. Hearne	687	339	786	73	10.56
Martin	753	404	791	73	10.61
Lohmann	1649	783	2280	209	10.190
Peel	1648	830	2091	171	12.39
Burton	847	370	1135	92	12.31
Woof	607	313	680	55	12.20
Flowers	824	451	857	66	12.65
Preston	687	310	1094	81	13.41
Attewell	1393	848	1235	91	13.52
Barlow	684	348	889	65	13.44
Bowley	644	346	824	59	13.57
Beaumont	857	456	1124	80	14. 4
Wright	1035	514	1233	86	14.29
A. Hide	933	459	1188	81	14.54
Barnes	1033	511	1434	97	14.76
Watson	775	420	918	61	15. 3
Wootton	674	308	855	54	15.45
Mr. S. M. J. Woods	785	292	1464	87	16.72
Mr. F. G. J. Ford	628	268	1075	61	17.38
Mr. W. G. Grace	1097	503	1691	93	18.17
Mr. C. A. Smith	638	268	1113	53	21

The list comprises 18 professionals and 4 amateurs.

1889.

BATTING IN FIRST-CLASS MATCHES.

For not less than Twenty Innings.

	Completed Innings.	Runs.	Most in an Innings.	Average.
Gunn	34	1299	118	38. 7
Shrewsbury	14	522	104	37. 4
Barnes	36	1249	130*	34.25
M. Read	25	847	136	33.22
Mr. W. G. Grace	43	1396	154	32.20
Mr. T. C. O'Brien	25	786	100*	31.11
Mr. J. Cranston	23	709	130	30.19
Mr. K. J. Key	35	1070	176*	30.20
A. Ward	27	822	114*	30.12
Mr. F. Marchant	23	669	176	29. 2
Abel	38	1095	138	28.31
Hall	36	966	86	26.30
Sugg	28	747	89	26.19
Mr. W. W. Read	32	805	115	25. 5
Mr. A. E. Stoddart	33	817	78*	24.25
Mr. F. G. J. Ford	20	495	123	24.15
Mr. E. A. Nepean	36	885	64*	24.21
Flowers	29	707	78	24.11

The list comprises 9 amateurs and 9 professionals.

BOWLING IN FIRST-CLASS MATCHES.

	Overs.	Maidens.	Runs.	Wickets.	Average.
Attewell	1314	654	1555	140	11.15
Briggs	1040	447	1646	140	11.106
Mold	679	262	1207	102	11.85
Watson	850	438	1139	90	12.59
Richardson	668	349	816	64	12.48
Wright	863	308	1466	114	12.98
Lohmann	1614	646	2714	202	13.88
Martin	980	404	1484	106	14
Shacklock	545	177	1133	80	14.13
Woof	548	182	1068	65	16.28
Mr. S. M. J. Woods	532	151	1239	74	16.55
Beaumont	716	274	1452	87	16.60
Peel	1229	479	2054	118	17.48
Mr. E. A. Nepean	567	129	1314	68	19.22
Mr. A. E. Stoddart	479	159	1081	52	20.41
A. Hide	610	224	1088	51	21.17
Mr. W. G. Grace	462	146	1014	44	23. 2
Roberts	661	272	1176	50	23.26

The list comprises 14 professionals and 4 amateurs.

1890.

BATTING IN FIRST-CLASS MATCHES.

For not less than Twenty-five Innings.

	Completed Innings.	Runs.	Most in an Innings.	Average.
Shrewsbury	38	1568	267	41.10
Gunn	47	1621	228	34.23
Abel	30	914	151*	30.14
Mr. J. Cranston	34	978	152	28.26
Mr. W. G. Grace	52	1476	109*	28.20
Mr. A. J. Webbe	35	995	134	28.15
Mr. W. W. Read	46	1169	94	25.19
Painter	27	683	119	25. 8
Mr. E. C. Streatfeild†	23	563	145	24.11
Mr. T. C. O'Brien	38	855	105	22.19
Mr. A. N. Hornby	30	672	75	22.12
G. G. Hearne	28	616	60	22
Quaife	36	791	156*	21.35
Lord Hawke	30	658	74	21.28
A. Ward	30	655	77*	21.25
Sugg	37	796	171	21.19
Hall	34	719	64	21. 5
M. Read	40	829	135	20.29
Ulyett	53	1093	107	20.33
Mr. G. McGregor	31	628	131	20. 8
Mr. E. M. Grace	29	574	96	19.23
Mr. F. Marchant	31	607	81	19.18
Lohmann	43	832	57	19.15
Mr. A. E. Stoddart	44	845	115	19. 9
Mr. K. J. Key	29	554	98	19. 3
Bean	35	668	100	19. 3
Mr. J. A. Dixon	30	571	109	19. 1
Mr. J. Shuter	34	645	53	18.33
Peel	44	817	83	18.25
Briggs	38	708	129*	18.24
Mr. C. J. M. Fox	26	477	58	18. 9
Mr. O. G. Radcliffe	35	635	93	18. 5
Mr. C. A. Smith	27	489	58*	18. 3
Barlow	27	489	92	18. 3
Mr. W. Newham	32	539	71	16.27

† Mr. Streatfeild batted in 26 innings and was 3 times not out.

The list comprises 19 amateurs and 16 professionals.

1890—*continued.*

BOWLING IN FIRST-CLASS MATCHES.

For not less than Fifty Wickets.

	Overs.	Maidens.	Runs.	Wickets.	Average.
Briggs	1113	... 456	... 1950	... 158	... 12.54
Attewell	1581	... 820	... 1874	... 151	... 12.62
Sharpe	1053	... 455	... 1754	... 139	... 12.86
Woof	440	... 174	... 814	... 63	... 12.58
Mr. S. M. J. Woods	360	... 120	... 775	... 59	... 13. 8
Peel	1552	... 714	... 2239	... 172	... 13. 3
Martin	1702	... 711	... 2481	... 190	... 13.11
Lohmann	1759	... 737	... 2998	... 220	... 13.138
Wainwright ...	461	... 171	... 812	... 59	... 13.45
Mold	893	... 300	... 1737	... 118	... 14.85
Mr. E. C. Streatfeild	571	... 240	... 1011	... 64	... 15.51
Watson	1041	... 561	... 1331	... 81	... 16.35
Flowers	643	... 256	... 1104	... 62	... 17.50
Wright	1007	... 439	... 1588	... 89	... 17.75
Shacklock	635	... 224	... 1319	... 72	... 18.23
Burton	564	... 190	... 996	... 54	... 18.24
Mr. W. G. Grace	609	... 212	... 1183	... 61	... 19.24
Mr. E. Smith ...	425	... 132	... 1051	... 52	.. 20.11
Roberts	855	... 332	... 1642	... 72	... 22.58
Mr. C. A. Smith	552	... 177	... 1211	... 50	... 24.11

The list comprises 15 professionals and 5 amateurs.

THE LEADING BATSMEN IN FIRST-CLASS CRICKET.

1871 TO 1880.

	Completed Innings.	Runs.	Average.
Mr. W. G. Grace	342	16877	49
Mr. J. M. Cotterill	50	1563	31
Mr. W. W. Read	71	2011	28
Hon. A. Lyttelton	92	2536	27
Mr. A. N. Hornby	214	5827	27
Mr. A. J. Webbe	142	3850	27
Mr. W. Yardley	96	2592	27
Mr. F. Penn	144	3826	26
Mr. G. F. Grace	241	6312	26
Lord Harris	181	4630	25
Mr. A. P. Lucas	139	3496	25
Lockwood	358	8720	24
Mr. A. G. Steel	66	1587	24
Daft	204	4892	23
Jupp	347	8200	23
Mr. I. D. Walker	236	5429	23
Charlwood	209	4714	22
Mr. F. Townsend	92	2033	22
Hon. Ivo Bligh	89	1944	21
Mr. E. M. Grace	111	2365	21
Ulyett	250	5248	20
Barnes	130	2702	20
Hon. Ed. Lyttelton	79	1656	20
Mr. G. H. Longman	86	1737	20
Mr. E. F. S. Tylecote	57	1147	20
Shrewsbury	158	3125	19
Mr. W. R. Gilbert	146	2802	19
Mr. A. W. Ridley	106	2033	19
A. Greenwood	211	4030	19
Barlow	158	2918	18
Oscroft	267	4916	18

The list comprises 21 amateurs and 10 professionals.

THE LEADING BOWLERS IN FIRST-CLASS CRICKET.

1871 TO 1880.

	Wickets.	Runs.	Average.
Rylott	304	3275	10
Mr. A. G. Steel	349	3867	11
Mycroft	661	7379	11
A. Shaw	1311	14956	11
Watson	453	5351	11

THE LEADING BOWLERS—1871 TO 1880—*continued.*

	Wickets.	Runs.	Average.
Peate	213	2600	12
W. McIntyre	454	5590	12
Bates	267	3365	12
Willsher	186	2407	12
Morley	1037	13750	13
Mr. D. Buchanan	184	2537	13
Southerton	957	13356	13
Mr. A. W. Ridley	209	2956	14
Emmett	647	9235	14
Mr. W. G. Grace	1174	16741	14
Hill	592	8670	14
Jas. Lillywhite	622	9469	15
Mr. A. Appleby	210	3557	16
Barratt	286	4914	17
J. C. Shaw	268	4748	17
Fillery	276	4886	17
Mr. G. F. Grace	261	5215	19
Street	360	7483	20

The list comprises 17 professionals and 6 amateurs.

THE LEADING BATSMEN IN FIRST-CLASS CRICKET.

1881 TO 1890.

	Completed Innings.	Runs.	Average.
Shrewsbury	221	8902	40
Mr. W. G. Grace	411	14541	35
Mr. C. T. Studd	105	3605	34
Mr. W. W. Read	367	12583	34
Mr. A. G. Steel	124	3945	31
Hon. A. Lyttelton	60	1759	29
Lord Harris	151	4339	28
Gunn	325	9146	28
Mr. W. L. Murdoch	164	4552	27
Mr. A. P. Lucas	98	2676	27
Mr. A. J. Webbe	226	6133	27
Mr. G. B. Studd	93	2503	26
Mr. W. H. Patterson	153	4126	26
Mr. K. J. Key	218	5826	26
Mr. S. W. Scott	95	2449	25
Ulyett	463	11847	25
Mr. A. N. Hornby	309	7850	25
Barnes	368	9217	25
Mr. I. D. Walker	95	2371	24
Mr. J. Cranston	101	2517	24

THE LEADING BATSMEN—1881 TO 1890—*continued*.

	Completed Innings.	Runs.	Average.
Mr. W. Newham	197	4852	24
Hall	355	8857	24
Mr. T. C. O'Brien	198	4803	24
Mr. A. E. Stoddart	136	3248	23
Abel	303	7125	23
Bates	308	7089	23
Mr. J. E. Barrett	57	1305	22
Mr. W. W. Rashleigh	98	2227	22
Mr. J. Shuter	306	6882	22
Lockwood	134	2974	22
Mr. L. Wilson	92	1932	21
Mr. E. F. S. Tylecote	63	1382	21
Mr. C. F. H. Leslie	70	1527	21
Mr. G. M. Kemp	64	1393	21
Mr. G. Giffen	156	3400	21
Mr. J. H. J. Scott	105	2275	21
Mr. C. I. Thornton	93	1987	21
Barlow	319	6781	21
Midwinter	99	2104	21
Mr. P. S. McDonnell	167	3549	21
Mr. J. Diver	119	2504	21
Lee	184	3869	21
Mr. F. G. J. Ford	92	1933	21
Mr. H. W. Bainbridge	81	1691	20
Mr. O. G. Radcliffe	159	3319	20
Flowers	328	6775	20
Mr. J. G. Walker	158	3257	20
Sugg	180	3708	20
Briggs	312	6384	20
Mr. J. E. K. Studd	76	1553	20
Mr. G. F. Vernon	195	3958	20
Mr. H. Whitfield	65	1318	20
Mr. G. J. Bonnor	182	3661	20
Quaife	164	3280	20
Mr. W. R. Gilbert	114	2277	19
Mr. W. E. Roller	166	3306	19
Robinson	166	3290	19
Scotton	244	4838	19
Mr. F. Marchant	163	3203	19
Mr. G. H. S. Trott	127	2485	19
G. G. Hearne	294	5699	19
Mr. A. C. Bannerman	161	3122	19
Lohmann	224	4336	19
Mr. J. H. Brain	168	3239	19
Grimshaw	171	3296	19
Mr. E. M. Grace	213	4068	19
Lord Hawke	248	4729	19
Mr. E. A. Nepean	86	1634	19

The list comprises 32 amateurs and 16 professionals.

THE LEADING BOWLERS IN FIRST-CLASS CRICKET.

1881 TO 1890.

	Wickets.	Runs.	Average.
Mr. C. T. B. Turner	529	6217	11
Crossland	285	3576	12
A. Shaw	366	4631	12
Attewell	814	10677	13
Morley	204	2705	13
Mr. F. R. Spofforth	532	7104	13
Mold	220	2941	13
Mr. H. F. Boyle	222	3033	13
Mr. J. J. Ferris	435	5941	13
Briggs	747	10232	13
Martin	436	6030	13
Watson	843	11626	13
Peate	853	11787	13
Emmett	623	8111	13
Lohmann	1069	14978	14
Barlow	714	10381	14
Flowers	747	11086	14
Peel	730	11435	15
Mr. T. W. Garrett	257	4043	15
Mr. S. M. J. Woods	222	3563	16
Wright	509	8386	16
Mr. G. E. Palmer	382	6306	16
Jones	231	3835	16
Bowley	256	4283	16
Burton	597	10112	16
Beaumont	448	7613	16
Barnes	612	10527	17
Mr. C. T. Studd	379	6552	17
Woof	611	10647	17
Mr. A. G. Steel	384	6695	17
A. Hearne	297	5213	17
Shacklock	282	4957	17
Wootton	606	10649	17
Barratt	412	7502	18
Mr. C. E. Horner	214	3901	18
Mr. G. Giffen	276	5121	18
Bates	478	9359	19
A. Hide	372	7370	19
G. G. Hearne	228	4647	20
Ulyett	372	7583	20
Mr. W. G. Grace	816	16696	20
J. Hide	348	7606	21
Mr. C. A. Smith	271	5939	21
Mr. S. Christopherson	241	5337	22
Roberts	203	4522	22
Mr. H. V. Page	201	4630	23
Mr. J. Robertson	298	7035	23
Humphreys	276	6922	25

The list comprises 32 professionals and 16 amateurs.

MR. W. G. GRACE'S BATTING AVERAGES.

In First-class Matches.

Year.	Completed Innings.	Runs.	Aver.	Year.	Completed Innings.	Runs.	Aver.
1864	7	402	57	1879	25	880	35
1865	13	319	24	1880	24	951	39
1866	15	640	42	1881	21	792	37
1867	5	154	30	1882	37	975	26
1868	9	588	65	1883	39	1352	34
1869	23	1320	57	1884	40	1361	34
1870	33	1808	54	1885	39	1688	43
1871	35	2739	78	1886	52	1846	35
1872	26	1485	57	1887	38	2062	54
1873	30	2139	71	1888	58	1886	32
1874	31	1658	53	1889	43	1396	32
1875	50	1814	36	1890	52	1476	28
1876	46	2622	62				
1877	37	1474	39		866	36,942	42
1878	38	1115	29				

MR. W. G. GRACE'S BOWLING AVERAGES.

In First-class Matches.

Year.	Wkts.	Runs.	Aver.	Year.	Wkts.	Runs.	Aver.
1865	23	281	12	1879	105	1414	13
1866	31	415	13	1880	85	1470	17
1867	39	255	9	1881	45	879	19
1868	44	639	14	1882	101	1745	17
1869	74	1187	16	1883	94	2077	22
1870	49	766	15	1884	82	1762	21
1871	78	1312	16	1885	118	2199	18
1872	56	688	12	1886	122	2439	19
1873	78	1004	12	1887	97	2078	21
1874	129	1658	12	1888	93	1691	18
1875	192	2472	12	1889	44	1014	23
1876	124	2388	19	1890	61	1183	19
1877	179	2231	12				
1878	148	2106	14		2291	37,353	16

MR. W. G. GRACE'S SCORES OF A HUNDRED AND UPWARDS IN FIRST-CLASS MATCHES.

1866.

224* England *v.* Surrey
173* Gentlemen of South *v.* Players of South

1868.

134* Gentlemen *v.* Players
130 South of Thames *v.* North of Thames
102* South of Thames *v.* North of Thames

1869.

180 Gentlemen of South *v.* Players of South
138* M.C.C. *v.* Surrey
127 M.C.C. *v.* Kent
122 South *v.* North
121 M.C.C. *v.* Notts
117 M.C.C. *v.* Oxford Univ.

1870.

215 Gentlemen *v.* Players
172 Glo'stershire *v.* M.C.C.
143 Glo'stershire *v.* Surrey
117* M.C.C. *v.* Notts.
109 Gentlemen *v.* Players

1871.

268 South *v.* North
217 Gentlemen *v.* Players
189* Single *v.* Married of England
181 M.C.C. *v.* Surrey
178 South *v.* North
162 Gentlemen of England *v.* Cambridge University
146 M.C.C. *v.* Surrey
118 Gentlemen of South *v.* Gentlemen of North
117 M.C.C. *v.* Kent
116 Glo'stershire *v.* Notts

1872.

170* England *v.* Notts and Yorkshire
150 Glo'stershire *v.* Yorkshire
117 Gentlemen *v.* Players
114 South *v.* North
112 Gentlemen *v.* Players
101 M.C.C. *v.* Yorkshire

1873.

192* South *v.* North
163 Gentlemen *v.* Players
160* Glo'stershire *v.* Surrey
158 Gentlemen *v.* Players
152 Eleven *v.* XV. of M.C.C.
145 Gentlemen of South *v.* Players of North
134 Gentlemen of South *v.* Players of South

1874.

179 Glo'stershire *v.* Sussex
167 Glo'stershire *v.* Yorkshire
150 Gentlemen of South *v.* Players of South
127 Glo'stershire *v.* Yorkshire
123 M.C.C. *v.* Kent
121 Glo'stershire and Kent *v.* England
110 Gentlemen *v.* Players
104 Gentlemen of South *v.* Players of South

1875.

152 Gentlemen *v.* Players
119 Glo'stershire *v.* Notts
111 Glo'stershire *v.* Yorkshire

1876.

344 M.C.C. *v.* Kent
318* Glo'stershire *v.* Yorkshire
177 Glo'stershire *v.* Notts

MR. W. G. GRACE'S SCORES OF A HUNDRED—*continued.*

1876—*continued.*

169 Gentlemen *v.* Players
126 United South *v.* United North
114* South *v.* North
104 Glo'stershire *v.* Sussex

1877.

261 South *v.* North
110 Glo'stershire and Yorkshire *v.* England

1878.

116 Glo'stershire *v.* Notts

1879.

123 Glo'stershire *v.* Surrey
102 Glo'stershire *v.* Notts
113 Glo'stershire *v.* Somerset

1880.

152 England *v.* Australia
106 Glo'stershire *v.* Lancashire

1881.

182 Glo'stershire *v.* Notts
100 Gentlemen *v.* Players

1883.

112 Glo'stershire *v.* Lancashire

1884.

116* Glo'stershire *v.* Australians
107 Gentlemen of England *v.* Australians
101 M.C.C. *v.* Australians

1885.

221* Glo'stershire *v.* Middlesex
174 Gentlemen *v.* Players
132 Glo'stershire *v.* Yorkshire
104 Glo'stershire *v.* Surrey

1886.

170 England *v.* Australia
148 Gentlemen of England *v.* Australians
110 Glo'stershire *v.* Australians
104 M.C.C. *v.* Oxford University

1887.

183* Glo'stershire *v.* Yorkshire
116* M.C.C. *v.* Cambridge University
113* Glo'stershire *v.* Notts
113 Glo'stershire *v.* Middlesex
101 Glo'stershire *v.* Kent
103* Glo'stershire *v.* Kent

1888.

215 Glo'stershire *v.* Sussex
165 Gentlemen of England *v.* Australians
148 Glo'stershire *v.* Yorkshire
153 Glo'stershire *v.* Yorkshire

1889.

154 South *v.* North
127* Glo'stershire *v.* Middlesex
101 Glo'stershire *v.* Middlesex

1890.

109* Glo'stershire *v.* Kent

AGAINST ODDS.

115	U.S.E.E. *v.* XXII. of Sleaford	1870
142	England *v.* XXII. of Toronto	1872
114	U.S.E.E. *v.* XXII. of Glasgow	1872
153	U.S.E.E. *v.* XXII. of Leinster	1874
126	England *v.* XXII. of Ballarat	1874
210	U.S.E.E. *v.* XVIII. of Hastings	1875
152	U.S.E.E. *v.* XVIII. of North Kent	1875
112	U.S.E.E. *v.* XVIII. of Trinity College, Dublin	1875
400*	U.S.E.E. *v.* XXII. of Grimsby	1876
124	U.S.E.E. *v.* XXII. of Stockport	1877
109	U.S.E.E. *v.* XXII. of Grange, Edinburgh ...	1877
122	United XI. *v.* XXII. of Market Bosworth ...	1882
111	Gloucestershire *v.* XXIV. Colts	1884

CURIOSITIES.

The first match in which hit-wicket appears was Hambledon *v.* England... 1773

A match was played at Bourne Park between the Duke of Dorset and Sir Horace Mann's Kent Eleven and Lord Tankerville's Surrey Eleven for £2,000, which Lord Tankerville's Eleven won 1773

The first match played with three stumps is supposed to have been Hambledon *v.* England 1777

The first Colts' match was Surrey *v.* Hants, in 1788

The first recorded match of the M.C.C. was *v.* White Conduit Club, 27th June 1788

The first match registered in the books of the M.C.C. was Middlesex *v.* Essex, at Lord's, 16th May 1791

A match was played between an Eleven of the Garrison of Dublin and an Eleven of All-Ireland for 1,000 guineas, which the Garrison won by an innings and 105 runs, 8th August 1792

A match between two Elevens on Horseback was played in 1800

The first match on the present Lord's Ground was Kent *v.* M.C.C. and Ground, 22nd June 1814

Little Dench, of Brighton, when long-stopping to George Brown, the fast bowler, protected himself by using a sack of straw fastened on to his chest 1825

The first match in which wides appear was Kent *v.* Sussex, at Brighton, 17th September 1827

Mr. Tramfer and his sheep-dog played two gentlemen of Middlesex, and won. The dog stood at the side of his master until the ball was hit, and was so quick at fielding that their opponents had great difficulty in scoring a single run 1827

The first match in which no-balls were scored was M.C.C. *v.* Middlesex, at Lord's, 17th May 1830

The first match between North and South was played at Lord's, 11th July 1836

The first match in which cards were printed was Gentlemen *v.* Players, at Old Lillywhite's Cricket Ground, Brighton, in 1838

The first match in which cards were printed at Lord's was Sussex *v.* M.C.C. and Ground, 26th June 1848

The first Canterbury Week began 1st June 1842
Lord Winterton's XI. beat 57 Labourers, 23rd August ... 1846
A swallow was killed by a ball bowled to the Earl of Winterton in 1847
The telegraph scoring-board was introduced at Lord's in ... 1848
The first match in which leg-byes were scored was at Sheffield, 17th September 1849
Double tie matches were played between—
Coleorton and Whitwick in 1853
Yardley Gobion and Castle Thorpe in 1863
I Zingari and Cranbury Park in 1864
A batsman hit a ball on to the back of a man who was running for him, and was caught out by the wicket-keeper 1854
Mr. Fiennes was given out, in the I Zingari *v.* Royal Artillery match at Woolwich, for playing a ball into the folds of his pads, which the wicket-keeper secured ... 1858
Caffyn, in compiling his score of 124 for the U.E.E. *v.* John Walker's XVI., broke three bats 1859
Mr. H. Payne, for Chalcot *v.* Bow, batted first in both innings, and scored all the runs for his side (24 and 10), and was not out both times 1859
The first match of an English team in Canada was played 24th September 1859
The first match of an English team in Australia was played 1st January 1862
Following innings, if 80 runs behind, was introduced in ... 1864
The wind was so strong that the bails had to be dispensed with in the A.E.E. *v.* Twenty-two of Scarborough match in 1864
The first match of an Aboriginal Eleven in England was *v.* Surrey Gentlemen, 25th May 1868
Swallows flitting across the wicket stopped the Gloucestershire *v.* Nottinghamshire match for a short time, at Trent Bridge, in 1875
The first match of an Australian Eleven in England was *v.* Notts, 20th May 1878
Jas. Lillywhite played in every Sussex County Match from ... ... 1862 to 1881
The largest gate at an English First-class Match was in the Surrey *v.* Notts match, at the Oval, when 24,450 paid for admission; and the total for the three days was 51,607, exclusive of members, August 1887

A match was played between Eleven of the Messrs. Leatham and the Wakefield Club, at Wakefield, 2nd August ... 1875

Scores—Leathams, 141; Wakefield, 45 first, 132 for 4 wickets second innings.

A match was played between Eleven of the Messrs. Leatham and Pontefract Club, at Pontefract, 6th August 1884

Scores—Leathams, 109 first innings, 72 for 4 wickets second; Pontefract, 60 first innings. Mr. A. E. Leatham captured 9 wickets; the other was run out.

Eleven members of the Messrs. Robinson, belonging to Somerset and Gloucestershire, played 35 matches from 1878 to 1890, winning 26 and losing 9.

Eleven members of the Messrs. Lucas, Lyttelton, Christopherson, Cæsar, Watney, and Brotherhood families have also played matches at one time or another.

The highest innings at the Oval was Surrey 698 *v.* Sussex, 9th August 1888

The first English team that visited South Africa sailed from London 21st November 1888

The first English team that visited India was Mr. G. F. Vernon's, which left London 31st October 1889

The Rule empowering a Captain to terminate his innings was first applied at Lord's in the M.C.C. and Ground *v.* Northumberland match, 10th August 1889

First-class matches have been finished in one day by—

North *v.* South, at Lord's, 15th July 1850
M.C.C. and Ground *v.* Surrey, at Lord's, 13th May ... 1872
Middlesex *v.* Oxford University, at Prince's, 18th June... 1874
North *v.* South, at Lord's, 17th May 1875
M.C.C. & Ground *v.* Oxford University, at Lord's, 24th May 1877
M.C.C. and Ground *v.* Australians, at Lord's, 27th May 1878
An England XI. *v.* Australians, at Birmingham, 26th May 1884
M.C.C. and Ground *v.* Lancashire, at Lord's, 18th May 1886
North *v.* South, at Lord's, 30th May 1887
Lancashire *v.* Surrey, at Manchester, 2nd August ... 1888

The Sergeants of the 2nd Battalion Grenadier Guards defeated the Sergeants of the Royal Artillery and Royal Engineers, at Bermuda, without losing a wicket in either innings, 11th February 1891

Scores: Sergeants R.A. & R.E., 34 first innings; 73 second. Grenadier Guards, 69 for no wicket, first innings (innings declared closed); 39 for no wicket, second.

CURIOSITIES OF BATTING.

James Broadbridge threw his bat at a wide ball and was caught by Mr. Ward at point 1829

Mr. E. Winter, in cutting at a ball, hit the top of the wicket so hard that the bails were driven into the stumps, where they stuck, although the wickets were almost in a horizontal position. Batsman not out 1832

The Hon. Robert Grimston used two bats when playing against Alfred Mynn—the larger to block Mynn's fast balls, the smaller to hit the other bowlers ... ...

Mr. Earle took four hours to make 11 runs against the A.E.E. 1846

Twenty-two of Hungerford got the A.E.E. out for 12 runs first innings; in the second George Parr took 4½ hours to make 28 1852

Mr. J. Rowley, for Manchester *v.* Liverpool, hit a 9, an 8, and a 7 in his score of 46 1861

Mr. Charles Payne hit a ball downhill, in a match at Tunbridge Wells, for which he ran 13 runs 1863

For XXII. of Castlemaine *v.* England, in Australia, Mr. Easton was batting two hours for 3 runs 1864

Mr. J. H. T. Roupell hit a 10, a 9, and an 8 on Parker's Piece, at Cambridge, in a score of 97 1865

Mr. G. Richards, for the Harrow Blues *v.* Civil Service, batted 77 minutes without scoring 1871

Mr. E. M. Grace averaged 142 runs per innings for Thornbury Club in 1872

Mr. E. M. Grace hit 259 runs in 100 minutes, out of a total of 331 for Thornbury Club in 1873

Mr. S. D. Smith for Marlborough College *v.* M.C.C., at Marlborough, hit 44 runs in 12 minutes 1873

Mr. W. G. Grace has never been dismissed in a first-class match without scoring, but he bagged a "brace" in the following matches:

For XXII. of Lansdown *v.* A.E.E. (Tinley the bowler), 28th May 1863

For U.S.E.E. *v.* XXII. of Cadoxton Club (Howitt the bowler), 21st May 1868

For Bedminster *v.* G.W. Ry., Swindon (Laverick the bowler), 7th May 1870

Shrewsbury, when playing for Shaw's team *v.* New South Wales, in Australia, was dismissed in both innings without scoring ... ... 18th and 19th February, 1887

Mr. C. T. B. Turner clean bowled him in both innings.

For Marlborough College *v.* Cheltenham College Mr. A. G. Steel added 48 runs to the total, and no other player scored while he did it... 1876

CURIOSITIES OF BOWLING.

William Bullen frequently bowled a ball a distance of 300 yards 1800

For Gentlemen of England *v.* Marylebone at Lord's, Holden bowled at both ends throughout the match 1818

Six wickets with consecutive balls have been captured by Wisden for A.E.E. *v.* XXII. of Canada and United States in 1859

By Mr. Brawn, for Godmanchester *v.* Willingham ... 1874

By Kirkland, for Bloxwick *v.* Cannock and Rugeley... 1890

R. C. Tinley, playing for the A.E.E. *v.* XVIII. of Hallam, captured all 17 wickets, second innings 1860

Mr. C. Absolon, playing for the United Master Butchers *v.* XX. of the Metropolitan Club, captured 18 wickets. The total of the innings was 4 runs, and 18 of the 20 failed to score 1861

In the Surrey *v.* Middlesex match at the Oval, all the Surrey Eleven bowled the first innings of Middlesex, 20th and 21st August 1866

In the England *v.* Australia match at the Oval, all the England XI. bowled, 11th August 1884

Mr. W. Gilby, playing for the Harrow United Club *v.* U.S.E.E., had only one run scored off his lob-bowling in 70 minutes 1867

Howitt, bowling for the U.A.E.E. against XXII. of the Hull Mechanics' Institution, hit a bail out of the ground a distance of 60 yards 1867

Mr. A. Dartnell, playing for Broad Green *v.* Thornton Heath, near Croydon, captured all 10 wickets, and the whole side was got rid of without scoring 1867

The Brigg Club dismissed an Eleven of Lea Ægir Club on their own ground in 3 overs for 3 runs 1876

Mr. H. F. Boyle captured 7 wickets with 8 balls for the Australians *v.* XVIII. of Elland at Leeds in 1878

Mr. H. Rotherham, bowling for Uppingham Rovers *v.* Gentlemen of Derbyshire, dismissed Mr. D. H. Docker with a ball which sent the bail a distance of 62 yards from the wicket 1881

Three wickets with successive balls have been captured repeatedly in a first-class match.

CURIOSITIES OF FIELDING.

William Yalden jumped over a fence, stumbled and caught the ball when on his back—about 1800

Capt. Adams, on the Old Phœnix Park Ground, jumped over an iron fence 3 ft. 10 high, and, while in the air, caught the ball with his left hand in 1844

R. C. Tinley, playing for the A.E.E. *v.* XXII. of Birmingham, caught 12 men at point in 1854

W. Caffyn, playing for the A.E.E. *v.* XXII. of Ipswich, threw in a ball from long-off which passed through the stumps and dislodged the bails at the bowler's end, and then travelled to the other wicket, passing through the stumps and dislodging the bails also 1853

In a match of three innings between the Gentlemen of Hampshire *v.* Gentlemen of Kent at Canterbury, wides and byes amounted to 145 out of a total of 615 runs ... 1857

Pooley stumped 4 and caught 8 for Surrey *v.* Sussex, at the Oval, July 6th and 7th, 1868; and stumped 4 and caught 4 for Surrey *v.* Kent (the following match), July 9th and 10th 1868

THE SIZE OF SOME OF THE PRINCIPAL GROUNDS IN ENGLAND.

	Whole Ground.	Match Enclosure, about
Lord's	12 Acres	6 Acres.
Oval	11 ,,	8 ,,
Gloucestershire County Ground	15 ,,	6 ,,
Old Trafford	7 ,,	5½ ,,
Brighton	10 ,,	6 ,,
Trent Bridge, Nottingham	10 ,,	8 ,,
Bramall Lane, Sheffield	11¾ ,,	8 ,,
St. Lawrence, Canterbury	7 ,,	5¾ ,,
Mote Park, Maidstone	5½ ,,	5 ,,
Birmingham	12 ,,	5½ ,,
Scarborough	7 ,,	6 ,,
Fenner's, Cambridge	8 ,,	6 ,,
The Parks, Oxford	10 ,,	5½ ,,

LAWS OF CRICKET.

As Revised by the Committee of the Marylebone Cricket Club, 1884 *and* 1889.

1. A match is played between two sides of eleven players each, unless otherwise agreed to; each side has two innings, taken alternately, except in the case provided for in Law 53. The choice of innings shall be decided by tossing. The Game.

2. The score shall be reckoned by runs. A run is scored— Runs.

 1st. So often as the batsmen after a hit, or at any time while the ball is in play, shall have crossed and made good their ground from end to end.

 2nd. For penalties under Laws 16, 34, 41, and allowances under 44.

Any run or runs so scored shall be duly recorded by scorers appointed for the purpose.

The side which scores the greatest number of runs wins the match. No match is won unless played out or given up, except in the case provided in Law 45.

3. Before the commencement of the match two Umpires shall be appointed, one for each end. Appointment o Umpires.

4. The Ball shall weigh not less than five ounces and a half, nor more than five ounces and three-quarters. It shall measure not less than nine inches, nor more than nine inches and one-quarter in circumference. At the beginning of each innings either side may demand a new ball. The Ball.

5. The Bat shall not exceed four inches and one-quarter in the widest part; it shall not be more than thirty-eight inches in length. The Bat.

6. The Wickets shall be pitched opposite and parallel to each other at a distance of twenty-two yards. Each wicket shall be eight inches in width, and consist of three stumps, with two bails upon the top. The stumps shall be of equal and sufficient size to prevent the ball from passing through, twenty-seven inches out of the ground. The bails shall be each four inches in length, and when in position on the top of the stumps, shall not project more than half-an-inch above them. The wickets shall not be changed during a match, unless the ground between them become unfit for play; and then only by consent of both sides. The Wickets.

The Bowling Crease. 7. The Bowling Crease shall be in a line with the stumps, six feet eight inches in length—the stumps in the centre,—with a return crease at each end, at right angles behind the wicket.

The Popping Crease. 8. The Popping Crease shall be marked four feet from the wicket, parallel to it, and be deemed unlimited in length.

The Ground. 9. The Ground shall not be rolled, watered, covered, mown, or beaten during a match, except before the commencement of each innings and of each day's play; when, unless the in-side object, the ground shall be swept and rolled for not more than ten minutes. This shall not prevent the batsman from beating the ground with his bat, nor the batsman nor bowler using sawdust in order to obtain a proper foothold.

The Bowler 10. The ball must be bowled; if thrown or jerked the umpire shall call "No Ball."

No Ball. 11. The Bowler shall deliver the ball with one foot on the ground behind the bowling crease, and within the return crease, otherwise the umpire shall call "No Ball."

Wide Ball. 12. If the bowler shall bowl the ball so high over or so wide of the wicket that, in the opinion of the umpire, it is not within reach of the striker, the umpire shall call "Wide Ball."

The Over. 13. The ball shall be bowled in Overs of five balls from each wicket alternately. When five balls have been bowled, and the ball is finally settled in the bowler's or wicket-keeper's hands, the umpire shall call "Over." Neither a "no ball" nor a "wide ball" shall be reckoned as one of the "over."

14. The bowler shall be allowed to change ends as often as he pleases, provided only that he does not bowl two overs consecutively in one innings.

15. The bowler may require the batsman at the wicket from which he is bowling to stand on that side of it which he may direct.

Scoring off No Balls and Wide Balls. 16. The striker may hit a "No Ball," and whatever runs result shall be added to his score; but he shall not be out from a "no ball," unless he be run out or break Laws 26, 27, 29, 30. All runs made from a "no ball," otherwise than from the bat, shall be scored "no balls," and if no run be made one run shall be added to that score. From a "Wide Ball" as many runs as are run shall be added to the score as "wide balls," and if no run be otherwise obtained one run shall be so added.

17. If the ball, not having been called "wide" or "no ball," pass the striker without touching his bat or person, and any runs be obtained, the umpire shall call "Bye;" but if the ball touch any part of the striker's person (hand excepted), and any run be obtained, the umpire shall call "Leg-bye," such runs to be scored "byes" and "leg-byes" respectively. Bye.

18. At the beginning of the match, and of each innings, the umpire at the bowler's wicket shall call "Play." From that time no trial ball shall be allowed to any bowler on the ground between the wickets; and when one of the batsmen is out, the use of the bat shall not be allowed to any person until the next batsman shall come in. Play.

19. A batsman shall be held to be "out of his ground," unless his bat in hand or some part of his person be grounded within the line of the popping crease. Definitions.

20. The wicket shall be held to be "down" when either of the bails is struck off, or if both bails be off, when a stump is struck out of the ground.

The STRIKER is out—

21. If the wicket be bowled down, even if the ball first touch the striker's bat or person;—"Bowled." The Striker.

22. Or, if the ball, from a stroke of the bat or hand, but not the wrist, be held before it touch the ground, although it be hugged to the body of the catcher;—"Caught."

23. Or, if in playing at the ball, provided it be not touched by the bat or hand, the striker be out of his ground, and the wicket be put down by the wicket-keeper with the ball or with hand or arm, with ball in hand;—"Stumped."

24. Or, if with any part of his person he stop the ball which, in the opinion of the umpire at the bowler's wicket, shall have been pitched in a straight line from it to the striker's wicket and would have hit it;—"Leg before wicket."

25. Or, if in playing at the ball he hit down his wicket with his bat or any part of his person or dress;—"Hit wicket."

26. Or, if under pretence of running, or otherwise, either of the batsmen wilfully prevent a ball from being caught;—"Obstructing the field."

27. Or, if the ball be struck, or be stopped by any part of his person, and he wilfully strike it again, except it be done for the purpose of guarding his wicket, which he may do with his bat, or any part of his person except his hands;—"Hit the ball twice."

Either BATSMAN is out—

The Batsman. 28. If in running, or at any other time, while the ball is in play, he be out of his ground, and his wicket be struck down by the ball after touching any fieldsman, or by the hand or arm, with ball in hand, of any fieldsman;—"Run out."

29. Or, if he touch with his hands or take up the ball while in play, unless at the request of the opposite side;—"Handled the ball."

30. Or, if he wilfully obstruct any fieldsman;—"Obstructing the field."

31. If the batsmen have crossed each other, he that runs for the wicket which is put down is out; if they have not crossed, he that has left the wicket which is put down is out.

32. The striker being caught no run shall be scored. A batsman being run out, that run which was being attempted shall not be scored.

33. A batsman being out from any cause, the ball shall be "Dead."

Lost Ball. 34. If a ball in play cannot be found or recovered, any fieldsman may call "Lost Ball," when the ball shall be "dead"; six runs shall be added to the score; but if more than six runs have been run before "lost ball" has been called, as many runs as have been run shall be scored.

35. After the ball shall have been finally settled in the wicket-keeper's or bowler's hand, it shall be "dead"; but when the bowler is about to deliver the ball, if the batsman at his wicket be out of his ground before actual delivery, the said bowler may run him out; but if the bowler throw at that wicket and any run result, it shall be scored "no ball."

36. A batsman shall not retire from his wicket and return to it to complete his innings after another has been in, without the consent of the opposite side.

Substitute. 37. A Substitute shall be allowed to field or run between wickets for any player who may, during the match, be incapacitated from illness or injury, but for no other reason, except with the consent of the opposite side.

38. In all cases where a substitute shall be allowed, the consent of the opposite side shall be obtained as to the person to act as substitute, and the place in the field which he shall take.

39. In case any substitute shall be allowed to run between wickets, the striker may be run out if either he or his substitute be out of his ground. If the striker be out of his ground while the ball is in play, the wicket which he has left may be put down and the striker given out, although the other batsman may have made good the ground at that end, and the striker and his substitute at the other end.

40. A batsman is liable to be out for any infringement of the Laws by his substitute.

41. The Fieldsman may stop the ball with any part of his person; but if he wilfully stop it otherwise, the ball shall be "dead," and five runs added to the score; whatever runs may have been made, five only shall be added. The Fieldsman

42. The Wicket-keeper shall stand behind the wicket. If he shall take the ball, for the purpose of stumping, before it has passed the wicket, or, if he shall incommode the striker by any noise or motion, or, if any part of his person be over or before the wicket, the striker shall not be out, excepting under Laws 26, 27, 28, 29, and 30. Wicket-keeper.

43. The Umpires are the sole judges of fair or unfair play, of the fitness of the ground, the weather, and the light for play. All disputes shall be determined by them, and if they disagree, the actual state of things shall continue. Duties of Umpires.

44. They shall pitch fair wickets, arrange boundaries where necessary, and the allowances to be made for them, and change ends after each side has had one innings.

45. They shall allow two minutes for each striker to come in, and ten minutes between each innings. When they shall call "Play," the side refusing to play shall lose the match.

46. They shall not order a batsman out unless appealed to by the other side.

47. The umpire at the bowler's wicket shall be appealed to before the other umpire in all cases, except those of stumping, hit wicket, run out at the striker's wicket, or, arising out of Law 42; but in any case in which an umpire is unable to give a decision, he shall appeal to the other umpire, whose decision shall be final.

48. If the umpire at the bowler's end be not satisfied of the absolute fairness o the delivery of any ball, he shall call "No Ball."

48*a*. The Umpire shall take especial care to call "No Ball" instantly upon delivery; "Wide Ball" as soon as it shall have passed the striker.

49. If either batsman run a short run, the Umpire shall call "One Short," and the run shall not be scored.

50. After the Umpire has called "Over," the ball is "dead," but an appeal may be made as to whether either batsman is out; such appeal, however, shall not be made after the delivery of the next ball, nor after any cessation of play.

51. No umpire shall be allowed to bet.

52. No umpire shall be changed during a match, unless with the consent of both sides, except in case of violation of Law 51; then either side may dismiss him.

Following Innings.

53. The side which goes in second shall follow their innings, if they have scored eighty runs less than the opposite side.

54. On the last day of a match, and in a one-day match at any time, the in-side may declare their innings at an end.

ONE-DAY MATCHES.

1. The side which goes in second shall follow their innings, if they have scored sixty runs less than the opposite side.

2. The match, unless played out, shall be decided by the first innings. Prior to the commencement of a match it may be agreed that the over consist of five or six balls.

SINGLE WICKET.

The Laws are, where they apply, the same as the above, with the following alterations and additions.

1. One wicket shall be pitched, as in Law 6, with a bowling stump opposite to it at a distance of twenty-two yards. The bowling crease shall be in a line with the bowling stump, and drawn according to Law 7.

2. When there shall be less than five players on a side, bounds shall be placed twenty-two yards each in a line from the off and leg-stump.

3. The ball must be hit before the bounds to entitle the striker to a run, which run cannot be obtained unless he touch the bowling stump or crease in a line with his bat, or some part of his person, or go beyond them, and return to the popping crease.

4. When the striker shall hit the ball, one of his feet must be on the ground behind the popping crease, otherwise the umpire shall call "No Hit" and no run shall be scored.

5. When there shall be less than five players on a side, neither byes, leg-byes, nor overthrows shall be allowed; nor shall the striker be caught out behind the wicket, nor stumped.

6. The fieldsman must return the ball so that it shall cross the ground between the wicket and the bowling stump, or between the bowling stump and the bounds; the striker may run till the ball be so returned.

7. After the striker shall have made one run, if he start again, he must touch the bowling stump or crease and turn before the ball cross the ground to entitle him to another.

8. The striker shall be entitled to three runs for lost ball, and the same number for ball wilfully stopped by a fieldsman otherwise than with any part of his person.

9. When there shall be more than four players on a side, there shall be no bounds. All hits, byes, leg-byes, and overthrows shall then be allowed.

10. There shall be no restriction as to the ball being bowled in overs; but no more than one minute shall be allowed between each ball.

RULES OF COUNTY CRICKET.

1. That no cricketer, whether amateur or professional, shall play for more than one county during the same season.

2. Every cricketer born in one county and residing in another shall be free to choose at the commencement of each season for which of those counties he will play, and shall, during that season, play for that county only.

3. A cricketer shall be qualified to play for any county in which he is residing and has resided for the previous two years; or a cricketer may elect to play for the county in which his family home is, so long as it remains open to him as an occasional residence. A man can play for his old county during the two years that he is qualifying for another.

4. That, should any question arise as to the residential qualification, the same should be left to the decision of the committee of the Marylebone Club.

FINIS.